A History of the Span
through Texts

MW00827036

'A meticulous and enlightening examination of a broad selection of texts, which are representative of Spanish during the last millennium and across the world . . . elegantly and succinctly presented. An indispensable tool for all those working or interested in the history of the Spanish language.'

Ralph Penny, Queen Mary and Westfield College, University of London

A History of the Spanish Language through Texts examines the evolution of the Spanish language from the Middle Ages to the present day.

Including chapters on Latin American Spanish, US Spanish, Judeo-Spanish and Creoles, the book looks at the spread of Castilian as well as at linguistically interesting non-standard developments. Pountain explores a wide range of texts, from poetry, through newspaper articles and political documents, to a Buñuel film script and a love letter.

A History of the Spanish Language through Texts presents the formal history of the language and its texts in a fresh and original way. The book has user-friendly textbook features such as a series of keypoints and a careful indexing and cross-referencing system. It can be used as a freestanding history of the language independently of the illustrative texts themselves.

Christopher J. Pountain is a University Lecturer in Romance Philology at the University of Cambridge and a Fellow of Queens' College. He has over twenty years' experience of teaching Spanish and Romance linguistics. His publications include *Using Spanish* (CUP 1992) and *Modern Spanish Grammar* (Routledge 1997).

A History of the Spanish Language through Texts

Christopher J. Pountain

Routledge
Taylor & Francis Group

LONDON AND NEW YORK

First published 2001 by Routledge
2 Park Square, Milton Park, Abingdon, Oxon, OX14 4RN

Simultaneously published in the USA and Canada
by Routledge
711 Third Avenue, New York, NY 10017

Routledge is an imprint of the Taylor and Francis Group

© 2001 Christopher J. Pountain

First issued in paperback 2013

Typeset in Baskerville by
Florence Production Ltd, Stoodleigh, Devon

All rights reserved. No part of this book may be reprinted or reproduced
or utilised in any form or by any electronic, mechanical, or other means,
now known or hereafter invented, including photocopying and recording,
or in any information storage or retrieval system, without permission in
writing from the publishers.

British Library Cataloguing in Publication Data
A catalogue record for this book is available from the British Library

Library of Congress Cataloging in Publication Data
Pountain, Christopher J.
    A history of the Spanish language through texts / Christopher J. Pountain.
      p. cm.
    Includes bibliographical references and indexes.
    1. Spanish language—History.   2. Spanish language—History—
    Sources.   I. Title.
    PC4075.P69 2000
    460′.9—dc21   00–038264

ISBN 978-0-415-18061-0 (hbk)

ISBN 978-0-415-70712-1 (pbk)

For Mary, Frances, Rosie and Matthew

Contents

XVI   The African connection   **236**

XVII Creoles and contact vernaculars   **245**

Illustrations

Maps

Transliteration and other notational conventions

Arabic transcription

The systems of equivalences used by the periodical *Al-Andalus*, widely followed in the Spanish-speaking world, are used in this book. Differing usage by authors has been adapted accordingly. The transliteration system for Arabic is given below; also given in this table are the slightly different transliterations adopted by Corominas and Pascual (1980–91) (Cor.), which the reader is likely to encounter frequently.

Arabic letter	Transliteration	Name of letter	Approximate phonetic value in Modern Arabic
ا	ʾ	*ʾalif* (strictly speaking, *ʾalif* is used as a 'carrier' for *hamza*: see below)	[ʔ]
ب	b	*bāʾ*	[b]
ت	t	*tāʾ*	[t]
ث	t̲	*t̲āʾ*	[θ]
ج	ŷ (Cor. ǧ)	*ŷīm*	[dʒ]
ح	ḥ (Cor. h)	*ḥāʾ*	[ħ] (voiceless pharyngeal)
خ	j (Cor. ḫ)	*jāʾ*	[x]
د	d	*dāl*	[d]
ذ	d̲	*d̲āl*	[ð]
ر	r	*rāʾ*	[r]
ز	z	*zāy*	[z]
س	s	*sīn*	[s]
ش	š	*šin*	[ʃ]
ص	ṣ	*ṣād*	[ṣ] ('emphatic', with centre of tongue lowered)
ض	ḍ	*ḍād*	[ḍ] ('emphatic', with centre of tongue lowered)
ط	ṭ	*ṭāʾ*	[ṭ] ('emphatic', with centre of tongue lowered)
ظ	z̧	*z̧āʾ*	[ð̧]('emphatic', with centre of tongue lowered)
ع	ʿ	*ʿayn*	[ʕ] (voiced pharyngeal)

Arabic letter	Transliteration	Name of letter	Approximate phonetic value in Modern Arabic
غ	g (Cor. ġ)	*ġayn*	[ɣ]
ف	f	*fāʾ*	[f]
ق	q	*qāf*	[q] (voiceless uvular)
ك	k	*kāf*	[k]
ل	l	*lām*	[l]
م	m	*mīm*	[m]
ن	n	*nūn*	[n]
ه	h	*hāʾ*	[h]
و	w (Cor. ụ when syllable-final)	*wāw*	[w]
ي	y (Cor. i̯ or à when syllable-final)	*yāʾ*	[j]
ء	ʾ	*hamza*	[ʔ]
ة	a̲ (Cor. -a) a̲t (Cor. -aᵗ)	*tāʾ marbūṭa*	represents the most common feminine ending, which is -*at* if followed by a vowel, and otherwise *a* or *ā*
◌َ	a	*fatḥa* (vowel mark)	[a]
◌ِ	i	*kasra* (vowel mark)	[i]
◌ُ	u	*damma* (vowel mark)	[u]
◌ا	ā		[aː]
◌ِي	ī		[iː]
◌ُو	ū		[uː]
◌ّ	mark of consonant doubling	*šadda*	

Phonetic symbols

The symbols used in this book are generally those of the International Phonetic Alphabet and so are not described further here. The signs [j] and [w] have been used to indicate both onglides and offglides, e.g. [je] and [ej], [we] and [aw].

A distinction is made between phonetic and phonemic transcription, the former being indicated, as is usual, by square brackets [ ], and the latter by obliques / /. Phonetic transcription is used when the point under discussion is primarily a matter of pronunciation, and phonemic transcription when systematic distinctions are implied. There is no extensive discussion of the phonemic status of particular sounds unless this is crucial to the matter in hand; it has been found more convenient to treat /w/ and /j/ as phonemic throughout (but see **Keypoint: vowels**, p. 296), and a distinction is made between /r/ and /ɾ/ only in intervocalic occurrence.

Latin

Vowel length is indicated where significant, in line with practice in modern Latin dictionaries (see **Keypoint: vowels**, p. 296). Citation forms are given in square brackets (see p. 12).

Other symbols

See p. 12 for an explanation of the use of the symbols <, >, ≤, ≥, ←, →, ? and √.

|| cognate with

° is used to indicate a construction in Latin or Old Castilian that is hypothesised and not directly attested.

* indicates an unacceptable construction.

Abbreviations

Ar.	Arabic
Cat.	Catalan
Du.	Dutch
Eng.	English
f.	folio
Fr.	French
Germ.	Germanic
Gr.	Greek
It.	Italian
l., ll.	line, lines
Lat.	Latin
MS	manuscript
MSp.	Modern Spanish
Oc.	Occitan
OCast.	Old Castilian
OFr.	Old French
p., pp.	person; page, pages
Pen.	Peninsular
pl.	plural
Ptg.	Portuguese
Rom.	Romanian
sg.	singular
Sp.	Spanish

Acknowledgements

The author and publishers would like to thank the following copyright holders for granting permission to reproduce their material:

Illustrations

MS Aemilianensis 60 f.72r, in Juan B. Olarte Ruiz (ed.), *Las Glosas Emilianenses*, Ministerio de Educación y Ciencia, 1977, reproduced by permission of the Ministerio de Educación y Cultura.

Genizah T-S H15.46 reproduced by permission of the Syndics of Cambridge University Library.

Celestina 1499, in *Tragicomedia de Calixto e Melibea*, Burgos: Fadrique de Basilea, 1499, f.4v, 1970, reproduced courtesy of The Hispanic Society of America, New York.

Vida de Santa Teresa de Jesús, Vicente de la Fuente (ed.), 1873, reproduced by permission of the Patrimonio Nacional. Copyright © Patrimonio Nacional.

Texts

Auto de los Reyes Magos, in Ramón Menéndez Pidal, 1971[2], *Crestomatía del Español Medieval*, I, reproduced by permission of Editorial Gredos, S.A.

Extracts from *Milagro de Teófilo*, in Brian Dutton, 1980 (2nd ed.), *Gonzalo de Berceo, Obras completas, 2: Los milagros de Nuestra Señora, estudio y edición crítica*, 2nd ed. revised (London: Tamesis), reproduced by permission of Boydell & Brewer Ltd.

Willis, Raymond S., Jr., 1934, *El libro de Alexandre. Texts of the Paris and Madrid Manuscripts prepared with an introduction.* Copyright © 1972 by Princeton University Press. Reprinted by permission of Princeton University Press.

Extract from *El País Internacional*, 25.9.89, reproduced by permission of *El País Internacional*.

Extract from 'El Sefaradizmo', Albert de Vidas, in *Aki Yerushalayim*, 50, reproduced by permission of *Aki Yerushalayim* and Albert de Vidas. (Originally appeared in *Erensia Sefardi*, 2:3, 1994.)

While the author and the publishers have made every effort to contact copyright holders of the material used in this volume, they would be happy to hear from anyone they were unable to contact.

This book owes an enormous debt to several scholars whose influence (even if not always accepted uncritically) will be apparent throughout the work: Joe Cremona, Martin Harris and Roger Wright. There is a further, and more particular, debt to a number of standard reference works, to which, in order to keep bibliographical references to a minimum, I have only acknowledged in detail where a contentious point is at issue: these works are indicated with an asterisk in the Bibliography, and are recommended as a basic reading list for students of the subject.

I owe a very special debt of gratitude to Ralph Penny, who painstakingly read the entire manuscript and made many helpful suggestions and corrections; needless to say, residual shortcomings are entirely mine. I would also like to record my thanks to my colleague Elsa de Hands, for help with Text 31, to my former student Yasmin Lilley, whose consuming interest in *caló* (Chapter XV) awakened mine, to Larry and Simone Navon, and to Avi Shivtiel of Cambridge University Library, who patiently helped me with the Hebrew (Chapter IV).

Finally, a special word of thanks to my long-suffering family, who have been subject to even greater abandonment than usual during the writing of this book, for which the dedication attempts to make amends.

Christopher J. Pountain
Cambridge, January 2000

I Preliminaries

About this book

One way of approaching the history of a language is to lay out in a formal fashion the main changes observable in phonetics and morphology, citing single word examples for the former and paradigms, or sets of morphological forms, for the latter. This method has followed from the belief that changes in these areas essentially conform to regular patterns which can be abstracted from such data. Vocabulary has rarely been approached in a similarly systematic way (indeed, many linguists would deny that it can be), and has thus been the almost exclusive preserve of compendious etymological dictionaries which have generally dealt with the semantic histories of words on an individual basis. Syntax was for a long time a relatively neglected area of historical linguistics, finding a natural home in neither of these formats. Textual references to individual examples are of course frequently given, but continuous texts are cited less often, and usually in the form of an appendix. *A History of the Spanish Language through Texts* reverses these priorities. Making the study of individual texts a starting point for the history of the language does not lend itself to a comprehensive and systematic account of phonological and morphological change; it is like turning jigsaw pieces out of a box rather than seeing the whole picture at once. It cannot be guaranteed, even with careful choice of texts, that all phonetic changes will be illustrated, and quite unrealistic to assume that even a representative selection of morphological forms will emerge. (At the same time, jigsaws are easiest to solve by looking at the picture on the box, and accordingly, I have described some of the more important formal features of the history of Spanish in a series of some forty Keypoints, which are listed on p. 262–97, and to which many of the points made in connection with individual texts are cross-referenced.)

What is the justification for such an approach? First, Romance linguistics occupies a unique status within historical linguistics precisely because of the wealth of its textual records, both in the parent language (Latin) and in the many Romance varieties observable from the Middle Ages down to the present day (see Malkiel 1974). The interpretation of texts as a source of data is therefore a skill which no Romance linguist can possibly ignore, the more so, because in fact it sometimes turns out that the jigsaw piece does not exactly correspond to the picture on the box – that is to say, the primary data is sometimes at odds with the overall formal historical account, which can then sometimes be seen to be idealised. Second, the study of texts embeds language in its cultural, social and historical matrix, a dimension which, while a hallmark of the work of the great Spanish philologist Ramón Menéndez Pidal (1869–1968), and recently reinstated by the insights of modern sociolinguistics, has been, and continues to be, very seriously neglected by some structuralist approaches. Third, the study of continuous texts allows us to pursue lexical histories in a more interesting way, since we can see vocabulary used in context, and to give a higher priority than is usual to syntax, since continuous texts are the only satisfactory source of syntactic data. Fourth, we will also be able to investigate questions of register and style, which have often been scarcely mentioned in formal histories, though such variation is increasingly recognised as being of crucial importance to an understanding of language change. Lastly, I dare hope that texts will provide an added stimulus to the study of the history of the Spanish language by bringing the language to life in a way that more abstract formal accounts of language evolution (tables of sound-changes and the like) cannot.

Texts

Texts have long been the preserve of editors who have had to satisfy the often conflicting criteria of faithfulness to original sources (palaeographic or 'diplomatic' editions) and the need to make a text easily accessible to modern readers whose interest is primarily literary or historical. Because of market forces in publishing, the latter concern has hitherto been dominant, and the range of readily available texts has been of a predominantly literary type. However, there have been a number of recent initiatives in the electronic publishing of early texts of a variety of genres in palaeographic editions (see Texts 10, 13 and 15), and there is no doubt that the digitisation of original source material and the consequent easy manipulation of large electronic corpora is revolutionising textual study.

In this book, examples of several different styles of editing will be found, although I have tried to base the versions given here on original documents or palaeographic editions wherever possible. The usual convention of marking the expansion of an abbreviation by italics and editorially reconstructed material in square brackets has been followed. Each text is followed by a translation which has been deliberately made as literal as possible, even, on occasions, at the expense of stylistic felicity. Comments have been numbered to facilitate cross-referencing and, except in one or two special cases, divided into three sections corresponding to (1) phonetics and phonology, (2) morphology and syntax and (3) vocabulary.

The choice of texts has naturally been difficult, and has been dictated by a number of criteria. The texts are representative of the history of Spanish in a number of ways: first and foremost, chronologically, spanning the period from the tenth century to the present day. I have also tried to use texts which are illustrative of different registers of Spanish, since the appreciation of register variation is important not only for the recent history of the language, which is better documented in this respect, but also as a basis for comparison with the texts which come from earlier periods, for which on the whole we have much less overt evidence of such variation. For the sixteenth, seventeenth and eighteenth centuries I have included samples of such important 'secondary' documents as grammars and other writings on language which purport to give more explicit information about the language of the time. Modern texts are also included, since, while indeed for the contemporary language we have a different, and for some linguists, the only, legitimate source of data available, namely, the judgements of native speakers, it is important to see the limitations of modern textual evidence in order to appreciate better the presumably similar limitations of such evidence from the past.

For the reasons mentioned above, many of the texts chosen are literary in nature, since there are many literary texts readily available in reliable editions. It can of course be plausibly objected that a history of a language which is based on literary texts is in an important sense elitist, since it is unlikely to take into account the spoken language or other written registers of the language such as legal or technical usage. This is an important objection which I fully accept, and which it is of crucial importance to bear in mind at every point in the exploitation of literary material. However, there are also advantages in using at least some literary material. Literary authors can be highly sensitive, consciously or subconsciously, to different linguistic registers, even if their representations of these registers are sometimes rather conventionalised (see especially Texts 13, 20, 22, 30, 31 and 37). Quite apart from their intrinsic merits, literary texts have for better or worse been widely used and discussed as source material in the philological tradition, and students of the history of the language may therefore reasonably be expected to be in a position to engage in that discussion. Lastly, the language of literature has often served as an important model for the standard language (see especially Texts 19 and 23), and has hence been an important factor in its development.

Further reading

Mondéjar (1980).

The 'Spanish language'

One of the things that will hopefully become apparent in this book is that it is extremely difficult to delineate in a linguistically rigorous way any notion of the 'Spanish language'. In the present day, the notion of the 'Spanish language' is often used, with some justification, to refer to the standardised language that has official status in a number of countries, including Spain, and under this view 'Spanish' would be equatable with the codification of vocabulary and grammar periodically made by the Real Academia Española. But such a view is in practice impossibly restricting. Official codifications of this kind always lag behind the reality of new words and turns of phrase which are constantly found in the use of native speakers. Furthermore, even within educated registers of usage within the 'Spanish-speaking world', there is much variation (one thinks immediately of the absence of *vosotros* and its corresponding verb forms in Latin America, the varying use of *lo~la* and *le* as direct object pronouns, and the very widespread phenomena of *seseo* and *yeísmo*). Our view of 'Spanish' might accordingly be broadened to encompass the language of all those who think of themselves as native speakers of Spanish, so admitting a degree of variation which can sometimes result in mutual incomprehensibility among speakers. However, there would still remain awkward questions of identity with such phenomena as *chicano* (Texts 32a and 32b), Judeo-Spanish (Texts 33 and 34), *caló* (Texts 35 and 36) and especially creoles (Texts 39 and 40). The rationale for giving all of these attention in this book is that from a historical point of view all these are developments in various ways of 'Spanish'. For the medieval period, the label 'Spanish' is in fact totally inappropriate (see Names below), and in addition to texts originating in Castile, some other well-known early documents which have an important bearing on the development of Romance in the Iberian Peninsula (Texts 1, 2 and 5a-d) have been included in this book.

I have already referred briefly to the question of register variation. The language of everyday speech, the formal written style of official documents, advertisements, sermons in church, etc., all have distinctive linguistic characteristics (some registers of the modern Peninsular language are explored in Texts 25 and 26). 'Spanish' in the broadest sense comprises all these registers. For any language which has been standardised and has a written tradition, as Spanish has, it is unsatisfactory to assume that any one register has priority or constitutes in some sense the 'real' language (see below, Data). However, in the question of the transition of 'Latin' to 'Romance', it has often been assumed that the spoken language must have absolute priority, and I will return to this question in Chapter II.

Data

An axiom of modern formal descriptive linguistics in the generative tradition is that native speakers will have intuitive judgements about forms and structures of the language they speak which are acceptable to them, and that this native speaker competence, rather than spontaneous use of language, or performance, constitutes the proper object of linguistic investigation. Modern sociolinguistics, on the other hand, has given primacy to performance in its quest to investigate variation as revealed in spontaneous speech. The data which can be extracted from texts is essentially performance data, although, with the exception of Text 28, the language of texts is far from spontaneous; on the contrary, it is often highly self-conscious (even when an author is simulating spontaneous speech, as in Texts 13, 15, 20, 22, 24, 27, 30 and 31). Although it is virtually impossible to extract information about speaker judgements for speakers long since dead, with the consequence that the investigation of competence is not really a feasible proposition for historical textual study, texts occasionally do, if judiciously interpreted, give us some insight in this direction (see especially Text 18). Furthermore, speakers may also have judgements about the acceptability of different linguistic forms in different contexts of use ('communicative competence'), and in particular educated speakers will also have judgements about which of a number of coexisting variants is 'correct', based on puristic teaching, aspiration to or affirmation of a particular social group, or personal prejudice: evidence of such judgements is to to be found in Texts 17 and 18.

A serious objection to the exploitation of texts as a source of data is posed by some sociolinguists (e.g. Labov 1994; Milroy 1992: 5), who claim that certain aspects of change can only be studied empirically in the spoken language of the present, since text-based data is uncontrolled (a position that is rejected by Romaine 1982: 14–21). To this it may be objected, first, that while such a position is strictly correct, written texts are the only direct source of data from the past, however imperfect, that we have available today, and, second, that while it is true that writing is secondary to speech, the written language is an important manifestation of language in any literate community, and that its study should therefore not be marginalised.

Names

Turning now to the historical perspective, we come up against a number of terminological problems. Even today, 'Spanish' continues to be known both as *español* and *castellano*, the latter term reflecting the fact that in origin 'Spanish' was the Romance variety of the area of Old Castile. These two terms currently have a number of connotations: *español* is sometimes resisted by those who wish to deny the association of the language with *España*, while *castellano* sometimes carries the notion of 'standard' Spanish; but mostly they may be regarded as interchangeably denoting 'Spanish'. The term *español* only really gained currency once the political notion of *España* came into existence with the union of the Castilian and Aragonese crowns in 1474 and the conquest of Granada in 1492, but *español* is clearly nothing more than *castellano* by another name (see Text 17), and so this double nomenclature is linguistically unimportant: in this book I shall likewise use both the terms 'Castilian' and 'Spanish', 'Castilian' being primarily reserved for the pre-1492 language and for contrast with other Romance varieties of the Iberian Peninsula, and 'Spanish' being used for the modern language and for contrast with other national Romance standards.

When did 'Spanish' begin?

Much more problematic is when 'Spanish'/'Castilian' began, the question begged by any history of the language. Any precise date or event is arbitrary (see 2.0), and it is tempting to regard the question as unimportant, since there is a continuum between 'spoken Latin' and 'spoken Romance' (see Chapter II, introduction). But there is an answer of sorts. Just as we may say that *español* begins when speakers become conscious of *España* and the fact that *español* is its official language, so the same point may be made about *romance* which is recognised as being different from Latin and *castellano* which is recognised as being different from, say, *aragonés* or *bable*. 'Castilian' may therefore be said to start at the point when there is a consciousness of 'Castile', and – very significantly for this book – when efforts are made to write down 'Castilian' in a way that is both different from Latin and different from other Romance dialects. There is further discussion of this question in connection with Texts 1 to 4.

Periodisation

An associated question is that of the periodisation of 'Spanish' (I shall henceforth use this term without quotation marks). Just about any proposal made concerning periodisation can be shown to be unsatisfactory, and yet attempting to write a history of the language without recourse to some general notions like 'Old Spanish', 'Golden-Age Spanish', etc., would be cumbersome even if it were feasible. The ideal solution of being able to characterise a particular phenomenon as being typical of, say, 'the speech of upper-class Toledans between 1320 and 1480' rather than to 'Old Spanish' or even 'fourteenth- and fifteenth-century Castilian' is impractical because of our lack for the most part of such precise knowledge. I shall therefore refer to three very broad and necessarily imprecise categories: 'Old Castilian', 'Golden-Age Spanish' and 'Modern Spanish'. The use of these terms should not be taken to imply that I believe that these are in any sense natural 'periods' of Spanish; they are simply labels of convenience.

Further reading

Eberenz (1991).

II Latin and Romance

Texts and the history of the Romance languages

The written word has always commanded huge respect. Romance linguists have often considered themselves doubly fortunate in having at their disposal not only a vast corpus of 'Romance' texts, but also an impressive body of literary and other texts in the parent language, Latin. The only severe problem, in fact, has been seen as what to do with the unsatisfactory state of affairs between the Classical Latin period and the appearance of the first texts apparently written in the Romance vernacular, when the language of documents often appears neither to be one thing nor the other, aspiring unsuccessfully to follow classical precept, but not overtly representing a vernacular. What happened during this, the so-called 'Vulgar Latin period', has been the subject of great speculation, to be resolved by comparing the textually attested forms of Latin and Romance and suggesting likely, if often unattested, intermediate forms. This sort of approach therefore assumes the following model for the history of Romance:

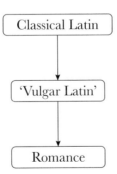

This model is unsatisfactory, however, in a number of important ways. In the first place, although there are frequent plausible correspondences between the attested forms of Classical Latin and Romance, there are many cases in which establishing such correspondences is difficult, in need of severe qualification, or downright impossible, leading to the inescapable conclusion that many Romance forms are simply not attested in Classical Latin at all (examples are given in Relating Latin and Romance below), so that our model would look like this:

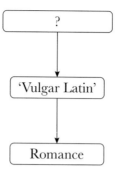

It also turns out that the Romance languages sometimes do not correspond in their inheritance of attested words: the notion 'head' is represented by Spanish *cabeza* (the Classical Latin neuter noun CAPĬTĬU[M] had the meaning of 'head covering'), by Italian *capo* (from Classical Latin CĂPŬT 'head') and by French *tête* (from Classical Latin TĔSTA 'earthen pot'): the conclusion must be that there was diversity in 'Vulgar Latin'. This suggests the following model:

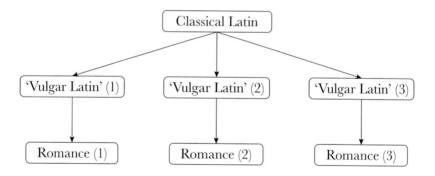

In fact, we need to ask some basic questions about the evolution of Latin into Romance. The majority of Latin/Romance speakers may be assumed to have been illiterate and uncultured, learning their mother tongue as an everyday means of communication. (This is not to imply they were necessarily unsophisticated or uninventive.) Their language would even in Imperial times have been quite different in nature from the cultured literary norm, especially in syntax and vocabulary. The evidence for this is not extensive, but it is compelling. We can see evidence of popular usage, or what indeed was termed *sermo vulgaris*, in the plays of Plautus (*c.* 254–184 BC) and the letters of Cicero (106–43 BC); in the rare workaday documents that have have come down to us (through disaster or accident) such as the inscriptions at Pompeii and Herculaneum, the towns buried in volcanic ash in 79 AD, or the fragments of bark letters found at Vindolanda near Hadrian's Wall, we can dimly observe a language significantly different from that of Latin literature. In other words, the source of Romance is not Classical Latin, but what we may now call more accurately 'Spoken Latin':

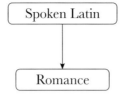

This is not to say that what we have so far been calling Classical Latin will not be of help in reconstructing Spoken Latin, but it must always be envisaged in that way, i.e., as a source of contributory evidence about the origins of the Romance languages rather than as the origin itself. Since Classical Latin is so well researched and documented, it is also useful to take it as a reference point, and ways in which that can be done are described below (Relating Latin and Romance).

We can improve our model still further by considering that there is also evidence of other 'styles' or 'registers' of Latin. Of especial importance to the Romance linguist is Christian Latin. The language of the early Church Fathers was characterised by their desire to be intelligible to ordinary people. Whilst the fathers were often cultured individuals who would have been at home in Classical Latin, they modified their language to make it, as we would say today, more 'user-friendly', and in their writing we can often perceive words, turns of phrase and syntactic patterns which resemble Romance rather than Classical Latin. Their language also contained a good deal of special terminology, often borrowed from Greek. In translations of the Scriptures into Latin from Greek they erred on the side of strict faithfulness to the Greek text and so introduced other kinds of modification into their Latin. This variety of Latin was of tremendous significance in Western Europe, since the church perpetuated the use of Latin in this way, and it is even possible that certain developments in Romance were influenced by it (see **Keypoint: learned and popular, semilearned and semipopular**, p. 277). We can now construe our model as follows:

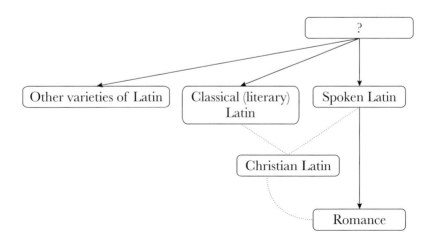

Still the picture is not complete. We must now turn our attention to our notion of 'Romance'. Not only did Spoken Latin dialectalise geographically so that different Romance varieties became discernible and were differentially labelled, but certain of these varieties were invested with prestige as a result of their adoption for administrative, legal and literary functions: it is in these that we have the beginnings of the modern Romance standard 'languages'. It was at this stage that these prestige varieties began to show similar characteristics to Latin in terms of the development of a number of variant styles or registers, so that we may once again suspect that the language of literature or the language of legal documents is not equatable with the language of everyday speech. There is another complication too: cultured authors of the Middle Ages and Renaissance came to be interested in Classical culture, especially at first in Classical Latin, and Classical Latin was quite clearly used as a source of lexical and stylistic, and arguably even syntactic, borrowing. The picture we may envisage is:

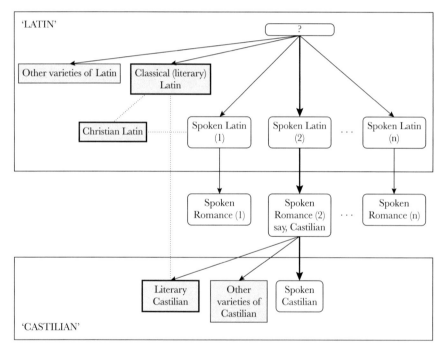

Even this diagram is a gross over-simplification of what we may construe as the reality of the evolution of Castilian. It attributes to 'Castilian' an identity and separability which is almost certainly inappropriate for the medieval period before the notion of a standard language emerged, and it gives no expression to the undeniable interaction between Romance varieties. However, it may be a useful preliminary challenge to such genealogical models of language evolution, which are still widely used. The thick arrowheads show what may be construed as the direct line of generational transmission from Spoken Latin to Spoken Castilian, while the shaded boxes show the principal types of extant texts. The enclosed areas denote what we may conveniently think of as comprising the general notions of 'Latin' and 'Castilian'. Broken lines show relations rather than chronological descent. The diagram also gives some (though nowhere near complete) expression to the role of variation in the evolution of languages which are used as vehicles of culture, as Latin and Castilian are, and it can quickly be seen that the texts at our disposal must not be thought of as being anything more than representative of particular varieties of 'Latin' and 'Romance' respectively.

Relating Latin and Romance

The simplest kind of relation between Latin and a Romance language is when a Latin word, having undergone clearly recognisable phonetic changes, yields a Romance form which has essentially the same meaning, e.g. PĀNE [PĀNIS] > Sp. *pan*. Most words, however, are much more problematical.

The Romance word may be very convincingly based on an attested Latin form, even though the phonetic changes it has undergone do not allow us to conclude that there is a complete identity with the Latin form. Sp. *pájaro* 'bird' derives clearly enough from Lat. PASSĔRE [PASSER] 'sparrow', but we must assume irregular phonetic changes of /ss/ to /ʃ/ and of /ĕ/ to /a/. Furthermore, there has been a change of noun type: from the Latin third declension (which yielded Spanish nouns with consonantal endings in the singular and plurals in *-es*) to the Spanish *-o* class (which normally derived from the Latin second declension). We know from textual evidence that the form *pássaro* existed in earlier Castilian; but if we require an exact parallel with a Latin form we have to assume the existence of a hypothetical ?PASSARU[S].

The lack of formal parallel with Latin is sometimes attributable to morphological, rather than phonetic, modification. Sp. *moler* is clearly associable with Lat. MŎLĔRE [MŎLO]; it has the same basic meaning of 'to grind', 'mill' and it resembles it phonetically in a very obvious way. But for *moler* we must presuppose an intermediate stage ?MŎLĔRE, that is to say, an analogical change of conjugation type, from the stem-stressed third conjugation to the inflection-stressed second conjugation, of the kind that happened very frequently in Spanish (Spanish does not in fact have any verbs deriving directly from the Latin third conjugation, in which the infinitive is stressed on the stem rather than the ending). In the same way, Sp. *morir* is very obviously derived from Lat. ?MŎRĪRE, but the classical form of the verb was MŎRĪ [MŎRĬOR], which was deponent (a class of verbs which were always passive in form). The deponents, and, indeed, the Latin passive inflexions, are totally defunct in Romance, and so it is plausible to assume that ?MORĪRE was an analogical non-deponent form. Another complication is that a Romance word may be traced back to an unattested morphological derivative of an attested Latin word. A well-known example of this is Sp. *compañero*, which has parallels in other Romance languages (Fr. *compagnon*, It. *compagno*). It is most probably based on the root PĀNIS 'bread' with the prefix COM- added; in the Spanish case, the suffix ĀRĬU[S] is also added. Whilst all these elements are known from attested Latin words, the particular combination ?COMPĀNĬĀRĬU[S] remains conjectural.

Sometimes the difficulty lies not so much with the phonetic or morphological form of the word as with its meaning or function. Sp. *alba* is clearly derivable from Lat. ALBA, the feminine form of ALBU[S] 'white', 'bright', and there are parallels in a number of other Romance languages (Fr. *aube*, It. *alba*), though the meaning of 'dawn' is unknown in Latin. Sp. *pero* 'but' appears to derive formally from Lat. PER HŌC, though the development of such an idiom with adversative meaning is not attested in Latin. Yet another example is Sp. *enhiesto* 'upright', which can plausibly be derived phonetically from Lat. ĪNFĔSTU[S], the meaning of which is 'hostile', 'dangerous', 'troublesome', but the semantic connection is harder to establish. It may be related to the use of ĪNFĔSTU[S] in such phrases as HASTĀ ĪNFĔSTĀ 'with lance couched' (Cor., II, 629–30).

There is a long tradition in Romance linguistics of labelling any such hypothesised form as 'Vulgar Latin', by which we should really understand hypothesised 'proto-Romance', and by writing reconstructed forms as ?PASSARU[S], ?MŎLĒRE, ?MŎRĪRE and ?COMPĀNĀRĬU[S] with an asterisk. I shall follow a rather different series of conventions in this book. I shall show all hypothetical forms with a question mark (this also releases the asterisk to indicate syntactic unacceptability, in line with modern generative usage), but I shall not use the term 'Vulgar Latin' to refer to them; instead I shall simply use the term 'Latin' for all such reconstructions. In tracing derivations I shall use the symbols '>' and '<' (the arrowhead indicates the chronological direction of movement) only where there is a plausibly exact formal parallel between the Romance word and Latin; where there is not, I shall show the attested Latin form as the source, but I shall use the sign '≥' to show that the Romance word has undergone something beyond the expected phonetic modification, or that it has undergone significant morphological readjustment. Semantic change is not marked as such, though it may be deduced from accompanying glosses given in single quotation marks. Where the Romance word is a morphological derivative of an attested Latin root, I shall show the latter preceded by a 'root' sign '√' and a full arrow '→' or '←'. The form of the Latin word most closely approximating to the Romance word is given as the source (see **Keypoint: the case-system of Latin**, p. 263); if it is not in its dictionary citation form (usually the nominative singular for nouns and the first person singular of the present tense for verbs), then this is given in square brackets. Thus:

PĀNE [PĀNIS] > *pan*
pájaro ≤ PASSĔRE [PASSER]
compañero ← √PĀNIS or ?COMPĀNĬĀRĬU[S] > *compañero*

Some forms, meanings and usages which are not attested in Classical Latin are attested in what are often referred to as 'Vulgar Latin texts'. This term has been used to characterise texts whose language, partially or principally, does not conform to the standards of literary usage observed in the canon of Latin literature. The Spanish word *sabueso* 'bloodhound' has no corresponding form in literary Latin, though it is paralleled in other Romance languages by such forms as It. *segugio* and OFr. *seus*; however, the form SIGUSIUM CĂNEM 'dog from Sigusium?' is attested in the *Lex Salica*, the codification of Salian Frankish law that dates from the sixth century. Spanish *después* probably derives from the phrase DĒ POST, which is indeed found in the sixth-century *Vitae Patrum*.

The origins of some Romance forms are rather more conjectural. Sp. *callar* may be supposed to derive from a hypothetical Latin form ?CALLARE which is plausibly the result of a borrowing from Gr. χαλάω 'to loose', 'drop', 'lower', which comes to have the specific association of 'to drop (the voice)'. Such forms as ?CALLARE are also often referred to as 'Vulgar Latin' forms.

'Latin', 'Vulgar Latin' and 'Romance'

In this book, then, no systematic distinction is made between 'Classical' and 'Vulgar' Latin when citing Latin words. This means that the term 'Latin' has a very broad application; but it is no broader than 'English', or 'Spanish', which like-wise embrace many periods, styles and registers of what is conventionally consid-ered the same language. My abandoning of this traditional distinction is in line with much recent thinking by both Romance and Latin scholars (Lloyd 1979; Wright 1982: 52–4), and I will give only a short justification here. The label 'Vulgar Latin' has been used with a multiplicity of meanings; most unfortunately, perhaps, it has been used to denote both reconstructed Latin (proto-Romance) and Latin which is attested only outside the language of classical literature. In the latter mean-ing, it has been applied very broadly indeed to cover anything from the graffiti on the walls of Pompeii to the language of the Vulgate Bible. It has also, as we have seen, been used as a synonym for 'spoken Latin'. There has often been an asso-ciated use of the term 'Vulgar Latin' as the intermediate evolutionary stage between 'Classical Latin' and the Romance languages. But it is more appropriate to see Latin as a language that was spoken over a very long period and a very extensive area, as a language which, like any other, underwent change and had much geo-graphical, social and stylistic variation. We might with advantage identify such notions as 'early Latin', 'late Latin', 'educated Latin', 'the Latin of Tarraconensis', and so on, although our knowledge of such variation is very partial. Even within 'Classical Latin', often represented as fairly immutable, there is evidence of such variation: classical scholars note a number of usages which are restricted to certain periods of Latin literature, and there are important differences in usage among authors and especially between Latin poetry and prose.

I will use the term 'Romance' in two ways. First, I will use it as a shorthand for the family of the Romance languages, that is, all those languages and dialects which derive historically from Latin. It is often convenient to speak of a feature which characterises the Romance languages but not Latin as a 'Romance phenom-enon': the disappearance of inflectional voice in the verb or the appearance of the definite article, for example. Second, the term 'Romance' is also used in opposition to 'Latin' to denote the medieval vernaculars, especially when two different systems of writing, one to represent Latin and the other to represent these vernaculars, emerged. In this second meaning, then, 'Romance' is of espe-cial significance in examining medieval texts.

1 A letter from the Visigothic period (seventh century?)

1.0 The Visigoths moved southwards to the Iberian Peninsula after the encroach-ment of the Franks on their kingdom of Toulouse at the beginning of the sixth cen-tury. There had been other Germanic peoples in the Peninsula before: in 409,

Swabians, Alans and Vandals arrived, although of these, only the Swabians established a lasting presence with a kingdom in the northwest. The Visigoths, who had
for many years lived in close contact with the Roman empire, were the most
Romanised of these peoples, to such an extent that from a linguistic point of view
they seem to have adopted the use of Latin/Romance, certainly in official documents, and probably in everyday speech as well. The first part of the Visigothic
period was characterised by a system of apartheid, with the two communities existing side by side, perhaps as much as anything else for religious reasons, since the
Visigoths were Arians while the native population continued allegiance to the
Roman church. Eventually, however, the Visigoths also adopted Roman Catholicism
and loosely united the Peninsula with Toledo as their capital – it is this situation to
which the notion of the 'Reconquest' later refers. The linguistic impact of Visigothic
on Hispano-Romance was consequently negligible; the Germanic loanwords in
Spanish are mostly common to a number of other Romance languages, and we may
assume that there were earlier borrowings into Latin (see, for example, 5d.3.3).

Further reading

Gamillscheg (1932); Thompson (1969).

The text

This text is taken from Gómez-Moreno (1954) and the English translation offered
is in essence an equivalent of his suggested Spanish version. The document comes
from a piece of slate which has been used on both sides, some of which has
flaked off at the edges. From the style of lettering it would seem to date from
the seventh century. It is thus a document which, whilst written in broad conformity with Latin spelling, might be expected to give some clues about the direction
in which spoken Latin was evolving in everyday, practical, use by this time. To
what extent it represents a stage in the evolution of Castilian, however, it is hard
to say, since dialectal features are not sufficiently distinctive.

> [domno] paulo faustinus saluto tvam
> [claritat]em et rogo te domne et comodo consu
> [etum es]t facere ut *per* te ipsut oliballa quollige
> [incell]a vt ipsos mancipios jn jvra iemento
> [peter]e debeas vt tibi fraudem non fa   5
> [cian]t illas cupas collige calas
>
> [r]ecortices et sigilla de tuo anvlo et uide
> [il]las tegolas cara tritas svnt de fibola quo
> [m]odo ego ipsas demisi illum meracium manda
> [d]e tiliata uenire ut ajvtet ibi unum quina   10
> et unum atmancio nostro[1]

---

1   This line was inserted between ll.10 and 11 in a smaller size of lettering, presumably indicating
    an afterthought or realisation of an omission.

de siriola pesitula at illa ammica tua
oris dirige prodi esto sic
tus custudiat

Translation

Faustinus to [the lord] Paulus: I greet Your [Excellency] and ask you, my Lord, even as it is the custom to do, yourself to collect the 'oliballa' [in the chamber] and that you should [take] an oath of the servants so that they do not deceive you. Collect the barrels which are stored; cork them again and seal them with your ring; and see the 'tegolas' that are crushed with the 'fibola', as I sent them. Order that Meracius to come from Tiliata (Tejeda) so that someone from Siriola can help there (and one Atmantius of ours). Send Pesitula and that Ammica of yours to the boundaries. May this be clear, and may he guard yours[?].

Phonetics and phonology

1.1.1 The variation in the spelling of Latin initial /kw/ and /k/ before /o/ (**comodo**, l.2, vs. **quo[m]odo**, ll.8–9); **quollige**, l.3, vs. **collige**, l.6) suggests both (a) that the Latin distinction between /k/ and /kw/ was no longer made in this context and (b) that the writer was aware of this, as a result of which he hyper-corrects the **c** of **collige** to **qu**. This is consistent with the very general reduction of the group /kwo/ to /ko/ in Spanish and indeed in Romance generally (cf. Lat. QUŌMŎDŎ > Sp. *como*, Fr. *comme*, It. *come*, Rom. *cum*, etc.). The same phenomenon may be present in **cara** (l.8) which probably corresponds to Lat. QUĀRĒ (cf. the Romance derivatives OCast. *ca* and Fr. *car*), though see below, 1.2.5.
   Keypoint: consonant groups (p. 267).

1.1.2 The spelling **domne** (l.2) appears to indicate a reduction of the Latin proparoxytone DŎMĬNE [DŎMĬNUS] by the syncope of the /ĭ/ vowel. This is exactly what happens in the Western Romance languages, cf. Sp. *dueño* < Lat. DŎMĬNU[S], *hombre* < Lat. HŎMĬNE [HŎMO]. The spelling here confirms us in our suspicion that such forms as ?/dŏmnu/ and ?/ŏmne/ existed at an intermediate stage.
   Keypoint: stress (p. 291).

1.1.3 The spelling **custudiat** (l.14) corresponding to Lat. CŬSTŌDĬAT [CŬSTŌDĬO] can be taken as evidence of the merger of tonic /ŭ/ and /ō/ which was a widespread feature of Romance, though the eventual result of this merger in Spanish was /o/. (MSp. *custodia* is in fact of learned origin.) Although their exact meaning is unclear (see 1.3.1), **fibola** and **tegolas** (l.8) are likely to correspond to Lat. FĬBŬLA and TĒGŬLAS [TĒGŬLA] respectively, suggesting a similar merger of /ŭ/ and /ō/ in atonic position (atonic /ū/ also merged with these). However, this phenomenon cannot be illustrated by modern evidence of the words in question, since TĒGŬLA underwent reduction of the proparoxytone by syncope of the atonic /u/ to yield MSp. *teja*, and FĬBŬLA as such does not survive at all in Spanish (*hebilla* with the same meaning 'buckle', 'clasp' derives from Lat. ?FĬBĔLLA, which is based on √FĬBŬLA, and *fibula* 'fibula', 'brooch' is of learned origin). The spelling **tus** (l.14) corresponding to Latin TŬOS [TŬUS] probably also reflects the same merger.

The parallel merger of atonic /ē/, /ī/ (and /ĭ/) may be indicated by the spelling **demisi** (l.9) corresponding to Lat. DĪMĪSI [DĬMĬTTO].

Keypoints: vowels (p. 296); **stress** (p. 291); **learned and popular, semilearned and semipopular** (p. 277).

1.1.4 Ajvtet (l.10) corresponds to Lat. ADIŪTET [ADIŪTO]. The /d/ + /j/ group palatalised in Spanish to /j/, cf. MSp. *ayude*, and this spelling indicates that process.

Keypoint: palatalisation (p. 280).

1.1.5 Other spelling 'mistakes' are not so easy to interpret. **Ipsut** (l.3) seems to be a rendering of Lat. IPSAM [IPSE] (see 1.2.3): this may have been a mistake induced by the presence of **ut** in the vicinity. **Jvra iemento** (l.4) is Lat. IŪRĀMENTU[M], and **quina** possibly corresponds to Lat. QUIVIS.

1.1.6 If it is correct to interpret **oliballa** (l.3) as having something to do with *olivas* 'olives', then the use of a *b* corresponding to Latin *v* (√OLĪVA) may be indicative of the fricativisation of Latin intervocalic /w/. The precise phonetic value of *b* here is uncertain, though the very use of the letter *b* with its bilabial associations suggests the possibility of [β].

Keypoint: the 'b/v' merger (p. 262).

1.1.7 The spelling of **atmancio nostro** (l.11), which, like the preceding **unum**, would have been accusative (ATMANTIUM NOSTRUM) in Classical Latin, and the problematic (see 1.1.6) **oliballa** (l.3), which, if the object of **quollige,** would have been an accusative, suggest a pronunciation of the final syllable with no final /m/. Indeed, final /m/ ceased to be pronounced centuries earlier:[2]

1.1.8 What is striking about this passage, however, is just how much is continued to be spelt in accordance with Latin practice.

Final /m/ is frequently represented in accusatives (**tvam**, l.1, **fraudem**, l.5, etc.), despite the evidence against its pronunciation given in 1.1.7.

---

2   See Wright (1982: 55–6) who quotes the observation of Velius Longus, writing in the second century:

> Sic enim dicitur *illum ego* et *omnium optimum*, *illum* et *omnium* aeque *m* terminat nec tamen in enuntiatione apparet … confitendum aliter scribi, aliter enuntiari …

'*Illum ego* and *omnium optimum* are said in such a way that although both *illum* and *omnium* both end in *m* it does not appear in pronunciation… so it is to be admitted that what is written in one way is pronounced in another …'

The distinction between double and single consonants is maintained (**sigilla** but **anvlo**, l.7) – unless **ammica** (l.12) is a misspelling of Lat. AMĪCA rather than a proper name.

There is no indication of lenition (**saluto**, l.1, corresponding to MSp. *saludo*, **cupas**, l.6, ‖ MSp. *cubas*, etc.).

Keypoint: lenition (p. 278).

Morphology and syntax

1.2.1 The phonological significance of **unum atmancio nostro** (l.11), discussed in 1.1.7, is closely bound up with the loss of Latin case distinctions: the writing of -*o* for -*um* suggests a lack of distinction between accusative and dative–ablative case (in Latin -UM and -O respectively in this instance). The case endings of Latin are otherwise apparently accurately represented in this text.

Keypoint: the case-system of Latin (p. 263).

1.2.2 The case-functions of the Latin genitive, dative and ablative cases came to be represented in Romance by prepositions, and something of that process of substitution can be seen here: **de tvo anvlo** (l.7) and **de fibola** (l.8) render the instrumental function of the Latin ablative. But the indirect object function of the dative is preserved in **paulo** from Lat. PAULŌ [PAULUS] (l.1) (though we cannot know exactly what originally stood before this word), and **oris**, apparently the dative-ablative plural ŌRĪS of Lat. ŌRA, possibly had a similar function. Maybe, then, there was still some sense of distinction between dative and accusative.

Keypoint: the case-system of Latin (p. 263).

1.2.3 Ipsut (l.3), **ipsos** (l.4), **illas** (l.6) and **illa** (l.12) are used with a frequency in excess of what is usual in literary Latin for the demonstratives ILLE and IPSE and in a way that sometimes suggests either the anaphoric or the defining functions of the Romance definite article, which in Spanish and most other Romance languages derived from the forms of Lat. ILLE. This is a feature of several 'vulgar' texts, and is extremely difficult to interpret. **Ipsut oliballa** . . . (l.3) and **illas cupas** . . . **calas** (l.6) seem to illustrate the use of **ipsut** and **illas** in a defining function: 'the "oliballa" [in the chamber]', 'the/those barrels which are stored'.

Ipsas in **ipsas demisi** (l.9) resembles in function a third person object pronoun of Romance (cf. MSp. *las envié*), though MSp. *las* has its origin in Lat. ILLAS [ILLE].

Keypoints: the definite article (p. 270); **demonstratives** (p. 270).

1.2.4 The expression **tvam [claritat]em** appears to be a way of referring deferentially to a second person. We shall see how, much later, similar third person expressions of the second person notion came to be used to indicate respect, one of which, *vuestra merced*, formed the basis of MSp. *usted* (see 18.2.1). Otherwise, the second person form used here is the Latin singular TU: there is no sign of the Latin plural VŌS being used with singular reference to indicate respect, a device widely adopted in Romance.

Keypoint: personal pronouns (p. 284).

1.2.5 Although the syntax is generally intelligible on the basis of Latin, there are some obscurities which cannot be elucidated by appeal to Romance patterns.

Ut per te ipsut oliballa quollige [incell]a (ll.3–4): what may be taken as the imperative **quollige** is incompatible with the **ut** construction (compare the use of the subjunctive **debeas**, l.5, in the parallel construction which follows).

The use of **cara** (l.8) is strange here, whether read as QUĀRE, QUĬĂ or as a relative pronoun, and it is difficult to gauge its exact meaning and function. The obscurity of this section also makes the exact value of **tritas svnt** (l.8) difficult to judge: it has been translated here as 'are crushed', but whether it is the equivalent of MSp. *son majadas, están majadas* or *han sido majadas* (the latter would correspond to the Latin perfect passive) is unclear.

Keypoint: the passive (p. 281).

Sic tus custudiat (ll.13–14): the verb **custudiat**, the subjunctive of CŬSTŌDĬO, seems to lack an obvious subject.

1.2.6 The word order is variable, and no consistent pattern emerges. The typical unmarked verb-final order of Latin is used in some instances (**vt tibi fraudem non fa[cian]t**, ll.5–6; **quo [m]odo ego ipsas demisi**, ll.8–9), but there is also verb-first order (**ut ajvtet ibi unum quina de siriola**, l.10). The same is true of clauses involving imperatives (verb-last: **illa ammica tua oris dirige**, ll.12–13; verb-first: **uide [il]las tegolas** . . . (ll.7–8). The apparent hyperbaton in l.6 (**illas cupas collige calas = illas cupas calas collige**?) is atypical of such utilitarian prose style.

Vocabulary

1.3.1 The choice of vocabulary (except of course for the proper nouns, such as **tiliata**, which has been identified with present-day Tejeda) does not obviously suggest a geographical provenance. Of the three words which are particularly problematic in meaning, only **oliballa** (l.3) is actually unknown; **fibola** and **tegolas** (l.8) are no doubt being used in a specialised way, the precise technical sense of which we can only guess at today.

III   Early Romance

The texts in this chapter are chosen because of their early date; they are not unequivocally representative of any one consistent geographical dialect, though their spellings indicate features which allow some conclusions about provenance to be drawn. They illustrate the problems typically encountered in assessing texts of this period.

2 From the Glosses of San Millán de la Cogolla (mid-tenth century?)

2.0 The San Millán glosses, which were originally dated by Menéndez Pidal to 977 (the Latin text which they gloss was copied about a century earlier) have sometimes been heralded as representing the birth of the Spanish language, but such a position is now emphatically not sustainable, and the date of their writing is also in question (Wright 1982: 195–6). While arguments about the primacy of this text revolve around the questions discussed in Chapter II under Names and Periodisation (what do we mean by 'Spanish'?, where are diachronic boundaries to be drawn?), one or two further observations on the matter are appropriate here. In the first place, the notion 'Spanish' as we understand it today scarcely existed at this time; the word *español* or *españón*, when first encountered, seems to designate the Christian inhabitants of the Iberian Peninsula, in order to distinguish them from Christians from other parts of Europe – it does not refer to language.[1] Second, the Romance of the glosses, has, as we shall see, marked non-Castilian dialectal features, and San Millán itself is situated in La Rioja, not in Castile (see Map 1, p. 21), so it is unlikely that we can equate it with 'Castilian' (similarly, it is not clear that *castellano* would have had any linguistic significance either at this time – see also in this connection 16.3.1). La Rioja oscillated between the crowns of León and Navarre in the tenth century and was only definitively incorporated into Castile in the mid-twelfth century. However, there is certainly enough evidence in the glosses to convince us that they are for the most part an

---

1   See Lapesa (1985a). *Espagnol* is first attested in Occitan at the end of the eleventh century. *Españon* is found in the *Poema de Fernán González* (*c*.1250) and in the P MS of the *Libro de Alexandre* (see Text 9).

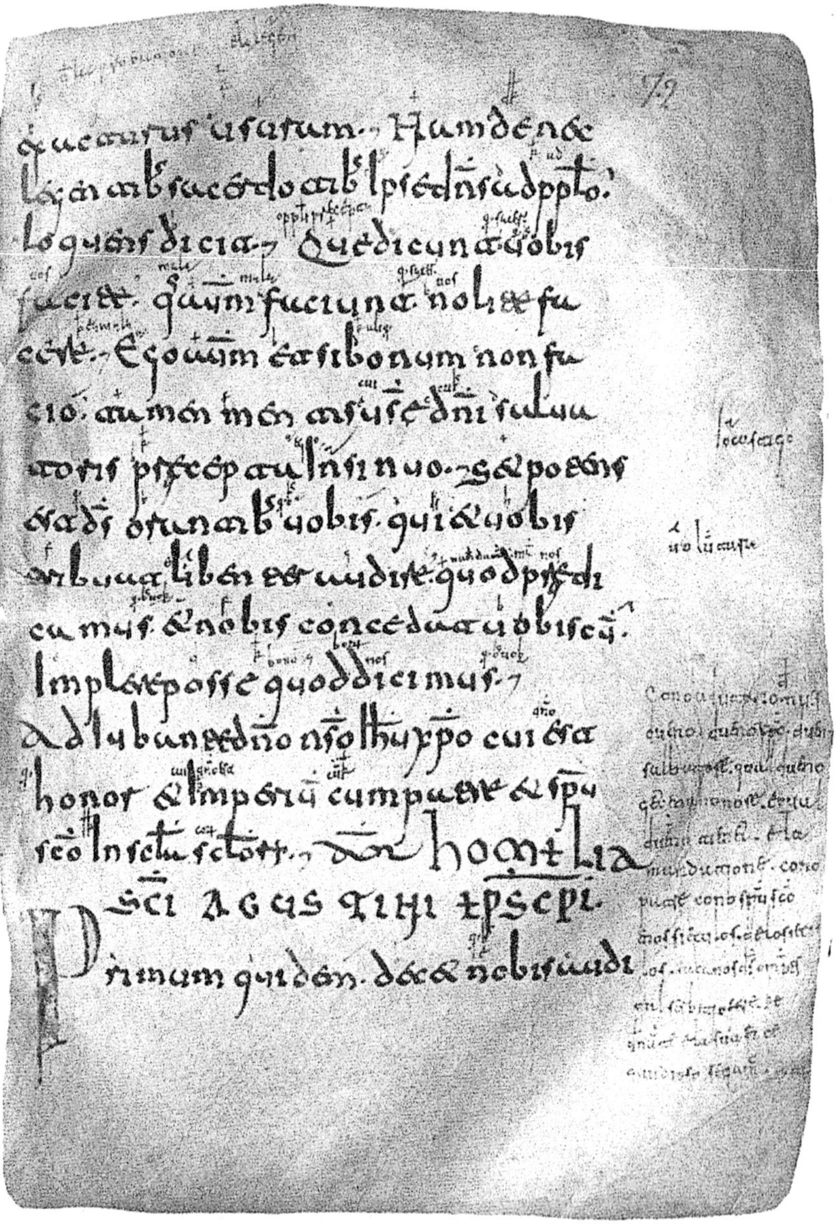

Plate 1 MS Aemilianensis f.72r (Text 2)

overt representation of Romance forms, and the Latin to which the glosses are appended is not the plainly heavily corrupted, Romance-like, 'Latin' of a legal text such as Text 3, but is a Christian Latin text (in the passage we shall examine, it is from a sermon by Caesarius of Arles).

Significant dates:

Castile		La Rioja		Aragon	
961	Semi-independence of Castile under Count Fernán González	923	Conquest of La Rioja by León	1035	Independence of Aragon under Ramiro I
1029	Union of Castile and Navarre	1167	Definitive union of La Rioja and Castile	1076–1134	Union of Navarre and Aragon under Pedro I and Alfonso I
1032	Union of Castile and León under Fernando I				

Map 1 The northern Iberian Peninsula, tenth to twelfth centuries

Apart from the lexical glosses which are reproduced here, parts of the manuscript contain other annotations which are only just beginning to be studied: the beginning of each sentence is marked with a dagger and within each sentence there are letters above words which may have indicated the order of the corresponding sentence in Romance. Latin relatives and nouns are also used to indicate the subject of verbs which do not have a subject expressed, the function of verb complements and the reference of pronouns.

An intriguing question is that of what purpose the glosses served. The most straightforward answer is that, rather like the annotations a student might make today in the margin of a book in a foreign language, they translate words which were not known, especially words which were crucial to understanding: this would be confirmed by such 'gist' translations as **kaderat** (l.3), which gives the general idea of **jncurrit anime detrimentum**, or **certe** (l.12), which renders the force of Latin **num**. On this assumption, it would be possible to use the glosses in a negative way, and to conclude, for instance, that if words like **adtendat** (l.1), **jncurrit** (l.3), **dissimulant** (l.7), **conmittunt** (l.8), **subuertere** (l.10), **litigare** (l.11), **jnsinuo** (l.15) needed glossing, then the forms corresponding to MSp. *atienda, incurre, disimulan, cometen, subvertir, lidiar, insinuar* either did not exist in the language of the time (this is very likely in the case of the learned words *incurre, disimulan, subvertir* and *insinuar*) or were not recognisable for phonetic or semantic reasons (*lidiar* had moved a long way from Lat. [LĪTĬGO] and had the more restricted meaning of 'to fight in battle', and possibly its modern meaning of 'to fight bulls'). But it appears that not all words and phrases which could have posed problems were glossed: in the passage below, the phrase **jn quo judicio judicaueritis judicauimini**, which must have been quite opaque to a Romance speaker of the time, is left without gloss. Another, related, possibility is that the glosses were made to facilitate the intelligible reading aloud of the text, a kind of crib-sheet for the assistance of the duty reader whose understanding of the text might otherwise have been hazy. Maybe they were to assist improvised exegesis of the text. Yet another scenario proposed is that the glosses are for the benefit of foreign visitors, so that they should know what the local Romance equivalents of certain phrases were: thus the last long 'gloss' in this passage may have been the local way of ending a sermon (which the local monks would have known anyway). The possibilities are many, and the debate ongoing. What is important for present purposes in our approach to this text is not to take too much for granted.

Further reading

Menéndez Pidal (1976) gives a palaeographic edition of the Glosses of San Millán and the slightly later Glosses of Santo Domingo de Silos (the latter in Castile itself, near Burgos, see Map 1, p. 21), and a description of the MSS. A facsimile edition was published by the Servicio de Publicaciones del Ministerio de Educación y Ciencia (1977). See also Emiliano (1993); Stengaard (1991a); Wright (1986).

The text

The extract comes from MS Aemilianensis 60, ff. 70v.–72r. and follows Menéndez Pidal (1971: 6–7).

> Adtendat [katet] unusquisq*ue* [q*ui* cataq*ui*] ne munera accipiendo alterius causam mala*m* faciat sua*m* pena*m* si jnjuste judicauerit; accipe pecunie lucrum et jncurrit [kaderat] anime detrimentu*m*. Non se circumueniat qui talis est [non e cuempetet elo uamne en iui]; jn illo enim jmpletur quod scriptu*m* est: jn quo judicio judicaueritis judicauimini. Forsita*m* [alq*ui*eras]   **5**
> quando jsta prędicamus aliqui contra nos jrascuntur et dicunt: jpsi qui hoc predicant hoc jmplere dissimulant [tardar an por jnplire]; jpsi sacerdotes, presuiteres et diacones talia plura conmittunt [tales muito fazen]; et quida*m*, fr*atre*s, alicotiens [alquanda beces] ueru*m* est, quod pej*us* est. Na*m* aliqui clerici et jnebriari se solent, et causas jnjuste subuertere [tran   **10**

tornare] et jn festiuitati*bus* causas dicere et litigare non erubescunt [no*n*ſe
bergudia*n* tramare].[2] Set num [certe] quid toti condemnandi sunt ...

    Saluatoris precepta jnsinuo [jocaſtigo] ... qui et nobis tribuat libenter   *15*
[uolu*n*taria] audire quod predicamus ... abjubante d*omi*no n*ost*ro Jhesu
Christo cui est honor et jmperiu*m* cum patre et S*piritu* S*an*cto jn s*e*c*u*la s*e*c*u*-
lor*um* [conoajutorio d*e* nueſtro dueno, dueno *Christo*, dueno Salbatore, qual
dueno get ena honore, equal due*n*no tienet ela mandatjone cono Patre, cono
S*piritu* S*an*cto, enoſ ſieculoſ deloſieculos. Facanoſ D*eu*ſ om*n*ipotes tal ſ   *20*
erbitjo fere ke d*en*a*n*te ela ſua face gaudioſo ſegam*us*. Am*em*][3]

Translation of the Latin text

Let everyone beware lest by accepting gifts from another, which is a sinful thing,
he makes his own punishment, if he has judged unjustly; by accepting a reward
of money he incurs damage to his soul. Such a person should not deceive himself;
for in him is fulfilled that which is written: as you judge so shall you be judged.
It may happen that when we preach these things there are people who are angry
with us and say: these men who preach this rule [only] pretend to observe it;
for priests and deacons commit many such [offences]; and indeed, brothers, sometimes this is the case, more is the pity. For some of the clergy are even wont to
get drunk and are not ashamed to destroy things without reason, and to utter
insults and to fight in their revelries. But surely all are to be condemned ...

    I teach the precepts of my Saviour ... may he freely grant us [you][4] to listen
to what we preach ... with the help of our Lord Jesus Christ, to whom is honour
and power with the Father and Holy Spirit for ever and ever.

    I will comment on each of the glosses in turn.

2.1 Katet (l.1) is the 3rd p.sg. present subjunctive of OCast. *catar* 'to look at' <
Lat. [CAPTO], the frequentative form of Lat. [CĂPĬO] 'to take', 'capture'. The
change in meaning is presumably a restriction to 'to take in with one's sight'.
Catar survives in Modern Spanish only in the prefixal forms *acatar* 'to heed',
'respect' and *percatarse de* 'to notice', 'realise'. The final /t/ of the Latin 3rd p.sg.
is still generally represented in the earliest texts, cf. here also **kaderat** (l.3), **cuempetet** (l.4), **get** (l.19), **tienet** (l.19), and was probably still articulated as [t] or
possibly [θ] (see also 4.2.11).

2.2 Quiscataqui (l.1) appears not to correspond exactly to any attested Romance
form, but it is a plausible interim neologism. It is apparently constructed from a
combination of Lat. QUIS 'who', Lat. ?CATA (< Gk. κατά, which was used to
render the distributive notion of 'by' in such expressions as 'two by two' and was
the origin of Sp. *cada* 'each') and Lat. QUI.

2   Follows Menéndez Pidal's reading with reagent: the *m* is unclear.
3   Before Menéndez Pidal this had been read as *omnipotens ... gaudiosos ...*
4   Understood as *uobis*, since *nobis* makes poor sense.

2.3 Kaderat (l.3) || MSp. *caerá* clearly illustrates the analytic Romance future. The intervocalic /d/ may still have been present, as suggested by the orthography (see 8.1.1 and 8.2.5). The 'gist' nature of the gloss is discussed in 2.0.

   Keypoint: future and conditional (p. 274).

2.4 Nonse cuempetet elo uamne ensiui (1.4) is a relatively long sequence with several interesting features.

2.4.1 Diphthongisation has taken place in two instances: **cuempetet** and **uamne** (compare also **nuestro**, ll.18–19, **due(n)no**); the first of these is in accordance with Castilian *cuente*, but the second is neither the Castilian diphthong (the spelling suggests [wa] rather than [we]) nor the eventual Castilian form (*ome~omne~ombre* in Old Castilian and *hombre* in Modern Spanish). Both the [wa] diphthong and the diphthongal development of HŎMĬNE [HŎMO] are further features associated with the eastern Peninsular dialects.

   Keypoint: vowels (p. 296).

2.4.2 Elo is the Romance definite article deriving from Lat. ILLU [ILLE, etc.]. There are further examples in the long gloss beginning on l.18 (**ela**, ll.19 and 21, as well as contracted forms of preposition + article, see below, 2.14.1). This form is again more typical of the eastern Peninsular dialects, where such masculine forms of the definite article as *lo* and *ro* are nowadays found in contrast to the *el* of Castile, where *lo* is the 'neuter' article (Alvar 1953: 215–8).

   Keypoints: the definite article (p. 270); **gender** (p. 275).

2.4.3 Ensiui is parallel to MSp. *en sí*; *sí* derives from Lat. dative form SIBI and may represent [siβi] with the intervocalic [β] still present; Mozarabic texts have the forms *mib* and *tib*. It is certainly Romance; Latin would have used the ablative after IN (IN SĒ).

   Keypoint: personal pronouns (p. 284).

2.4.4 The exact meaning of **cuempetet** is hard to determine: the gloss presumably means something like 'a man should not rely on his own judgement'. *Contar* < Lat. [CŎMPŬTO] 'to calculate' must have evolved semantically through the stages 'to count off' → 'to count on', 'rely on'; it also developed in a slightly different semantic direction to 'to give an account of' → 'to relate'.

2.5 Alquieras 'perhaps' (l.5). This may be accounted for in two different ways. First, the form *-quiera* has been used productively in the morphology of Castilian to indicate universal relatives (*cuandoquiera, cualquiera, quienquiera*, etc. – these were more numerous in Latin, where they were marked by -CUMQUE). It was the further extension of *-quiera* that gave rise to *siquiera* and OCast. **alquieras**, whose final /s/ may have been analogical with the final /s/ of a number of Old Castilian adverbs (see 4.2.14, 6.3.8). Alternatively, **alquieras** can be derived from Lat. ?ĀLĬ(U)D QUAERAS [QUAERO] '?you may want something else'.

   Keypoint: adverbs (p. 262).

2.6 Tardarsan por jmplire (l.7) appears not to translate the Latin exactly, but to have the meaning 'they tarry, are slow, in observing'.

2.6.1 Tardarsan illustrates the analytic Romance future and the placing of the reflexive clitic pronoun between the infinitive stem and the inflection.
   Keypoints: future and conditional (p. 274); **clitic pronoun position** (p. 264).

2.6.2 Jnplire (≤ Lat. [IMPLÉO] 'to fill'; 'to satisfy') is cognate with MSp. *henchir* 'to swell', 'fill': the spelling may reflect an absence of palatalisation of the /pl/ group, which is a feature of many eastern Peninsular Romance varieties. It is used here in the sense of 'to fulfil', a notion which is rendered in Modern Spanish by the morphologically and semantically closely related *cumplir* ≤ [COMPLĔO] 'to fill'; 'to complete'. The physical sense of 'to fill' has come to be rendered in Spanish by the derived form *llenar* (← Lat. adjective √PLĒNU[S] 'full'), which has greater morphological transparency.

2.6.3 The infinitive is consistently spelt with a final *-e* (cf. **transtornare**, ll.10–11, **tramare**, l.12, **fere**, l.21).
   Keypoint: final *-e* (p. 273).

2.7 Tales muitos fazen (l.8). Lat. MULTU[S] yields *mucho* in Castilian, with an individual palatalisation of the /lt/ group to /tʃ/ which is not shared with neighbouring dialect areas. The form *muito* therefore suggests a non-Castilian development (cf. Ptg. *muito*).
   Keypoints: palatalisation (p. 280); **consonant groups** (p. 267).

2.8 Alquandas beces (l.9) 'sometimes'. The spelling **beces** < Lat. VĬCĒS [VĬCIS] 'changes', 'turns' suggests the merger of Latin initial /b/ and /w/ (see also 3.1.3 and 7.1.6); compare also **Salbatore** (l.18), where /b/ similarly represents the result of Lat. /w/, in this case postconsonantally. *Vez* generalised its meaning to that of 'time', 'occasion', and came to be used in a number of analytic time expressions (MSp. *alguna vez, raras veces, muchas veces, de vez en cuando*, etc.). The equivalent to **alquandas beces** in Modern Spanish is *algunas veces*; **alquandas** appears to derive either from the Latin adjective [ĂLĬQUANTUS] which in the plural had the meaning 'some', or even from the adverb ĂLĬQUANDO 'sometimes' reanalysed as an adjective. *Alguno* < Lat. ĂLĬCŪNUS 'something', *alguien* < Lat. ĂLĬQUEM [ĂLĬQUIS] 'someone' (see 18.2.8) and *algo* < Lat. ?ĂLĬQUOD 'something' are the only Modern Spanish survivors of a number of Latin words beginning with ĂLĬ- which indicated the indefinite notion of 'some (other)'; other such forms in Old Castilian were *alguandre* 'never' < Lat. ĂLĬQUANDO 'sometimes' and *alondre* or *algodre* < Lat. ĂLĬUNDĚ 'somewhere else'.
   Keypoint: the 'b/v' merger (p. 262); **adverbs** (p. 262).

2.9 Transtornare ll.10–11 'to overturn' is a morphological derivative of √TORNO 'to turn' which survives in MSp. *trastornar*. (See also 2.6.3.)

2.10 Nonse bergudian tramare (l.11).

2.10.1 Se bergudian ‖ MSp. *se avergüenzan* (for the 'verbal' *a-* prefix, see 9.3.3) is a morphological derivative of Lat. √VĒRĒCUNDĬA 'shame'. The corresponding Latin verb was the deponent VĔRĒCUNDOR. Such inherently intransitive verbs are often rendered in Romance by a verb which is reflexive in form.

    Keypoint: the reflexive (p. 288).

2.10.2 Tramare is a morphological derivative of Lat. √TRĀMA 'weft', 'woof (in weaving)', probably evolving through the associational stages 'to weave' → 'to invent', 'to plot' (the Modern Spanish meaning) → 'to cause difficulties, disturbance' (the likely meaning here).

2.11 Certe (l.12) has the appearance of a Latin gloss corresponding to Lat. CERTĒ [CERTUS]: it does not represent the diphthong of Castilian *cierto*, and the Latin -*e* adverbial inflection was abandoned in Romance, cf. 4.2.14.

    Keypoints: adverbs (p. 262); **vowels** (p. 296).

2.12 Jocastigo (l.15).

2.12.1 Jo < Lat. ĔGŎ suggests the very general weakening of the intervocalic /g/ in this word in Romance and the consequent creation of a sequence ?/eo/, with shift of stress in some areas, including Castilian, from /éo/ to /eó/ realised as [jo].

    Keypoint: personal pronouns (p. 284).

2.12.2 Castigo < Lat. CASTĪGO is here to be understood as having moved away from the Latin meaning of 'to reprove', 'to punish', 'to correct' to 'to warn' → 'to teach'; it is quite widely used with the meaning of 'to warn' in Old Castilian, though the modern meaning has reverted to that of the original Latin, perhaps as a result of learned pressure.

    Keypoint: learned and popular, semilearned and semipopular (p. 277).

2.13 Uoluntaria (l.16) may also be a Latin gloss (the corresponding Latin adverb would have been VOLUNTARIĒ): popular phonetic development would have changed the /aria/ ending to /era/), and as a feminine adjective it does not make literal sense. *Voluntad* was no doubt current at the time, however, so **uoluntaria** would no doubt have had the advantage of being more readily comprehensible by comparison with the obsolete **libenter**.

    Keypoint: adverbs (p. 262).

2.14 The long gloss beginning on l.15 has many points of interest.

2.14.1 Conoajutorio (l.18), **ena** (l.19), **cono** (l.19), **enos** (l.20), show a non-Castilian contraction of the prepositions *con* and *en* with the definite article.

2.14.2 Qual (l.18) < Lat. QUĀLE [QUĀLIS] is used adjectivally, as in Latin, though it later comes to have an exclusively pronominal usage (see 9.2.4).
    Keypoint: relatives (p. 289).

2.14.3 Get (l.19) < Lat. EST [SUM] 'to be' probably indicates a pronunciation [jet]; such a diphthongal development of this verb form is found quite widely in Romance, and significantly in several of the Romance dialect neighbours of Castilian, though Castilian itself has *es*.

2.14.4 Honore (l.19) is treated as feminine here, as were a number of other nouns ending in *-or* in Old Castilian (see 11.2.7), though in Latin HŎNORE [HŎNOR or HŎNOS] was masculine.
    Keypoint: gender (p. 275).

2.14.5 Final *-e* is shown consistently here (**Salbatore**, **honore**, **mandatjone**, **face**, as well, as already noted in 2.6.3, in infinitives).
    Keypoint: final *-e* (p. 273).

2.14.6 Segamus (l.21) < Lat. SĒDĔĀMUS [SĔDĔO] corresponds to Castilian *seamos*. The *g* may represent [j], as it no doubt does in *get* (2.14.3).

2.14.7 We have already seen (2.4.1) that diphthongisation of Lat. /ŏ/ is evidenced in this text, and similarly there is evidence for Lat. /ĕ/ having diphthongised to [je] (**tienet** < Lat. TĔNET [TĔNĔO], **sieculos** < Lat. SAECŬLOS, the analogical masculine plural of the originally neuter SAECŬLU[M], l.20). For further observations on **sieculos**, see 2.15 below.
    Keypoints: vowels (p. 296); **gender** (p. 275).

2.14.8 Omnipotes (l.20) < Lat. OMNĬPŎTENS suggests the reduction of the /ns/ group to /s/, (see 3.1.6), although there are problems with seeing this as the exact representation of a Romance form (see 2.15 below).
    Keypoint: consonant groups (p. 267).

2.14.9 Fere (l.21) is the 'reduced' infinitival form of Lat. FACĔRE [FACĬO] typical of the eastern Peninsular dialects (cf. Cat. *fer*). See also 9.2.6.

2.14.10 Denante (l.21). See 8.3.6.

2.15 We must be very cautious about assuming that any of these glosses approach a phonemic representation of the Romance of the time or that they were forms in common usage. In **conoajutorio** and **Salbatore** there is no evidence of the lenition of the intervocalic /t/ of Lat. ADIŪTŌRĬU[M] and SALVĀTORE [SALVĀTOR]. **Honore** is written with an initial *h* which was certainly absent in pronunciation. **Spiritu** does not have the expected prothetic /e/ (cf. MSp. *espíritu* and 3.1.2). **Sieculos**, whilst exhibiting diphthongisation, appears to be an unreduced proparoxytone; the proparoxytone has been reduced in MSp. *siglo*, though this too has oddities in its phonetic history, since the /k'l/ group regularly became

/ʒ/ in Old Castilian, as in Lat. SPĔCŬLU[M] > *espejo*, OCast. [espeʒo]; 'semi-learned' restraint is often called upon to explain this. **Omnipotes** is an obsolete nominative form of the present participle OMNĬPŎTENS – we would expect the Romance form to derive from the 'minimum' generalised form (see **Keypoint: the case-system of Latin**, p. 263) OMNĬPŎTENTE. **Gaudioso** ← √GAUDĬU[M] represents as *au* the Latin diphthong /au/ which generally monophthongised to /o/, cf. AURU[M] 'gold' > MSp. *oro*, and as *di* the group /dj/ which in Castilian changed to /j/, cf. RĂDĬU[S] > MSp. *rayo*; furthermore Lat. ?GAUDĬŌSU[S], whilst a plausible morphological derivative attested elsewhere (e.g. Fr. *joyeux*), does not appear to have yielded a direct descendant in Ibero-Romance. The transition relative (see 18.2.4) construction with **qual** (l.18) is of a kind that would be more expected in the Latinate syntax of the cultivated prose of the fifteenth century (see Texts 13 and 15) than in the Romance of this period.

   Keypoints: vowels (p. 296); **consonant groups** (p. 267); **lenition** (p. 278); **stress** (p. 291); **learned and popular, semilearned and semipopular** (p. 277).

3 The Valpuesta document (1011)

3.0 This is a document from Valpuesta, in the judicial area of Villarcayo (Burgos) (see Map 1, p. 21). It can be dated exactly to 1011, and is one of the longest such legal documents from this period.

   We must bear in mind a number of circumstances in trying to assess this text linguistically. It is a legal document, and we may compare it with similar documents from other ages, including our own. It is concerned with clarity first and foremost, and there is no pursuit of stylistic effect. It contains many phrases which we may take to be conventional legal formulae, the meaning of which would probably have been quite clear to lawyers. We may also suppose that it would have been read aloud to the parties to the agreement in a way which they could fully understand. We are struck by the fact that some phrases appear to be written in Latin; though the Latin is 'incorrect' by classical standards, it presents features which are unlikely to have been current in the local Romance of the time. For example, the very first phrase uses the classical spelling **ego** (l.1), which had almost certainly by this time become [jo] or [ío] and **uxor** 'wife' which had no doubt been replaced by [muʒer] < Lat. MŬLĬĔRE [MŬLĬĔR]; the possessive **mea** follows rather than precedes the noun; the dative **nobis** is used with **placuit** though in Romance *nos* would have served as both direct and indirect object case; the syntax (**ego** and **uxor mea** in the nominative corresponding to **nobis** in the dative) appears 'loose'. Next comes the word **expontanias** which very definitely suggests a Romance pronunciation of Lat. SPONTĀNĔAS [SPONTĀNĔU[S]] as [espontaneas], with the characteristic prothetic /e/ of Castilian and many other Romance dialects (see 3.1.2). Yet the word order and the absence of a preposition in **expontanias nostras uolumtates** suggests a Latin formula. As we read on, we have the impression of the text having been drafted in Romance, though often written in a Latinate way. **Mazanares** (l.14) is unquestionably a Romance, not a Latin, word (for its derivation, see 3.3.9 below); and the frequent use of **ille** and **ipse** correspond well to the Romance use of the definite article.

The interpretation of such texts as this has recently been much discussed, and I am broadly following Wright (1982) in my suggestions about this document. We must bear in mind that there was probably not an obvious distinction felt between 'Latin' and 'Romance' at this time. There were no doubt on the other hand different 'styles' or registers of language, as there are in any speech community: the language of the Mass, the language in which a monk might talk to a visitor from Provence, the language landowners used amongst themselves, the language used among the peasants – and the language of legal documents such as this. When things needed to be written down (and compared to today, probably very little did), scribes followed a broadly Latin spelling system, the only one with which they were familiar. This is not, in fact, so different from modern English spelling, where because of the weight of tradition many words are spelt as if they were Middle English (*night* for [naɪt]): English speakers learn to read these words logographically, i.e., by recognising them as whole patterns, a kind of phonetically based mnemonic device. It is therefore not too far-fetched to suggest that **ego** might have been read aloud as [jo] in eleventh-century Castile. Moreover, it was only in the wake of the Council of Burgos in 1080, when the Roman liturgy was introduced into Spain, and with it the Carolingian reforms of medieval Latin, that there was a concern to write Latin 'correctly'. But it is more difficult to conjecture how the indubitably archaic **uxor mea** would have been read. Here we need to consider the special needs of lawyers. Again a modern parallel may be drawn: legal documents in English until quite recently contained phrases like *Now this document witnesseth . . .*, *Know ye all men by these presents . . .* which were consuetudinal formulae; husbands and wives promise *to have and to hold from this day forth*; the modern Spanish constitution contains future subjunctive forms which are obsolete in speech. Thus the survival of 'Latin' words and expressions, even morphology and syntax, in legal documents is readily explained, and we may surmise that, as today with modern performances of Shakespeare's plays, the language of former times was given a pronunciation which accommodated it to the current usage.

I have spent some time on this contentious question because it is crucial in establishing the limitations of what can and cannot be deduced from documents such as this. They are certainly not to be taken at face value; we must always bear firmly in mind the social circumstances in which they were produced, and the needs which they met.

Further reading

Wright (1982) and (1991).

The text

The text is taken from Menéndez Pidal (1976: 33–4), generally following the abridgement in Menéndez Pidal (1971: 14). There are two manuscript versions extant, and the most linguistically significant discrepancies between these are shown here in braces.

Ego Gomez Didaz et uxor mea Oſtrozia placuit nobiſ expontaniaſ noſtraſ
uolumtateſ ut conkambiauimuſ et uindimus {uend.} noſtra billa {uilla} Onia
cum ſuaſ kaſaſ et ſuoſ omneſ abitanteſ jn ea et terraſ et uineaſ et
ortus et arbuſta et totuſ pomiferoſ qui jn ea ſunt et molinoſ et peſcariaſ
et kannariekaſ jn flumine Ueſka ... per ſuoſ terminoſ ... jllo ſemdario   5
de Sancti Romani et per jlla defeſa de domna Eilo et per egleſia Sancti
Micalli de Pando et per jllo lombo de Petra ficta et deſcende ad Sancti
Andre, ... per portiello {per illo portiello} de Abienzo ... per jllo collato
de Orzaleſ et per ſuma ſerra de Petra Pionia et ad lomba que dicent
Gallielo ...   10
Et accepimuſ ... precio uel conkambiatjone de te ... id eſt uilla in termino
de Kaſtella que dicent Tobeira, ... terras, uineaſ, molinoſ cum ſuiſ aquiſ,
kannareſ .UIIII. {nobem} qui ſunt jn flumine Ebro {Hebro} ubi dicent Bado
longo ... terras et kaſſaſ et ortaleſ et mazanareſ cum pratiſ, paſcuiſ ...,
de jlla uia qui diſcurrit de Fredaſ ad jlla cote de jlla Lopeira usque ad jllo   15
ad terminu de jllo monte que dicen Eſura ad jlla Monneka; et de parte
Kannozeto, de kanaliella Eſpeſſa uſque ad jpsa Lopeira {Lopera} ... Et jpſ
a terra et jpso mazanare qui eſt latuſ rio qui diſcurrit de Kadrectaſ ...

Translation

(The placenames have been modernised in this translation; only those not followed
by a question mark are definitely identifiable.)

Of our own free wills it pleases us, myself, Gómez Díaz, and my wife, Ostrocia, to
exchange and sell our farm of Oña, together with its dwellings and its inhabitants
there within, its land, vineyards, orchards, shrubs and all the fruit trees which are
within, the mills, fishponds and fishpond canals on the river Oca ... along its
boundaries ... [which are] the track of San Román(?), the pastureland belonging
to Doña Eilo, the church of San Miguel de Pando and the ridge of Piedrafita(?)
and down to San Andrés, ... the pass of Abienzo(?) ... the col of Orzales(?), the
top of Piedra Pionia(?) and to the ridge called Gallielo(?) ...

  And we accept as a price or exchange from you ... that is, the farm on the
boundary of Castile called Tovera, ... lands, vineyards, mills with their waters, nine
canals which are on the river Ebro at the place called Badolongo (=Vadillo?) ...
lands, houses, market gardens, apple orchards with meadowlands, pasturelands ...,
from the road with goes from Frías to the land of the Lopeira(?) as far as the one on
the boundary of the moorland called Esura(?) to the Muñeca(?); and from the
district(?) of Cañoceto(?), from Canaliella Espesa(?) to the Lopeira(?) ... and the
land and the apple orchard which is by the river which flows from Las Caderechas.

Phonetics and phonology

3.1.1 It is clear that a number of expected Romance phenomena are not entirely
represented by the spelling of this document. Diphthongisation is confirmed by
such spellings as **portiello** (l.8) and **kanaliella** (l.17), but is not consistently indi-
cated (**terras** || MSp. *tierras*, ll.3 and 12; **serra** || MSp. *sierra*, l.9; **nostra** || MSp.

nuestra, 1.2). Palatalisation is evidenced in **mazanare** (1.18) ← (Lat. √MATĬĀNUS (see 3.3.9 below) but a semi-etymological spelling remains in **Kadrectas** ‖ MSp. *Caderechas* (1.18); even the most elementary combinations of consonant + [j] are represented in the Latin way (**uineas** ‖ MSp. *viñas*, 1.3). Lenition is not represented: **collato** ‖ MSp. *collado* (1.8), **latus** ‖ MSp. *lado* (1.18, see below 3.2.3).

 Keypoints: vowels (p. 296); **palatalisation** (p. 280); **lenition** (p. 278).

3.1.2 I have commented above (3.0) on **expontanias** (1.1) < SPONTĀNĚAS [SPONTĂNĒUS], which indicates the addition of a prothetic /e/- to an initial group consisting of /s/ + consonant. There is another example of this phenomenon in **Espessa** (1.17) < SPĬSSA [SPĬSSUS]. The initial group *s* + consonant is still inadmissible in Modern Spanish, hence the form of borrowings such as *estrés*, *esnob* < Eng. *stress*, *snob*.

 Keypoint: consonant groups (p. 267).

3.1.3 In **billa** (1.2) < Lat. VILLA, *b* represents the result of Lat. /w/, probably the bilabial articulation [β] (cf. 2.8, 7.1.6), (the more etymological spelling **uilla** is found in the other MS copy).

 Keypoint: the 'b/v' merger (p. 262).

3.1.4 Abitantes (1.3) < Lat. HĂBĬTANTES [HĂBĬTO] and **ortus** (1.4) < Lat. HŎRTOS [HŎRTUS] provide clear evidence of the loss of initial /h/ – as we would expect, since this loss had already taken place within Latin (Allen 1978: 43–5).

3.1.5 Pescarias ‖ MSp. *pesqueras* (1.4) < Lat. ?PĬSCĀRĬAS [√PĬSCIS] and **semdario** ‖ MSp. *sendero* (1.5) < Lat. SEMĬTĀRĬU[S] have spellings which reflect the original Latin form in their ending *-ario/a(s)* but otherwise show expected phonetic changes: in **pescaria** unstressed /ĭ/ has changed to /e/; in **semdario** /t/ has undergone lenition to /d/ and there is syncope of Latin unstressed /i/ in the second syllable; **eglesia** ‖ MSp. *iglesia*, 1.6, < Lat. ECCLĒSĬA, shows assimilation of /k/ to /g/ before a voiced consonant. The -ĀRĬU[S] ending probably passed through the intermediate stage of ?[ejɾu] before eventually becoming [eɾo] in Castilian, and this stage is in fact suggested here by the spelling of the proper names **Tobeira** (1.12) and **Lopeira {Lopera}** (1.17).

 Keypoint: consonant groups (p. 267).

3.1.6 Defesa ‖ MSp. *dehesa* (1.6) < Lat. DĒFENSA [√DĒFENDO] provides evidence of the reduction of the internal /ns/ group to /s/ which is widespread in Romance (cf. Lat. MENSA > Sp. *mesa*, Lat. MENSE [MENSIS] > Sp. *mes*).

 Keypoint: consonant groups (p. 267).

3.1.7 Domna ‖ MSp. *doña* (1.6) < Lat. DŎMĬNA shows reduction of the proparoxytone, but no overt evidence of the expected palatalisation of the resulting /mn/ group to /ɲ/ (see 3.1.1).

 Keypoints: consonant groups (p. 267); **stress** (p. 291); **palatalisation** (p. 280).

3.1.8 As noted in 3.1.1, **portiello** (l.8) and **kanaliella** (l.17) provide evidence of the diphthongisation of the /ĕ/ of the Latin suffix -ĔLLU[S], and we may therefore suppose that the same phenomenon had affected the inconsistently spelt **Kastella** (l.12), which is indeed frequently found in early Old Castilian with the spelling *Castiella*. The *-iello/a* suffix was eventually to change to *-illo/a* in Castilian, probably as a result of the reduction of the diphthong before a palatal consonant.

Keypoint: **vowels** (p. 296).

3.1.9 On the history of the /mb/ group, evidenced in **conkambiauimus** (l.2) and **lombo** (l.7), **lomba** (l.9), see 32a.1.4.

Morphology and syntax

3.2.1 Of great interest in such texts is the frequency of **illo/a(s)** < Lat. √ILLE and **ipso/a(s)** < Lat. √IPSE, which seem to be used in some of the functions of the definite article of Romance. **Illo/a** is more frequent than **ipso/a** in this text. The use of **illo** is interesting in view of the fact that Castilian eventually adopts the form *el* rather than *lo* for the masculine singular; in Castilian, *lo* forms the so-called 'neuter' article with adjectives. In neighbouring Romance dialects, the article has a more straightforward gender-inflection pattern, e.g. Ptg. *o, a, os, as* or the *elo, ela, elos, elas* system suggested by the Glosses of San Millán (see Text 2). As regards usage, **illo/a** and **ipso/a** often have here what seems to be a defining function, e.g. **illo semdario de Sancti Romani, illa defesa de domna Eilo** (ll.5–6), **illa uia qui discurrit de Fredas** (l.15), but the marking of this function is not invariable, and we also find **ad lomba que dicent Gallielo** (ll.9–10), **latus rio qui discurrit de Kadrectas** (l.18). The construction **usque ad illo ad terminu de jllo monte** . . . (ll.15–16) cannot be taken at face value since it seems to be neither Latin nor Romance in nature (cf. MSp. *el/aquél en el límite* . . .); it is likely to be a scribal error in which **ad** is erroneously used a second time.

Keypoints: **the definite article** (p. 270); **gender** (p. 275).

3.2.2 Although the Latin case-system is preserved to a certain extent (**jn flumine Ueska**, l.5, **cum suis aquis**, l.12, showing **in** and **cum** 'correctly' with the ablative form), there are many 'errors': **cum suas kasas** (l.3) with an apparent accusative instead of an ablative, **ad Sancti Andre** (ll.7–8), where the genitive **Sancti** is lacking the accusative noun on which to depend, e.g. *ecclesiam*. Use of the Latin cases is presumably fossilised and inherited in this style of written language through legal formulae, as indeed is the word **flumine** itself, see 3.3.3 below.

There is a case distinction between **qui** (**qui discurrit de Kadrectas**, l.18), where **qui** is a subject pronoun, and **que** (**que dicent Gallielo**, ll.9–10), where **que** has an object function. Note that case is not the basis of later distinctions observed between *qui* and *que* in some texts (see 8.2.2).

Keypoints: **the case-system of Latin** (p. 263); **relatives** (p. 289).

3.2.3 **Latus** (l.18), corresponding to Lat. LĂTUS, the etymon of MSp. *lado* 'side', is here used prepositionally ('by the side of'); this use is also attested in the Old Castilian expressions *al lados de, allados de*, but it has not survived in Castilian. LĂTUS, which was a neuter noun of the 3rd declension in Latin, was reanalysed as a second declension noun, as the now regular plural form *lados* shows (the Latin plural form was LĂTĔRA); OCast. *al lados de* appears to preserve the singular meaning of LĂTUS.

   Keypoint: the case-system of Latin (p. 263).

Vocabulary

3.3.1 Conkambiauimus (l.2) and **conkambiatjone** (l.11) are prefixal creations (cf. 9.3.1) from √[CAMBĬO], a post-classical verb of Celtic origin meaning 'to exchange'. **Concambiar** itself has not survived, though we can find similar prefixal creations *recambiar* and *intercambiar* in Modern Spanish.

3.3.2 Kasas (l.3) 'houses'? < Lat. [CĂSA] 'hut', 'cabin' is an example of the change in meaning of a word as a result of amelioration through self-deprecation: CĂSA in Latin had lowly connotations by comparison with DŎMU[S] 'house', and it may have become a familiar way of referring to a house which eventually became the canonical term in a number of Romance areas. See also 9.3.6, 15.3.5, 22.3.2, 25.3.2 and 29.3.1.

3.3.3 We see here a number of words for the notion of 'watercourse'. **Flumine** < FLŪMĬNE [FLŪMEN] (ll.5 and 13) is in all probability, as noted in 3.2.2, an archaism, since it has not survived in Castilian, but it may be distinct in meaning from **rio** (l.18), which is clearly referring to a much smaller stream than either the Oca or the Ebro. Castilian now makes no distinction between large rivers and tributaries, using *río* < Lat. RĪVU[S] 'stream', 'channel' to encompass both notions (Latin is rich in such general words for 'river' with FLŪVĬU[S], FLŪMEN and AMNIS). For the notion of a small stream, Castilian has *arroyo*, which derives from a pre-Roman source. There are also a number of words here deriving from the root √[CĂNĀLIS] 'waterpipe', 'channel': **kannariekas** (l.5), **kannares** (l.13) (these no doubt as a result of crossed etymology with CANNA > MSp. *caña* 'cane used as a pipe') and **kanaliella** (l.14). Presumably all these were man-made and had specific functions, **kannarieka** (‖ MSp. *cañariega*) being regularly used for a canal feeding a mill's fishpond.

3.3.4 Defesa (l.6) < DĒFENSA, a Late Latin noun formed from DĒFENSUM, the supine of DĒFENDO 'to repel', 'to ward off'; 'to defend', here has the meaning of 'pastureland', as does its descendant MSp. *dehesa*. This semantic history is one of more specific association with 'land which is set aside (for pasturing)'.

3.3.5 Both **lombo** (l.7) and **lomba** (l.9) are found here, both deriving from LŬMBU[S] 'loin', 'back of an animal'. We see here the creation of a gender opposition which is clearly not based on reference to sex. In Modern Spanish the feminine *lomba* survives as *loma* 'hillock'; *lomo*, whilst retaining as its predominant meaning that of 'back of an animal', also has the geographical meaning of 'loin of a hill'. The creation and exploitation of a gender opposition of this kind is quite common in Castilian, the feminine term often denoting something larger or broader than the masculine: *cuenca* 'basin (a geographical feature)' < Lat. CŎNCHA 'shell' is larger than *cuenco* 'earthenware bowl' (see also 30.3.1).

   Keypoint: gender (p. 275).

3.3.6 Serra (l.9) < Lat. SĔRRA 'saw' is here used in its metaphorically extended meaning of 'mountain range' (because of the visual similarities between the teeth of a saw and mountains).

3.3.7 Collato (l.8) is a morphological derivative of Lat. √COLLIS 'hill', with the differentiated meaning of 'col', 'saddle (the dip or high-level pass between two hills)'.

3.3.8 Ubi (l.13) could be read as OCast. *o* (see 6.3.9).

3.3.9 Manzanare (l.18) is a morphological derivative of √*manzana* (for the history of this word see **Keypoint: vocabulary** (p. 292)). The suffix *-ar* or *-al* (*-al* is more common in Latin America) meaning 'collection of plants', 'grove' derives from the Latin suffix -ĀLIS and has been very productive in the history of Spanish, used not only with original Latin words (e.g. *trigo* 'wheat' < Lat. TRĬTĬCU[M], *trigal* 'wheatfield') but also with neologisms such as *manzana* and foreign borrowings such as *naranja* (*naranjal*) and *maíz* (*maizal*).

3.3.10 For **usque ad** (l.15), see 8.3.11.

4 From the *Auto de los Reyes Magos* (twelfth century)

4.0 The *Auto de los Reyes Magos* is an intriguing but highly problematic text. The text is copied on the back of two of the last sheets of a twelfth-century codex which belonged to the cathedral of Toledo and is now in the Biblioteca Nacional. The natural conclusion is that it was a mystery play written for performance in the cathedral. It is linguistically extremely important, since it is clearly an early attempt to represent Romance. But the Romance is inconsistently written, and so there has been much speculation about who might have written or copied it.

The linguistic composition of Toledo in the twelfth century was complex. Toledo was a city of considerable prestige as the former capital of the Visigothic kingdom (see Chapter II) and the geographical centre of the Peninsula. Evidence of the three cultures – Christian, Jewish and Muslim – that coexisted there can be seen to this day in the old city. Though reconquered by Castile in 1085 and so coming naturally within the extended Castilian speech-community, it is likely that there remained within Toledo a sizeable Mozarabic population who would originally have used a different kind of Romance (see Chapter IV), and it is possible that the scribe was such a person, the more so since the document has no identifiable learned features. On the other hand, there also came to Toledo a large number of immigrants from north of the Pyrenees whose native languages were French (*francien*), Occitan or Gascon. The possibilities for inter-Romance borrowing, and, in particular, for non-Castilian colouring of a text as it was being copied by a non-Castilian native speaker, are therefore manifold, and much scholarship has been devoted to trying to disentangle the many apparently contradictory threads in the *Auto*.

Further reading

Lapesa (1985b); Sola-Solé (1975).

The text

The text is given here as in Menéndez Pidal (1971: I, 71–2).

[CASPAR, solo]
¡Dioſ criador, qual marauila,
no ſe qual eſ acheſta ſtrela!
Agora primas la e ueida,
poco timpo a que eſ nacida.
¿Nacido eſ el Criador   5
que eſ de la gentes ſenior?
Non eſ uerdad, non ſe que digo;
todo eſto non uale uno figo.
Otra nocte me lo catare;
si eſ uertad, bine lo ſabre.   10
[Pausa.]
¿Bine eſ uertad lo que io digo?
En todo, en todo lo prohio.
¿Non pudet ſeer otra ſennal?
Acheſto eſ i non eſ al;
nacido eſ Dios, por uer, de fembra   15
in acheſt meſ de december.
Ala ire o que fure, aoralo e,
por Dios de todos lo terne.

[BALTASAR, solo]
Eſta strela non ſe dond uinet,
quin la trae o quin la tine.   20
¿Por que eſ acheſta sennal?
en moſ diaſ [no] ui atal.
Certas nacido eſ en tirra
aquel qui en pace i en guera
senior a a ſeer da oriente
de todos hata in occidente.   25
Por tres nocheſ me lo uere
i maſ de uero lo ſabre.
[Pausa.]
En todo, en todo es nacido
Non ſe ſi algo e ueido.   30
Ire, lo aorare,
i pregare i rogare.

Translation

Caspar: God the Creator, what a marvel, I do not know which this star is! I have seen it just now for the first time; it was born a short time ago. Is the Creator who is Lord of all people born? It is not true, I do not know what I am saying; all this is worthless [talk]. I will keep watch for another night; I will know if it is true. [Pause.] Can what I am saying be true? I insist on everything, on everything. Can it not be another sign? [No:] it is this and no other; for certain, God is born of woman in this month of December. I will go to where he is; I will worship him; I will acknowledge him to be the God of all.

Balthasar: I do not know where this star comes from, who brought it or who is keeping it [there]. What is the meaning of this sign? I never saw the like in all my days. For certain, there is born on earth the one who in peace and war is to be Lord of all from east to west. I will keep watch for three nights and know more certainly. [Pause.] Indeed, indeed, he is born; I do not know if I have seen something significant. I will go, I will worship him and pray and beseech [him].

Phonetics and phonology

4.1.1 The text clearly has features we associate with Castilian.

The spelling **prohio** (l.12) < Lat. ?PERFĬDĬO or ?PRŌFĬDĬO (see below 4.3.3) is apparently an early representation of the movement of one of the allophones of OCast. /f/ (or ?/ɸ/) towards [h] (see also 10.1.2), though /f/ is more often represented by *f*, cf. **fembra** (l.15) – compare also **hata** (l.26) < Ar. *ḥattā*, cf. 8.1.7). However, since the f>h change was also a feature of Gascon (where it in fact occurs in all contexts), such spellings as *prohio* have also been seen as possible evidence of Gascon involvement in the text's transmission.

Keypoint: the f>h change (p. 271).

Fembra (l.15) < Lat. FĒMĬNA. The reduction of the proparoxytone /femina/ to ?/femna/ would have produced a consonantal group /m'n/ which in Castilian underwent a distinctive change to /mbr/. The change of /m'n/ to /mbr/ illustrates two processes: the dissimilation of the sequence of two nasal consonants and the addition to the sequence /mr/ of a homorganic plosive /b/ (for a similar process involving /d/, see 7.1.5).

Keypoints: stress (p. 291); **consonant groups** (p. 267).

Noches (l.27) < Lat. NOCTES [NOX] shows the typical Castilian palatalisation of the /kt/ group to /tʃ/, cf. 14.1.1, 15.1.3. (Note, however, that *ch* is also used to represent /k/, e.g. **achesta**, 1.2.)

Keypoint: palatalisation (p. 280).

4.1.2 At the same time, some of the spellings appear to be Latinate: **noche** (see above, 4.1.1) is also represented as **nocte** (l.9); the spelling **uertad** (l.10 and 11) for **uerdad** (l.7), is closer to that of Lat. VĒRĬTĀTE [VERĬTĀS] and **in** (ll.16 and 26) for **en** (ll.12, 22, 23, 24 and 29) corresponds to Lat. IN. The problematic **december** (l.16 – see below 4.1.3) is also identical in spelling with Lat. DĚCEMBER.

4.1.3 December (l.16) has been interpreted as representing a Gascon form such as *desembre*, which would enable a strict rhyme with **fembra** if the final vowels of both words are similarly pronounced (Lapesa, 1985b: 149–50). Such a rhyme would have been possible in a number of Occitan areas.

4.1.4 Since the *Auto* is in verse, much attention has been paid to resolving the apparent irregularities of metre and assonance, and much depends on how strictly we imagine that such constraints were observed. No amount of ingenuity seems able to resolve the irretrievable metrical irregularity of ll.17–18, for instance, and so we perhaps should be suspicious generally of using metre in this text to determine whether particular groups of vowels were construed as being diphthongal, in hiatus or in *sinalefa*. With regard to assonance, we have already considered (4.1.3) some of the problems of resolving ll.15 and 16. Lines 1 and 2 (**marauila** || MSp. *maravilla* < Lat. MĪRĀBĬLIA [MĪRĀBĬLIS] and **strela** || MSp. *estrella* < Lat. STELLA) are also anomalous, and not readily resolvable.[5]

4.1.5 Although diphthongs are not explicitly represented, it seems very likely that *i* and *u* sometimes represent diphthongs such as [je] and [we]. The rhyme of **tirra** and **guera** (ll.23–4) could be resolved by reading **tirra** as [tjera], for instance, and it is hence likely that **timpo** (l.4), **bine** (ll.10 and 11) and **quin** (l.20) were respectively [tjempo], [bjene] and [kjen]; the *u* of **pudet** (l.13) and **fure** (l.17) probably similarly represented a diphthong, although its precise phonetic nature ([wo] or [we]) cannot be established. If this conclusion is correct (and it is generally accepted as such), then it should make us wary of viewing the scribe or scribes' spelling as entirely phonemic.

  Keypoint: vowels (p. 296).

4.1.6 *l* appears to represent /l/ or /ʎ/. The *l* of **marauila** < Lat. MĪRĀBĬLIA [MĪRĀBĬLIS] has a clear /lj/ source and so most probably corresponds to /ʎ/ (this word did not undergo the more usual Castilian development of /lj/ to /ʒ/, see 9.1.4), and we may hence see the *l* of **strela** (l.2) < Lat. STELLA and **ala** (l.17) ≤ Lat. ILLĀC as representing /ʎ/ too (cf. 7.1.6). The *ni* of **senior** (ll.6 and 25) < Lat. SĔNĬŌRE [SĔNĬOR] no doubt represents /ɲ/, as does *nn* in **sennal** (ll.13 and 21) < Lat. SIGNĀLE [SIGNĀLIS].

  Keypoints: palatalisation (p. 280); **consonant groups** (p. 267).

4.1.7 **Strela** (l.2) shows no orthographical evidence of the prothetic /e/ that is so characteristic of the western Romance languages (see 3.1.2), although the /e/ may have been assimilated to the preceding vowel through *sinalefa* (*achesta_(e)strela*).

4.1.8 **Agora** (l.3) < HĀC HŌRĀ 'at this time' here is spelt with *g*, which represents the regular result of the lenition of intervocalic /k/ to /g/ (probably pronounced [ɣ] in Old Castilian as in Modern Spanish). The form *agora* survived until the sixteenth century, but the intervocalic [ɣ] then weakened further to the point of disappearance (the *h* of MSp. *ahora* is purely orthographic), perhaps facilitated by the toleration in Castilian of hiatus (in careful speech *ahora* is still syllabified /a-o-ra/, though in faster speech diphthongal pronunciations such as [awra] can be heard today).

---

5 Since *marauila* later rhymes with *nacida*, Lapesa (1985b:146) regards *marauila* as representing two different variants, the one here being most probably ?[maraβeʎa].

The spelling **aorar** (ll.17 and 31) < Lat. [ĂDŌRO] suggests a more advanced lenition of intervocalic /d/ through ?[ð] to the point of complete elision, cf. 11.1.5.
   Keypoint: lenition (p. 278).

4.1.9 Non (l.7, etc.) < Lat. NŌN has a final /n/ unlike MSp. *no*. The full form *non* continued to be used until the fifteenth century, though in the *Cantar de Mio Cid*, *no* was the variant found before apocopated clitic pronouns (e.g. *nol = no le*), in final position, and sometimes before *lo* and *nos* (Menéndez Pidal 1908–11: 192).

Morphology and syntax

4.2.1 Though the 'full' forms of the demonstrative prevail (**achesta**, ll.2 and 21, **achesto**, l.14, **achest**, l.16), there is also one 'reduced' form (**esto**, l.8); such variation is typical of Old Castilian (see also 7.2.2). The demonstrative is used as the antecedent to a relative clause (**aquel qui**, l.24, see also 6.2.7, 15.2.3).
   Keypoints: demonstratives (p. 270); **relatives** (p. 289).

4.2.2 The development of **agora** (l.3) < Lat. HĀC HORĀ is an example of the creation in Romance of a synthetic adverb from a form which had greater morphological transparency in Latin.
   Keypoint: adverbs (p. 262).

4.2.3 Ueida (ll.3 and 30) is an analogically regularised past participle of *ve(e)r* (the CL past participle of VĬDĔO was VĪSUM, see 11.3.9). MSp. *visto* derives from a Latin form ?VĪSTU[M], which is analogical with a number of irregular Latin past participles ending in -TU[M] and was current from earliest texts; the formation of a noun *vista* '(something) seen' from this participle may have contributed to its being preferred. (ll.3, 15, 22 and 30). Another analogically regularised past participle is **nacida** (l.4); in the classical language the past participle NATU[M] of NASCOR was irregular.

   In the perfect verb form **e ueida** (l.3), the past participle agrees with the direct object of the verb **la** (= **achesta strela**). Such agreement is common, though not invariable, in Old Castilian until the fourteenth century, when the past participle in compound verb forms becomes invariable (Macpherson 1967). See also 6.2.4 and 8.2.10.

4.2.4 Poco timpo a que (l.4) shows the use of *aver* (‖ MSp. *haber*) in such time expressions; see 11.2.1.

4.2.5 In **es nacida** (l.4), *ser* is used as the perfect auxiliary of the intransitive verb *nacer* (see 10.2.6).
   Keypoint: the perfect (p. 282).

4.2.6 La gentes (l.6) must presumably be read as *las gentes*. Although *las gentes* may be given the meaning 'peoples' here, it could also be used in Old Castilian, as in modern colloquial Latin American Spanish, with the general collective meaning of 'people' (cf. 11.2.5).

4.2.7 Me lo catare (l.9) and **me lo uere** (l.27) provide evidence of the early use of the 'intensifying' or 'nuance' value of the reflexive in Castilian (cf. 25.2.10).
   Keypoint: the reflexive (p. 288).

4.2.8 Fure (l.17) is a future subjunctive form, used here in a relative clause with an indefinite antecedent ('wherever he may be'), cf. 18.2.10, 21.2.1, 22.2.5, 28.2.4. For the use of *ser* in this context, see 10.2.1.
   Keypoint: the future subjunctive (p. 275).

4.2.9 Terne (l.18) is an example of a metathesised future stem (cf. 11.2.11, 19.2.3).
   Keypoint: future stems (p.274).

4.2.10 Dond (l.19) is used here in the elative sense of 'from where', 'whence' (see 6.3.9).

4.2.11 There is some variation in the representation of the third person singular inflection. The spellings **pudet** (l.13) and **uinet** (l.19) suggest the preservation of a final consonant (see 2.1), but the -*t* is absent in other third person singular forms, e.g. **uale** (l.8), **fure** (l.17), and, perhaps most significantly, in **tine** (l.20), which rhymes which **uinet**. It is difficult to know what conclusion to draw from this. Was there really a corresponding variation in pronunciation, or was the /t/ so lightly articulated (as [ᵟ] or [θ]) that speakers were sometimes not conscious of it? Or is the variation in the spelling only, the -*t* forms being a remnant of a more traditional spelling custom, or even an awareness of Latin?

4.2.12 The possessive **mos** (l.22) has aroused a good deal of speculation: because the spelling recalls versions of this possessive in the *jarŷas* (see Texts 5a-d), it has been suggested that it is a Mozarabic feature of this text (Lapesa 1985b:141).
   Keypoint: possessives (p. 287).

4.2.13 Esta strela non se dond uinet (l.19) shows topicalisation of **esta strela** (see 10.2.10).

4.2.14 Primas (l.3) and **certas** (l.23) are adverbs, and belong to a minor class of Old Castilian synthetic adverbs formed from an adjective with an inflectional -*as* (see also 2.5 and 6.3.8): a final -*s* is also found in *entonces* < ?IN TUNCE and *quizá(s)* < ?*quisabe* (Cor., IV, 738–40). The pattern never became more productive (the idioms *de veras* and *de buenas a primeras* which survive in Modern Spanish may have been formed in a similar way) and soon disappeared.
   Keypoint: adverbs (p.262).

4.2.15 The position of clitic pronouns with verbs shows an interesting variation between ll. 17 and 31. Line 31 has **lo aorare**, thus apparently placing the clitic unusually immediately after a likely intonational break, while the expected **aoralo e** appears in the structurally very similar l.17. It is probably justifiable to regard l.31 as anomalous, therefore, the more so since it is over-short: there may originally have been an additional word here.
   Keypoint: clitic pronoun position (p. 264).

Vocabulary

4.3.1 Primas (see above 4.2.14) seems clearly to be formed from the Latin adjective √PRĪMU[S] 'first', though it was PRĪMĀRĬU[S] 'in the first rank' which yielded the adjective *primero* in Castilian.

4.3.2 Non uale uno figo (l.8) *lit.* 'it is not worth a fig' probably belongs to colloquial register and is perhaps encouraged by the necessity of rhyme with **digo**; it calls to mind a large number of similar negative expressions used in the Romance languages (e.g. *pas* 'step', *mie* 'crumb', *point* 'dot' in Fr.) some of which became grammaticalised: thus Sp. *nada* 'nothing' is presumed to derive from an ellipsis of ?(RĒS ~ CAUSA) NĀTA 'thing born', first used as the object of a negated verb.

4.3.3 Prohio (see above 4.1.1) is, despite its phonetic form, most obviously derived from Lat. √PERFĬDĬA 'bad faith'; the verb ?PERFĬDĬO appears to have moved into the associated area of 'to be obstinate' (not necessarily with a pejorative overtone), and then to 'to insist', the meaning here. In Modern Spanish *porfiar* has added the meaning 'to persist' (cf. 20.3.3).[6]

4.3.4 Al (l.14), a shortened form of Lat. ĂLĬ(U)D 'something else', is extremely common in Old Castilian texts. Modern Spanish has abandoned it in favour of the analytic *otra cosa* (see 13.3.10).

4.3.5 Por uer (l.15) has sometimes been seen as an Arabism, parallel to the Arabic expression *bi-l-ḥaqq* found in the *jarỹas* (see Text 5), though Lapesa (1985b: 148) points to other such expressions with *por* and its cognates in other Romance languages (cf. also Eng. *for sure*). *Vero* < Lat. VĒRU[S] 'true' is indeed overtaken in the course of the history of Spanish by *verdadero*, which is a morphological derivative of the noun *verdad* < Lat. VĒRĬTĀTE [VĒRĬTĀS]; but *vero* is common enough in early texts, and the device of using *por* with an adjective to express an adverbial notion is well established in Castilian. *Vero* survives in Modern Spanish only in the set phrase *Veracruz* 'True Cross' (the Mexican placename).
   Keypoint: adverbs (p. 262).

4.3.6 In l.32 there are two near synonyms, **pregar** < Lat. [?PRĔCO] (the classical form was the deponent PRĔCOR 'to ask', 'to pray') and **rogar** < Lat. [RŎGO] 'to ask'. **Rogar** has survived into the modern language expressing the notion of 'to pray (for something)', and (in formal register) the original broader meaning of 'to ask', while **pregar** is a very uncommon word in Old Castilian, and may here be motivated stylistically by a desire to vary the vocabulary in the speech of the second king. The semantic field of 'to ask (for)' is extremely rich in Spanish: MSp. *pedir* < Lat. [PĔTO] 'to make for (a place)'; 'to aspire to (something)'; 'to ask for' has a constant presence throughout the history of the language,

---

6   Cor., IV, 613–5, suggests that the link between the Latin meaning of 'bad faith' and 'obstinacy' is to do with obstinacy in heresy, and on this basis sees it as a semilearned word.

while *demandar* < Lat. [DĒMANDO] 'to remit', 'assign' → 'to expect (something from somebody)' → 'to seek' → 'to ask for', though enjoying some popularity in Old Castilian, especially in its meaning of 'to seek' (see 5b.3.3), is now restricted to the legal meaning of 'to sue'.

4.3.7 For **catar** (l.9) see 2.1; for **terne** [**tener**] (l.18) see 11.3.4; for **seer** (l.25) see 6.3.6; for **hata** (l.26) see 8.3.11.

IV   Al-Andalus

The Arab presence in the Peninsula

The loose political unity of the Visigothic kingdom was brought to an end by the invasion of the Peninsula by Arab forces under Tariq ibn Ziyad, the governor of Tangier, in 711. The Arab occupation was rapid, facilitated by the internal weaknesses of the Visigothic state and the tolerant attitude of the new masters towards Christians and Jews. Under the Umayyad dynasty, the zenith of which was marked by the reign of the Caliph 'Abd al-Rahman III (912–61) from his capital of Cordoba, the adoption of Islam and the Arabic language became general within Al-Andalus (the Arabic name for Spain). But the use of Romance vernaculars, collectively known nowadays as Mozarabic, appears to have continued, especially in a domestic environment, and, indeed, there were even Christian writers from Al-Andalus who continued to use written Latin: as late as the mid-eleventh century the Pseudo-Isidore Chronicle was written in Toledo.

Mozarabic

Relatively little is known about the Mozarabic dialects of Romance, since, so far as we can tell, none has survived in the sense of supplying the basis for a modern Romance dialect (however, there may be Mozarabic loanwords, or even linguistic features, in Castilian: see 15.1.4). The so-called 'Reconquest' of Al-Andalus by the Christian states of the north, which began with the resistance to the Arabs at Covadonga in 718 by the Visigothic Asturian leader Pelayo and culminated in the fall of Granada in 1492 to the forces of Castile and Aragon, had as its chief linguistic consequence the imposition, by resettlement, of the northern Romance dialects on the rest of the Peninsula and the death of Mozarabic (see Map 2, p. 43). It is for this reason that the dialect map of the Iberian Peninsula, reflecting as it does the progress of the Reconquest, is quite unlike that of France or Italy, where the original dialectalisation of Latin over a wide area can still be perceived in the patterning of isoglosses.

Strictly speaking, then, the Mozarabic dialects should be ignored in a history of the Spanish language, since Mozarabic is not obviously an ancestor, or intermediate stage, of Castilian. From the point of view of textual interpretation, however, Mozarabic texts offer us a significantly different perspective on the development of Romance from the texts we have examined in Chapter III, since they are written not in the Roman alphabet but in Arabic or Hebrew script, and within the context of an Arabic cultural matrix. This means that we can largely disregard the problems of etymologically motivated spellings with which we tangled repeatedly in our examination of Texts 2, 3 and 4. The even more impor-

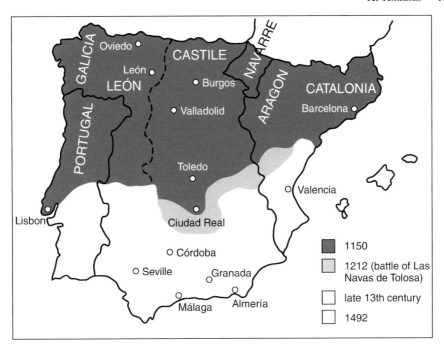

Map 2 The progress of the Reconquest

derable lexical, syntactic and stylistic debt of the texts in Roman script to legal and ecclesiastical Latin can also be safely ruled out.

The texts in Arabic and Hebrew script offer their own problems, however. These languages have consonantal systems which are very different from those of the early Romance languages, and they do not represent vowels other than [w]~[u] (Arabic *wāw* ‏و‎, Hebrew *vav* ‏ו‎), [j]~[i] (Arabic *yā'* ‏ي‎, Hebrew *yod* ‏י‎) and what may be taken to be [a] (Arabic *'alif* ‏ا‎, Hebrew *aleph* ‏א‎: this is in fact a consonantal sign to which a vowel is 'attached'). Furthermore, as with the northern texts, there is sometimes more than one manuscript version. All the Mozarabic texts that have come down to us are short and fragmentary (sometimes just odd words in a document, such as the Romance plant-names in a botanical treatise), and often very difficult to interpret.

The texts below are the final lines (*jarŷas*) of lyric poems called *muwaššaḥat*, a verse form cultivated apparently exclusively by Arabic and Hebrew poets within Al-Andalus. The *jarŷa* sums up the *muwaššaḥ*; it purports to be uttered by someone other than the poet and is popular in style: hence the occasional use of Romance, which, as we have seen, was a domestic, unofficial language within Al-Andalus. Some of these *jarŷas* occur in more than one *muwaššaḥ* and are also echoed in purely Romance sources, which suggests that they were the product of an ongoing oral tradition. I reproduce each *jarŷa* first in its original form, then in Roman transliteration, then in a reconstructed form, followed by a translation. It is important to see this process of transliteration and reconstruction, which have often been taken for granted in the citation of Mozarabic data. Italics are used in the reconstructed versions to indicate reconstructed material or discrepancies from the original.

Further reading

Asín Palacios (1943); Galmés de Fuentes (1983); García Gómez (1975); Heger (1960); Jones (1988); Lapesa (1960); Stern (1948).

5a: A *muwaššaḥ* of Abū Bakr Yaḥya ibn Baqī (died 1145); a poem of condolence to Moše ben 'Ezra on the occasion of the death of his brother Yehūda, by Yehūda Halevi (died *c.*1170)

This is a particularly difficult text to reconstruct, and several quite different Romance reconstructions have been proposed.

The text

This *jarŷa* occurs in both an Arabic and a Hebrew source. The Arabic is from the Ibn Bušrā MS no. 166 and was first reproduced by García Gómez (1952: 96) on the basis of a copy of the MS (see also Stern 1953: 5–6, and Heger 1960: 68). The version here follows Jones (1988: 101–5). The Hebrew, from Yehūda Halevi, *Dīwān*, I, 168–9, of which four manuscript versions survive, is reproduced by Stern (1948: 315). The alternatives in the Arabic have been suggested as a result of comparison with the Hebrew versions.

Original Arabic text

نبذ ليشقه ايون شنل

حصرى مو قرحون برل

Transliteration

nbḏ (bnḏ) lyšqa[1] 'ywn šnl (šn'la̠ or šnyla)
ḥṣry (km knd or ksknd or bsrnd) mw qrḥwn[2] brl

One of the original Hebrew texts

בניד לפשכה אדיון שנאלה   כם כנד מו קרגון פוראלה

Transliteration

bnyd lpškh 'dywn šn'lh   km knd mw qrgwn pwr'lh

---

1   **lyšqa** may be read as **lbšqa** if *yā'* (medial -ـيـ-) is read as *bā'* (medial -ـبـ-).
2   **qrḥwn** can be read as **qrŷwn** if *ḥā'* (ح) is read as *ŷīm* (ج).

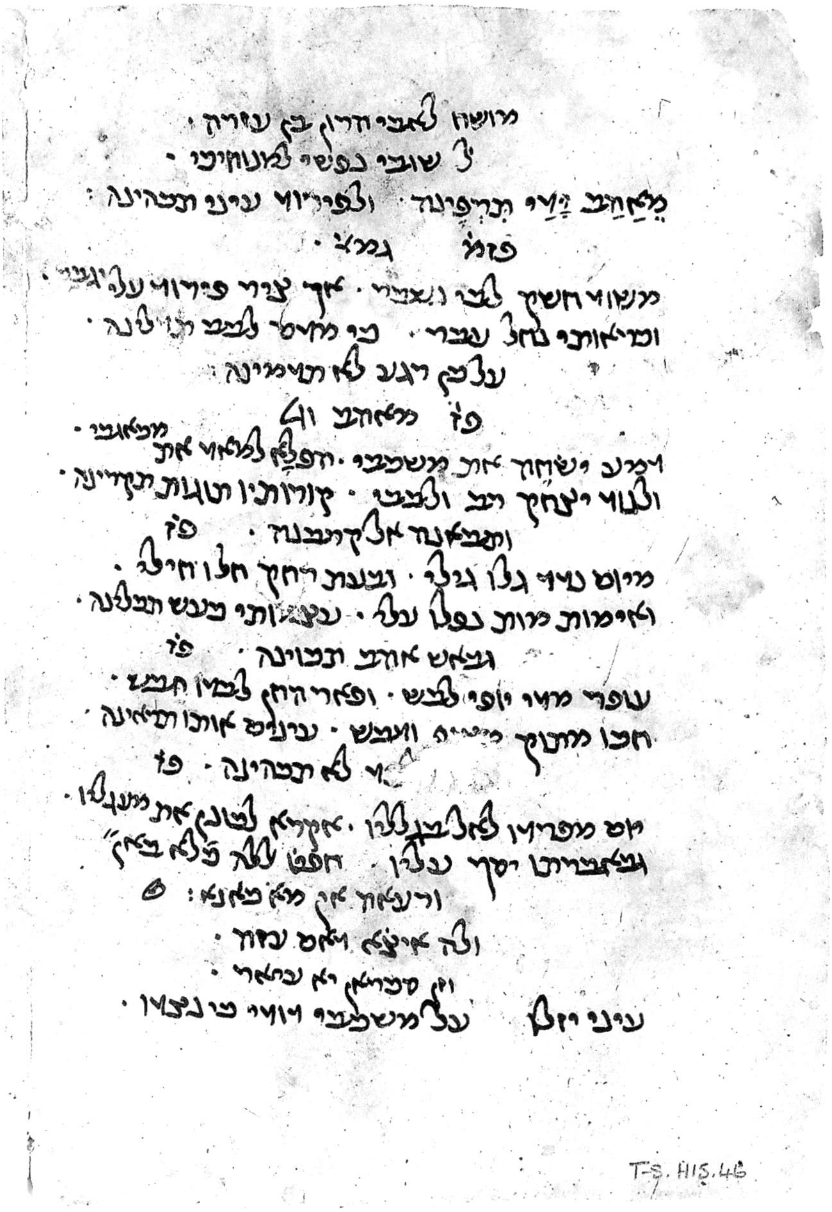

Plate 2 Genizah T-S 1115.46 (containing one of the Hebrew versions of Text 5a) Courtesy of the Syndics of Cambridge University Library.

Reconstruction

> b**e**n**i**d l**a** *p*ašqa (ay) **a**un š**i**n el**l**i
> ka**ṣ**r**a**ndo(?)[3] mu q**o**raŷun *p***o**r e**l**li

Translation

The festival comes, (alas,) still without him, breaking my heart because of him.

It can quickly be seen that a number of adjustments have had to be made in reconstruction to provide a version that is intelligible at all in Romance.

Having established the considerable problems inherent in these texts, I now turn to an examination of three *jarŷas* which offer interesting Romance data.

5b A poem in praise of Isḥāq ben Qrispīn by Yehūda Halevi (died *c.*1170)

The text

Yehūda Halevi, *Dīwān*, I, 163–4, as edited by Stern (1948: 313); see also Heger (1960: 65) and García Gómez (1975: 415).

Original Hebrew text

כם כנתניר אמומאלי   גריד בשאי ירמנאלש
אדבלארי דמנדארי   שן אלחביב נן בבראיו

Transliteration

> gryd bš'y yrmn'lš   km kntnyr 'mwm'ly
> šn 'lḥbyb nn bbr'yw   'dbl'ry dmnd'ry

Reconstruction

> g**a**rid b**o**š ay y**e**rman**e**ll**a**š   k**o**m**o** k**o**nt**e**nir a m**e**u male
> š**i**n al-ḥabib n**o**n b**i**b**i**r**e**yu   adb**o**lar**e**y(**u**)[4] dem**a**nd**a**re

Translation

Tell me, oh little sisters, how to contain my grief; without my lover I will not live; I will fly away to seek him.

---

3   Variously reconstructed, not surprisingly, as k**o**m**o** k**a**nd**o** 'as when', k**o**m k**a**n**e**d 'how [it = my heart] burns', l**a**ṣr**a**ndo 'wounding'.
4   Alternatively reconstructed as **adoblarey** and **ad ob l'irey**, see Alarcos 1953.

Phonetics and phonology

5b.1.1 No distinction is made between /b/ and /β/ in these texts. This does not necessarily indicate an absence of phonological distinction, however, since neither Hebrew nor Arabic had a sound [β] or [v] (the [v] of Modern Hebrew *vav* ו is a later development).

Keypoint: the 'b/v' merger (p. 262).

5b.1.2 /s/ is consistently represented by Heb. *shin* שׁ, with no distinction between שׂ [s] and שׁ [ʃ]. This has been taken to imply a lack of distinction in Mozarabic itself between /s/ and /ʃ/, a feature sometimes encountered in modern Judeo-Spanish (see Texts 33 and 34); furthermore, it has led some scholars to suggest that words which undergo an apparently arbitrary change of /s/ to /ʃ/ in Castilian, e.g. *jabón* 'soap' < OCast. /ʃaβon/ < Lat. ?SAPŌNE [SĀPO] ≤Germ. *saipo* (cf. Fr. *savon*) are of Mozarabic origin (see 15.1.4).[5] The representation of Romance sibilants in Semitic scripts is a particularly complex matter to resolve, since while Romance distinguished the voiceless alveolar–palatal affricate /ts/ (*ç*), the apico–alveolar /ṣ/ (*s* or *ss*), the palatal /ʃ/ (*x*) (and for some dialects, including Castilian, the palatal affricate /tʃ/ (*ch*)), Arabic script distinguished the alveolar /s/ (*sīn* س), the palatal /ʃ/ (*šīn* ش) and the 'reinforced' alveolar /ṣ/ (Ar. *ṣād* ص), and Hebrew script distinguished *shin* שׁ and *samech* ס. Ar. *šīn* ش Heb. *shin* שׁ were perhaps closer phonetically to the apical /ṣ/ of Romance; in *aljamiado* texts, Ar. *sīn* could س render Romance /ts/ (see also 14.1.2).

Keypoint: the sibilants of Old Castilian (p. 290).

5b.1.3 Yermaneḷḷaš (‖ MSp. *hermanillas*) < Lat. √GERMĀNA shows the palatalisation of Latin initial [g] to [j] before a front vowel, which, interestingly, is probably an intermediate stage of the Castilian development: Castilian eventually loses this element altogether when the first syllable of the word is unstressed, as here (MSp. *hermana*), though it retains [j] in a stressed syllable, e.g. GĔNĔRU [GĔNER] > *yerno*.

Keypoint: palatalisation (p. 280).

5b.1.4 Male and **demandare** show preservation of a final vowel (no doubt /e/), which was lost in these contexts in Castilian (*mal, demandar*), cf. 2.6.3, 2.14.5.

Keypoint: final -*e* (p. 273).

Morphology and syntax

5b.2.1 Of considerable interest is the form **bibireyu**, which with the final *vav* seems to indicate the preservation in this dialect of the final -*o* of the analytic future form deriving from Lat. ?VĪVĪRE [VĪVO] HĂBĔO. (Such evidence is absent, however, in the neighbouring – and problematic – **adbolarey**(*u*), in which no final *vav* is represented.)

Keypoint: future and conditional (p. 273).

---

5   On this question see Valle (1996).

5b.2.2 Mɛu ‖ MSp. *mío* was used before a noun in the medieval language, as here.
   Keypoint: possessives (p. 287).

5b.2.3 The form **a** looks very like the 'personal' *a* of Castilian, albeit rather surprisingly used with an abstract noun object.
   Keypoint: 'personal' *a* (p. 283).

Vocabulary

5b.3.1 Ḥabib 'friend', 'lover' is an Arabic noun much used in this literature.

5b.3.2 Garid is now generally thought to derive from Lat. [GARRĬO] 'to speak' (Cor., III, 109–11); it appears to be the usual word for this concept in the *jarŷas*. Only its past participle, *garrido*, has survived in Castilian, where it has undergone a great number of associational changes, ranging through 'spoken' → ?'speaking a lot', and then via a number of pejorative meanings such as 'empty-headed', 'shameless' to its fifteenth-century meaning of 'beautiful'.

5b.3.3 Dɛmandare 'to seek' (< Lat. [DĒMANDO]) is also regularly used with this meaning in Old Castilian. The meaning of 'to ask' in Fr. *demander* and of 'to demand', 'to require', 'to sue' in MSp. *demandar* can be seen as associated with the meaning 'to seek'.

5c A poem probably in honour of Abū Ibrāhīm Samuel ben Yosef ibn Negrella, a vizir in Granada, by Yosef al-Kātib 'Joseph the Scribe' (prior to 1042)

The text

Edited by Stern (1948: 331), from MS Oxford hebr. e. 100, folio 40. Stern suggests that this is the first known Hebrew *muwaššaḥ* which has a Romance *jarŷa*. See also Heger (1960: 107) and García Gómez (1975: 422).

Original Hebrew text

תנת אמארי תנת אמארי   חביב תנת אמארי

אנפרמירון וליוש גידש (גיוש)   ידולן תן מאלי

Transliteration

   tnt 'm'ry tnt 'm'ry   ḥbyb tnt 'm'ry
   'nfrmyrwn wlywš gydš (or gywš)   ydwln tn m'ly

Reconstruction

   tan tɛ amaraẏ   ḥabib tan tɛ amaraẏ
   enfɛrmɛron (or enfɛrmiron) olyoš *cuitaš / gueraš / nidioš?*   ya dolɛn tan male

Translation

I will love you so, lover, I will love you so; my eyes have grown ill with sorrows (*or* cure [them]?); they hurt so badly.

Phonetics and phonology

5c.1.1 Dolen (|| MSp. *duelen*) has been reconstructed to show an apparent absence of diphthongisation of Lat. /ŏ/. Yet because of the paucity of the information about vowels supplied by these texts, this is not the only interpretation of the original, and we might well reconstruct this word as **dwelen** or **dwolen**, i.e., with diphthongisation. **Olyoš**, on the other hand, has often been reconstructed as **welyoš**, although there appears to be no more evidence for the diphthong than in **dolen**. (Stern's practice was to reconstruct word-initial *yod* ﻳ and *vav* ﻭ consistently as *ye* and *we*.) If **welyoš** were indeed the form that is represented here, it would imply that in this dialect Lat. /ŏ/ diphthongised before a palatal consonant /ʎ/, a context in which diphthongisation is avoided in Castilian. Developments like [weʎos] are attested in both the Leonese and Aragonese dialect areas, so **welyoš** is not an implausible reconstruction here.

    Keypoints: consonant groups (p. 267), **vowels** (p. 296); **palatalisation** (p. 280).

5c.1.2 Enfermeron has been reconstructed with /e/ or /i/ in the inflection (to reflect Heb. *yod* ﻳ). While it is again imprudent to draw very firm conclusions about the representation of vowels, this does seem to be a different development from that of Castilian, which has /a/.

5d An anonymous *jarŷa*

The text

From the Ibn Bušrā MS, no. 259 (see Text 5a), as reproduced in Jones (1988: 111–16); see also García Gómez (1952: 102); Stern (1953: 28–93) and Heger (1960: 136).

Original Arabic text

ممّ أيْ حبيبِ

شلجَمله شقرله

القلْ الب

ابْكله حمرلة

Transliteration

> m^amm 'ay ḥbybⁱ
> šlŷ^amla̲⁶ šqrla̲
> 'lql 'lb
> 'bkla̲⁷ ḥmrla̲

Reconstruction

> mamm*a* ay ḥabibi
> šol-ŷuma*ll*a šaqra*ll*a
> *e*l-qu*w*a*ll*o albo
> *e* (or l*a*) boka*ll*a ḥamra*ll*a

Translation

Mother, what a lover! His hair [is] fair, [his] neck [is] white and [his] little mouth [is] red!

Phonetics and phonology

5d.1.1 Quwallo: the reconstruction **qu*w*ello** was proposed by García Gómez (1975: 177) in order to supply a missing syllable required by the metre. At first sight this appears to be evidence of diphthongisation; yet the /we/ diphthong we know from other Hispanic dialects constitutes, as a diphthong necessarily does, one syllable only. The exact value of the stressed vowel in the words **ŷuma*ll*a**, **šaqra*ll*a**, **boka*ll*a** and **ḥamra*ll*a** is impossible to determine. There is no *prima facie* evidence of diphthongisation of /e/ in what is in all probability the diminutive ending /eʎa/ (see 3.1.8); yet in a number of Hispanic dialects of the Leonese, Castilian and Aragonese areas this did yield a diphthongal result /jeʎa/, later reducing in Castilian to /iʎa/.

Morphology and syntax

5d.2.1 The diminutive suffix /eʎa/ (if such it is, see 5d.1.1) is attached not only to Romance stems (**boka*ll*a** from *boca*) but also to Arabic stems (**ŷuma*ll*a**, **šaqra*ll*a**, **ḥamra*ll*a** – see 5d.3.2). Such morphological productivity is frequently found in borrowings and is a sign that a stem has been integrated into the host linguistic system.

Vocabulary

5d.3.1 Mamm*a* apparently corresponds to MSp. *mamá*, and is frequently so reconstructed, though Hitchcock (1977) views some instances of *mama* in the *jarŷas* as

---

6   The *fatḥa* could alternatively be read as being over the *mīm* (p̃).
7   The initial *'alif* (‌١) could be a *lām* (ل).

wishful thinking, on the grounds that *mama* is not otherwise attested in Spanish until the late fifteenth century.

5d.3.2 There are several Arabic words: **ŷuma*ll*a** derives from Ar. *ŷumma* 'thick head of hair', **šaqra*ll*a** from Ar. *šaqrā* 'fair' and **ḥamra*ll*a** from **ḥamrā'** 'red'. This last word is well known from the name *Alhambra* (*qalat al-ḥamra*, literally 'the red fortress' because of the ferruginous clay used in the mortar with which it was built). It has otherwise left no permanent trace in Castilian, though several other Arabic colour terms have been fully integrated, most obviously *azul* ← Ar. √*lāzaward* 'lapis lazuli' and *carmesí* ← Ar. √*qarmaz* 'cochineal' (both these words deriving ultimately from Persian). The history of these words shows one powerful reason for borrowing in the area of colour, namely, the adoption of the name of a dye or characteristic object associated with a colour which was supplied from abroad.

5d.3.3 Another colour term, **albo**, from Lat. ALBU[S] 'white', is of considerable interest, since this word has generally been replaced in Romance (in the standard Romance languages, it survives as the canonical word for 'white' only in Rom. *alb*). *Albo* is found in Castilian only in very early texts (it was later reintroduced as a learned word with a very limited usage) and in the morphological derivatives *alba* 'dawn' and *enjalbegar* 'to whitewash', the latter from a conjectural Lat. ?[EXALBĬCO]; the notion of 'white' is rendered by *blanco*, from a Germanic loanword *blank* (see 1.0).

5d.3.4 Boka*ll*a derives from Lat. √BŬCCA 'cheek', which supplies the word for 'mouth' in a number of Romance languages (e.g. Sp. *boca*, Fr. *bouche*). This is part of an interesting series of changes in meaning in words denoting neighbouring parts of the face, which may be represented as follows:

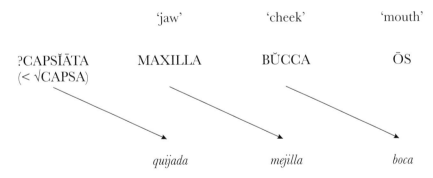

A number of factors probably contributed to bring about these changes. The Latin word for 'mouth', ŌS, was a phonetically weak word which was prone to replacement; BŬCCA, as well as denoting 'cheek', was also used in Latin as a slang word for 'mouth' (amongst other things, it denoted 'mouth full of food'), so we may be seeing here the adoption of a colloquial or lower register word to express a common notion. *Quijada* < CAPSĬĀTA is clearly a metaphorical creation based on the characteristic shape of the jaw bones.

The prestige of Arabic

The subsequent history of the Reconquest and the rise of Christian, Romance-speaking Spain as a world power may cause us to forget that for several centuries Muslim, Arabic-speaking Al-Andalus was a strong presence in the Peninsula both in political and cultural terms. The next text to be examined, though it comes from a time of major territorial advances by the Christian kingdoms of the north, reflects something of the cultural prestige of Al-Andalus. In the early thirteenth century, written literature in Castilian was scarce and Castile was increasingly inclined to recognise and take an interest in the cultural richness of the Arab world, which unlike Castilian had a venerable literary tradition. The circumstances were thus favourable for Arabic exercising a major linguistic influence on Castilian.

6 A faith for life. *Calila e Dimna* (first half of the thirteenth century)

6.0 *Calila e Dimna* was a well-known collection of ancient stories, some of which date back to the Sanskrit *Panchatantra*. The eighth-century translation into Arabic from Persian by Ibn al-Muqaffa' was widely known and has been translated into many languages. Although this Castilian version follows the Arabic fairly closely, and although a number of imitative features can be identified, this is very far from being a slavishly literal translation. The actual mechanism of its translation has been much discussed; at the end of MS A there is the remark 'Et fue sacado de arávigo en latín, et romançado por mandado del infante don Alfonso [i.e. the future Alfonso X, el Sabio] . . .', which has been variously understood. Everything hinges on what is meant by *latín*: is it indeed 'Latin', in which case a Latin version would have acted as an intermediary between Arabic and Castilian, or is it to be understood as *latín romance*, i.e., the Romance vernacular, in which case translation was made direct into Castilian? The many parallels with the Arabic original have persuaded a number of scholars that the latter is the more likely scenario. There are two MSS which concern us: MS A (Escorial h–III–9) is in a hand dated variously between the late fourteenth century and the mid-fifteenth century, MS B (Escorial x–III–4) is thought to be fourteenth century; both appear to be copies of the original Alfonsine version, though they are not identical. Establishing an edition is therefore not at all straightforward.

The text

This extract, which comes from Chapter II of the work and recounts in autobiographical form the story of the doctor Borzouyeh, follows the edition of Alemany Bolufer (1915). Passages in italics are particular to MS B; underlined passages are those which have no parallel in the Arabic text. This is not a totally palaeographic edition: the use of *u, v, i, y* and *j* follows modern orthographical custom; abbreviations are expanded and modern accentuation is used. I have made the minor corrections suggested in the Cacho Blecua and Lacarra (1987) edition.

Further reading

Alemany Bolufer (1915); Cacho Blecua and Lacarra (1987); Galmés de Fuentes (1955–56) (this long article, which analyses the text of the story of Borzouyeh in detail, is recommended for those who know some Arabic and want to follow up the complex question of influence at a syntactic level more fully).

> **Et yo, después que me guardé de non creer las cosas de que non era seguro de non caer en peligro de muerte, <u>dexéme de todas las cosas dubdosas et</u> metíme en fazer pesquisas de las leyes [et] en buscar la(s) más derecha(s). Et non fallé en ninguno de aquellos con quien yo fablé esto buena respuesta, quel yo (non) deviese creer. Et dixe <u>en mi coraçón</u>: 5 "Tengo por seso, pues así es, de obligar ala ley de míos padres".**
>
> **Pero fue buscando si avería aesto alguna escusaçión e non la fallé. Et membróme el dicho de un omne que comía feo e era tragón, e dixéronle que comía mal e feo, et él dixo: "Así comían mis padres e mis abuelos".**
>
> **Et non fallé ninguna escusaçión porque non deviese fincar en la ley del 10 padre, et quíseme dexar de todo e meterme a fazer pesquisas de las leyes *et preguntar por ellas* e estudiar en ellas. Et estorvóme la fin que es çerca e la muerte que acaesçe tan aína como cerrar el ojo e abrirlo. *Et avía fechas algunas obras que non sabría si eran buenas,* onde por aventura mientra me trabajase de pesquerir las leyes detenermeía de fazer algunt bien, et 15 morría ante que viese lo que quería.**

Translation

And taking care not to trust in anything if I was not sure that it would not place me in mortal danger, I abandoned all doubtful things and set about enquiring into religions and seeking out the most just. And I did not get a satisfactory reply in which I could trust from any of those with whom I spoke about this. And I said to myself, 'Since this is so, I think it is wise to obey the religion of my fathers'.

But I kept looking to see if there was any excuse for [abandoning] it, and I did not find one. And I remembered the saying of a man who ate in an ugly fashion and was a glutton, and people told him he ate in an ugly fashion and was a glutton, and he said, 'My parents and my grandparents ate in this way'.

And I found no reason not to remain in the religion of my father, and [yet] I wanted to abandon it all and enquire into religions and ask about them and study them. And I was disturbed by the end [of life] which is close at hand, and death which occurs as quickly as the closing and opening of an eye. And [I was afraid that] I might have done some things, uncertain as to whether they were good works or not, as a result of which perhaps while I endeavoured to investigate religions I would be deflected from doing some [other] good work, and would die before I saw what I wished.

Phonetics and phonology

6.1.1 Dubdosas (l.3). A complex consonant group /bd/ has been created by the syncope of a syllable; the word is a neologistic adjectival formation from Lat. √DŬBĬTO 'to doubt'. Such groups occur quite frequently in Old Castilian, but are later simplified; Castilian resists the occurrence of plosive consonants (/p/, /t/, /k/, /b/, /d/, /g/) in implosive or final position, and they tend to occur nowadays in more recent learned or foreign words (e.g. *ábside*, *técnico*).
    Keypoint: consonant groups (p. 267).

6.1.2 In **pesquerir** (l.15) ≤ Lat. [PERQUAERO] the development of PER- > *pes-* is probably explicable as dissimilation, to avoid two instances of /r/ in close proximity.

6.1.3 Omne (l.8) is one of a number of variant developments of Lat. HŎMĬNE [HŎMO], which appear in Old Castilian texts. The group /m'n/ more regularly became /mbr/, as reflected in the variant *hombre*, which as it happens has yielded the standard Modern Spanish form.
    Keypoints: stress (p. 291); **consonant groups** (p. 267); **vowels** (p. 296).

6.1.4 The development of **membró** (l.8) ≤ MĔMŎRĀVIT [MĔMŎRO] is an example of the insertion of a homorganic plosive /b/ between /m/ and /r/, as in the change of /m'n/ to /mbr/ in Castilian (see 4.1.1 and 6.1.3). See 5d.3.2 and 8.1.7 for examples of this phenomenon in borrowings from Arabic (*al-ḥamra* > *Alhambra*, *al-jumra* > *alfombra*).

6.1.5 Algunt (l.15). There is no etymological source for the final *t* (see 2.8). Such spellings are frequent in Old Castilian: the scribe may have the impression that the final nasal closes to a homorganic plosive.

Morphology and syntax

6.2.1 There is variation in the form of possessives: **la ley de míos padres** (l.6); **mis padres e mis abuelos** (l.9). *Míos* and *mis* are later distinguished as, respectively, tonic and atonic forms of the possessive.
    Keypoint: possessives (p. 287).

6.2.2 Fue buscando (l.7). This is a periphrastic verb-form (*ir* + gerund); it is difficult to say to what extent **fue** retains its full lexical meaning of 'went' or has been grammaticalised, as has happened in Modern Spanish, to the point at which the paraphrase has the predominantly aspectual meaning of 'to keep on doing'.
    Keypoint: periphrastic verb forms (p. 283).

6.2.3 Comía feo (l.8). The adjective **feo** is used here as an adverb of manner, as has been made clear in the translation 'in an ugly fashion'. The use of adjectives as adverbs is relatively limited in the written language of today, though it is common in spoken register.
    Keypoint: adverbs (p. 262).

6.2.4 Avía fechas algunas obras (ll.13–14). The past participle of the analytic pluperfect agrees with the direct object of the verb, **algunas obras** (cf. 4.2.3, 8.2.10). The choice of the analytic pluperfect with its imperfect inflection may be encouraged here by the other verb forms in the sentence: the conditional **sabría**, also with an imperfect inflection, and the imperfect itself, **eran**.

    Keypoints: the perfect (p. 282); **the pluperfects of Old Castilian** (p. 286).

6.2.5 Avería (l.7), **detener(me)ía** (l.15), **morría** (l.16). These are conditional verb forms, all occurring after the indirect question complementiser **si** and referring to future in the past time. The exact function of another of the conditionals in this text, **sabría** (l.13), is more difficult to construe; it may be appropriate to read it as 'I might (not) have known'. From the point of view of morphological form, while **sabría** is identical to its Modern Spanish descendant, **morría** (‖ MSp. *moriría*) has a syncopated stem (see 8.2.5), and **avería** (‖ MSp. *habría*) has a full stem. The form **detenermeía** (MSp. *me detendría*) retains the full stem because of the insertion of the clitic pronoun between the infinitive and the conditional inflection.

    Keypoints: future stems (p. 274); **future and conditional** (p. 274); **clitic pronoun position** (p. 264).

6.2.6 La fin (l.12). The feminine gender was common in Old Castilian and persisted as late as the sixteenth century, though MSp. *fin* is masculine.

    Keypoint: gender (p. 275).

6.2.7 There are a number of complex relative clauses in this passage, occasioned by the difficulties of translation from Arabic. Arabic relativisation is different in type from that of Romance: the relativising element is sometimes identical to a demonstrative; it can be accompanied by a preposition and carry case-marking. In such cases Arabic relative structures pose considerable problems for Castilian syntax, which must resort to a full noun such as **las cosas** in **de non creer las cosas de que non era seguro de non caer en peligro de muerte** (ll.1–2) or a demonstrative (cf. 4.2.1, 15.2.3) such as **aquellos** in **en ninguno de aquellos con quien yo fablé esto** (l.4).

    Note here the use of the apparently singular **quien**: the analogical plural form *quienes* (cf. MSp. *aquellos con quienes hablaba*) did not make its appearance until the sixteenth century (see also 7.2.4, 24.2.6).

    Another complex relative structure is seen in **avía fechas algunas obras que non sabría si eran buenas** (ll.13–4), where the relative pronoun **que** pertains not to the verb in the same clause (**sabría**), but to the verb in the dependent clause, **eran** (**buenas**). Such relativisation, whilst often found in colloquial Spanish today, is considered unacceptable by many speakers, or at least stylistically inelegant.

    Keypoint: relatives (p. 289).

6.2.8 Arabic has no reflexive pronoun; where reflexivity has to be made clear, an intensive noun is used. Reflexivity is often rendered in translation into Castilian by a similar device, and this is what has happened in **dixe en mi coraçón** (l.5), the equivalent of MSp. *me dije*, even though in this particular case there is no intensive noun used in the original Arabic.

6.2.9 In **estudiar en ellas** (l.12), a dative/accusative idea in Arabic is rendered by a prepositional object construction in Castilian; in fact, *estudiarlas* would have rendered the meaning adequately.

6.2.10 The frequency of **et** paralleling Ar. *wa*, particularly when it is used at the beginning of a sentence, is a striking feature of this text.

Vocabulary

6.3.1 Ley (l.6, etc.) is used here in the restricted sense of 'religion', i.e. '(God's) law'.

6.3.2 Derechas (l.4) < Lat. DĪRĒCTAS [DĪRĒCTUS] or [DĒRĒCTUS] 'straight', 'upright' here has the more abstract meaning of 'just'; in this sense it is also used as a noun meaning '(what is) right', hence 'law', and also comes to be used for 'right' as opposed to 'left' (this notion was expressed by Lat. DĔXTERU [DĔXTER] which gives Sp. *diestro*, still found with this meaning in Old Castilian).

6.3.3 Escusaçión (l.7, etc.) < Lat. EXCŪSĀTĬONE [EXCŪSĀTĬO] is found commonly in Old Castilian; it subsequently appears to have given way, in the sixteenth century and later, to the modern *excusa*, which is a more popular morphological derivative of Lat. [EXCŪSO]. Although *escusa* is found as early as Berceo with its modern meaning, in Old Castilian *escuso/a* is predominantly used as an adjective meaning 'secret', 'apart' (Cor., I, 47).
   Keypoint: **learned and popular, semilearned and semipopular** (p. 277).

6.3.4 Membró (l.8) < Lat. MĔMŎRĀVIT [MĔMŎRO] 'to call to mind' was very widely used from the twelfth to the fourteenth century, but then yielded to competition from *recordar* < Lat. ?[RĔCŎRDO] 'to remember', 'recollect' (the CL form [RĔCŎRDOR] was deponent) and *acordarse* (this latter verb appears to have been based on *recordar*, see Cor., IV, 826–9); Valdés mentions *membrar* as belonging exclusively to poetic language in the early sixteenth century. This is an example of the pruning of an area of vocabulary in which there is considerable synonymic overlap; besides MĔMŎRO and RĔCŎRDOR, Latin had the verbs MĔMĬNI 'to remember', 'bear in mind' and RĔMĬNISCOR 'to recall'.

6.3.5 Tragón (l.8). The source of this word is uncertain; Cor., V, 580–4, derives the morphologically related verb *tragar* 'to swallow' from Lat. √DRĂCŌNE [DRĂCO] 'dragon', 'voracious monster'. If this is correct, it illustrates semantic change due to hyperbole, or exaggeration.

6.3.6 Fincar (l.10) < Lat. [FĪGĬCO] 'to fix', 'nail' (the corresponding Classical form is [FĪGO]). *Fincar* was common in Old Castilian in the meaning of 'to remain', and was one of a number of semantically weakened verbs denoting little more than 'being (in a place)' (*estar* < Lat. [STO] 'to stand', *quedar(se)* < Lat. [QUIETO] 'to quieten' and *seer* < Lat. [SEDĔO] 'to be seated', of which the first two have survived into Modern Spanish). The demise of **fincar** is probably another example of the pruning of a rich semantic area.

6.3.7 Aína (l.13) < Lat. (not Classical) ĂGĪNA 'activity', 'haste', a morpholog-ical derivative of the verb √[ĂGO] 'to do', is a common adverb in Old Castilian; the reason for its subsequent disappearance (as late as the seventeenth century) was probably competition from the morphologically more transparent *rápidamente*.

6.3.8 Mientra (l.14) is a shortened form of *demientra*, a variant development of *domientre* (see 8.2.8), deriving from Lat. (not Classical) DŬM ĬNTĔRIM, an idiomatic combination of conjunction and adverb which would have been tauto-logous in Classical Latin: 'while', 'meanwhile'. *Mientras* has turned out to be a versa-tile form in Spanish, functioning as a conjunction in its own right (also with *que* in the contrastive meaning of 'whereas', 'whilst') and even as an adverb 'meanwhile' (particularly in modern journalistic register). The final *-s*, without direct source in Latin, is common to several adverbs in Old Castilian (see 2.5, 4.2.14) and so may be analogical.

    Keypoint: adverbs (p. 262).

6.3.9 Onde (l.14) < Lat. ŬNDĔ 'whence'. Latin distinguished between the forms ŬNDĔ (elative) 'from where', 'whence', ŬBI (locative) '(at) where' and QUŌ (allative) 'to where', 'whither' (cf. 33.3.2). Here, **onde** is being used in precisely the elative sense of ŬNDĔ as a relative. There is a considerable amount of movement, still ongoing (see 27.2.1, 30.2.6), in this semantic area in Romance. Modern Spanish locative *donde* in fact derives from Lat. ?DE ŬNDĔ, which would have been literally tautologous in Classical Latin ('from from where'). We also find *do* with locative meaning in Old Castilian poetic register (< Lat. ?DE ŬBI, cf. 8.2.11), and occasionally *o* (< Lat. ŬBI itself). The reasons for such change may have been (a) strengthening of forms which were phonetically weak, and (b) pruning of super-fluous semantic distinctions (compare the loss of *whence* and *whither* in English) which could in any case be expressed analytically when needed (MSp. *donde* (locative) / *de donde* (elative)/*adonde* (allative)), a device which also achieves greater morpho-logical transparency. The volatility of this area may also be encouraged by the fact that ŬBI and ŬNDĔ are unusual in not exhibiting the initial phoneme sequence /kw/ or /k/ that characterises other interrogatives and relatives.

V Early literature in Castilian
Dialect diversity and mixture

The first substantial works of Romance creative literature in the Iberian Peninsula date from the early thirteenth century. As we shall see, they are all in their various ways works of some sophistication and artifice, and for this reason they cannot be taken as simple manifestations of the speech of the time so much as a specialised literary register of the Romance of the Castilian territories. It is also highly likely that they already owe some debt to learned Latin influence, although intense imitation of Latin for its own sake would only come much later (see especially Texts 13 and 15). Another striking feature of these texts is the apparent mixture of dialectal features they represent. Such features may be due to the original author, the scribe, or the succession of copyists who intervened in the production of the texts which survive today. The scope for the introduction of idiosyncrasy and inconsistency, as well as simple transcriptional error, was enormous. We must also remember that there was no notion of any literary standard language at this time: no agreed system of spelling, no dictionaries or grammars of the vernacular. The ways in which these texts are written down are therefore perhaps most appropriately seen as early experiments in the representation of Romance using Roman script: while we can plausibly assume that such alphabetical representation is generally phonemic in nature, we must always bear in mind that a scribe's primary intention was not to give a modern reader information about the language of the time. It is most important constantly to have these matters in mind, since the texts exemplified in this chapter have sometimes been used rather uncritically as a source of Old Castilian data.

7 A father's farewell to his wife and daughters, from the *Cantar de mio Cid* (late twelfth century–early thirteenth century)

7.0 The *Cantar* (or *Poema*) *de mio Cid* is an enormously important text linguistically. It has been variously dated as early as 1140 and as late as 1207; it is a long text, running to some 3730 lines, and is the first work of creative literature in what may reasonably be called Castilian (though by comparison with the later Alfonsine 'standard' – see Text 10 – it has some features which might be regarded as non-Castilian). It is important to bear its literary characteristics in mind when assessing the text linguistically. It is an epic poem celebrating, in a suitably modified version of events which exalts the protagonist to the status of folk-hero, the deeds of the Cid

Ruy Díaz de Vivar during the last two decades of the eleventh century: his expulsion from Castile by Alfonso VI (reigned 1072–1109), his adventuring against the Moors, the marriage of his daughters to the cowardly Infantes de Carrión and their subsequent humiliation by their husbands, the case presented against the Infantes by the Cid and his daughters' eventual marriages into the royal houses of Navarre and Aragon. In all likelihood it was performed orally and transmitted orally from reciter to reciter before eventually being written down; its style is characterised by certain set phrases, variation in the use of past tenses and accommodation of lines to fit the poetic medium, especially with regard to assonance and caesura. We may thus confidently suppose that in the late twelfth or early thirteenth century its language was stylistically marked and probably also somewhat archaic in nature.

The text

There is only one MS, which is now in the Biblioteca Nacional. The *explicit* reads as follows:

> Per Abbat le escrivio en el mes de mayo
> en era de mill and C.C. xL.v. años

This date has been the subject of extensive discussion. At first sight sight it would seem to represent 1207 (the equivalent of 1245 in the Julian calendar, which was used until the fourteenth century in Spain); but palaeographic evidence places the MS in the fourteenth century, and there are also amendments in later hands. It is probably a copy of a thirteenth-century MS now lost. The version of the text given here follows Menéndez Pidal (1961), ll.268–84. The long lines 2 and 15 are clearly each intended as two lines of poetry, and the split is shown by ‖. Most modern editions show the caesura, which I have indicated here by |; as will be seen, the position of the caesura can have important linguistic implications.

Further reading

The *Cantar* has quite naturally been the object of a vast number of studies, literary, linguistic and historical. The compendious linguistic treatment of Menéndez Pidal (1908–11) has in many respects not been bettered, and remains a fundamental starting point for a study of the language of the *Cantar*. The modern editions by Smith (1972) and Michael (1976) are both highly instructive from palaeographic, linguistic and literary points of view. For an interesting attempt at dating the *Cantar* on the basis of linguistic evidence, see Pattison (1967). On specific linguistic questions relevant to this extract see especially Gilman (1961) and Montgomery (1991).

Merçed ya çid | barba tan complida
Fem[1] ante uos | yo & u*ue*stras ffijas ‖ yffantes[2] son | & de dias chicas[3]

---

1   The first corrector adds an **e** above the **m**.
2   The first corrector adds a tilde (~) above the **y**.
3   Only legible with reagent.

Con aqueſtas mys duenas⁴ | de quien ſo yo ſeruida
Yo lo veo | q*ue* eſtades uos en yda
E nos deuos | partir nos hemos en vida   *5*
Dandnos conſeio | por amor de ſanc*t*a Maria
En clino las manos | en la⁵ barba velida
A las ſus fijas | enbraço las prendia
Legolas al coraço*n* | ca mucho las q*ue*ria
Lora delos oios | ta*n* fuerte mientre Sospira   *10*
Ya doña Ximena | la mi mug*ier* tan co*m*plida
Com*m*o a la mi alma | yo tanto vos q*ue*ria
Ya lo vedes | q*ue* partir nos emos en vida⁶
Yo yre & uos | fincaredes remanida
Plega aDios | & a ſanc*t*a Maria ‖ q*ue* aun co*n* miſ manos | caſe
    eſtas miſ fijas   *15*
O q*ue* de ventura | & algunos dias vida
E uos⁷ mug*ier* ondrada | de my ſeades ſeruida

Translation

'Mercy, oh Cid, you of the splendid beard! Here I stand before you, I and your
daughters – they are children and young in days – together with these my ladies
by whom I am served. I see that you are on your way and we must part from
you in this life. Give us comfort, for the love of Saint Mary!'

The handsomely bearded one stretched out his hands and took his daughters in
his arms; he drew them to his heart, for he loved them dearly; he wept and sighed
very deeply: 'Oh Doña Jimena, my most excellent wife, I love you as much as my
own soul. You see that we must part in this life: I am to go and you are to remain.
May it please God and Saint Mary that I may still marry these my daughters with
my own hands, or that He may give good fortune and some days longer of life, and
that you, honoured woman, may be served by me!'

Phonetics and phonology

7.1.1 The phoneme /ʒ/ has various orthographical representations here: **j** in **ffijas**
(l.2) < Lat. FĪLĬAS [FĪLĬA], **i** in **conseio** (l.6) < Lat. CONSĬLĬU[M] and **gi** in
mugier (ll.11 and 17) < Lat. MŬLĬĔRE [MŬLĬĔR].
    Keypoint: the sibilants of Old Castilian (p. 290).

---

4 The first corrector places a tilde on the **ue**.
5 **ſ** has been added here.
6 The copyist originally put **en vida** before **emos**, but then deleted it. This is a heavily amended
    line: **nemos** was written above **emos** originally, which has led some scholars to reconstruct the
    word as *tenemos*.
7 Later amended to **Y vos** in black ink.

7.1.2 It is likely that the initial /l/ in **Lego(las)** (l.9) ≤ Lat. (AP)PLĬCĀVIT [(AP)PLĬCO] and **Lora** (l.10) < Lat. PLŌRAT [PLŌRO] represents the palatal consonant /ʎ/. The subjunctive form **plega** (l.15) ≤ Lat. PLĂCĔAT [PLĂCĔO] gives no such indication of palatalisation, however, a feature which is sometimes attributed to semilearned influence on the development of *placer*.

  Keypoints: **palatalisation** (p. 280); **learned and popular, semilearned and semipopular** (p. 277).

7.1.3 **Complida** (l.11) and **sospira** (l.10) show the regular development of the atonic /ō/ and /ŭ/ in Lat. CŌMPLĬTA [COMPLĔO] and SŬSPĪRAT [SŬSPĪRO] to /o/. The later spellings *cumplida* and *suspira* may reflect the particular outcome of a strong tendency evidenced in the variant spellings of Old Castilian to neutralise the opposition between atonic /o/ and /u/ (see 9.1.7, 10.1.5).

  Keypoint: **vowels** (p. 296).

7.1.4 **Duenas** (l.3) < Lat. DŎMĬNAS [DŎMĬNA] is likely, particularly in view of the later amendment, to represent a pronunciation [dweɲas], as in Modern Spanish (cf. 3.1.7).

  Keypoints: **consonant groups** (p. 267); **palatalisation** (p. 280); **stress** (p. 291).

7.1.5 **Ondrada** (l.17) < Lat. HŎNŌRATA [HŎNŌRO] shows the development of a homorganic plosive (/d/) to ease the articulation of the /nr/ group which resulted from the syncope of the /ō/ (see 4.1.1, 6.1.4, 19.2.3).

  Keypoint: **consonant groups** (p. 267).

7.1.6 In **velida** (l.7), possibly ← √BELLU[S] (see 7.3.6 below), an initial *v* corresponds to Lat. /b/, suggesting merger in initial position of Latin /b/ and /w/, cf. 2.8, 3.1.3. The Modern Spanish spelling *bellida* is etymological. The single **l** must once again be taken as a representation of the palatal /ʎ/ (see 7.1.2 and cf. 4.1.6).

  Keypoints: **the 'b/v' merger** (p. 262); **palatalisation** (p. 280).

Morphology and syntax

7.2.1 For the variation in the use of possessives with and without the definite article (e.g. **uuestras ffijas** (l.2), **las sus fijas** (l.8), see 8.2.7.

  Keypoint: **possessives** (p. 287).

7.2.2 **Aquestas** (l.3) is the full form of the Romance 'first person' demonstrative, deriving from Lat. ?ACC(U) ISTAS [ISTE]. There are many instances of this in the *Cantar*: both full and reduced forms (e.g. *estas*) are amply attested, though the latter are already in the majority.

  Keypoint: **demonstratives** (p. 270).

7.2.3 **De quien so yo seruida** (l.3) and **de my seades seruida** (l.17) show the agentive use of *de* in Old Castilian in contrast to Modern Spanish, where *por* is more usual. *De* as an agentive preposition does however survive in Modern Spanish in some stative passive usages, e.g. *acompañado de su esposa*, cf. 24.2.4.

7.2.4 Quien (l.3) derives from Lat. QUEM, the masculine accusative singular form of the relative pronoun and also of the personal-referring interrogative ('who?') and indefinite ('anyone') pronoun QUIS. In Old Castilian *quien* is in variation with *qui*, which was also person-referring (but see 8.2.2): in the *Cantar de Mio Cid*, *qui* appears twenty-three times in such functions and *quien* eight times. (See also 6.2.7.)

   Keypoint: relatives (p. 289).

7.2.5 So (l.3) < Lat. SUM, 1st p.sg. present indicative of ESSE [SUM] 'to be', is a common form in Old Castilian; in Modern Spanish such monosyllabic first persons have an added -*y*. See 33.2.2.

   Keypoint: monosyllabic verb forms (p. 280).

7.2.6 The inflections -*ades* and -*edes* (**estades**, l.4 and **fincaredes**, l.14) are the expected developments of the Latin inflections -ĀTIS and -ĒTIS, in which the intervocalic /t/ has become /d/ as a result of lenition. The /d/ was later progressively lost to yield the Modern Spanish inflections -*áis* and -*éis*.[8] See also 9.2.2, 13.2.2, 14.2.1.

7.2.7 For the positioning of clitic pronouns with respect to the verb, and in particular the intercalated clitic pronoun in **partir nos hemos** (l.5), see 2.6.1 and 4.2.15.

   Keypoint: clitic pronoun position (p. 264).

7.2.8 Spanish, like Latin, does not obligatorily express a subject with a finite verb, since the subject notion is implicit in the verbal inflection (such languages are often called pro-drop languages in modern linguistic terminology). Subject pronouns are used in pro-drop languages for emphasis or contrast, a phenomenon we can observe clearly here: <u>Yo</u> lo veo que estades <u>uos</u> en yda (l.4); <u>yo</u> yre & <u>uos</u> fincaredes remanida (l.14).

7.2.9 A particular feature of the *Cantar de mio Cid* is the variety of tenses used to express past time. In ll.7–10 we see, successively, a preterite (**en clino**), an imperfect (**prendia**), another preterite (**lego**), and two presents (**lora**, **sospira**) (I ignore **queria** on l.9 which refers to a state of affairs and where consequently the imperfect is expected). The use of the present as a past narrative tense is common in all periods; it is the use of the imperfect, **prendia**, that is particularly striking here. It is likely that the variation in tense responded to the poet's desire to make the recitation more vivid and to avoid the monotonous repetition of preterites in what, after all, was mainly a third person past narrative; furthermore, as perhaps here, the use of different tenses may have made the demands of assonance easier to satisfy (**prendia** and **sospira** fit the *i-a* assonance of this *laisse*).

---

8   The complex history of the fall of /d/ in the -*des* second person plural inflection, which affected proparoxytonically stressed forms first, is discussed in Lloyd (1987: 358–9). Cuervo (1893) is still also relevant to this issue.

7.2.10 A las sus fijas enbraço las prendia (l.8); **a la mi alma tanto yo vos queria** (l.12) show use of the 'personal' *a*, which has come to be a very distinctive feature of Spanish syntax.

  Keypoint: 'personal' *a* (p. 283).

7.2.11 Another feature of **A las sus fijas enbraço las prendia** (l.8) is the left-dislocation of the direct object (**las sus fijas**) and the presence of a coreferential direct object pronoun (**las**). Such manipulation of word order is very frequent in Spanish, and is possibly facilitated by the use of the 'personal' *a* (see 7.2.10), which signals the object. In Modern Spanish the left-dislocation of a direct or indirect object noun or noun phrase normally entails the use of a 'resumptive' object pronoun: e.g.

(For a later example of this phenomenon, see 16.2.3.) There is another example of a 'redundant' pronoun construction in ll.4 and 13, where **lo** is used to refer to the clauses beginning with **que** . . .; these clauses may in fact have been thought of as being right-dislocated, since they follow the caesura: thus (exemplifying from l.4):

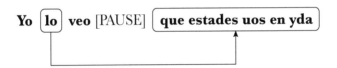

7.2.12 For the form of the adverb **fuerte mientre** (l.10), here written as two separate words, see 8.2.8.

  Keypoint: adverbs (p. 262).

7.2.13 Plega (l.15) is the 3rd p.sg. present subjunctive of *placer* < Lat. PLĂCĔAT [PLĂCĔO] 'to please' (see above 7.1.2). This is an anomalous development which would regularly have yielded /pladza/ in Old Castilian; however, there is much analogical influence among frequently used verbs of the *-er* and *-ir* conjugations (see 28.2.2). The form preferred in Modern Spanish in the compounds of *placer* (*placer* itself is as a verb now obsolete) is *-plazca*, which is analogical with the inchoative stem verbs ending in -ESCO (cf. *conozca* from *conocer* < Lat. [COGNOSCO] and 7.3.9, 9.3.12). There has also been an analogical change in the preterite form of *placer*, which in Old Castilian is, in the 3rd p.sg., *plogo* (an expected development, in fact, of Lat. PLĂCŬIT, cf. HĂBŬIT [HĂBĔO] > OCast. *ovo*, cf. 8.2.1); this has been replaced in the MSp. *-placer* compounds by the analogically regularised *-plació*.

  Keypoint: preterite stems (p. 287).

Vocabulary

7.3.1 Some borrowings from Arabic can be observed. **Ya** (ll.1 and 11) corresponds to Ar. *yā*, with the same function. The title **Çid** (l.1) is in origin an Arabic title *sidi* 'lord'. **Fem** (l.2) is a combination of *fe* from Ar. *hā* 'look, there (he) is' (also found as *ahe*: the *f* of *fe* represents the *hā'* ○ of Arabic, cf. 8.1.7) and the clitic pronoun *me*; later, as a result of the reanalysis of *fe* (> /he/ > /e/) as a part of the Castilian verb *haber*, forms such as *hemos aquí*, *heis aquí*, were generated, though in Modern Spanish only the invariable *he aquí* 'here is/are' survives with any frequency.

7.3.2 Ante (l.2) is used here in the spatial sense of MSp. *delante de* (see 8.3.5).

7.3.3 Yffantes (l.2) < Lat. INFANTES [INFANS] 'incapable of speech', 'small child'. The word seems to be used here in the general sense of 'children' (not just small children). In Castilian, *infante* and its gender-hypercharacterised feminine derivative *infanta* have since specialised in meaning to mean 'son/daughter of noble' → 'son/daughter of the king' (perhaps as a result of a semantic calque from Ar. *walad*, which had the meaning both of 'boy', 'son' and 'heir to the throne').

7.3.4 Chicas (l.2). *Chico* has long been a rival to *pequeño* in Castilian to denote the notion of 'small'. *Chico* is possibly derived from Lat. CICCU[S] 'membrane surrounding the seeds of a pomegranate', which came to mean 'something small and insignificant'. The Classical Latin word for 'small', PARVU[S], was very generally replaced in Romance; *pequeño* derives from a form ?PĬCĬNNU[S], which is probably a variant form of the attested PĬTĬNNU[S]. Such words seem to be the products of expressive combinations of front consonants and high vowels rather than to derive from any identifiable full lexical source – a kind of sound symbolism. It is perhaps not coincidental that *chico* also exhibits this property (see also 30.3.3).

7.3.5 Barba tan complida 'he of the spendid beard' (l.1), **barba velida** 'he of the handsome beard' (l.7) are epic-style soubriquets for the Cid. Another feature of the epic style is the use of such formulaic expressions as **lorar de los oios** (l.10).

7.3.6 Velida (l.7) (∥ MSp. *bellida*, see above 7.3.5) is uncommon in Modern Spanish, though it survives in the surname *Bellido*. It may be a crossed etymology between BELLU[S] 'beautiful' and MELLĪTU[S] 'sweet' (Cor., I, 561–2).

7.3.7 Lego (l.9) (∥ MSp. *llegó*) is, like its Latin etymon (AP)PLĬCAVIT [(AP)PLĬCO] 'to add to', 'to apply to', used transitively in Old Castilian in the meaning of 'to draw (someone/something) close'; it later comes to have the corresponding intransitive meaning of 'to get near to', 'to arrive', a meaning sometimes conveyed by *arribar* in Old Castilian (see 8.3.3).

7.3.8 Queria (l.9) ⩽ Lat. QUAERĒBAT [QUAERO] 'to search for' replaces VŎLO 'to want' in Hispano-Romance. Here we see the widening of this meaning to include the notion of 'to love'. It is perhaps significant that such usage is here with the 'personal *a*' (see above 7.2.10), since, as can be seen in Modern Spanish, the *a* provides a basis for distinguishing these two meanings: *quiere una secretaria* 'he wants a secretary', *quiere a una secretaria* 'he loves a secretary'.

   Keypoint: 'personal' *a* (p. 282)

7.3.9 Fincaredes remanida (l.14). This is an apparently tautologous expression; perhaps the reinforcement of *fincar* is necessary because of the weakening of its full lexical meaning of 'to remain' (see 6.3.6), which was a feature of its development towards the status of a copular verb. *Remanecer* < [?RĔMĂNESCO], an inchoative form of Lat. RĔMĂNĔO 'to remain', was substituted by *permanecer*, a similar formation from the closely related Lat. ?PERMĂNESCO, the inchoative form of √PERMĂNĔO; *permanecer* may have been reinforced by the later learned borrowings *permanente* and *permanencia*, to which it was transparently related morphologically.

8 A sinner repents. Gonzalo de Berceo, *Los milagros de Nuestra Señora* (first half of thirteenth century).

8.0 Gonzalo de Berceo, a native of La Rioja, lived from approximately 1198 to 1267. His best-known work is the one from which this text is taken, the *Milagros de Nuestra Señora*, a series of poems illustrating the Virgin's successful intercession on behalf of sinners who repent and call on her aid. This is cultured poetry, generically known as the *mester de clerecía* 'the service of learning', drawing on Latin and foreign sources, and we can see even at this early stage of the literary language a number of points of learned influence, especially in vocabulary. Yet Berceo also drew on oral sources for his compositions, and his declared aim (though we must bear in mind the conventional modesty which was the stock-in-trade of the troubadour tradition) was to write in a language which was accessible to everyone:

   Quiero fer una prosa en roman paladino
   en cual suele el pueblo fablar a su vecino
   ca non son tan letrado por fer otro latino
   bien valdra como creo un vaso de bon vino.

'I want to tell a tale in the plain Romance in which folk normally talk to their neighbours, for I'm not educated enough to make another Latin version: it'll be worth a glass of good wine, I think.'

   The phrase *roman paladino* reminds us that the principal linguistic differentiation at this time was between 'Latin' and 'Romance'. Although different regional varieties of Romance are clearly visible in all the texts in this chapter, it is probably not appropriate to speak yet of 'Castilian', and certainly not of any uniformity within 'Castilian' (for further discussion see Chapter VI). By Berceo's time, La Rioja was firmly incorporated into the kingdom of Castile, and so the *Milagros* is usually counted as Castilian literature. However, this text betrays a number of features of the Romance of the La Rioja area (see especially 8.1.1, 8.1.6, 8.2.2,

8.2.5 and 8.2.9), which may be compared with the language of Text 2, from the Riojan monastery of San Millán, which dates from over two centuries earlier. However, even to speak of 'Riojan' as a uniform Romance variety would be mistaken: Alvar (1976: 83–4) rather tortuously attempts to reconcile the notion of a 'dialecto riojano' with the presence of a 'pluralidad de normas lingüísticas' in the La Rioja area.

The text

The following text consists of stanzas 751–2, 764 and 766–7 from the *Milagro de Teófilo*, and is taken from Dutton (1980). There are two MS sources for the *Milagros*: a partial fourteenth-century one (MS F) now in the possession of the Real Academia Española, and another (MS I) belonging to Santo Domingo de Silos, dating from the eighteenth century. Despite the late date of the latter, it appears to be a reasonably faithful copy of a lost thirteenth-century MS, and it is this that Dutton basically follows. Material in italics is based on MS F; I have added the other MS F variants in braces. Material in non-bold is Dutton's own editorial emendation. Punctuation and accentuation are editorial, and there is a good deal of judicious regularisation which will be referred to as necessary in the commentary.

Further reading

Alvar (1976), Dutton (1980), Gerli (1992), Penny (1997).

Disso entre sí misme {mismo}: «Mesquino, malfadado,
del otero qe sovi {estoui} ¿quí me ha derribado?
La alma *h*e perdida, el cuerpo despreciado,
el bien qe *h*e perdido no lo veré cobrado.

Mesquino peccador, non veo do ribar,   5
non trovaré {fallare} qi quiera por mí a Dios rogar;
morré como qi yaze en medio de la mar, -
qe non vede terrenno {terreno} do pueda escapar.

Non quiero por los piedes la cabeza desar,
a la Madre gloriosa me quiero acostar;   10
cadré a los sos {sus} piedes delante so {el su} altar,
atendiendo su gracia, allí quiero finar.

Maguer la denegué como loco sendío,
que sovi {fui} engannado por un falso judío,
firmemientre {-mente}[9] lo creo, enna {en la} su mercet fío,   15
qe d'ella nació Christus qe fue Salvador mío.

---

9 With **fui** the line is a syllable short; Dutton surmises that it may have been the eighteenth-century copyist's error in interpreting the long *s* (ſ) as *f*.

Que vaya al su tiemplo {templo} cras de buena mannana,
venir.m {-me} *h*á lo qe veno {uino} a la egiptïana,
qe priso {tomo} grand porfazo como mala villana,
fasta qe la Gloriosa li fo {fue} entremediana.   ***20***

Translation

He said to himself, 'Wretch, ill-fated one, from the heights on which I stood,
who has brought me down? I have lost my soul and despised my body; the good
I have lost I will not see recovered.

'Miserable sinner [that I am], I see nowhere to go; I will not find anyone to
pray to God for me; I will die like one who is lying in the middle of the sea,
who sees no land to which he may escape.

'I will not abandon my head on account of my feet; I will go to the glorious
Mother; I will fall at her feet before her altar, waiting for her grace – there I
will end my days.

'Although I denied her, like a madman without sense, I was deceived by a false
Jew; firmly I believe, in her mercy I trust, that of her Christ was born, who was
my Saviour.

'Let me go to her church early tomorrow morning; there will come to me
what came to the Egyptian woman [i.e., St Mary of Egypt], who stood greatly
accused of being an evildoer until the Glorious One acted as her intermediary.'

Phonetics and phonology

8.1.1 Vede (1.8) < Lat. VĬDET [VĬDĒO], **piedes** (1.11) < Lat. PĔDĒS [PĒS].
Lenition brings about the complete elision of intervocalic /d/ in some Castilian
words (cf. 11.1.5), yielding in these cases the corresponding Modern Spanish
forms *ve* and *pies*. The preservation of /d/ is a feature of more easterly Peninsular
dialects.
Keypoint: lenition (p. 278).

8.1.2 While **engannado** (1.14) < Lat. ?INGANNĀTU[M] √[GANNĬO]) and
mannana (1.17) < Lat. ?MĀNĔĀNA (see below 8.3.9) presumably represent
/engaɲado/ and /maɲana/, as in Modern Spanish, /ɲ/ being the expected
development of both /nn/ and /nj/, it is unlikely that **nn** consistently represents
/ɲ/ in this text. There is no source for /ɲ/ in **terrenno** (1.8) < Lat.
TERRĒNU[M], and it is unlikely that **enna** (1.15, see 8.2.9) would have been
phonetically [eɲa] from what we know of modern dialectal developments.
Keypoint: palatalisation (p. 280).

8.1.3. The Latin /ks/ group represented by the letter *X* palatalised to /ʃ/, usually
also spelt *x* (see 12.1.1), in Old Castilian, but in Berceo *ss* and sometimes *s* are
more often used, hiding the distinction between /s/ and /ʃ/ which was no doubt
present: thus **disso** (1.1) ⩽ Lat. DĪXIT [DĪCO], **desar** (1.9) < Lat. ?DĒ(LA)XARE
(√LAXO).
Keypoint: consonant groups (p. 267); **palatalisation** (p. 280).

8.1.4 Mercet (l.15) < Lat. MERCĒDE [MERCES]. Final /e/ was lost in differing contexts in the various Romance languages: here we have a context which permits such loss in Castilian. The resultant final /d/ may be presumed to have fricativised to [ð] as a result of lenition whilst still intervocalic, but it still proves a somewhat volatile element in Modern Spanish, where pronunciations vary from complete suppression (cf. 29.1.1) to the devoiced fricative [θ] and the very careful standard (but minority) pronunciation [ð]. It is difficult to know exactly what the orthographical *-t* represents here: most likely a voiceless sound such as [θ], although it is not impossible to imagine [t], which is a development typical of some of the eastern Peninsular dialects.

   Keypoint: final *-e* (p. 273).

8.1.5 The I MS **tiemplo** (l.17) < Lat. TĔMPLU[M] shows an apparently regular diphthongisation of the Latin /ĕ/. The Modern Spanish form, however, like that of the F MS, is *templo*, which may show semilearned accommodation to TĔMPLUM itself. It is also possible, however, that *tiemplo* and *templo* were variant developments: such variation seems to have been reasonably common in syllables ending in a nasal consonant.

   Keypoint: vowels (p. 296).

8.1.6 The irregular first person preterite form **sovi** (ll.2 and 14) and the third person clitic pronoun **li** (l.20) show a final /i/ (< Lat. /ī/ in these inflections) in contrast to Castilian /e/, which is a marked Riojan feature of this text. Since this feature is specific to certain morphological forms and is not a generalised phonetic phenomenon (statistically, this is so, and Dutton's editorial policy has been to present a regularised picture in this respect), it is reasonable to suspect that analogical pressure is at work. The final /i/ of the preterite may be analogical with the stressed *-i* of the regular *-er/-ir* preterites, for instance.

8.1.7 Fasta (l.20) < Ar. *ḥattā* 'until'. The /st/ group is probably the result of the dissimilation of the Arabic double consonant: Berceo also uses the form *fata*, cf. Ptg. *até*, in which this problematic group is simplified.

   OCast. *f* poses a number of problems in its phonetic interpretation. It represents, as here, Ar. /ħ/ (*ḥā' ح*), but also the /x/ (*jā' خ*) of Arabic borrowings such as *alfombra* < Ar. *al-jumra* /alxumɾa/, as well as /h/ (*hā' ه*) (see 7.3.1). It is also used for derivations from Lat. /f/, both those which eventually became /h/ and subsequently fell altogether (e.g. **malfadado**, l.1, < Lat. √FĀTU[M] ‖ MSp. *malhadado*) and those which remained as /f/ (e.g. **fío**, l.15, < Lat. FĪDO). It is unlikely that Old Castilian preserved the Arabic sounds [ħ] and [x], which would have been quite foreign to the sound-system of the time (MSp. /x/ < OCast. /ʃ/ and /ʒ/ is a later development and nothing to do with Arabic); they would have been adapted to the closest sound available. Whatever sound or sounds *f* may have represented at the time of this text, OCast. /f/ was eventually destined to split by the sixteenth century into /f/ and /h/, broadly according to phonetic context. All these circumstances can be reconciled if we construe *f* as representing a phoneme whose central pronunciation was the bilabial fricative [ɸ], which was sufficiently fricative to be a possible pronunciation of Lat. /f/ and sufficiently aspirate to render the [h], [x] and [ħ] of Arabic loanwords.

   Keypoint: the f>h change (p. 271).

Morphology and syntax

8.2.1 A number of irregular preterites have forms which are different from those of Modern Spanish and indeed from those encountered in many other Old Castilian texts: **sovi** (ll.2 and 14), **veno** (l.18), **priso** (l.19), **fo** (l.20). **Sovi** is the preterite of *seer* (see 6.3.6) ≤ Lat. [SĔDĔO] (the corresponding Latin perfect form was SĒDĬT) and appears to have been created by analogy with the preterite of *haber* (Lat. HĂBUĪ [HĂBĔO]), which via an intermediate form ?/auβi/ yielded OCast. *ove* ≥ MSp. *hube*. **Priso** is formed from the reduced supine form PRE(HE)NSU[M] of Lat. [PRĔHENDO] (cf. the Modern Spanish adjective *preso*); MSp. *prendió* shows analogical regularisation. **Veno** and **fo** differ only slightly from the more usual Old Castilian forms *vino* and *fue*, which are also in origin the Modern Spanish forms and are used in the F MS.

   Keypoint: preterite stems (p. 287).

8.2.2 Quí (l.2), **qi quiera** (l.6), **qui** (l.7). Castilian distinguishes human reference in interrogative, relative and indefinite pronouns by the use of *quien* < Lat. QUEM, the accusative of QUIS: *¿quién?*, *quienquiera*, *quien* (see 7.2.4). The use of **qui** here is most probably a Riojan feature.

8.2.3 In the construction **del otero qe sovi** (l.2) the preposition *en* is not used (cf. standard MSp. *del otero en el que (estuve)*). Although the omission of the preposition would be considered imprecise according to later normative grammatical precepts, the sense is in fact pragmatically obvious, and such omissions are still frequent in modern spoken usage.

8.2.4 La alma (l.3). Initial *a-* in feminine words has often favoured the use of *el* rather than *la* as the definite article in Spanish (see 13.2.9 and 16.2.6); in Modern Spanish *el* is restricted to cases where the initial *a-* is stressed (thus *el águila* but *la antorcha*). There is apparently no such allomorphic variation in this text.

8.2.5 Morré (l.7), **cadré** (l.11). These future forms have syncopated stems, and are irregular by comparison with their Modern Spanish counterparts *moriré* and *caeré* (cf. 11.2.11). For *morré*, see 6.2.5. *Caer* < Lat. [CĂDO] loses the intervocalic /d/ by lenition in Castilian and a hiatic vowel group /ae/ is created. The eastern Hispanic dialects are generally resistant to hiatus, and what may be taken as the Riojan form *cader* is regularly found in Berceo, its syncopated future stem being *cadr-* formed like *podr-* from *poder* in Castilian. Note here the very clear modal meaning of the future: **cadré** occurs in parallel with three *querer* + infinitive expressions in this stanza, and indicates the speaker's intention.

   Keypoints: future and conditional (p. 274); **future stems** (p. 274).

8.2.6 Me quiero acostar (l.10). This is an instance of clitic-climbing: the clitic pronoun **me**, which semantically is the reflexive object of *acostar*, stands before the auxiliary verb *querer* (cf. 21.2.4).
    Keypoint: clitic pronoun position (p. 264).

8.2.7 Variation in the form of possessives and the presence or absence of the definite article is apparent here as in Text 7 (see 7.2.1): **los sos piedes**, **so altar** (l.11), **su gracia** (l.12), **(la) su mercet** (l.15), **Salvador mío** (l.16), **el su tiemplo** (l.17). It is possible that some of this variation is exploited by the poet to satisfy assonance and metre, since semantic distinctions are difficult to perceive.[10]
    Keypoint: possessives (p. 287).

8.2.8 Firmemientre (l.15). This is an example of *-mientre* ≤ Lat. MENTĒ being used to create an adverb from an adjective (for other examples see 7.2.12 and 10.1.4). The *-mientre* form itself must be regarded as a popular phonetic development of Lat. MENTĒ with diphthongisation; the epenthesis of *-r-* is probably due to analogical pressure from other adverbial expressions ending in *-re*, of which there were a number in Old Castilian, e.g. *siempre* 'always', *alguandre* 'never' (see 2.8), *(do)mientre* . . . 'while . . .'. The later preference for *-mente* (cf. the F MS) has been attributed to the learned influence of Latin (Alvar and Mariner 1967: 18); it certainly cannot be seen as a subsequent development of *-mientre* (see also 10.1.4).
    Keypoint: adverbs (p. 262).

8.2.9 Enna (l.15) is a contracted form of *en* + *la*, and betrays the Riojan origins of this text (cf. 2.14.1). Castilian is resistant to such contractions of preposition and article, *al* and *del* being the only ones found in Modern Spanish.

8.2.10 In **la alma he perdida** (l.3), the past participle of the compound perfect agrees with the preceding direct object (cf. 4.2.3 and 6.2.4). Despite the left-dislocation of the direct object, there is no 'resumptive' pronoun, in contrast with l.4 (see 7.2.11).

8.2.11 For **do** (ll.5 and 8), see 6.3.9; for **venir.m há** (l.18), see **Keypoint: clitic pronoun position** (p. 264).

Vocabulary

8.3.1 Mesquino (l.1) (‖ MSp. *mezquino*) is a borrowing from Ar. *miskīn* 'poor', 'miserable', and it is in this sense that it is used here. We can imagine that its adoption in Romance is a consequence of its frequency in Arabic as a term of pity or abuse. In Modern Spanish it has undergone transfer to the associated pejorative meaning of 'mean', 'niggardly'.

---

10 Alvar and Pottier (1983: 101 n.21) speak of a tendency in Berceo to use the article with the possessive, and of an association between the absence of the article and 'inherent possession' (parts of the body), but this is not apparent in this short extract.

8.3.2 Otero (l.2) is one of a number of words for 'hill' in Castilian. Others are *cerro* < Lat. CĬRRU[S] 'lock', 'ringlet', 'fringe', which undergoes restriction to 'horse's mane', and then by association takes on the meaning of 'animal's back' (where a horse's mane is), then by metaphor 'raised part of land'; and *cuesta* < Lat. CŎSTA 'rib', 'side', which similarly develops by metaphor the meaning of 'sloping land'. **Otero** < Lat. ?ALTĀRĬU[S] (√ALTU[S] 'high') is a popular word which has undergone all the expected phonetic changes (vocalisation of implosive /l/ to [u], subsequent monophthongisation of the resultant diphthong [aw] to [o], metathesis of /**arju**/ to /**ajru**/ and monophthongisation of [aj] to [e]); the corresponding adjective *oto* (cf. Fr. *haut*) is found in placenames such as *Colloto*, although it has not survived in Castilian, where the adjectival form is the more conservative variant development *alto*.

8.3.3 Derribar (l.2) is a morphological derivative of Lat. √RĪPA 'river-bank'. It presumably originally had the meaning of 'to push off a bank or slope'. From √RĪPA also derives the verb **ribar** (l.5), which presumably originally had the meaning 'to approach a bank', and is used in exactly this meaning here; MSp. *arribar* < Lat. [?ADRĪPO] continues the specialised maritime meaning of 'to get into port'.

8.3.4 Trovar (l.6). The semantic history of this verb is an example of widening of meaning. It is now generally considered (see Cor., V, 666) that its origin is in Lat. [?(CON)TRŎPO] 'to speak figuratively', which then comes to mean 'to invent verses' (hence *trobador* 'troubador', 'one who invents verses'), and then 'to find (in general)'.

8.3.5 Delante (l.11). The Latin preposition ANTĔ, which is found as *ante* from early Castilian texts, also forms the basis of two compound prepositions in Castilian: *antes de* and *delante de*. The three are semantically discriminated: *ante* 'faced with'; 'before (in some special contexts, such as *ante el tribunal*)', *antes de* 'before (temporal)', *delante de* 'in front of (spatial)'. *Delante* (here without *de*) itself probably has its origins in Lat. ?DĒ IN ANTĔ, the first /n/ of which undergoes dissimilation to /l/; *antes*, which is also used adverbially, adds /s/ probably by analogy with other adverbs (see 2.5, 4.2.14, 6.3.8).
    Keypoint: adverbs (p. 262).

8.3.6 Finar (l.12) may be seen either as a form of Lat. [FĪNĬO] which has been analogically assimilated to the majority *-ar* conjugation or as a morphological derivative of the noun FĪNIS 'end'. It was common in Old Castilian in the meaning of 'to die', a euphemistic value which was also a feature of Lat. FĪNĬO. The notion of 'dying' is especially prone to such euphemistic substitution (cf. MSp. *fallecer*, discussed in 9.3.12). The specialised meaning of **finar** may have been facilitated by the fact that the more usual way of rendering the notion of 'to finish' in Old Castilian was with the verb *acabar*.

8.3.7 Maguer (l.13) is one of a number of words for 'although' in Old Castilian; others are *comoquiera que* (see 11.3.14) and *aunque*. None of the Latin concessive conjunctions, such as TĂMETSI, QUAMQUAM and QUAMVĪS survive; this may be due to the relative infrequency of such subordinating structures in popular speech. **Maguer** itself derives from Gr. μακάϱιε 'fortunate', 'happy', which probably moved to a function rather like that of optative *ojalá* and then to 'although'. Optative and concessive are related in that both envisage an imagined situation, and it cannot be coincidental that the reverse movement with *ojalá* (from optative to concessive) has occurred in some areas of Latin America, a phenomenon also found occasionally in Golden Age Spanish (Kany 1951: 381 and Cor., III, 764–8). See also 33.3.1.[11]

8.3.8 Loco sendío (l.13). This expression appears to be tautologous, since both adjectives mean 'mad'; it may have been a set phrase. The origin of **loco** is uncertain, possibly from Arabic; *sendío (sandío)* appears to be structurally associated with the pitying exclamation Lat. SANCTE DĔUS (Cor., V, 147–50).

8.3.9 Cras de buenna mannana (l.17). **Cras** < Lat. CRĀS 'tomorrow' is frequent in Old Castilian and continues as an archaism in Golden-Age Spanish. Perhaps because of its phonetic weakness as a monosyllable, it has been replaced very generally in Romance, and in Spanish, by *mañana* < Lat. ?MĀNĔĀNA, based on √MĀNE 'early', which presumably undergoes transfer of meaning to 'early (in the day)' → 'morning' → 'tomorrow (in the morning)'. Here, there is an idiomatic association with *mañana* in the phrase *de buena mannana* 'early tomorrow morning'.

8.3.10 Porfazo (l.19) 'insult', 'humiliation', is a noun formed from Lat. ?√[POSTFĂCĬO], a neologism based on idiomatic association with the phrase POST FĂCĬE[M] [MALDICO] 'to talk about someone behind their back'.

8.3.11 Fasta (l.20) < Ar. *ḥattā* 'until'. Unlike the vast majority of Arabic loanwords in Spanish, this is a preposition with a very general 'grammatical' function rather than a 'lexical' word (noun, adjective or verb) with a very specific meaning, and therefore does not seem to be culturally peculiar to Al-Andalus. Why, then, should it have been borrowed? Two factors may be relevant. First, we may note that the notion of 'until' is expressed very variably in the Romance languages (cf. Fr. *jusqu'à* < Lat. USQUE AD, It. *fino* ← Lat. √FĪNIS and such creations as Oc. *troa* < Lat. ?INTĔR HOC AD). It does not seem that there was a general Romance term for this notion, therefore; perhaps because of lack of morphological transparency, Classical Latin DUM, DŌNĔC and QUŎĂD were abandoned in favour of more analytic alternatives. Second, in the particular case of the Ibero-Romance languages, it could have been familiarity with valedictory formulae that gave the Arabic preposition currency (cf. the wealth of such expressions in Modern Spanish: *hasta luego, hasta mañana, hasta la vista*, etc.).

8.3.12 For the use of **sovi** (l.2) < Lat. SĒDĬT [SĔDĔO], see 6.3.6.

---

11 Variation in the expression of concession has attracted a good deal of attention. See especially Rivarola (1976), and, for a recent text-based study of *maguer*, Montero Cartelle (1992).

9 Moral instruction from Aristotle, from the *Libro de Alexandre* (thirteenth century)

9.0 Authorship of the *Libro de Alexandre* has been variously attributed to Berceo, Alfonso X and Juan Lorenzo de Astorga: whoever the author was, he was an educated and well-read person, and we will therefore not be surprised to find learned features in his poetic language. The story of Alexander the Great was clearly an inspiring subject for the time, no doubt because it provided an example of great kingship; the extract we look at here, which forms part of the material covered by the G' MS (see below), is from Aristotle's advice to the young Alexander. The major source of the *Libro de Alexandre* was the late twelfth-century Medieval Latin *Alexandreis* of Gautier de Châtillon, which was a favourite set text in medieval schools, to such an extent that it was preferred to the classics; but there is also a debt to the French *Roman d'Alexandre*, as well as to classical sources (Pritchard 1986: 7). The multiple sources of the text must therefore constantly be borne in mind. The *Libro de Alexandre* was an enormously influential work, clearly admired by fifteenth- and sixteenth-century Castilian writers, so it is important in the ongoing tradition of literary writing in Castilian. These factors contribute significantly to its complexity, since not only do we have to disentangle the linguistic debt to the Latin and French models, if any, but also contend with the diversity of the surviving versions, which are the product of extensive copying.

The text

The *Libro de Alexandre* poses considerable intrinsic problems for editors and philologists. There are two principal MS sources: the older O[suna] MS, thought to have been copied at the end of the thirteenth century or the beginning of the fourteenth century, appears to have some stanzas missing; the more complete P[aris] MS dates from the fifteenth century. There are a number of other surviving MS fragments: the G' MS consists of a number of stanzas from the first part of the poem included by Gutierre Díez de Gamés in *El Victorial* (early fifteenth century). As can easily be seen from the short extract given here, these two MSS have much material in common, yet are far from identical: they are most probably the product of different copyings of a common ancestor, but the many striking differences between them make the establishment of an edition difficult. While the P MS exhibits a number of features which suggest an origin to the east of Castile, the O MS carries indications of a more westerly provenance. Detailed analysis of a section of the work by Alarcos Llorach (1948) led him to conclude that such dialectal features are the work of copyists and that the original version of the poem would have been in Castilian. All the MSS contain obvious mistakes in copying: to mention some of the clearest cases in the extract below, l.5 of the O MS is too short; **se ombre buelve** in l.13 of the O MS is an unlikely word order; l.18 of the G' MS does not rhyme convincingly.

To illustrate the problems of textual reconstruction and the assessment of non-Castilian features, the O, P and G' MSS versions are given, following the edition of Willis (1934).

Começo don Ariſtotil || cuemo ombre bien letrado

fijo a bona edat || ſodes embiado

de ſeer ombre bueno || tenedes lo bien guiſado

si leuar lo *qui*ſierdes || cuemo auedes co*m*peçado

Ffijo ereſ de reÿ || aſ grant clerizia

en ti ueo aguçia || qual pora mi qu*er*ria

de peq*ue*nez moſtraſte || muÿ grant cauallaria

de q*ua*ntoſ oÿ uiuen || tieneſ grant meioria

Siempre faz con co*n*ſeio || q*ua*nto q*ue* fer ouieres

ffabla co*n* tuſ ua∫∫allos || q*ua*nto fazer q*ui*ſieres

sertan mas leales || ſi lo aſſÿ fezieres

Enpeço Ariſtotiles com*m*o oñe bien honrrado

fijo dixol en buena hedat ſodes vos llegado

pora ſeyer oñe bueno tu lo aſ aguſſado

ſy leuar lo quijeres com*m*o lo aſ enpeçado

Fillo eres de Rey tu aſ grañt clereſoria

en ti veo agudeoa q*ua*l *pa*ra mj querria

de peq*ue*ño demueſtras muÿ grañt cauallaria

de q*ua*ntoσ oÿ bjuen tu aſ melloria

Sienpre fes con conſello q*ua*nto de fer oujeres

fabla co*n* tus vaſallos q*ua*nto q*ue* fer quijſieres

ſerante maſ leales ſy aſi lo fiſieres

começo Ariſtotiles como onbre bien lenguado

e dixo fijo a buena hedad heres llegado

de ser honbre bueno faslo bien aguisado

sy lleuarlo quijeres como as começado

hijo eres de Rey e as gran clerezja

de pequeñes demueſtras muy gran cavallerja

en ti veo acuçia qual para mj queRia

de quantos ay biben traes gran mejorja

sienpre fas con consejo quanto fazer quijeres

habla con tus vasallos lo que fazer quijeres

sertean mas leales sy lo asi fizjeres

5

10

sobre todo te cura || mucho [[de no]] amar mugiereſ	σobre todo te guarda de amor de mugeres	sobre todo te guarda de muncho amar mugeres
Ca deſque ſe ombre buelue || co*n* ellas vna vez	Deſque ſe buelue el om̃e en [e]llas vna veṣ	despues que ſe e*n*buelue onbre con ellas vna bez
siempre ua arriedro || & òſiempr*e* pierde prez	ſienpre maſ va aRiedro e maſ pierde ſu pres	sjenpre va aRiedro e pierde todo el prez
puede p*er*der ſu alma || q*ue* a Dios mucho g*ra*uez	puede perder ſu alma e Dios lo aborres	e puede perder su alma pues Dios le aboResçe
et puede en grant ocaſion || caer muȳ de rafez	puede caher en grañt ocaſion toſte e Rafes	puede *en* gran ocaçion caer mūy de Refez
En poder de uil ombre || non metaſ tu fazienda	En poder de ujl om̃e no*n* metas tu faṣjenda	en poder de vil honbre no pongas tu fazjenda
ca darta mala caga || nu*m*qua pre*n*draſ emienda	q*ue* darta mala çaga nu*n*ca prendras emjenda	ca te dara mal a çaga do nunca apren-deras en mj hedad
ffaleçer te ha a la cota || como la mala re*n*ta	falleçerte ha a la cueyta com*mo* el cauallo mala Rie*n*da	falleçer te a la cuyta como la mala Rienda
echar ta en logar || onde Dios te defienda	echarteha en lugar onde fijo Dios te defienda	metertea e*n* lugar donde Djos te defienda

Further reading

Alarcos Llorach (1948); Cañas (1988) (an accessible modern scholarly edition with a good introduction and glossary); Willis (1934).

Translation of the O MS text

Aristotle began in the manner of a well-read man: 'Son, you have been sent at a good time; you are well prepared to be a good man, if you will carry on as you have begun.

'You are the son of a king; you have great learning; in you I detect a shrewdness I could wish for myself. As a child you showed very great nobility; you have the advantage of all others alive today.

'Whatever you have to do, do it after taking counsel; discuss with your vassals anything you want to do. They will be more loyal to you if you act thus. Above all, take great care not to be a womaniser.

'For when a man once goes with women, he regresses and always loses renown; he can lose his soul, which is greatly grieving to God, and he can very easily fall down on a great occasion.

'Do not place your business in the power of a base man, for he will serve you badly and you will never get satisfaction; he will fail you in time of trouble like a bad rein; it will throw you into a place from which may God protect you.'

Phonetics and phonology

9.1.1 Cuemo (ll.1 and 4) is a variant development of Lat. QUŌMŎDŎ alongside **com(m)o** in the O and G' MSS. The most likely scenario for the evolution of **cuemo** is that an original [wo] in ?/kwom(od)o/ changed to [we] in line with the ?[wo] which was probably an intermediate stage in the diphthongisation of Lat. /ŏ/ (e.g. Lat. BŎNU[S] > ?[bwono] > [bweno]; but see 1.1.1).
   Keypoint: vowels (p. 296).

9.1.2 Ombre (ll.1, 13 and 17) is the regular Castilian development of Lat. HŎMINE [HŎMO] (see 6.1.3), though the P MS has the form **om̄e** (expandable as *omne*), a variant regularly encountered in Old Castilian texts.
   Keypoint: consonant groups (p. 267).

9.1.3 Bona (l.2), **bueno** (l.3) < Lat. BŎNA [BŎNUS]. We cannot regard the spelling **bona** as reflecting a pronunciation [bona], in view of the general attestation of the expected Castilian diphthongisation in this text.
   Keypoint: vowels (p. 296).

9.1.4 Fijo (l.2), **ffijo** (l.5). There is not necessarily any particular significance in the double *f*, which often simply indicated a capital letter.[12] In the O and P MSS *f* or

12 See, however, Blake (1988).

ff consistently represents the phoneme ?/ɸ/, though in the later G' MS we find **hijo** (l.5) and **habla** (l.10) as against **fijo** (ll.2 and 20), **fas** (l.9), **fazer** (ll.9 and 10), **fizjeres** (l.11). The *h* here may represent [h], or even zero (Penny 1990), but is more likely to be a feature of the pronunciation of the time of the MS rather than of the time of the composition of the poem. An important difference between the O MS and the P MS is seen in the result of the palatalisation of the /lj/ group of Lat. FĪLĬU[S]: whereas **fijo** in the O MS indicates a pronunciation [fiʒo], the **fillo** spelling of P (l.5) suggests [fiʎo]; compare also O **meioria** [meʒoria]/P **melloria** (l.8) [meʎoria] < Lat. √MĚLĬOR, O **conseio** [konseʒo]/P **consello** [konseʎo] (l.9) < Lat. CONSĬLĬU[M]. [lj] > [ʒ] is a peculiarly Castilian development (see 7.1.1), and the preservation of [lj] as [ʎ] is certainly non-Castilian (though see 4.1.6). Yet the P MS is not consistent, for we also find **fijo** (l.2) and **mugeres** (as O **mugieres**) < Lat. MŬLĬĔRES [MŬLĬĔR].

Keypoints: the **f>h change** (p. 271); **palatalisation** (p. 280).

9.1.5 Seer (l.3) suggests the greater tolerance of Castilian towards vowels in hiatus as against the P MS **seyer**, the spelling of which suggests the presence of a semi-vowel separating the two /e/ vowels. As noted in 8.2.5, the avoidance of hiatus is a feature of the more easterly Peninsular dialects.

9.1.6 Leuar (l.4) later became **llevar** in Castilian (as in the G' MS) as a result of a reanalysis of the stem of the verb **levar**, which is originally radical-changing. The successive stages can be envisaged as follows. Latin /ĕ/ (1) diphthongises under stress to /je/ (2); the sequence /lje/ is reanalysed as /ʎe/ (3), and finally the stem /ʎeβ/ generalises to the whole verb paradigm (4):

(1)	*(2)*	*(3)*	*(4)*
LĔVŌ	/ljeβo/	/ʎeβo/	*llevo*
LĔVĀS	/ljeβas/	/ʎeβas/	*llevas*
LĔVAT	/ljeβa/	/ʎeβa/	*lleva*
LĔVĀMUS	/leβamos/	/leβamos/	*llevamos*
LĔVĀTIS	/leβades/	/leβades/	*lleváis*
LĔVANT	/ljeβan/	/ʎeβan/	*llevan*

9.1.7 Clerizia (l.5), **fezieres** (l.11), **logar** (l.20). We may note that variant vowel spellings of **cleressia**, **fizieres** and **lugar** in the P and G' MSS which foreshadow the later Spanish forms *clerecía*, *hicieres* and *lugar*. In Old Castilian, there is often such variation in atonic vowels, *e* alternating with *i* and *o* with *u*; this may be indicative of a tendency to neutralise the atonic distinctions between /e/ and /i/ and between /o/ and /u/, a process which was, in the event, not carried through. See also 10.1.5, 11.1.8, 13.1.5, 21.1.3 and 28.1.3.

Keypoint: **vowels** (p. 296).

9.1.8 Clerizia (l.5), **prez** (l.14), **rafez** (l.16), **fazienda** (l.17) in the O MS contrast in their sibilant consonant spellings with **cleressia**, **pres**, **rafes** and **fasienda** in the P MS. The variant spellings of such words (even sometimes within the same

MS) is one of the chief problems in establishing the problematic history of the distribution and origins of OCast. /ts/ and /dz/.

Keypoints: palatalisation (p. 280); **lenition** (p. 278); **the sibilants of Old Castilian** (p. 290).

Morphology and syntax

9.2.1 The O and P MSS show a rather surprising change from the polite **vos** form to the more familiar **tu** form of address in the course of Aristotle's speech. Both start with **vos**: **sodes** (l.2); O continues this through stanza 1 (**tenedes, quisierdes, auedes**) while P switches immediately (**as aguisado, quieres, as enpeçado**). The G' MS consistently has **tu** forms throughout. *Tu* would have been the expected form of address from a respected tutor to a young pupil, though *vos* was the form of respect used to the king.

Keypoint: personal pronouns (p. 284).

9.2.2 Quisierdes (l.4). This is a future subjunctive form deriving from the future perfect indicative of Latin (QUAESĪVERITIS [QUAERO]), and here used in the crucial syntactic context which was in all likelihood the basis of this categorial shift, the protasis of a future-referring conditional sentence.

Keypoint: conditional sentences (p. 265); **the future subjunctive** (p. 275).

9.2.3 O **aguçia** and P **agudeza** (l.6) are differing morphological derivatives of *agudo* < Lat. ACŪTU[S], exploiting the *-ia* and *-eza* endings respectively.

9.2.4 Qual (l.6). **Qual** is here used as a relative pronoun (cf. 2.14.2), but as yet without the definite article.

Keypoint: relatives (p. 289).

9.2.5 Pora (l.6) is the ancestor of MSp. *para* (a form which in fact appears in the P and G' MSS).

Keypoint: *por* and *para* (p. 286).

9.2.6 Fer (l.9) and **fazer** (l.10) both derive from Lat. [FĂCĬO]. The reduced form (cf. Fr. *faire*, It. *fare*) seems to be a non-Castilian feature (see 2.14.9); in the O MS the two forms are used in close proximity: the inconsistency could be the result of genuine variation or, more probably, of a copyist's amendment (**quanto que fer quisieres** in the P MS is syntactically odd – see 9.2.8).

9.2.7 Quanto (ll.9 and 10) < Lat. QUANTU[M] functioned as a relative (as *cuanto* still does in Modern Spanish in formal registers) with the meaning of 'everything that' (*todo lo que*).

Keypoint: relatives (p. 289).

9.2.8 Que fer ouieres (l.9) resembles the use of *que* in MSp. *tener que hacer* 'to have to do'. The use of *que* in the modal auxiliary expression *tener que* + infinitive is unusual in Spanish, since such complements more commonly involve a preposition (as in **de fer** in the P MS) rather than a complementiser: cf. 13.2.5. The origin of Sp. *que* may be an ellipsis of a structure such as *tener (algo) que (está por) hacer* 'to have something that is to be done'. (The possibilities for the subsequent reanalysis of the *que hacer* phrase can be seen in the adjectival (*un ejercicio que corregir*) and nominal (*un quehacer doméstico*) use of *que* + infinitive in Modern Spanish.)

9.2.9 Futures with intercalated clitic pronouns are evident in **sertan** (l.11), **darta** (l.18), **ffaleçer te ha** (l.19) and **echar ta** (l.20). The P MS **serante** (l.11), whilst likewise showing avoidance of an initial position for the clitic pronoun, interestingly has an order (the clitic following the whole future form *serán*) which is not widely encountered before the sixteenth century. In the G' MS the pronoun **te** precedes the future in **te dara** (l.18); either this is a later amendment or the **ca** conjunction is here considered 'strong' enough to allow the clitic to precede the verb, unlike in the O and P MSS.

In **te cura** (l.12), the clitic pronoun precedes the imperative form, which would be impossible in Modern Spanish (*cúrate*); the preceding position is here made possible, in accordance with the Old Castilian rule, because the pronoun is not in initial position, since it is preceded by the adverbial **sobre todo** (see also 10.2.9).

Keypoint: **clitic pronoun position** (p. 264).

9.2.10 Si lo assy fezieres (l.11), **desque se ombre buelve con ellas una vez** (l.13). The clitic pronoun is separated from the verb here (by **asaz** and **ombre** respectively) in a way which is impossible in standard Modern Spanish (see also 10.2.5, 11.2.3).

Keypoint: **clitic pronoun position** (p. 264).

9.2.11 Ombre (l.13). This may literally mean simply 'a man' (especially in view of the context!), but *ombre* (particularly if used without an article) in Old Castilian can also have the general indefinite meaning of 'people', 'one'.

Vocabulary

9.3.1 The first stanza reveals a number of words for 'to begin'. **Começo** (O l.1) derives from Lat. [?COMĬNĬTĬO], the COM- prefix being an intensifying device (cf. *comer* < Lat. [?COMĔDO], ĔDO being the usual Latin verb for 'to eat'). **Enpeço** (P l.1) has a complex semantic history: it appears to be based on a possible Celtic borrowing into Latin ?PĔTTĬA 'piece', from which derives MSp. *pieza*; *empezar* < ?IN + PĔTTĬARE probably went through the associational stages of 'to cut into pieces' → 'to cut off a piece' → '(to cut off a piece and) begin to use it' → 'to begin (to use something)'. **Compeçar** (O l.4) appears to be a crossed etymology between **começar** and **empeçar**. This is an interesting case of the toleration of near synonymy, since not only have both *comenzar* and *empezar* survived into Modern Spanish with little appreciable difference in meaning between them, but the semantic field of 'beginning' remains very rich today, with the learned additions *iniciar* and *principiar* and auxiliary expressions such as *ponerse a* + infinitive and *echarse a* + infinitive.

9.3.2 For seer (l.3), see 6.3.6.

9.3.3 Guisado (O l.3) and **agujsado** (P and G' l.3) are derived from a Germanic root √*wisa* (cognate with Eng. *wise* 'way', 'manner') which was probably borrowed into Latin. The *a-* prefix appears in several Spanish verbs (e.g. *arrepentirse, acatar, acontecer, acosar, amenazar*), especially verbs which have, as does *aguisar*, a causative meaning (see also 2.10.1, 10.3.3, 13.3.3). OCast. *guisar* has the general meaning of 'to prepare'; the word subsequently underwent restriction of meaning via 'to prepare (by seasoning or cooking)' to the more restricted meaning of 'to stew'.

9.3.4 Leuar (1.4) < Lat. [LĔVO] 'to raise' has developed its meaning from 'to lift up (and carry)' → 'to carry' and 'to wear'. The notion of 'to raise' is rendered by a morphological derivative, *levantar*, formed from the Lat. present participle LĔVANTE[M] [LĔVO] 'raising'.

9.3.5 Clerizia (l.5) derives from the Greek √κληρος, which was borrowed into Latin as CLĒRU[S] 'body of priests', 'clergy' (MSp. *clero*); it meant 'learning', the clergy being the literate, learned class *par excellence* of medieval society. The second stanza of the *Libro de Alexandre* begins:

> Mester traigo fermoso, non es de joglaria,
> mester es sin pecado, ca es de clerezía
> fablar curso rimado por la quaderna vía,
> a sílabas contadas, ca es grant maestría.

'I bring a beautiful skill, it is not *joglaría* [i.e. troubadour poetry], it is a sinless skill, for it is learned to speak a sequence rhyming in quatrains with regular syllables; it is a great art.'

9.3.6 Caualleria 'chivalry', 'nobility' (l.7) is a morphological derivative created by the addition of the very productive suffixes *-ero* and *-ía* to the stem Lat. √CĂBALLU[S], which in the classical language had the pejorative meaning of 'workhorse' or 'nag', but which, probably as a result of amelioration by self-deprecation (see 3.3.2, 22.3.2, 25.3.2, 29.3.1), became the generic word for 'horse', without any such nuance, in later usage, as the evidence of Fr. *cheval*, It. *cavallo*, etc., and even loanwords such as Welsh *cefyll*, show. (Lat. ĔQUU[S] 'horse' survived, in the feminine, ĔQUA, as Sp. *yegua* 'mare'.)

9.3.7 Ffabla (l.10, ‖ MSp. *habla*) derives from an analogically regularised form FĀBŬLAT of the Latin deponent verb [FĀBŬLOR] 'to talk', 'to converse', 'to chatter', a verb of rather more restricted meaning than the Lat. LŎQUOR, which universally disappeared in favour of more semantically marked alternatives (cf. Fr. *parler* < Lat. [PĂRĂBŎLO] 'to tell stories', based on Gr. √παραβολή 'comparison', 'parable', which is also the basis of Sp. *palabra* 'word'). Another verb which enters this semantic field in Castilian is *platicar* (< Lat. ?[PRACTĬCO] based on Gr. √πρακτικός 'fit', 'busy'), which must have gone through the associational development 'to be familiar (with)' → 'to have dealings (with people)' → 'to have conversation (with people)'; *platicar* has become the commonest word for the notion of 'to talk' in Latin-American Spanish.

9.3.8 Arriedro (l.14) < Lat. AD RĔTRŌ 'backwards'. This adverb (cognate with Fr. *arrière*) was current until the Golden Age. The notion is rendered analytically in Modern Spanish by *hacia atrás*.
   Keypoint: adverbs (p. 262).

9.3.9 Prez (l.14) 'honour', 'esteem' < Lat. PRĔTĬU[M] 'worth', 'value'. This word is common in Old Castilian down to the fifteenth century. It is an Occitan borrowing; *precio* 'price', the development which has survived into Modern Spanish, is often regarded as a semilearned word, since it retains the /j/ in the /tsjo/ ending rather than its developing to /tso/ or /ts/ (Cor., IV, 631).
   Keypoints: learned and popular, semilearned and semipopular (p. 277); **palatalisation** (p. 280).

9.3.10 Toste (P l.16) 'quickly' is a borrowing from Occitan or French and is cognate with Fr. *tôt*; the use of such a word may represent another 'eastern' feature of the P MS. Its origin is Lat. TOSTU[M], the past participle of TORRĔO 'to burn', 'to roast', which underwent the associational changes 'burnt' → 'lively' → 'quickly'.

9.3.11 Rafez (l.16) 'easily' is a borrowing from Ar. *rajīṣ* 'supple', 'tender'; 'inexpensive', 'base', 'mean', and the cultural basis for such a borrowing is not difficult to appreciate. The semantic area of 'easy' is one which sees a good deal of movement in Old Castilian: see 11.3.12. Another Arabic borrowing here is **çaga** (l.18) < Ar. *sāqa* 'rearguard', originally belonging to the semantic field of military terms, though becoming more general in application and still used in Modern Spanish in a number of expressions, including *a la zaga* 'at the rear'. Here it seems to have an even more general meaning of '(end) result', 'outcome'.

9.3.12 Ffaleçer (l.19) derives from an inchoative form ?[FALLESCO] of Lat. FALLO 'to make invisible' (cf. 7.2.13, 7.3.9); we must assume a change in meaning to 'to become invisible' as an intermediate step towards the Old Castilian meaning of 'to be lacking', 'to fail' (a notion rendered in Modern Spanish by *faltar*, which was a verbal formation from *falta* < Lat. ?FALLĬTA, the analogical feminine past participle of the same verb). In Modern Spanish, *fallecer* has undergone a further change in meaning through euphemism for the notion of 'to die' (see 8.3.6).

VI The Castilian norm

Alfonso X (reigned 1252–84) is often credited with having carried out the first standardisation of Castilian. This view needs considerable qualification. It certainly does not amount to anything like the rationalist standardisation that was to take place in the eighteenth century as a result of the work of the Real Academia Española (see Text 23); at most, it implies the development of a house style by the scribes of the Royal Scriptorium, in the development of which it is likely, however, that the King did frequently intervene in person. In the introduction to the *Libro de la Ochava Espera* (1276), a famous passage records that the king

> tolló las razones que entendió eran sobejanas et dobladas et que non eran en castellano drecho, et puso las otras que entendió que complían; et cuanto en el lenguaje, endreçólo él por sise

Some of the terms here need comment. Although *castellano drecho* has been equated with the supposed Alfonsine 'standard', it is difficult to know exactly what is meant by it, since it is not in fact a frequently used term in Alfonsine prose: it probably implied stylistic felicity rather than conformity to some court linguistic 'standard'. The word *castellano* was often used contrastively, to indicate the kind of vernacular (*romance*, as opposed to Latin) spoken in Castile, so *castellano drecho* could imply that words which were not in use in Castile were amended; we must bear in mind that a number of non-Castilians worked on the translations which were made under Alfonso's auspices. There is indeed evidence that in the course of the Alfonsine period the incidence of obvious Aragonesisms, Occitanisms, etc., which were common in earlier texts from Castile (see Chapter V), decreased; but it would be unwise to interpret *castellano drecho* as necessarily a standard imposed *within* Castile.

The term *lenguaje* (see 18.3.3) seems to have meant a way of speaking or expressing oneself; in modern linguistic terms we might interpret it as appropriateness of register, though in Alfonso's time there was also a notion of appropriateness of particular languages, Latin typically being used for communication with non-Castilian speakers and Galician for lyric poetry (Alfonso himself composed the *Cantigas de Santa María* in Galician). The matching of language to communicative purpose is probably what lies behind a number of significant linguistic developments which took place in and around the Alfonsine period, chief amongst which is the use of the vernacular for official purposes in preference to Latin. To understand why the vernacular was used in this way we must look at the circumstances of thirteenth-century Castile.

Alfonso's father Fernando III had opted for the drawing up of *fueros* (legal codes) for newly reconquered territories in Castilian rather than Latin, for the purely practical reason that Latin was scarcely known in Al-Andalus by this time. The similar use of Castilian in the great Alfonsine codification of laws known as the *Siete Partidas* was to have a knock-on effect in the education of lawyers. In the translation of works from Arabic, Castilian was again the natural language to choose. Jewish translators were used for this work, each working in tandem with a Christian who composed the text; Jews did not know Latin and, moreover, found it offensive as the language of the Christian liturgy, so Castilian was the language used. The translation of the scientific works coincided with a time of general reorganisation in university curricula, so that Castilian came to have prestige in this area too. It must also be borne in mind that in Spain at this time Arabic probably had as much prestige as a language of culture and learning as Latin (see Chapter IV), so that Latin was not necessarily the obvious vehicle of learned literature. Alfonso's concern for the transmission of knowledge (not to mention the legitimising of the position of Castile and himself as its king) almost certainly motivated the drawing up of chronicles in Castilian from a compendia of Latin sources.

Thus it was that a huge increase in the use of Castilian and in the corpus of written texts in Castilian took place during the thirteenth century. Although a cautionary note has been sounded concerning the notion of the establishment of a standard, the Alfonsine corpus certainly provided a consistent linguistic norm for subsequent literary activity, and the spelling system was to remain substantially unaltered until the eighteenth century (see Text 23).

The language of these texts can, broadly speaking, be equated with educated Toledan usage, which various factors contributed to establishing as the prestige variety of the day. Although the royal court followed an itinerant king, Toledo was the nearest thing to a fixed capital in late medieval Castile. It was regarded as the historic capital of Spain, since it had been the Visigothic centre of administration. More crucially, it was the locus of Alfonso's school of translators, who achieved international renown and received scholars from all over the western world. Tradition also has it (Alonso 1949: 66–7) that Alfonso decreed that any case of dispute over the interpretation of a Castilian word in the *Siete Partidas* was to be resolved according to the usage of the city of Toledo. (This may, however, have been wishful thinking by later commentators who saw in the sixteenth century the yielding of the Toledan norm to that of Madrid, see Text 17.)

10 The Moorish invasion of Spain. Alfonso X, el Sabio, *Primera crónica general* (late thirteenth century).

10.0 The *Primera crónica general* was compiled in several stages. The Prólogo and Chapters 1–108 are dated by Menéndez Pidal (1955) to around 1270; the rest, though probably begun shortly afterwards, was interrupted by work on the *General estoria* and was ultimately revised during the reign of Sancho IV. It is thus possible to observe in this chronicle the evolution of the consistent Toledan 'house style' mentioned above. The extract below, from Chapter 556, which forms part of the account of the invasion of Spain by the Moors, is in the later style and so may be taken to be an example of mature *castellano drecho*. The source of the material in this chapter is Rodrigo of Toledo (see Sánchez Alonso, 1925); the original Latin of this text survives, although it is known that there was also a Castilian version made, which is now unfortunately lost.

The text

The text, from ff.191r-191v of the Escorial MS Y.i.2, appears, with minor modification, as transcribed palaeographically in Kasten *et al.* (1997). In particular, it has been possible to show original punctuation in this text, the only omission being the *calderón* or paragraph mark ('). Some of the major variants encountered in other versions are given in footnotes.

Further reading

Lapesa (1985c); Menéndez Pidal (1955); Niederehe (1987).

DE COMO LOS MOROS ENTRARON EN ESPANNA LA SEGUNDA UEZ.

Andados tres annos del Regnado del Rey Rodrigo q*ue* fue. En la era de sietecientos & cinquaenta & dos.[1] Q*u*ando andaua ell anno de la encarnacion en siete cientos & quatorze. & el dell imperio de Leo en uno. Enuio Vlid[2] rey de los Alaraues por Muça q*ue* fuesse a ell a tierra de Affri[quia][3] o ell era. & muça fue alla. & dexo en tierra de Affrica por sennor en su   5 logar. a tarif abenciet q*ue* era tuerto de[4] un[5] [oi]o. & mandol Muça q*ue* ayudasse al cuende Julian yl mostrasse amiztad. Este tarif dio al cuende Julian doze mill omnes pora todo fecho. E el cuende paso[6] los aq*ue*nd mar asconduda mientre en Naues de mercaderos pocos a pocos. por tal q*ue* ge lo non ente*n*diessen. & pues q*ue* fueron todos passados a Espanna; ayun-   10 taron se en un mo*n*t q*ue* oy dia lieua nombre daq*ue*l moro. & dizen le en arauigo Gebaltarif. & los xpr*is*tianos Gibaltar. Ca gebel[7] en arauigo; tanto quiere dezir como monte. & esta passada fue; en el mes q*ue* dizen en Arauigo Regel[8]. E el rey Rodrigo quando lo sopo; enuio contra ellos un su sobrino. q*ue* auie nombre yennego con gra*n*d poder. & lidio con los moros   15 muchas uezes. mas siempr*e*l uencien. & al cabo mataron le. & dalli adelante tomaro*n* los moros atreuimiento & esfuerço. El cuende Julian guio

1   *annos*
2   *Vulit*
3   *Africa, Friquia, Francia, Arabia*
4   *el* added
5   Another *un* has been used and subsequently deleted here by the scribe.
6   *passo*
7   *gabel, gebal*
8   *rregeb, regel, rogel, ragel*

los por la prouincia Bethica q*ue* es tierra de Seuilla & por la prouincia de
Luzenna. La hueste de los godos luego[9] comienco[10] empeço de seer mal
andante. Ca por la luenga paz q*ue* ouieran desacostumbrandosse darmas;   **20**
non sabien ya nada de los grandes fechos q*ue* los godos fizieran en otro
tiempo & eran tornados uiles & flacos & couardes & non pudieron soffrir
la batalla. & tornaron las espaldas a sus enemigos. E non se podiendo
amparar ni*n* foyr; moriron y todos.

Translation

Concerning how the Moors came to Spain a second time.

After three years of the reign of King Rodrigo had elapsed, in the year 752,
when it was 714 years since the birth of our Lord and one year of Leo's [Pope
Leo II] reign had elapsed, Ulid, king of the Alaraves, sent for Muça to come to
him in the land of Africa where he was. And Muça went there, and left as lord
in his stead in Africa Tarif Abenciet, who was blind in one eye. And Muça
ordered him to help Count Julián and show him friendship. This Tarif gave
Count Julián 12,000 men to have at his disposal. And the count gradually took
them secretly across the sea, hidden in merchant vessels, so that no one should
know, and when they had all been taken over to Spain, they gathered on a hill
which today bears the name of that Moor, and is called in Arabic Gebaltarif,
and [by] the Christians Gibaltar [modern Gibraltar] (for *gebel* in Arabic means
'hill'). This passage took place in the month called *Regel* in Arabic. And when
King Rodrigo learnt of this, he sent a nephew of his called Íñigo against them
with great power, and he fought with the Moors many times, but they always
defeated him, and in the end they killed him. Count Julián guided them through
the province of Baetica, that is to say, the lands of Seville, and through the
province of Luceña [Badajoz to the Algarve]. The Goths' army then began to
be unfortunate. For due to the long peace which they had enjoyed, during which
they had become unaccustomed to arms, they knew nothing of the great deeds
which the Goths had done in former times and had become base, weak and
cowardly and could not stand up to battles. And they turned their backs on their
enemies, and, being unable either to help each other or to flee, they all died
there.

Phonetics and phonology

10.1.1 Although in *castellano drecho* there is a general resistance to the extensive
loss of final /e/ which can be observed in earlier Castilian texts of more northerly
origin, there is in this passage still some evidence of the phenomenon: **mandol**
= *mandóle* (l.7) (but at the end of a phrase **mataron le**, l.17), **yl** = *y le* (l.8), **aquend**
= *aquende* (l.9), **mont** = *monte* (l.12) (but **monte**, l.14), **siemprel** = *siempre le* (l.17).
Keypoint: final -*e* (p. 273).

9   *en, en este, de* added
10 *comienço*

10.1.2 Initial /f/ (?/ɸ/) is consistently written as *f*: **fechos** (1.22) (|| MSp. *hechos*), **fizieran** (1.22) (|| MSp. *hicieran*), **foyr** (1.25) (|| MSp. *huir*).
    Keypoint: the f>h change (p. 271).

10.1.3 A distinction between /b/ and ?/β/ appears to be made orthographically. The initial *v (u)* of **uezes** (1.17) (|| MSp. *veces*), **uencien** (1.17) (|| MSp. *vencían*) and **uiles** (1.23) corresponds to the initial /w/ of Lat. [VĬCIS], [VINCO] and [VĪLIS] and the initial *b* of **batalla** (1.24) corresponds to the initial /b/ of Lat. BATTŬĀLĬA. Intervocalically, *u* is used for the results of both Latin /b/ and /w/ and *b* for the results of Lat. /p/: the *u* of **andaua** (1.2) (|| MSp. *andaba*) corresponds to Lat. /b/ (the etymology of the stem of this verb form is uncertain,[11] but the **-aua** inflection derives from the Latin imperfect inflection -ĀBAT); the *u* of **Naues** (1.9) corresponds to Lat. /w/ ([NĀVIS]) and the *b* of **cabo** (1.17) to Lat. /p/ (CĂPŬT).
    Keypoint: the 'b/v' merger (p. 262).

10.1.4 Diphthongisation is visible in two or three words which in their modern Spanish forms have no diphthong: **cuende** (1.9) (|| MSp. *conde*) < Lat. CŎMĬTE [CŎMĔS] and **sietecientos** (1.2) < Lat. ?SEPTE[M] CENTOS [CENTUM]. The non-diphthongal variants which were eventually preferred may be explained as follows. In the case of MSp. *conde*, a following implosive nasal consonant blocks diphthongisation. MSp. *setecientos* may be the result of non-diphthongisation in the first, unstressed syllable, or the first diphthong may have been reduced by a process of dissimilation, in order to avoid two /je/ sequences in the same word. For the adverbial inflection **-mientre** (1.10) and its replacement by MSp. *-mente*, see 8.2.8.
    Keypoint: vowels (p. 295).

10.1.5 The varying spellings of the verb forms **pudieron** (1.23) and **podiendo** (1.24) provide evidence of a tendency to neutralise the opposition between /o/ and /u/ atonically (see 9.1.7). In a number of words, atonic *o* corresponds to a modern *u*, suggesting that atonic [o] has tended to close to [u] as the language further developed: **logar** = *lugar* (1.7), **ouieran** = *hubieran* (1.21), **soffrir** = *sufrir* (1.23), **foyr** = *huir* (1.25), **moriron** = *murieron* (1.25), though analogical pressure has also probably been at work in the verbs. There is a very strong tendency in Spanish for verbs in *-ir* to have a stem vowel in /u/ rather than /o/ (even the two common verbs which do have /o/, *morir* and *dormir*, have /u/ in some forms, e.g., *murió, murieron, muriendo*); and a stressed /u/ is common in the stems of several irregular preterites (e.g. *anduve, estuve, pude, puse, tuve*, plus the many *-uje* preterites of verbs in *-ucir*, in addition to *supe* and *hube* – see also 11.1.8).[12]

10.1.6 Flacos (1.23) < Lat. FLACCŌS [FLACCUS] is one of a relatively small number of words in Spanish which derive from a Latin word beginning with the

---

11 Lat. AMBŬLO 'to walk' corresponds semantically, but ?AMBĬTO 'to go round' is closer in phonetic terms.
12 On this last point, see Lloyd's (1987: 365–7) hypothesis that high (close) vowels come to be associated with perfective aspect in a kind of sound symbolism.

/fl/ group. Although this group palatalises to /ʎ/ in one instance (Lat. FLAMMA > MSp. *llama* 'flame'), it remains as /fl/ in several other words, of which this is one.[13]

Keypoint: consonant groups (p.267); **palatalisation** (p. 280).

10.1.7 For **non** (l.11), see 11.1.1.

Morphology and syntax

10.2.1 In the phrase **o ell era** (l.6), *ser* is still used to indicate location (cf. 4.2.8, 12.2.10), though there was already a growing tendency in Castilian to use *estar* for this purpose with animate subjects.

Keypoint: *ser* and *estar* (p. 290).

10.2.2 Dexo . . . a tarif abenciet (ll.6–7). This is an early example of the 'personal *a*', the use of which was not yet general (cf. **enuio contra ellos un su sobrino**, ll.15–16); it was favoured particularly with personal pronouns and proper nouns.

Keypoint: 'personal' *a* (p. 000).

10.2.3 Aquend (l.9) 'on this side of' is a complex preposition which derives from Lat. ?ACCU + HINC + DE (see **Keypoint: demonstratives** (p. 270), and 20.3.2). The *aqu-* element is the reinforcer familiar from demonstratives and general adverbs of place *aquí* and *acá*; HINC had the meaning 'from here', and the addition of *de* converts the adverb *aquen* into a complex preposition meaning 'on this side of'. Its antonym was *allende* ⩽ Lat. ?ILLINC DE 'on the far side of', and the two forms were used especially in relation to stretches of water.

10.2.4 Asconduda (l.10). Latin second conjugation (-ĒRE) verbs whose perfects ended in -U must have developed past participles in -ŪTUM, e.g. ?TĔNŪTUM rather than the Classical form TENTUM from TĔNĒRE [TĔNĔO], cf. Fr. *tenu*, It, *tenuto*, Rom. *ţinut*. This kind of past participle ending was analogically extended in Romance, so that, for example, VENDO, whose past participle in Latin was VENDĬTUM, yielded Fr. *vendu* and It. *venduto*, which suggests a common form ?VENDŪTUM. While Old Castilian exhibits a number of such formations (*sabudo*, *tenudo*, *vençudo* are commonly encountered), further analogical pressure eventually leads to their complete regularisation as *-ido* forms, yielding *sabido*, *tenido*, *vencido* in Modern Spanish.

10.2.5 There are a number of points of interest in the phrase **ge lo non entendiessen** (ll.10–11). First, the sequence **ge lo** is probably a development of Lat. ILLĪ ĬLLU [ILLE] via ?/(e)(ʎelo/, /ʎ/ changing to the fricative /ʒ/ in a way which anticipates Latin American *rehilamiento* (see Chapter XII introduction); in the modern language *ge* has developed, probably by a false analogy, to *se*. Second,

---

13 For discussion of this interesting question, which makes the provision of a 'rule' for the development of Latin initial /fl/ problematic, see Lloyd (1987: 226–7).

the position of the negative **non** appears between the clitic pronoun sequence and the verb; this is a feature sometimes found in northern Castilian texts of this period (see 9.2.10). Third, the function of **ge** (= *le*) itself is not totally clear: it seems to be an 'ethical dative', i.e., literally, 'so that they should not realise it concerning him', a device which is very heavily exploited in Castilian.

Keypoint: **clitic pronoun positio**n (p. 264).

10.2.6 Eran tornados uiles (l.23). Many intransitive verbs took *ser* as their perfect auxiliary in Old Castilian (cf. 4.2.5), the past participle agreeing in number and gender with the subject (a feature still visible in different degrees in modern French and Italian); this form is the pluperfect of *tornar*. The range of verbs taking *ser* in Spanish gradually reduces until by the end of the sixteenth century only *nacer, morir, ir* and *pasar* are used with *ser*; in the modern language *haber* has generalised to every verb (Pountain 1985). See also 12.2.7.

10.2.7 In **mataron le** (l.17) and **siemprel(e) uencien** (l.17), a direct object referring to a person is pronominalised as *le* rather than *lo*, a phenomenon known as *leísmo*. *Leísmo* is of long standing in Castilian, and continues in areas of Old Castile to the present day; it may be connected with the use of the personal *a*, since it is the personal nature of the direct object that is an essential trigger for both phenomena.[14] **Le** is used to refer to a place in **dizen le** (l.12), which shows an extension of *leísmo* beyond 'personal' reference.

Keypoints: **'personal'** *a* (p. 283); **personal pronouns** (p. 284).

10.2.8 Un su sobrino (ll.15–16). The use of the 'short' possessive here in conjunction with the indefinite article renders the idea of 'one of his nephews', 'a nephew of his', which in later Spanish came to be expressed by a postposed 'long' form (*un sobrino suyo*).

Keypoint: **possessives** (p. 287).

10.2.9 Non se podiendo (l.24). At this time, the position of the clitic pronoun with non-finite parts of the verb followed essentially the same rule as for finite verbs: here, because it is preceded by a negative, **se** appears before **podiendo** (see also 9.2.9).

Keypoint: **clitic pronoun position** (p. 264).

10.2.10 Two features of word order may be noted.

In **Enuio Vlid rey de los Alaraues por Muça** . . . (ll.4–5) the verb appears first. This word order is very common in Spanish, especially when the verb is relatively short and the subject long; indeed, in the modern language it is the normal order in a number of circumstances, particularly with verbs like *gustar, encantar*, etc., which typically have a subject and an indirect pronoun object, e.g. *Me gustan las películas de horror*, and with intransitive verbs which express the idea of existence, e.g. *Existen muchas organizaciones de este tipo*.

---

14 This, at least, is true of the basis for *leísmo* in the northern prestige norm, though there are a number of other bases for *leísmo* (Fernández Ordóñez 1994)

In **E el rey Rodrigo quando lo sopo** . . . (l.15) the topic of the sentence, **el rey Rodrigo**, stands first (rather than *Quando lo sopo el rey Rodrigo*). Such topicalisation is a typical feature of Spanish, especially in the spoken language (see 25.2.8 and 28.2.5), though Latin may also have provided the model in this case, since such constructions as CAESAR CUM VIDISSET . . . 'when Caesar saw . . .' were common in classical prose.

10.2.11 Auie nombre yennego (l.16). Modern Spanish would require a preposition here to mark the apposition of **nombre** and **yennego**: *tenía el nombre de Íñigo*.

10.2.12 Y (l.25) < Lat. ĬBI behaves as a clitic pronoun. It gave way to the phonologically more distinctive form *allí* (see 20.3.2), which functioned as a full adverb.
   Keypoints: adverbs (p.000); **clitic pronoun position** (p. 000).

10.2.13 For **pora** (l.9), see 9.2.5 and Keypoint: *por* **and** *para* (p. 286); for **lieua** (l.12) see 9.1.6; for **auie** (l.16), **uencien** (l.17) see **Keypoint: the imperfect endings of Old Castilian,** (p. 277); for **ouieran** (l.21), see **Keypoint: the pluperfects of Old Castilian,** (p. 286).

Vocabulary

10.3.1 Tuerto (l.7) derives from Lat. TŎRTU[M], the past participle of TŎRQUĔO 'to twist' (which as ?[TŎRCĔO] was the origin of Sp. *torcer*). *Torcer* developed the analogical past participle *torcido*, while *tuerto* came to have the restricted adjectival meaning of 'twisted in sight', 'squinting', a value it still has in Berceo, and then the related meaning of 'one-eyed'. At this time the meaning was probably not yet unequivocally 'one-eyed', and so the explanatory phrase **tuerto de un oio**, which strikes a modern reader as tautologous, is used.

10.3.2 Auer (|| MSp. *haber*) < Lat. [HǍBĔO] is used as a verb of possession in **auie nombre yennego** (l.16) and **la luenga paz que ouieran** (l.21). The Modern Spanish verb *tener* derived from Lat. [TĔNĔO], which had the rather more specific meaning of 'to hold'; the semantic movement observable in *tener* is an example of semantic weakening. *Haber* and *tener* coexist with slightly shifting meanings in the semantic field of 'possession' throughout Old Castilian (Seifert 1930, and see also 12.3.1).

10.3.3 Atreuimiento (l.18) is a morphological derivative, using the very productive suffix *-miento*, of *atreverse*, which derives from a reflexive use of Lat. [TRĪBŬO] 'to attribute (to oneself)', and develops the more particular meaning of 'to attribute (to oneself) the ability to do something', being especially applied to situations of risk or danger, and hence coming to mean 'to dare'. The addition of an initial *a-* is a procedure common to a large number of Spanish verbs (see 9.3.3, 13.3.3).

10.3.4 Hueste (l.20) 'army' < Lat. HOSTE [HOSTIS] has been superseded in Modern Spanish by the learned borrowing *ejército* < Lat. EXERCĬTU[S], which first made its appearance in the fifteenth century.

10.3.5 Luenga (l.21) < Lat. LŎNGA [LŎNGUS], was the normal word for the notion of 'long' until the fifteenth century, when it was replaced by *largo*. *Largo* derives from Lat. LARGU[S] 'abundant', 'numerous' and comes to have a more specific meaning in a number of Romance languages (the cognate Fr. *large* and It. *largo* both have the meaning 'broad', this notion being represented in Spanish by *ancho*, which similarly became more specific in meaning than its etymon Lat. AMPLU[S] 'large', 'ample').

10.3.6 Amparar (l.25) probably derives from Lat. ?[ANTĔPĂRO] 'to prepare beforehand', hence 'to help (with preparations)'. The notion of 'to help' is a rich semantic field in Spanish; other exponents of this notion are *ayudar* < Lat. [ADIŪTO], the frequentative form of ADIŬVO 'to help', and *socorrer* < Lat. [SUCCŬRRO] 'to hasten to help'. All three verbs have survived into the modern language, though *ayudar* is the most widely used, with *amparar* now having the connotation of 'to protect'.

10.3.7 For **lidiar** (l.16) see 2.0.

11 The fox and the crow. Don Juan Manuel, *El Conde Lucanor* (1335)

11.0 Don Juan Manuel (1282–1348) was a nephew of Alfonso X (see Text 10). He was a complex character, who, in the midst of a sometimes turbulent career of political intrigue, devoted several years of his life to writing, though unfortunately only about half his works have survived. *El Conde Lucanor* was written in 1335, and is a very important text from both a linguistic and literary point of view. Don Juan Manuel's style is very accessible: he uses a good deal of popular vocabulary and a generally paratactic though elegant syntax; he also develops the use of dialogue in third person narrative and avoids ostentatious Latin quotation and imitation. He was very conscious of language and the possible corruptions of textual transmission; in the prologue to *El Conde Lucanor* he writes:

> Et porque don Iohan vio & sabe que en los libros contesçe muchos yerros en los transladar, porque las letras semejan unas a otras, cuydando por la una letra que es otra, en escriviéndolo, múdasse toda la razón & por aventura confóndesse, & los que después fallan aquello escripto, ponen la culpa al que fizo el libro; & porque don Iohan se reçeló desto, ruega a los que leyeren qualquier libro que fuere trasladado del que él compuso, o de los libros que él fizo, que si fallaren alguna palabra mal puesta, que non pongan la culpa a él, fasta que bean el libro mismo que don Iohan fizo, que es emendado, en muchos logares, de su letra.

(Indeed, we would do well to bear this passage in mind constantly in our assessment of early texts.) The moral exemplariness of the tales in *El Conde Lucanor* and the concern not to give offence with erotic content (unlike Boccaccio in the *Decameron*, written a few years later) is strongly echoed in Cervantes's *Novelas Ejemplares* and it is not surprising to find that *El Conde Lucanor* was a work much admired in the Golden Age; it was published in Seville in 1575 and again in Madrid in 1642. The stories come from various sources, including *Calila e Dimna* (see Text 6); the tale of the fox and the crow, from which the passage below is taken, is one of Aesop's fables.

The text

Unfortunately, we cannot be sure that we are really seeing Don Juan Manuel's own work intact, since the oldest MS source available is the S MS in the Biblioteca Nacional, which is written in a fifteenth-century hand. It is on this MS that Blecua (1969), which I follow here, is based. Punctuation, accentuation and word divisions are modern; abbreviations (except for *ñ*) have been expanded, and no distinction is made between *u* and *v*.

Further reading

Blecua (1969); Huerta Tejadas (1954–6).

Don Cuervo, muy gran tiempo ha que oy fablar de vós & de la vuestra nobleza, & de la vuestra apostura. & commo quiera que vos mucho busqué, non fue la voluntat de Dios, nin la mi ventura, que vos pudiesse fallar fasta agora, & agora que vos veo, entiendo que a mucho más bien en vós de quanto me dizían. & porque veades que non vos lo digo por   **5** lesonia, también commo vos diré las aposturas que en vós entiendo, tam[bién] vos diré las cosas en que las gentes tienen que non sodes tan apuesto. Todas las gentes tienen que la color de las vuestras péñolas & de los oios & del pico, & de los pies & de las uñas, que todo es prieto, & [por]que la cosa prieta non es tan apuesta commo la de otra color, & vós   **10** sodes todo prieto, tienen las gentes que es mengua de vuestra apostura, & non entienden cómmo yerran en ello mucho; ca commo quier que las vuestras péñolas son prietas, tan prieta & tan luzia es aquella pretura, que torna en india, commo péñolas de pavón, que es la más fremosa ave del mundo; & commo quier que los vuestros ojos son prietos, quanto para   **15** oios, mucho son más fremosos que otros oios ningunos, ca la propriedat del oio non es sinon ver, & porque toda cosa prieta conorta el viso, para los oios, los prietos son los mejores, & por ende son más loados los oios de la ganzela, que son más prietos que de ninguna otra animalia. Otrosí, el vuestro pico & las vuestras manos & uñas son fuertes más que de   **20** ninguna ave tanmaña commo vós. Otrosí, en l' vuestro buelo avedes tan grant ligereza, que vos enbarga el viento de yr contra él por rezio que sea, lo que otra ave non puede fazer tan ligeramente commo vós. & bien tengo que, pues Dios todas las cosas faze con razón, que non consintría que, pues en todo sodes tan complido, que oviese en vos mengua de no   **25** cantar mejor que ninguna otra ave. & pues Dios me fizo tanta merçet que vos veo, & sé que ha en vós más bien de quanto nunca de vós oy, si yo pudiesse oyr de vós el vuestro canto, para siempre me ternía por de buena ventura.

Translation

Sir Crow, I have heard tell of your nobility and elegance for a very long time. And although I have sought you a great deal, it has not been the will of God, nor my fortune, to be able to find you until now, and now that I see you, I understand that there is much more merit in you than people told me. And so that you may see that I do not say this out of flattery, in addition to telling you the elegant features I understand there to be in you, I will also tell you the things in which people consider that you are not so elegant. Everyone considers that the colour of your feathers, your eyes and your beak, your feet and your claws, is all black, and that black things are not as elegant as those of another colour, and since you are all black, people consider that it is a deficiency in your elegance, and they do not understand how much they are mistaken in this; for although your feathers are black, so black and shiny is that blackness, that it verges on deep blue, like the feathers of a peacock, which is the most beautiful bird in the world; and although your eyes are black, as for eyes, they are much more beautiful than any others, for the function of the eye is simply to see, and because every dark thing eases the sight, black [eyes] are the best, and for this reason the eyes of the gazelle, which are blacker than those of any other animal, are praised. Furthermore, your beak, hands and claws are stronger than those of any other bird of comparable size. Also, in your flight you have such great agility, that it prevents the wind impeding it however strongly it may be blowing, something which no other bird can do as well as you. And I firmly consider that, since God makes everything with reason, he would not allow, since in everything [else] you are so accomplished, that there should be in you the lack of not singing better than any other bird. And since God has granted me so great a mercy as to see you, and I know that in you there is more good than ever I heard of you, if I could hear your song from you I would consider myself fortunate for ever.

Phonetics and phonology

11.1.1 Nin (l.3) ≤ Lat. NĔC has a final /n/ which was probably created by analogy with **non** (l.3) < Lat. NŌN (see 4.1.9 and 27.3.1). Both **nin** and **non** have lost the final /n/ in Modern Spanish.

11.1.2 In the development of **uñas** (l.9) < Lat. ŬNGŬLAS [ŬNGŬLA] 'hoof', 'claw', 'talon' the complex consonantal group /ngl/ created by the reduction of proparoxytones palatalised to /ɲ/, an extreme case of assimilation.
    Keypoints: stress (p. 291); **palatalisation** (p. 280).

11.1.3 The spelling **voluntat** (l.3) < Lat. VŎLUNTĀTE [VŎLUNTAS] may indicate the devoicing of the final consonant to ?[θ], cf. 8.1.4. Note also in this text the parallel example of **propriedat** (l.16) < Lat. PROPRĬĔTĀTE [PROPRĬĔTAS].
    Keypoints: lenition (p. 278); **final -*e*** (p. 273).

11.1.4 Fremosa (l.14), **fremosos** (l.16) < Lat. FORMŌSA, FORMŌSŌS [FORMŌSUS] show metathesis of /r/ and the preceding vowel and dissimilation of the first /o/ to /e/. The same dissimilation is apparent in the eventually preferred variant *fermoso* (‖ MSp. *hermoso*).

11.1.5 Loado (1.18) < Lat. LAUDĀTU[M] [LAUDO] shows the disappearance of the intervocalic /d/ of Latin as a result of lenition and the consequent creation of a hiatic vowel group /oa/.
   Keypoint: lenition (p. 278).

11.1.6 Animalia (1.19) < the Latin plural form ĂNĬMĀLĬA [ĂNĬMĂL] here preserves the Latin spelling, though it was clearly construed as a singular noun. There is a good deal of variation observable in the development of this word in Old Castilian. Modern Spanish has inherited *alimaña* (see below 15.3.3) with metathesis of /l/ and /n/; *alimaria*, another metathesised form with the introduction of /r/, perhaps for the sake of dissimilation, is also attested.

11.1.7 The spelling of **buelo** (1.21) < Lat. √VŎLO suggests a lack of distinction between ?/β/ and /b/ in initial position (cf. 2.8, 3.1.3, 7.1.6).
   Keypoint: the 'b/v' merger (p. 262).

11.1.8 For the implications of the spellings **dizían** (1.5), **lesonia** (1.6), **complido** and **oviese** (1.25), corresponding to MSp. *decían, lisonja, cumplido* and *hubiese*, see 7.1.3, 9.1.7, 10.1.5).
   Keypoint: vowels (p. 296).

11.1.9 Siempre (1.28) < Lat. SEMPĔR shows metathesis of the final /er/ group; this may be brought about by the original greater frequency of vocalic endings in Romance, though analogical pressure may also be involved, since the ending -*re* was common to a number of adverbs in Old Castilian (see 8.2.8).
   Keypoint: adverbs (p. 262).

11.1.10 Dios (1.24) appears to derive, atypically for a Romance noun, from the nominative form Lat. DĔUS. In the Jewish community, however, the form *Dio* seems to have been preferred, maybe because the final /s/ was interpreted as a marker of the 'plurality' of the Christian Trinity ('three persons in one God': Father, Son and Holy Spirit).

11.1.11 Ganzela (1.19) < Ar. *gazāl*, here has an epenthetic /n/ (cf. *manzana* ← Lat. √MATĬU[S] and *ansi(na)* ← Lat. SĪC, see 21.1.4, 27.3.1, 33.3.2, 40.3.2), though the modern form is *gacela*.

11.1.12 Conorta (1.17) < Lat. [CONFORTO] 'to strengthen', shows evidence of the weakening and loss of word-internal Lat. /f/, cf. 4.1.1. In this particular case, such loss may have been facilitated by the absence of a need for a morphologically transparent relation with *fuerte* < Lat. FORTE [FORTIS] 'strong' after the meaning of CONFORTO shifted to that of 'to ease'.
   Keypoint: the f>h change (p. 271).

Morphology and syntax

11.2.1 Muy grant tiempo ha (l.1) shows the use of *haber* in the expression of 'time since when'; *ha* and its corresponding imperfect form could either precede or follow the noun. In Classical Latin this notion was most frequently rendered by the accusative case; the use of an impersonal verb in Romance (cf. Fr. *il y a*, It. *fa*) can be seen as a strategy for creating an analytic alternative to the use of a case-inflection (Latin also sometimes used a prepositional phrase with ĂBHINC). *Haber* is the verb regularly used in such constructions in Old Castilian; the modern usage with *hacer* dates from the late sixteenth century (see Kany 1951: 217–20).

Another impersonal use of *haber* can be seen in a **mucho más bien** (l.4) and **ha en vós** (l.27), where *(h)a* is used to express the existential notion of 'there is', rendered in Modern Spanish by *hay*.

11.2.2 Vos (l.2) is the usual Old Castilian form of the atonic pronoun, still conserving the initial consonantal phoneme (pronounced ?[β]). By the time of Valdés, *os* had become current; Valdés records that *vos* is found only in written documents by his day (the first half of the sixteenth century) and that the *v* is 'superflua' (Lope Blanch 1969: 87).

11.2.3 In **vos mucho busqué** (ll.2–3), **mucho** is intercalated between the clitic pronoun and the verb, which is not possible in Modern Spanish. See 9.2.10 and 10.2.5.
   Keypoint: clitic pronoun position (p. 264).

11.2.4 The syntax of comparisons involving a clause differs slightly from Modern Spanish in that **quanto** rather than the MSp. *lo que* (or *el que*, etc., if a specific noun is in the original term of the comparison) is used: **ha en vós más bien de quanto nunca de vós oý** (l.27, cf. also l.6). As in Modern Spanish, **de** is the comparative preposition used when a clause is involved, in contrast to the **que** which appears in comparisons of like with like (compare **mucho son más fremosos que otros oios ningunos**, l.16).

11.2.5 Las gentes (l.7) is here used in the general collective sense of 'people' (see 4.2.6).

11.2.6 Porque veades . . . (l.5) is to be understood as 'so that you may see . . .'; **porque** at this time has the meaning of 'so that', 'in order that', that would later be rendered by *para que* as *para* encroached on the semantic domain of *por*.
   Keypoint: *por* and *para* (p. 286).

11.2.7 Color (ll.8 and 10) is here feminine in gender, though Lat. CŎLŌRE [CŎLOR] was masculine. There was in the Romance languages some variation in the gender of nouns in -ŌRE; *color* and *calor* were regularly feminine in Old Castilian and are still treated as such in some Castilian dialects. In Modern Spanish the vast majority have reverted to the masculine in standard usage (MSp. *labor* is a conspicuous exception). Cf. 2.14.4.
   Keypoint: gender (p. 274).

11.2.8 Ello (l.12) illustrates the use of the Spanish neuter to refer to a proposition (here, the opinion **es mengua de vuestra apostura**). **Lo que** (l.23) is the neuter relative, referring to the preceding clause.
    Keypoint: **gender** (p. 275).

11.2.9 A feature of the sometimes plain, almost colloquial, style of *El Conde Lucanor* is seen in the repetition of **que** in ll. 23–4 (**& bien tengo que**, . . ., **que non consintría que**, . . ., **que oviese en vós** . . .); presentation of the complements of *tener* and *consentir* is interrupted by an adverbial clause and the writer/speaker must repeat **que** in order to re-establish the complement construction.

11.2.10 The frequent use of **pues** in ll.24, 25 and 26 foreshadows the extensive use Modern Spanish makes of this word in colloquial register as a general filler (see 25.2.4). Here, however, it is a causal conjunction, though it has evolved considerably from the Latin prepositional meaning of POST 'after', presumably first becoming a temporal conjunction ('then', 'afterwards') and then moving on to a causal meaning as a result of the natural association between temporal and logical consequence.

11.2.11 Consintría (l.24) is an example of a syncopated future stem, and **ternía** (l.28) is a metathesised future stem (see also 4.2.9).
    Keypoint: **future stems** (p. 274).

11.2.12 Si yo pudiesse . . . **me ternía** (ll.27–8). This sequence of tense (imperfect subjunctive in the protasis, conditional in the apodosis) was usual in Old Castilian in a conditional sentence referring to a future condition which is unlikely to be fulfilled.
    Keypoint: **conditional sentences** (p. 265).

11.2.13 For the variation in the use of possessives with and without the definite article (e.g. **la vuestra nobleza**, ll.1–2, **vuestra apostura**, l.11), see 8.2.7 and **Keypoint: possessives** (p. 287); for the use of **vos** as a second person pronoun of respect, see **Keypoint: personal pronouns** (p. 284); for the use of the second person verb forms in -**des**, see 7.2.6.

Vocabulary

11.3.1 Apostura (l.2) and **apuesto** (l.8) are morphological derivatives of the past participle *apuesto* < Lat. APPŎSĬTU[M] [APPŌNO] 'having been added'. There is a general associational development in these words through the very general notions of 'something added' → 'what is put on' → 'adornment'.

11.3.2 Fallar (l.4) has a complex semantic history. It is thought to have its origin in Lat. [AFFLO] 'to blow on', 'towards', which goes through the associational changes of meaning 'to smell the track (e.g. of an animal)' → 'to find (in hunting)' → 'to find (general)'. But the phonetic development is not straightforward, and an intermediate metathesis of ?[afʎar(e)] ⩾ [faʎar(e)] must be assumed (Cor.,

III, 308). The notion of 'to find' appears to have been variously expressed in later Latin (cf. *trobar*, 8.3.4), and in Castilian there has been ongoing variation; *encontrar*, a morphological derivative of Lat. √CONTRĀ 'against', has perhaps passed through the associational stages 'to stand against', 'confront' → 'to seek to meet' → 'to find', and has largely replaced *hallar* today in spoken register.

11.3.3 Entiendo (l.4) undergoes a similarly complex semantic shift. Its origin is Lat. [ĬNTĚNDO] 'to extend' → 'to direct (one's attention) towards (something)', which became associated with the idea of 'to perceive', 'understand'.

11.3.4 Tienen (l.8) is here used in the sense of 'to hold (an opinion)', 'believe'.

11.3.5 Péñolas (l.8) derives from Lat. [PĬNNŬLA], a diminutive form of PĬNNA 'feather'. The meaning 'wing' is reached by synecdoche. Since PĬNNA also came to mean, by metaphorical extension, 'battlements' in Latin and, as Sp. *peña*, further develops to mean 'hilltop' → 'rock', the use of the diminutive for the notion of 'feather' achieves semantic discrimination.

11.3.6 Two colour terms in this text tell us a good deal about word creation within this semantic field, which has a very volatile history in Romance. **Prieto** (l.9) is a back-formation from *apretar* < Lat. [APPĚCTŎRO] 'to clasp to one's chest' → 'to squeeze', 'compress', which presumably passed through the associational stages 'thick' → 'dark' → 'black'. **Prieto** and **negro**, the latter < NĬGRU [NĬGER], which was probably the canonical term for 'black' in Classical Latin (the classical language also had ĀTER, which was particularly associated with the notion 'funereal'), were both used in Old Castilian, where their referential domains are difficult to chart exactly. **India** (l.14) (*indio* in the 1575 Seville edition; *índigo* is a later borrowing) was the name of the indigo plant from which the characteristic dark blue dye was extracted, and is typical of many cases in which the name of an object with, or in some way supplying, a characteristic colour becomes the name of the colour itself.

11.3.7 Mengua (l.11) is a morphological derivative of Lat. ?√MINGUO, which was an analogically regularised form of MĬNŬO 'to diminish'. **Mengua** has extended its meaning by association from 'diminution' to include the notion of 'lack' (see also 13.3.11).

11.3.8 Luzio (l.14) 'glossy', is from Lat. LŪCĬDU[S] 'clear', 'bright', 'lucid'; the doublet development *lúcido*, with the same meaning as the Classical Latin word, is a learned borrowing dating from the fifteenth century.

11.3.9 Viso (l.17) < Lat. VĪSU[M] 'appearance' is used here in the meaning of 'sense of sight'. This is rendered in Modern Spanish by *vista*, which has extended its meaning from that of 'something seen' to encompass a number of other notions associated with sight. MSp. *viso* has the Latin sense of 'appearance'; 'sheen', which may indicate that it is a learned restitution.

11.3.10 Otrosí (ll.19 and 21) 'also', 'furthermore' is cognate with Fr. *aussi*, It. *altresì* (< Lat. ?ALTERU [ALTĔR] SĪC); it survives in Modern Spanish only in legal register.

11.3.11 Tanmaña (l.21) < Lat. TAM MAGNU[S] *lit.* 'as great', is used here, as was its Latin etymon, as a comparative form (*tanmaña . . . commo . . .*). MSp. *tamaño* as a noun meaning 'size' is first attested in the seventeenth century.

11.3.12 Ligereza (l.20) must be a borrowing based on Fr. *léger* < Lat. ?LĔVĂRĬU[S] (itself a morphological derivative of Lat. √LĔVIS). Old Castilian in fact did have its own derivative based on √LĔVIS, *liviano* < ? LĔVĬĀNU[S] (*leve* itself is a later learned borrowing), used with the meaning 'light'. *Ligero* also had the meaning 'easy' (as here **ligereza** is 'ease'), the opposite of OCast. *grave* 'difficult'; these words were later replaced by the learned words *fácil* < Lat. FĂCĬLIS and *difícil* < Lat. DIFFĬCĬLIS, which have diffused to all registers in the modern language. See 9.3.11.

Keypoint: learned and popular, popular and semipopular (p. 277).

11.3.13 Enbarga (l.22) is from Lat. ?[IMBARRĬCO], itself a morphological derivative of a root √BARRA of uncertain origin, possibly Celtic.

11.3.14 Commo quiera que (l.2) was one of a number of a concessive conjunctions used in Old Castilian, and was the principal rival to *maguer (que)* (see 8.3.7) until the end of the fourteenth century, when *aunque* underwent a dramatic increase in frequency (Montero Cartelle 1993:175).

VII Prose documents in Castilian from the fifteenth century

The texts examined in this chapter have been chosen from amongst the vast range available in this period to reflect a number of styles, registers and different kinds of source.

12 Death from the plague, from the Memoirs of Doña Leonor López de Córdoba (early fifteenth century).

12.0 Doña Leonor López de Córdoba was the daughter of Don Martín López de Córdoba, Maestre de Calatrava, who in the late fourteenth century supported King Pedro the Cruel against his bastard brother, Enrique de Trastamara; the latter defeated and murdered Pedro and ordered Don Martín's execution and the incarceration of his family and household in Seville. Only Doña Leonor and her husband survived this ordeal, and the remainder of their lives was beset with difficulties. This poignant document gives Doña Leonor's account of those turbulent years; the extract below relates to the plague in Andalusia in 1400–1.

The document is unusual in that it is in effect a short autobiography, written by (or, rather, at the dictation of) a woman, and that it has many features which suggest the spontaneity of what we may take to be the everyday spoken language of the noble classes of the time. At the same time, we must not underestimate the formality of the document. It begins in notarial fashion, Doña Leonor being concerned to set the record straight for the benefit of her descendants with precise details of her lineage, marriage settlement, etc.; we must bear in mind that no doubt it was a notary who wrote it down at (presumably slow) dictation speed, and so it cannot be regarded as a literal transcript of speech. Although this extract comes from the more narrative part of the document, there are notarial tones in such usages as the combination of demonstrative and possessive in **aquel mi fijo** (l.6) and in the absolute use of the gerund in **haviendo muerto todos los dichos** (l.13) (as well as in the use of **los dichos** 'the aforementioned' itself, a typical anaphoric device of legal register).

The text

How far we can trust the MS is doubtful: the original is lost, and the text reproduced here, from Ayerbe-Chaux (1977), is a palaeographic transcription (conserving capital letters and punctuation) of an eighteenth-century MS in the Biblioteca Colombina which purports to be a copy of the original, though the Marqués de la Fuensanta's 1883 edition of another (also lost) eighteenth-century copy shows some discrepancies with the Colombina MS.

> **Yo abie grande devocion en estas palabras, rezaba cada noche esta Oracion, rog*ando* á Dios me quisiese librar á mi, y á mis fijos; é si alguno obiese de llevar, llebase el mayor p*or* q*ue* era mui doliente; é plugo á Dios que una noche no fallaba q*uie*n velase aquel Mozo Doliente, p*or* q*ue* havian muerto todos los q*ue* hasta entonzes le havian velado, é vino á mi 5 aquel mi fijo, q*ue* le decian Juan Fern*andez* de Henestrosa, como su Abuelo, q*ue* era de hedad de doze años, y quatro meses é dixome: S*eñ*ora no ay q*uie*n vele á Alonso estanoche? é dijele: Velarlo[1] vos por Amor de Dios; y respondiome: S*eñ*ora agora q*ue* hán muerto Otros quereis que me mate? é yo dixele: p*or* la Caridad que yo fago, Dios habrá piedad de mi; 10 é mi hijo por no salir de mi mandamiento lo fué á velar, é p*or* mis pecados aq*ue*lla noche [le dió la pestilencia e otro dia le enterré,][2] y el emfermo vivió desp*ues* hav*ie*ndo muerto todos los dichos; é D*oñ*a Theresa, muger de D*on* Alfonso Fern*andez* mi Primo hubo mui gran enojo, p*or* q*ue* moria mi fijo p*or* tal Ocacion en su Casa, y la muerte en la Voca lo 15 mandaba sacar de ella, y yo estaba tan traspasada de pesar, q*ue* no podia hablar del corrim*ien*to que aquellos Señores me hacian; y el triste de mi hijo dezia; decid á mi S*eñ*ora Doña Theresa q*ue* no me haga echar q*ue* agora saldrá mi anima p*ar*a el Cielo, y aquella noche falleció, y se enterró en S*an*ta Maria La Coronada, que es en la Villa. 20

Translation

I held these words in great devotion; I prayed this prayer every night, asking God to deliver me and my children, and that, if he had to take anyone, he might take the elder, because he was in great suffering. And it pleased God that one night there was no one to watch over that sick boy, because all those who had watched over him hitherto had died, and my son, the one called Juan Fernández de Henestrosa like his grandfather, came to me and said to me, 'Madam, is there no one to watch over Alonso tonight?' And I said to him, 'You watch over him for the love of God'; and he answered me, 'Madam, when others have died do you want me to die?' and I said to him, 'For the charitable works I do, God will have pity on me.' And my son, so as not to go against my command, went to watch over him, and for my sins, he [Alonso] gave him [Juan] the plague that night, and the next day I buried him [Juan]; and the sick boy lived though all the aforementioned people died. And Doña Teresa, the wife of Don Alfonso Fernández, my cousin, was very cross because my son was dying for such a reason in her house, and with death in her voice she ordered him to be taken out of it. And I was so overcome by grief that I could not speak of the embarrassment

1 Corrected to *Veladle* or *Veladlo* by nineteenth-century editors.
2 Missing in the MS used by Fuensanta.

that lady and gentleman gave me. And my poor son said, 'Tell my lady Doña Teresa not to put me out, for my soul is now leaving for heaven'; and that night he died. And he was buried in Santa María la Coronada, which is in the town.

Phonetics and Phonology

12.1.1 There is a great deal of inconsistency in spelling, which may well have been introduced by later copyists. The following points show just how difficult it is to extract satisfactory phonological data from a text of this kind.

There is indiscriminate use of *b* and *v*: there is no distinction intervocalically shown in **obiese** (1.3) < Lat. HĂBUISSET [HĂBĔO] and **llebase** (1.3) < Lat. LĔVĀVISSET [LĔVO], and the spelling **voca** (1.15) < Lat. BŬCCA suggests a lack of distinction initially as well.

Keypoint: the 'b/v' merger (p. 262).

Both *x* and *j* are used to represent the palatal result of Lat. /ks/ in **dixo** (1.7) ⩽ DĪXIT [DĪCO] and **dije** (1.8), **dixe** (1.10) ⩽ Lat. DĪXĪ [DĪCO]. Since in Old Castilian *x* generally represented /ʃ/ and *j* represented /ʒ/, this might be taken to indicate a merger of the ʃ/ʒ opposition as a result of the devoicing of /ʒ/; alternatively, the spelling with *j* may be a later introduction. Similarly, *c* and *z* are used indiscriminately (**dezia** and **decid**, 1.18), which could similarly suggest a merger of the ts/dz opposition.

Keypoints: consonant groups (p. 267); **palatalisation** (p. 280); **the sibilants of Old Castilian** (p. 290).

The same kind of point may be made concerning the use of *f* and *h*, since we have **fago** (1.10) but **hacian** (1.17), **fijo** (1.6) but **hijo** (1.11); note also **hasta** (1.5) (see 8.1.7) and **hablar** (1.17). If such spellings are not simply later amendments, the use of *h* could suggest an aspirate articulation ?[h].

Keypoint: the f>h change (p. 271).

H is used in the etymological spellings of the forms of *haber*, which are generally spelt with an *h* (though note the inconsistent **abie**, l.1; again, the use of *h* in such spellings was more typical of later orthographical practice. The *h* is used erroneously in **hedad** (1.7) < Lat. AETĀTE [AETAS]. This would suggest that *h* had no phonetic value at all, a conclusion which, however, sits uncomfortably with the value ?[h] for *h* proposed above, and substantiating Penny's (1990) view that *h* has no phonetic value (see 9.1.4). However, it must again be underlined that the spelling of this text may have undergone a number of post-fifteenth-century modifications.

Finally, the spelling **ocacion** (1.15) < Lat. OCCĀSĬŌNE [OCCĀSĬO] might be taken to indicate a neutralisation of /ts/ and /s/; this is the phenomenon which later will be familiar as Andalusian *ceceo* (see 27.1.1).

Keypoint: the sibilants of Old Castilian (p. 290).

12.1.2 The spelling **emfermo** (1.13) < Lat. INFIRMU[S] shows how *m* is used here in a context where the opposition between /n/ and /m/ is neutralised (before /f/, where its phonetic realisation is in fact the labiodental [ɱ]). This

neutralisation, which takes place before all consonants, leads to a sometimes arbitrary choice being made between *m* and *n* in the conventions of Spanish spelling:
thus in Modern Spanish, [m] is represented by *m* in *impacible* [impaθible] but by
n in *enviar* [embjaɾ].

12.1.3 The spelling -*eis* in the second person plural verb form **quereis** (l.9) appears
to indicate an early reduction of the -*edes* inflection (see 7.2.6, 13.2.2).

Morphology and syntax

12.2.1 Although the morphology and syntax of a copied text might be expected
to have survived more intact than spelling, some features seem to be less reliable
than others.

At first sight **abie** (l.1) appears to be an example of the -*ié* imperfect of Old
Castilian. However, the -*ié* inflection is not normally found in the 1st p.sg., and
all other imperfects in this text are of the -*ía* type; it is therefore to be concluded
that this is a copyist's invention or error.

Keypoint: the imperfect endings of Old Castilian (p. 277).

There is some variation between *lo* and *le* as a direct object pronoun: **le havian
velado** (l.5) but **lo fué á velar** (l.11). Again, this is a feature on which it would
have been easy for a copyist subconsciously to impose his own usage, though
leísmo is common in Old Castilian texts.

Keypoint: personal pronouns (p. 284).

12.2.2 Grande (l.1) does not here show apocope to *gran* before the noun. Modern
Spanish continues to show some variation in the use of *gran* and *grande* before
the noun, *grande* having the more distinctive meaning of 'great' (*el grande hombre*
'the great man'), and such a difference in meaning may have been present in
Old Castilian too.

12.2.3 The complementiser **que** is omitted in the indirect command **rogando á Dios
me quisiese librar a mi** . . . (l.2). This is a feature which persists in formal register
in Modern Spanish; it seems to have been more prevalent in the earlier language,
and occurs very widely in the Golden Age (see 17.2.5, 21.2.6, 22.2.6, 23.2.4).

12.2.4 The use of 'personal' *a* in this text appears to vary:
With *a*:

   me quisiesse librar á mi, y á mis fijos (l.2)
   quien vele á Alonso (l.8)

Without *a*:

   si alguno obiese de llevar (ll.2–3)
   llebase el mayor (l.3)
   velase aquel Mozo Doliente (l.4)

A plausible way of construing the use of *a* at this time is that it was used with personal pronouns (**mi**) and with proper names (**Alonso**); **mis fijos** takes **a** as a result of its syntactic coordination and semantic contrast with **á mi**.
    Keypoint: 'personal' *a* (p. 283).

12.2.5 Vos is used here as the second person singular pronoun of address between mother and son. The imperative form **velarlo** (l.8) which was 'corrected' to **veladlo** by nineteenth-century editors may not in fact be in need of correction: the infinitive often functions as a second person plural and general imperative in colloquial usage in Modern Spanish.
    Keypoint: personal pronouns (p. 284).

12.2.6 The relative construction in l.6, **aquel mi fijo, que le decian** . . ., in which the **le** is coreferential with the relative pronoun in referring to **fijo**, would be judged of marginal acceptability in standard written usage in Modern Spanish, though such sentences are frequently encountered in spoken register. The use of the object pronoun avoids the need to use a complex prepositional relative such as *a quien*. See in this connection 6.2.7.

12.2.7 The past participle **muerto** (l.9) of the intransitive verb *morir* is here used with the perfect auxiliary **haber**, which gradually generalised to become the universal perfect auxiliary in Modern Spanish (see also 10.2.6).

12.2.8 The construction **el triste de mi hijo** (ll.17–18) shows the use of the Romance preposition **de** to render the Latin appositional function of the genitive case in a noun + noun phrase such as SCĔLUS VĬRI 'you scoundrel of a man'; the use of the adjective in place of the first noun is made possible by the nominalisation of the adjective, which is signalled by the use of the definite article (Lapesa 1962).

12.2.9 Se enterró (l.19) is a clear example of a reflexive used as a passive: 'was buried', cf. 16.2.1.
    Keypoint: the reflexive (p. 288).

12.2.10 The distribution of *ser* and *estar* is quite different from that of Modern Spanish. Although **estar** is used with a past participle to indicate a state (**estaba tan traspasada de pesar**, l.16), it is not yet used universally with locative adverbs (**es en la Villa**, l.20, cf. 10.2.1), nor with adjectives denoting a state rather than an inherent property (**era doliente**, l.3).
    Keypoint: *ser* and *estar* (p. 290).

12.2.11 For **plugo** (l.3, preterite of *placer*), see 7.2.13.

Vocabulary

12.3.1 Aver (|| MSp. *haber*) is used as the verb of possession in this text, though its objects are restricted to abstract nouns (**devocion**, l.1, **piedad**, l.10). See 10.3.2.

12.3.2 The original meaning of **rezaba** (l.1) < Lat. RĔCĬTĀBAT [RĔCĬTO] 'to read aloud', 'recite' is still preserved in such usages as MSp. *reza el letrero* 'the sign reads', but it more usually has the more specific meaning of 'to say (a prayer)'. In this text it is, as in Latin, transitive, with the object **oracion**, but so strong is the association with such an object that **rezar** eventually comes to carry this meaning within itself, and so develops an intransitive usage, as in Modern Spanish. For the closely associated notion of *rogar* (cf. **rogando**, l.2) 'to pray', 'to ask', see 4.3.6.

12.3.3 Velase (l.4) < Lat. VĬGĬLĀVISSET [VĬGĬLO] 'to keep watch' is the popular derivation of this word; *vigilar* is a later learned doublet development, first attested in the eighteenth century. This is a typical example of how a relatively fine semantic distinction has been introduced into Spanish by this means: *velar* tends to have the benign connotations of 'to watch over', 'look after', and is strongly associated with the idea of keeping awake all night; *vigilar* is used more in the sense of 'to protect', 'invigilate', and has rather more defensive connotations.

12.3.4 The noun **enojo** (l.14), a morphological derivative of Lat. √[ĬNŎDĬO] 'to inspire horror' probably underwent some semantic attenuation, construable as 'to cause to be horrified' → 'to cause to be angry', 'annoyed'. This is a particularly well-endowed semantic field in Modern Spanish and includes learned words such as *irritar* < Lat. [IRRĪTO] and *molestar* ← Lat. √MŎLESTU[S] 'troublesome'; another near-synonym, *enfadar*, which is preferred to *enojar* in Peninsular, though not Latin-American usage, is a relatively late borrowing from Galician/Portuguese, becoming current only in the late sixteenth century (Pountain 1994).

12.3.5 Ocacion (l.15, ‖ MSp. *ocasión*) < Lat. OCCĀSĬŎNE [OCCĀSĬO] here has its typical Old Castilian meaning of 'accident', 'misfortune', being attested with this meaning as early as the *Cantar de mio Cid* (see Text 7). Its modern meaning of 'occasion' is in fact closer to that of Latin, and possibly a result of learned pressure.
Keypoint: learned and popular, semilearned and semipopular (p. 277).

12.3.6 Pesar (l.16) is a nominal usage of the Latin infinitive PENSĀRE [PENSO] 'to weigh'. This verb had a remarkable semantic development. Two forms, *pesar* and *pensar*, derive from it, the first preserving the meaning of 'to weigh' and extending to the metaphorical meaning of 'to weigh (heavily on)' → 'to grieve', which is the meaning in question here. PENSO also had in Latin the metaphorical meaning of 'to weigh (in the mind)', 'to consider', and it is from this that *pensar* 'to think' derives. The meanings 'to weigh' → 'to grieve' and 'to think' hence appear to have been discriminated by a different phonetic development (see Wright 1982: 27–9).
Keypoint: learned and popular, semilearned and semipopular (p. 277).

12.3.7 The verb *correr* has evolved from Lat. [CŬRRO] 'to run' to have a very wide range of meanings in Spanish. The noun **corrimiento** (l.17) is glossed by Covarrubias (1977) [1611] as 'confusión, vergüenza', and derives from one of the causative transitive meanings of *correr* 'to embarrass' (probably associated with the notion of 'to make (the blood) run', 'to make a person blush').

12.3.8 The learned form **anima** (l.19) < Lat. ĂNĬMA 'wind', 'soul', is encountered from the earliest texts and coexisted with the popular doublet development *alma*.
   Keypoint: learned and semilearned, popular and semipopular (p. 277).

12.3.9 For **falleció [fallecer]** (l.19) in the meaning of 'to die', see 9.3.12.

13 A mistress's complaint. Alfonso Martínez de Toledo, *Arcipreste de Talavera o Corbacho* (mid-fifteenth century)

13.0 Alfonso Martínez de Toledo (1398–1470?) was chaplain to Juan II of Castile. The *Corbacho*, which purports to be a critique of human weakness and exaltation of divine love, is unacceptably misogynistic for a modern reader (it is in a tradition of such writing, Boccaccio's *Corbaccio*, its namesake, being a precursor, and parts of the *Celestina*, see Text 15, a successor), but from a linguistic point of view it is a most important text because of the Arcipreste's manipulation of different registers and especially because of his attempt to represent direct speech. In the extract below, a passage of direct speech is followed by a moral reflection which is in more cultured Latinate style, though the author often also mixes popular and cultured register.

The text

There is one MS source in the Library of the Escorial, which is a copy dated 1466; the work was subsequently published five times between 1498 and 1547. These printed editions suggest that another MS or MSS may have been extant, and variants in the 1500 Toledo edition are given in square brackets. Otherwise the text follows the palaeographic edition by Naylor (1983), with punctuation and modern accentuation added by González Muela (1970). Naylor has not distinguished between types of *s* or between *r* and *rr* used initially.

Further reading

A work of fundamental importance on fifteenth-century style is Lida de Malkiel (1950). González Muela's (1954) study of the use of the infinitive is also of particular interest.

> E el Amjgada dize A su Amjgo: '¡Ay de mj! Más me valjera ser casada;
> qu*e* fuera más honrrada y en mayor estima tenjda. ¡Perdý me, cuytada, qu*e*
> en ora mala vos creý [conocí]! No*n* es esto lo qu*e* vos me prometist*es*, nj*n*
> lo qu*e* me Jurastes; qu*e* no*n* he ganado el dinero qu*an*do me lo Avés
> Arrebatado, dizje*n*do qu*e* devés y qu*e* Jugast*es*. Y com*m*o vn rufián   5
> Amenazando v*ue*stro so*n*brero, dando coçes en él, diziendo: 'A ty lo digo,

sonbrero' ¡donde me he yo enpeñado y envergonçado muchas vezes por vos, buscando para pagar vuestras debdas A baratos! Ya non lo puedo bastar, & ¿dónde lo tengo de Aver, Amjgo, ya? ¡dios perdone al que mjs menguas conplja & mjs trabaJos cobría! Non queda ya synón que me ponga 10 A la verguença con Aquéllas del públjco [público partido]. ¡Guay de mj, captiua! ¿Asý medran las otras? ¡Landre, Señor, rrauja y dolor de costado!'. Estas y otras maneras de fablar tyenen las mugeres: de las otras murmurar, detraer & mal fablar, & quexar se de sý mesmas, que fazer otra cosa ynposyble les sería. Esto proujene de vso malo & luenga mente continuado, 15 non conosçiendo su defaljmjento; que es vn pecado muy terrible la persona non conosçer a sý, nin A su falljmjento.

Translation

And the concubine says to her man-friend: 'Woe is me! I would have been better off married, for I would have been more greatly honoured and held in higher esteem. Alas, I am undone, for I believed you in an evil hour! This is not what you promised me, nor what you swore to me; I have hardly earned money before you have snatched it from me, saying that you have debts and you have been gambling. And [you're] like a hooligan threatening your hat, kicking it and saying, "I'm telling you, hat": I've got myself into debt and shame often on your account, seeking to pay off your debts and deals! I can't put up with it any longer, and when am I going to get it back, friend, eh? May God forgive him who supplied what I lacked and covered up my deeds. There's nothing for it now but for me to expose myself to shame along with prostitutes. Woe is me, poor unfortunate! Do other girls prosper in this way? Lord, what a pox, rage and pain in the side!' Women have these and other ways of speaking, of gossiping about others, disparaging and speaking ill of them, and of complaining about themselves, for doing anything else is impossible for them. This comes from an evil habit which has continued over a long period, since they are unaware of their defect; for it is a very terrible sin for a person not to know himself nor his defects.

Phonetics and phonology

13.1.1 Sonbrero (l.6) is a morphological derivative of *sombra* 'shadow' ≤ Lat. UMBRA. The initial /s/ of *sombra* may have been added as a result of analogy with its antonym *sol*, the structural association with which in such phrases as *sol y sombra* was frequent.

13.1.2 Landre (l.12) < Lat. ?GLANDĬNE (the CL accusative form was GLANDEM) [GLANS] illustrates the loss of /g/ in the relatively few words inherited from Latin beginning with the /gl/ group (another example is *latir* 'to beat' < Lat. [GLATTĬO] 'to yap').
  Keypoint: consonant groups (p. 267).

13.1.3 Debdas (l.8) < Lat. DĒBĬTAS [DĒBĔO] shows preservation of the complex group /bd/ produced by the voicing of intervocalic /t/ (cf. 3.1.5) and the reduction of proparoxytones; in MSp. *deuda*, the implosive /b/ has vocalised to /u/. A complex group /pt/ is evident in **captiva** [**captivo**] (l.12) < CAPTĪVU[S] 'captive'; this, however, may represent a learned restitution of the /p/, since the spellings *cativo* and *cautivo*, showing respectively simplification of the /pt/ group and vocalisation of the implosive /p/, are both attested in Old Castilian; *cautivo* is the form that has survived into the modern language, cf. 18.3.5.

   Keypoint: consonant groups (p. 267).

13.1.4 Guay (l.11) has been derived from Germanic *wai* 'alas'; here it seems to be in variation with the simple **ay** (l.1), which appears to be a conventionalised expressive exclamation with no identifiable source.

13.1.5 For the final /n/ in **non** (ll. 3 and 8), **synón** (l.10) and **nin** (ll.3 and 17), see 11.1.1. For the atonic /o/ in **conplía** and **cobría** (l.10) corresponding to MSp. *cumplía*, *cubría*, see 9.1.7. For **mesmas** (l.14), see **Keypoint: *mismo*** (p. 279).

Morphology and syntax

13.2.1 Valjera and **fuera** (ll.1–2). The *-ra* verb form, originally a pluperfect indicative form in Old Castilian, like its Latin etymon (e.g. *amara* < Lat. ĂMĀVERAT [ĂMO]), came to be used in past counterfactual conditionals in both protasis and apodosis; here it is used in the apodosis of what may be interpreted as either a past or present counterfactual conditional apodosis, since there is no protasis or *si*-clause (see 20.2.4, 23.2.2).

   Keypoint: conditional sentences (p. 264); **the pluperfects of Old Castilian** (p. 286).

13.2.2 The forms **avés** and **devés** (ll.4–5) show the reduction of the *-edes* inflection of Old Castilian (see 7.2.6, 12.1.3). A number of variant developments of the second person plural form can be observed in later Old Castilian and in the Golden Age; the one that has eventually been adopted in Modern Spanish has the /ei/ diphthong (*habéis*, *debéis*), but the forms seen here are the ancestors of the best-known of the Latin-American *voseo* verb forms, the *porteño* form of the *voseo* (see 13.2.8 below and also 30.2.1).

13.2.3 Prometistes (l.3) and **jugastes** (l.5) do not yet have the analogical *-eis* ending (cf. 17.2.2): compare MSp. *prometisteis*, *jugasteis*; this appears to have developed during the sixteenth and seventeenth centuries (Alvar and Pottier 1983: 206–7).

13.2.4 The gerund is used quite extensively in the *Corbacho*. In direct speech it seems to be a way of avoiding the more cumbersome use of a relative or adverbial clause with a finite verb and is a short step from paratactic syntax: ll.5–6 (**Y commo vn rufián Amenazando vuestro sonbrero, dando coçes en él, diziendo** . . .) might be recast as °*Amenazás vuestro sonbrero commo un rufián; das coçes en él, y decís* . . . The gerund may also be used for the sake of the greater vividness conveyed by its progressive aspect. In the final moralising section,

conosçiendo has no overt subject (the subject must be understood as 'women'), and it is part of a series of non-finite forms of the verb – the others are infinitives, see below 13.2.7 – which often in the *Corbacho* give the impression of 'loose' syntax.

13.2.5 Tengo de aver (l.9) has the preposition **de** rather than the modern *que* (see 9.2.8).

13.2.6 In **dios perdone al que mjs menguas conplja & mjs trabajos cobría** (ll.9–10) the object (**menguas, trabajos**) precedes the verb (**conplja, cobría**). This feature is often associated with Latinate syntax (in Latin the verb preferentially stood at the end of a clause). There is also a rhetorical 'balancing' of the two relative clauses here which the inverted structure highlights. Placing the verb after its prepositional object is seen in ll.13–14, **de las otras murmurar**, **detraer & mal fablar**, where the sequence of verbs is consequently given a position of stronger stress.

13.2.7 The syntax of the infinitive in the *Corbacho* is complex. The Arcipreste often imitates Latin uses of the infinitive, especially the 'accusative and infinitive' complement structure of Latin which was used after verbs of saying and thinking, cf. 15.2.2. In ll.16–17 we also see a parallel to the so-called 'nominative and infinitive' complement type of Latin: the subject complement of **es un pecado muy terrible** is **la persona non conosçer a sý**, within which **la persona** is the subject of the infinitive **conosçer**. In Modern Spanish such a complement would be represented by a full clause structure introduced by *que*, e.g. *el que una persona no se conozca es un pecado muy terrible* (cf. 21.2.7).

13.2.8 The woman here addresses her man-friend as **vos**, which, while originally a form of respect, came increasingly to be the form used among equals, while **tú** was reserved for God, children and insults (**tú** is here used by the ruffian cursing his hat). Very considerable reorganisation of the system of second person address was subsequently to take place with the appearance of third person expressions used with second-person reference (see 18.2.1), but the extension of **vos** to more intimate use, as here, is no doubt the origin of the Latin-American *voseo* (see 30.2.1).

   Keypoint: personal pronouns (p. 284).

13.2.9 For the use of **el** with **amigada** (l.1), see 8.2.4 and 16.2.6.

Vocabulary

13.3.1 Arrebatado (l.5) is based on Ar. √*ribāṭ* '(sudden) attack against the infidels' a culturally specific concept that was a natural candidate for borrowing. The dominant idea seems to have been that of sudden attack, hence 'snatching a victory'; although *arrebatar una victoria* can still be used in this way, *arrebatar* itself has broadened to mean 'to snatch' in general.

13.3.2 Coçes (l.6) 'kick' shows metonymy from its Lat. etymon CALCE [CALX] 'heel' to 'a blow given with the foot'. The notion of 'heel' comes to be rendered by *talón*, which is from Lat. √TĀLU[S] 'rear part of the foot', 'ankle-bone', and the notion of 'ankle' by *tobillo* < Lat. ?TŪBĔLLU(S) < √TŪBER 'swelling' (the characteristic shape of the ankle-bone). This is an example of a structural movement within a semantic area which contains referential overlap:

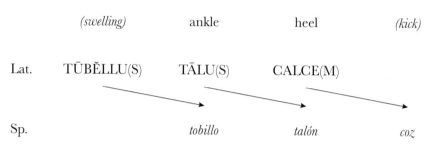

13.3.3 Amenazando (l.6) is a morphological derivative of Lat. ?√MĬNĀCĬA 'threat' (Classical Latin had MĬNĀTĬO 'threat' and MĬNĀCE [MĬNĀX] 'threatening', but no corresponding noun or verb; Romance makes good this deficiency). The Castilian verb has the common *a-* prefix (see 2.10.1, 9.3.3, 10.3.3).

13.3.4 Enpeñado (l.7) is a morphological derivative of Lat. √PIGNU[S] 'something given as security'; OCast. *empeñar* preserves the meaning 'to pawn' but has extended this to the more general meaning of 'to pledge'; the reflexive has undergone an associational change independently of the non-reflexive verb through the stages 'to pledge oneself' → 'to persist in' → 'to endeavour to'.

13.3.5 Baratos (l.8) is a word of unknown origin. In Old Castilian, *baratar* had the meaning of 'to do business', and the noun here clearly has the meaning of 'business', 'deal'. The Modern Spanish meaning of *barato* used adjectivally as 'cheap' is probably an ellipsis of *(buen) barato* 'a good deal' (cf. Fr. *de bon marché*).

13.3.6 The common verb **bastar** (l.9) is an instance of a Greek borrowing into Latin. Gr. βαστάζειν 'to carry', 'sustain (a weight)', borrowed as ?BASTĂRE, generalised its meaning to the associated implication of 'to be (strong) enough (to carry, etc.)'.

13.3.7 Captiua (l.12), see above, 13.1.3, has extended its meaning to the associated notion of 'unfortunate (because a captive)'.

13.3.8 Landre (l.12) (see above 13.1.2) 'mast', 'acorn', undergoes a metaphorical change of meaning to denote 'tumour', 'bubo' and hence 'bubonic plague'. (It is sobering to bear in mind the reality of the threat of plague at this time, see Text 12; **landre** forms the basis of many common curses.)

13.3.9 Quexar se (l.14) derives from Lat. ?QUASSĬĀRE, a variant of Lat. [QUASSO] 'to hit violently', 'break': see 14.3.7. It must have become associated with the personal notion of 'to afflict', and is also used transitively in this sense in Old Castilian. As a reflexive, the only usage in which it has survived since the fifteenth century, it means 'to bemoan' (at first not necessarily with a sense of grievance), and then 'to complain'.

13.3.10 Otra cosa (l.14) is found here instead of OCast. *al* (see 4.3.4).

13.3.11 For **tenjda** (l.2), see 4.3.7 and 11.3.4; for **donde** (l.9) in the meaning of 'whence', see 4.2.10; **menguas** (l.10) see 11.3.7.

14 Aljamiado aromatherapy. An *aljamiado* document from Ocaña (late fourteenth–early fifteenth century)

14.0 *Aljamiado* texts are being increasingly recognised as a valuable source of information about the Romance languages of the Iberian Peninsula, since, as we have already seen in connections with Texts 5a–d, representation of Romance in a non-Roman script removes a number of problems of interpretation. *Aljamiado* texts are also independent of the Christian Latin linguistic and cultural traditions, being firmly embedded in Islamic culture; the cures in this text involve ritual exorcisms in Arabic and verses from the Qur'an, as well as as many Arabic words (see 14.3.1 below). They can therefore plausibly be regarded as being more objective representations of Romance. This text is particularly valuable to us because it does seem unequivocally to represent a Castilian variety (perhaps with some admixture of Leonese features), whereas many other well-known *aljamiado* texts hail from Aragonese-speaking areas.

The text

This MS was found when a building in Ocaña, in the province of Toledo, was demolished in 1969. It dates from the late fourteenth or early fifteenth century. The text in bold is taken from Martínez Ruiz (1974). Martínez Ruiz has made some accommodation to the spelling conventions of Castilian in order to make the text more approachable; but since this does not always give a sense of the Arabic, I have added my own transcription of his interpretation in Arabic characters of the original manuscript, which is also given in the same article. Long *a* (*ā*) represents the a vowel mark followed by *'alif* (ا), which is the usual equivalent for Castilian /e/; long *i* (*ī*) represents the *i* vowel mark followed by *yā'* (ﻴ-); a sequence of the *u* vowel mark followed by *wāw* (و') is transcribed as *ū* when no other vowel follows and otherwise as *uw*; all vowels are written as full vowels, even when they are clearly being used as consonant separators. *Šīn* (ش) is consistently transcribed as *š*, *ŷīm* (ج) as *ŷ* and *bā'* (ب) as *b*. The *tā' marbūṭa* or feminine ending mark of Arabic (ﺔ) is transcribed by *a*, and the one instance of the *ä* ending is transcribed as *at*. % indicates a break signalled by punctuation.

Text in Arabic script

تُمَرِذَاشْ أَنَ اِشْقُذِيلَّه بَلَنْقَه ِا اِشْكِرِبِرلُوَاذِ(؟)

شْ ِاشْتُشْ نُنْبِرِشْ شُبْرَاذِ جُشْ ِانِيلَّ قُنُنْ قَلَمْ تُمَذْ أَنَ(؟) قُجَرَ

ذَا مَذِرَ نُوَابَه ِا أَنْ بُقُو ذَ الصَّفْرَنْ ِا آغُوَا رُشَذَ ِا اِجَنْلُو

ِانْلَ قَجَرِ ِا فَزَالً ذُ قُمْ تِنْطَه ِا شِئُنْ أُبِيَارَا اَغُوَا رُشَذَ

شِيَه قُنْ آغُوَا ذَالْ اَلْوَضُوا ِا ذِشْ فَرَاشْ لَذِ يِجَ اِشْكِرِبْتُرَ قُنْ

اَغُوَا رُشَذَ ا ذَالْ الْوَضُوا ِا شِيَه اِلْغُوَظَة قُوَانْة كَابَه اِنْ

قَشْقَرَ ذَ أَنْ وبُوا ذَلِ غَلِنَه ِابِلَ قَذْ ذِيَه ِا نْجَا ِا الْكَاكِذَ

رَا ذِيلُ بُرْ بِيرْ ذَا ۤ لِكَالَّه قَنْتِنَذْ أُنْتَاتْلَا لُشْ بَاجُشْ

قُنِلَّ قَذَ بَاغَذَ ٪ أُتْرُشْ اَتْرُشْ اَرَسِيُنْ ذَا شْتُشْ

نُنْبِرِشْ لِ ِاشْكِرِبِذَاشْ ِانْ بَرْغَمِنُو بِرْجِنْ ذَا بَازَارُّ شِلُ

أُبِيَارَا ِا شِنَنْ شِيَه ذَا أَتْرُ قُنْلْ ذِاجُو اَلصَّفْرَنْ ِا آغُوَ رُّ

شَذَ ِا بُنِذْ جَالُ ِانْبِنُوا قُلْرَذُ ِانْدَارَاجُوا ذَ الْ قُرَصُونْ قُشِذُ

قُنْ هِلُو ذَالِزُشْ ذَاتَا شِذُرَاشْ ٪ أُتْرُشْ شَتُشْ شَهُو

مَارِيشْ قُنْكَا لَ ِا بِذَاشْ ذِا شَهُمَرْ شُنْ ِاشْتُشْ ِالْمِيعَه

ِا لِنُوَالَّوَا ِا شَنْتَلُو قُلْرَذُ ِاِنْسِيَانْصُو مَجُوا ِا اَلْهُزَاهَه

ِا قَشْتُورِيُ ِا شَنْتَلُو بَلَنْتُوا ٪ أُتْرُشْ نَرْلَا اذَاشْ

قَذَ مَنَّه اَ قُمَارْ أَنْ وبُوا بِيِسْ رِّلُوا اَتَذُ قُنْ ِانْسِيَانْشُ

مَجُو مُلِذُ ٪ تُنُشْ لُشْ قُمَارَاشْ ذَا منشم ا ذا

ِارِّيُشْ ٪ ِا أُرْطَلِارشْ لَا شِيَنْ بِنَذُشْ ِا لَاجاكِشْ

شَاُبْ قَرْنَارُ أُ غَلِينَه ِا أُبَاجَه ٪

Transliteration

(The top line in each pair of lines is the literal transcription, the bottom line in bold is Martínez Ruiz's version.)

tumariḏāš una iškuḏīlla balanqa iškiribirluwāḏi

Tomaredes una esqudilla blanqa i esk[i]ribirlo ade *1*

š ištuš nunbiriš šubrāḏiŷuš in illa qunun qalam tumaḏ una quŷara

s estos nonbres sobredichos en ella qon un qalam, tomad una quchara *2* dā madira nuwāba ' un buqū da 'lṣṣafaran i aghuwā rušada iŷiadlū

de madera nuʷeva i un poqo de alṣṣafaran i aguʷa rosada i echadlo   *3*

inla qaŷar i fazāl du qumu tinṭa i šinun ubiyārā aghuwā rušada

en la quchara i fazeldo qomo tinṭa, i si no ubiera aguʷa rosada   *4*

šiya qun aghuwā ḍāl alwaḍū' i diśfarāš ladiŷa iškiribṭura qun

sea q n aguʷa del alwaḍuʷ, i desfarás la dicha escriptura qon   *5*

aghuwā rušadā ḍāl 'lwaḍū' i šiya ilghuwa ṭaat quw ānaṭa kāba in

aguʷa rosada del alwaḍuʷ i sea el aguʷa tanta quʷanta kepa en   *6*

qašqara da un wibū' dali[?] ghalina i bibalu qada diya i nuŷā lukākida

qásqara de un wevo de gallina, bebalo qada diʸa i noche, i lo ke keda   *7*

rā ḍīllu bur bibir dā alik'lla qantidad untānlā luš bāŷuš

ra d'ello por beber de akella qantidad untanla los baŷos   *8*

qunillu qada bāghada %[3] utruši āšṭa urasiyun da ištuš

con ello qada vegada. Otrosí esta oración de estos   *9*

nunbiriš li iškiribiridāš in barghaminū birŷin ḍā bāzārru šilu

nonbres le esk[i]riberedes en pergamino virŷen de bezerro, si lo   *10*

īubiyārā i ši nan šiya ḍā utru qunil ḍī' ŷū alṣṣafran i aghuwa rru

īubiʸera, i si non, sea de otro, qon el dicho alṣṣafaran i aguʷa ro   *11*

šada i bunidŷālu inbinū' quluradu ind[?]ārāŷū' ḍāl quraṣūn qušidu

sada i ponedŷelo en vino qolorado en derecho del qoraṣón qosido   *12*

qun hilū ḍālizuš ḍātāšiḍurāš % utruši šatuš šahū

qon hilo de lizos de tesedores. Otrosí sahu   *13*

māriy[u]š qunkā lā biḍāš ḍāšahumar šun ištuš ilmī'a i

merios qon ke le pidas de sahumar son estos al my'a   *14*

linuwā[?]lliwā i šandālū quluradu i yinsiyānṣu maŷū' i alhuzāma i

i linolio i sándalo bᵃlanqo, i inçienṣo macho i alhuzema   *15*

qaštuwriyu i šandalū balanqū' % utruši ḍarlāidāš

i qastorio i sándalo bᵃlanqo. Otrosí darledes   *16*

qada manana a qumār un wibū' biyin rraluwa ašadu qun insiyānšu

qada mañana a qomer un wevo biʸen ralo asado qon inçienso   *17*

maŷū mulidu % tuduš luš qumārāš ḍ' mnšm ' ḍ'

macho molido. Todos los qomerás de monte i de   *18*

irriyuš % i urṭali'zš lā šiyan biḍaduš i lā ŷ 'kiš

rios, i orṭalizas le sean vedadas [salvo] i leche i karne   *19*

šalbu qarnāru u ghaliyna i ubāŷa %

salvo qarnero o gallina u oveŷa.   *20*

Translation

Take a white bowl and write the aforementioned names on it with a reed pen; take a new wooden spoon and a little saffron and rose water and put it on the spoon and make it into a kind of ink. If there is no rose water, let it be with the water used for ritual washing, and use as much water as will go in a hen's eggshell. [The patient] should drink it each day and night, and on every occasion anoint his lower regions with what remains undrunk. Also, write this prayer with these

---

3   % would appear to indicate the end of sentence.

names on virgin calfskin parchment, if there is any available, and if there is not, on some other kind, with the aforementioned saffron and rose water, and place it in red wine on the right hand side of the heart, sewn with weaver's thread. Also, the aromatic smokes with which you must ask him to cense himself are these: balsam, linseed and white sandalwood, 'male' incense [i.e., naturally distilled from the tree], lavender, castoreum and white sandalwood. Also, every morning you will give him a very lightly cooked egg with ground 'male' incense. Eat everything from moorland and rivers; vegetables should be forbidden him, and milk and meat, except for beef, chicken or mutton.

Phonetics and phonology

14.1.1 A number of phonetic features instantly place this text in the Castilian area: the development of the Lat. /kt/ group to what may be taken as /tʃ/ (**leche**, l.19 < Lat. LACTE/LĀC, cf. 4.1.1, 15.1.3), the development of the Lat. /m'n/ group to /mbr/ (**nonbres**, l.2 < Lat. NŌMĬNES [NŌMEN], cf. 4.1.1), and the suggestion of the incipient change of /f/(?/ɸ/) to /h/ (see 14.1.3 below).
  Keypoint: consonant groups (p. 267).

14.1.2 Of great interest is the representation of the medieval sibilants of Castilian (see also 5b.1.2). The following correspondences can be seen:

Proposed phoneme	Arabic letter	Name of Arabic letter	Martínez Ruiz's Roman letter transcription	Example
/s/	ش	šīn	s	**otrosí**
/z/	ش	šīn	s	**rosada**
/ts/	س or ص	sīn or ṣād	ç or ṣ	**oración; qorasón**
/dz/	ز	zāy	z	**bezerro**
/ʃ/	ش	šīn	s	**tesedores**
/ʒ/	ج	ŷīm	ŷ	**baŷos**
/tʃ/	ج	ŷīm	ch	**quchara**

As is usual in such texts, Romance /s/ is represented by *šīn*: this is the nearest Arabic sound to the apico–alveolar articulation [ṣ] that we must presume for OCast. /s/, which has continued down into present-day standard Peninsular usage. The use of *šīn* in this way does not permit a contrast between /s/ and /ʃ/; but /ʃ/ is relatively infrequent, and it was no doubt much more crucial to distinguish between /s/ and the more common /ts/, whose predorsal quality is reflected in Arabic *sīn* or *ṣād*. A clear distinction, reflecting the presence or absence of voicing, was made between /ts/ and /dz/; but there is no such clear distinction in this text between /s/ and /z/ (/z/ is sometimes represented by *ŷīm* in *aljamiado* texts). The affricate value of /ts/ and /dz/ is not reflected, but we may put this down to the fact that Arabic did not have a suitable consonant available. There is no distinction between /tʃ/ and /ʒ/, which are both represented by *ŷīm*, again, perhaps, because of the difficulty of representing the affricate, though in other *aljamiado* texts /tʃ/ is often represented by a doubled *ŷīm* (*ŷīm* with *šadda*, ﺝ̌). In view of the considerable problems of representing the Old Castilian sibilants with Arabic characters, it is not surprising that some distinctions were sacrificed.

Keypoint: the sibilants of Old Castilian (p. 290).

14.1.3 /f/ (?/ɸ/) is very strikingly here represented by both the aspirate *hā'* ﻫ and the labiodental *fā'* ﻑ: thus we see both **hilo** (l.13) < Lat. FĪLU[M] and **fazeldo** (l.4) < Lat. [FĂCĬO]. Since the variation occurs in the same context (here, initial position), and there is also an example (in the text as a whole, not in the extract given here) of the same word being spelt in different ways (both **safumeriʸo**, and **sahumeriʸo** ≤ Lat. √?SUBFŬMO), the most likely conclusion to be drawn is that an attempt is being made to represent a sound such as [ɸ], which has similarities to both [h] and [f], but which is neither.

Keypoint: the f>h change (p. 271).

14.1.4 In other cases, too, there is no one-to-one match between Arabic letter and Romance phoneme. Arabic *bā'* ﺏ is used for /b/, /β/ and /p/; this could suggest a neutralisation of the b/β ('b/v') opposition, though it must be remembered that there is no ready equivalent for [v] in Arabic (Modern Arabic transcribes the [v] of foreign words by *fā'* ﻑ), cf. 5b.1.1. Arabic *tā'* ﺕ and *ṭā'* ﻁ are used indiscriminately to represent /t/, *dāl* ﺩ and *ḍāl* ﺽ for /d/ and *kāf* ﻙ and *qāf* ﻕ for /k/. The palatalised consonants of Romance are represented by the corresponding doubled Arabic letters (with *šadda*): thus double *lām* ﻝ = /ʎ/ and double *nūn* ﻥ̌ = /ɲ/.

Keypoint: the 'b/v' merger (p. 262).

14.1.5 In Arabic, a syllable cannot begin with a consonant sequence, and so a bridging vowel is often introduced: thus /eskribirlo/ is **eskⁱribirlo** (l.1) and /blanko/ is **baⁱlanqo** (l.15). A similar strategy is adopted with sequences of two vowels in hiatus, and a semivowel *y* or *w* is used: thus **diʸa** for /dia/ (l.7). The same thing also happens with some diphthongal groups, e.g. **nuʷeva** for /nueβa/ (l.3) and **biʸen** for /bien/ (l.17). It is not clear to what extent these are spelling conventions or a feature of *aljamiado* pronunciation.

Morphology and syntax

14.2.1 The intervocalic /d/ of the *-des* second person plural verb ending is still present in paroxytonically stressed words (thus **tomaredes**, l.1); it was to be lost in the course of the fifteenth century (see 7.2.6, 13.2.2), though it remained for longer in proparoxytonically stressed words (see 17.2.2).

14.2.2 There is variation in the expression of the imperative: both the future tense (e.g. **eskⁱriberedes**, l.10) and the morphological imperative **tomad** (l.2) are used.

14.2.3 There is oscillation between the singular and plural (*tú* and *vos*) forms: **darledes** (l.16) but **qomerás** (l.18), in close proximity. This is no doubt a consequence of oscillation in the mind of the writer between a particular case and a general treatment. In a similar way, a third person verb is often to be understood as having as its subject the patient who is undergoing treatment, e.g. **bebalo** (l.7).
    Keypoint: **personal pronouns** (p. 284).

14.2.4 Metathesis has taken place in the combination of imperative and clitic pronoun in **fazeldo** (‖ MSp. *hacedlo*, l.4), though the existence of **echadlo** (l.3) shows that this was not invariable (cf. 20.2.9).

14.2.5 The -*ra* verb form is used in the protasis of a conditional sentence (**si no ubiera aguʷa** . . ., l.4, see 20.2.4). **Kedara** (ll.7–8) is probably more appropriately read as the future subjunctive *kedare*.
    Keypoint: **conditional sentences** (p. 265).

14.2.6 A characteristic feature of Castilian is the clitic pronoun sequence *ŷelo* (**ponedŷelo**, l.12): see 10.2.5.
    Keypoint: **clitic pronoun position** (p. 264).

14.2.7 There is dissimilation of the conjunction *o* to **u** before a word beginning with /o/ (**u oveŷa**, l.20), though no representation of the corresponding dissimilation of *y* to *e* before a word beginning with /i/ (**i inçiensọ**, l.15).

Vocabulary

14.3.1 There are a number of Arabic words used within this Romance text: **waḍū** (l.5) 'ritual ablution', **my'a** (l.14), probably a kind of resin made from myrrh, **juzāmạ** (l.15) 'lavender' and **za'farān** (l.11) 'saffron'. The last two are familiar from MSp. *alhucema* (which, however, did not in the end displace *espliego* with the same meaning < Lat. SPĪCŬLU[M] 'sharp point', 'spear') and *azafrán*. All these words show total incorporation into Romance insofar as, in common with so many Arabic loans in Spanish, they retain the Arabic definite article *al-* as part of the noun itself (compare **del alwaḍuʷ**, l.5, where the presence of the Romance definite article clearly shows that the Arabic *al-* is construed as belonging to the noun stem). The word **qalam** 'reed pen' (l.2), still the standard word for 'pen' in Arabic, is in fact a borrowing into Arabic from Gr. κάλαμος; the same word borrowed into Latin as CĂLĂMUS was coincidentally to yield in Spanish the learned borrowing *cálamo* 'reed', 'reed pipe' and 'pen' in high poetic register.

14.3.2 Vegada (l.9) < Lat. VĬCĀTA was a rival to *vez* < Lat. VĬCE [VĬCIS] in Old Castilian; *vegada* was adopted as the standard word for 'time', 'occasion' in Catalan.

14.3.3 Ralo (l.17) derives from Lat. RĀRU[S]; the conversion of the second /r/ to /l/ is a result of dissimilation of the two occurrences of /r/. Sp. *raro*, its learned doublet, is first attested only in the late fifteenth century. As so often, it is the popular form *ralo* which has the more 'concrete' meaning of 'sparse', 'bare'; nowadays it is somewhat restricted (to beards, teeth, etc.), but formerly it was more widely applicable, to the extent of being regarded as the opposite of *espeso* (Covarrubias Orozco 1977 [1611]:895).

Keypoint: learned and popular, semilearned and semipopular (p. 277).

14.3.4 Esqudilla (l.1) < Lat. SCŬTĚLLA 'little dish' has survived dialectally in Modern Spanish and has the meaning of 'large cup' in Latin America, but is now less common in the standard language.

14.3.5 Tinṭa (l.4) < Lat. TINCTA, the past participle of TINGO 'to dye', developed a specific association with writing and so in Spanish became the word for the coloured liquid used for writing, i.e. 'ink'. As an adjective, it eventually developed a specific association with wine, in the meaning 'red' (though in this text **qolorado**, l.12, is the word used for wine, see 14.3.6).

14.3.6 Qolorado (l.12) < Lat. CŎLŌRĀTU[S] 'coloured', seems to have become the canonical term for the colour 'red' between the fifteenth and seventeenth centuries. (Earlier, *bermejo* was commonly used with this function) *Colorado* still has this value in much of Latin America, whereas in the Peninsula it has yielded place to *rojo*. The semantic field of 'red' is particularly rich in Spanish, and there has been much change in the choice of canonical term for the colour; the co-occurrence of the colour adjective with a noun in texts, as here (**vino qolorado**) supplies valuable evidence about the use and precise nuance of these words, which are otherwise very difficult to discriminate.

14.3.7 Qáscara (l.4) is a back-formation from the verb *cascar* < Lat. ?QUASSĬCĀRE √QUASSO) 'to shake', 'break' (cf. 13.3.9). It is an interesting development from a number of points of view: semantically, it seems to owe its origin to association with the necessary action of cracking that produces the shell or husk, and has extended its meaning to the outer covering of a number of fruits (not just those which necessitate cracking); morphologically, it does not form part of a productive process of derivation, and furthermore it is an unusual example of an apparently spontaneously created proparoxytone.

14.3.8 The word **Vedar** (**vedadas** l.19) < Lat. VĚTĀTĀS [VĚTO] 'to forbid', 'prohibit' has largely been replaced in Modern Spanish by the learned word *prohibir*, which is first attested as late as the sixteenth century. This is an example of the success of a learned borrowing at the expense of a word of popular origin.

Keypoint: learned and popular, semilearned and semipopular (p. 277).

15 Mad with love. Fernando de Rojas, *La Celestina* (1499)

15.0 The *Celestina*, the first version of which was published in 1499, is one of the milestones of Spanish literature, the product of both literary imagination and scholarship. Linguistically it is a complex text because it subtly combines popular and learned elements in a medium which purports to be a drama, and hence a representation of direct speech. The extract selected is one of the conversations between a young noble, Calisto, and his servant Sempronio. Direct speech is suggested by a number of racy features: short questions and exclamations, and some colloquialisms. However, it is also a structured disputation, laced with classical allusions which are manipulated just as expertly by the servant as the master, and with features of syntax and vocabulary which are associated with cultured prose.

We have now reached the period of incunabula, the dawn of printing, which was to revolutionise the dissemination of texts, and their nature. Yet though our source is a printed text, we must not necessarily expect greater consistency in spelling, or absence of 'scribal' error. Moreover, the *Celestina* is known to us in a number of printed versions, amongst which there are many discrepancies, and this makes the establishing of a definitive text a wellnigh impossible task. None the less, the variation encountered is highly interesting for the historical linguist.

The text

The text is transcribed from the first known edition, printed by Fadrique de Basilea in Burgos perhaps in 1499, fols. 4r to 4v. A facsimile of this edition published by the Hispanic Society of America, to whom the book belongs, was reprinted in 1970. I follow the transcription given in Corfis and O'Neill (1997), in which many other versions of the *Celestina* can also be consulted.

Further reading

Criado de Val (1955); Marciales (1985); Russell (1991); Whinnom (1966).

Ca*listo*: q*u*e me reprobas.
Se*mpronio*: q*u*e sometes la dignidad del hombre ala imperfecio*n* de la flaca muger.
Ca*listo*: muger: o grosero: dios dios.
Sem[*pronio.*]: & assi lo crees o burlas.
Ca*listo*: q*u*e burlo: por dios la creo: por dios la co*n*fiesso: & no creo que ay   5
    otro soberano enel cielo avn q*u*e entre nos otros mora.
Se*mpronio*: ha ha ha: oystes que blasfemia: vistes q*u*e ceguedad.
Ca*listo*: de q*u*e te ries.
Se*mpronio*: riome q*u*e no pensaua q*u*e hauia peor inue*n*cion de pecado q*u*e en
    sodoma.   10
Ca*listo*: como.
Se*mpronio.* porq*u*e aque*l*los procuraron abominable vso co*n*los angeles no
    conoscidos: & tu conel que co*n*fiessas ser dios.
Ca*listo*: maldito seas q*u*e fecho me has reyr lo que no pe*n*se ogaño.
Se*mpronio*: pues q*u*e: toda tu vida auias de llorar.   15
Ca*listo*: si.
Se*mpronio*: porque.
Ca*listo*: porq*u*e amo a aquella ante q*u*ien ta*n* i*n*digno me hallo: q*u*e no la
    espero alca*n*çar.

Se*mpronio*: o pusilanimo: o fi d*e* puta q*ue* nembrot: que magno alexa*n*dre: los   *20*
   quales no solo del señorio del mu*n*do: mas del cielo se juzgaron ser
   dignos.
Ca*listo*: no te oy bie*n* esso q*ue* dixiste torna di lo no procedas.
Se*mpronio*: dixe q*ue* tu que tienes mas coraço*n* q*ue* nembrot ni alexa*n*dre deses-
   peras de alcançar vna muger. muchas delas quales en gra*n*des estados consti-   *25*
   tuydas se sometieron alos pechos & resollos de viles azemileros: & otras a
   brutos animales: no has leydo de pasife co*n*el toro. de minerua co*n*el can.
Ca*listo*: No lo creo hablillas son.
Se*mpronio*: lo de tu abuela co*n*el ximio fablilla fue testigo es el cuchillo d*e* tu
   abuelo.   *30*
Ca*listo*: maldito sea este necio & q*ue* porradas dize.

Translation

C: What are you criticising me for?
S: For submitting the dignity of a man to the imperfection of a weak woman.
C: Woman? You ill-bred lout! A god(dess), a god(dess)!
S: Do you really believe that? Or are you joking?
C: Joking? I believe that she is a god(dess), I acknowledge her as a god(dess), and
   I believe that there is no other sovereign in heaven, even though she dwells
   among us.
S: (Ha, ha, ha! Did you ever hear such blasphemy? Did you ever see such blindness?)
C: What are you laughing about?
S: I'm laughing, because I didn't think there was a worse invention of sin than in
   Sodom.
C: How so?
S: Because they tried to commit abominations with angels in disguise, and you [try
   to do so] with the person you acknowledge to be a god(dess).
C: Damn you! You've made me laugh, something I didn't expect to do this year.
S: What for? Were you going to weep all your life long?
C: Yes.
S: Why?
C: Because I love one of whom I am so unworthy that I have no hope of possessing
   her.
S: (Oh, you coward, oh, you bastard! Just think of Nimrod and Alexander the Great,
   who thought themselves worthy not only to rule the world but heaven as well!)
C: I didn't hear what you said. Once again, say it, don't carry on [saying some-
   thing else].
S: I said that you, who have a stouter heart than either Nimrod or Alexander, are
   despairing of possessing a woman, many of whom, though they were of high
   rank, yielded to the breasts and breathings of base muleteers, and others to brute
   beasts. Haven't you read about Pasiphae and the bull, or Minerva and the dog?
C: I don't believe it; they are old wives' tales.
S: Was the story of your grandmother and the monkey an old wives' tale? The wit-
   ness to it is your cuckold of a grandfather.
C: Damn this idiot; what rubbish he talks!

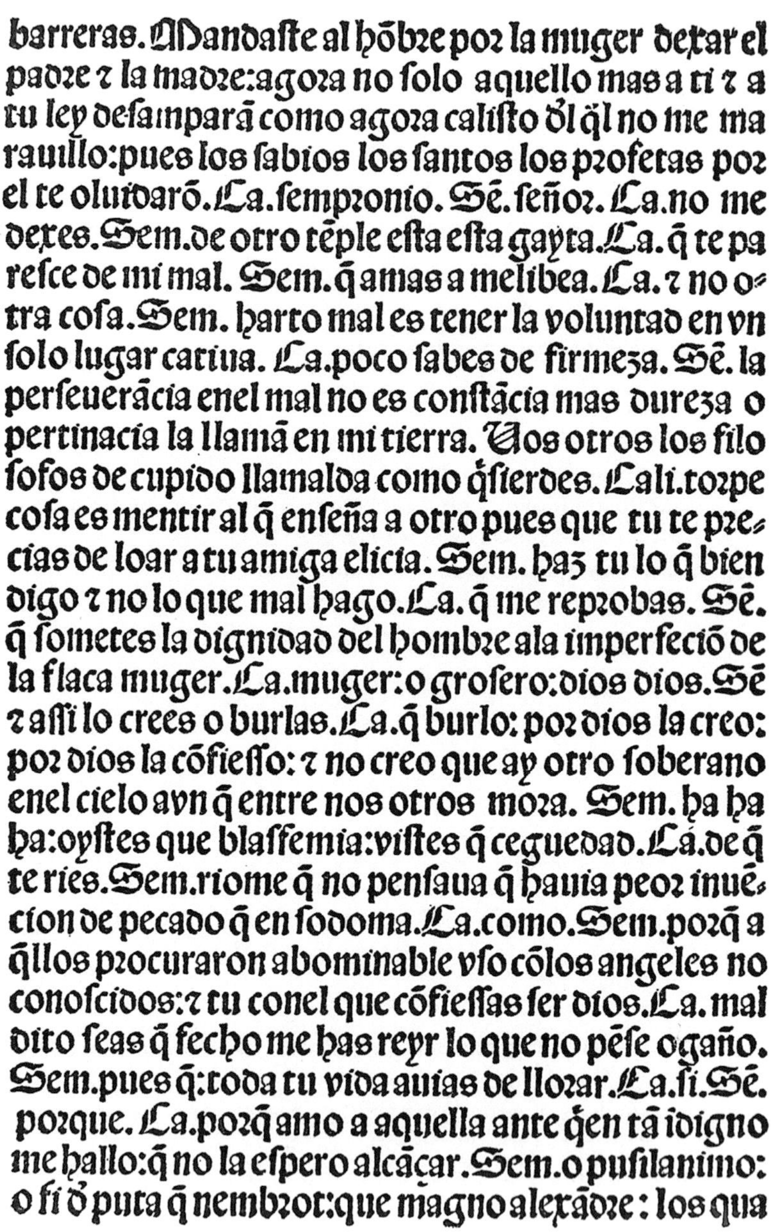

barreras.ODandaſte al hōbꝛe poꝛ la muger deꭇar el
padꝛe ⁊ la madꝛe:agoꝛa no ſolo aquello mas a ti ⁊ a
tu ley deſamparā como agoꝛa caliſto dl ꭇl no me ma
rauillo:pues los ſabios los ſantos los pꝛofetas poꝛ
el te oluidarō.Ca.ſempꝛonio.Sē.ſeñoꝛ.Ca.no me
deꭇes.Sem.de otro tēple eſta eſta gayta.Ca.ꝗ̃ te pa
reſce de mi mal.Sem.ꝗ̃ amas a melibea.Ca.⁊ no o⸗
tra coſa.Sem. harto mal es tener la voluntad en vn
ſolo lugar catiua.Ca.poco ſabes de firmeza.Sē. la
perſeuerācia enel mal no es conſtācia mas dureza o
pertinacia la llamā en mi tierra.Uos otros los filo
ſoſos de cupido llamalda como ꝗ̃ſierdes.Cali.toꝛpe
coſa es mentir al ꝗ̃ enſeña a otro pues que tu te pꝛe⸗
cias de loar a tu amiga elicia.Sem. haz tu lo ꝗ̃ bien
digo ⁊ no lo que mal hago.Ca.ꝗ̃ me repꝛobas.Sē.
ꝗ̃ ſometes la dignidad del hombꝛe ala imperfeciō de
la flaca muger.Ca.muger:o groſero:dios dios.Sē
⁊ aſſi lo crees o burlas.Ca.ꝗ̃ burlo: poꝛ dios la creo:
poꝛ dios la cōfieſſo: ⁊ no creo que ay otro ſoberano
enel cielo avn ꝗ̃ entre nos otros moꝛa. Sem. ha ha
ha:oyſtes que blaſſemia:viſtes ꝗ̃ ceguedad.Cá.de ꝗ̃
te ries.Sem.riome ꝗ̃ no penſaua ꝗ̃ hauia peoꝛ inuē⸗
cion de pecado ꝗ̃ en ſodoma.Ca.como.Sem.poꝛꝗ̃ a
ꝗ̃llos pꝛocuraron abominable vſo cōlos angeles no
conoſcidos:⁊ tu conel que cōfieſſas ſer dios.Ca. mal
dito ſeas ꝗ̃ fecho me has reyr lo que no pēſe ogaño.
Sem.pues ꝗ̃:toda tu vida auias de lloꝛar.Ca.ſi.Sē.
poꝛque.Ca.poꝛꝗ̃ amo a aquella ante ꝗ̃en tā idigno
me hallo:ꝗ̃ no la eſpero alcācar.Sem.o puſilanimo:
o ſi d puta ꝗ̃ nembꝛot:que magno aleꭇādꝛe: los qua

Plate 3 Tragicomedia de Calixto e Melibea, Burgos: Fadrique de Basilea, 1499, f.4v
(Text 15). Courtesy of The Hispanic Society of America, New York.

Phonetics and phonology

15.1.1 The spelling **imperfecion** (l.2) suggests the semipopular simplification of the consonantal group /kts/ of the learned borrowing *imperfección*.
   Keypoint: learned and popular, semilearned and semipopular (p. 277).

15.1.2 Initial *f* continues to be systematically used, with sporadic occurrences of *h*: **hallo** (l.18, see 11.3.2) and **hablillas** (l.28, see 9.3.7), suggesting that the initial ?/ɸ/ of Old Castilian is being weakened.
   Keypoint: the f>h change (p. 271).

15.1.3 The past participle **maldito** (l.14) < Lat. MĂLĔDICTU[M] [MĂLĔDĬCO] had a number of variant forms in Old Castilian. The popular phonetic evolution of the /kt/ group was to /tʃ/, as in the simple past participle *dicho* < DICTU[M] [DĪCO], cf. 4.1.1, 14.1.1, and this development is also found in many of the compounds of *dicho*: *entredicho, susodicho, contradicho, redicho*. Although the variant *maldicho* is attested in Old Castilian, MSp. *maldecir* (and its antonym *bendecir*, with which it clearly develops in parallel) have both analogically regularised past participles (*ha maldecido, fue maldecido*) and semipopular adjectival past participles *maldito* and *bendito* (with simplification of the /kt/ group to /t/). A number of verbs in Castilian have such doublet past participles, the learned form being always the one which is used adjectivally: some examples are *absorbido/absorto, corrompido/corrupto*.
   Keypoint: consonant groups (p. 267); **palatalisation** (p. 280).

15.1.4 Ximio (l.29) || MSp. *simio* < Lat. SĪMĬU[M] is one of a number of examples of an initial Latin /s/ developing to a palatal /ʃ/ in Old Castilian. These examples have been explained in a number of ways. Some are deemed to be borrowings from Mozarabic, on the grounds that Latin /s/ was regularly represented as /ʃ/ in Mozarabic texts (see 5b.1.2); others as back formations from morphologically related forms which had suffered phonetic modification for other reasons, e.g. *jugo* 'juice' < Lat. SŪCU[S] affected by the development of Lat. ?EXSŪCARE > *enjugar* 'to extract the juice from' → 'to dry'; others, such as *ximio*, have no ready explanation. They may simply have been variant pronunciations (Italian likewise has *scimmia*): we should also bear in mind that the three voiceless sibilant phonemes of Old Castilian (/ts/, /s/ and /ʃ/) were phonetically very close, and there is in fact evidence of a good deal of apparently fairly random exchange amongst them. Valle (1996) puts forward the hypothesis that [ʃ] was a rural pronunciation which underwent partial lexical diffusion before the Modern Spanish forms became fixed.
   Keypoint: the sibilants of Old Castilian (p. 290).

Morphology and syntax

15.2.1 The Modern Spanish rule requiring a subjunctive in the complement of a negated verb of saying or thinking (e.g. *no me parece que tengan dinero*) apparently does not hold here: on l.5 an indicative is used after **no creo**, and on l.9 after **no pensaua**.

15.2.2 There are a number of learned syntactic features.

In **la flaca muger** (l.2) and **brutos animales** (l.27), the adjective preceding the noun denotes a non-distinctive quality of the noun. The range of such epithets, as they are known in classical rhetoric, of which this device is probably an imitation, increases in Castilian prose from the fifteenth century onwards, and continues to be cultivated in formal written style, often with very subtle semantic effects in Modern Spanish (see 18.2.3, 26.2.1).

The Latinate 'accusative and infinitive' construction with verbs of saying and thinking can be seen in **el que confiessas ser dios** (l.13) and **se juzgaron ser dignos** (ll.21–2), cf. 13.2.7. The second of these is easily rendered in Modern Spanish with the full clause construction (*juzgaron que eran dignos*), but the first, which is itself a relative clause, is not so readily transposable (cf. the awkward and strictly ungrammatical *el que confiesas que es Dios*); this reveals that the 'accusative and infinitive' construction did have expressive advantages in Spanish, as well as being a feature associated with cultured prose (Pountain 1998b).

The inversion of past participle and auxiliary verb in **que fecho me as reyr** (l.14) is a feature sometimes associated with Latinate syntax, in which verbs were often moved to the end of their clause. Another example of this phenomenon is the inversion of adjective complement and verb in **ante quien tan indigno me hallo** (l.18).

15.2.3 The use of demonstratives as relative clause antecedents persists (**esso que dixiste**, l.23, cf. 4.2.1), though we also find **lo que no pensé ogaño** (l.14). The use of a demonstrative facilitates complex relativisation with prepositions: **aquella ante quien tan indigno me hallo** (l.18). See, in another connection, 6.2.7.
    Keypoint: relatives (p. 289).

15.2.4 Lo de (l.29) displays a typical use of the Castilian neuter in its meaning of 'the matter of'.
    Keypoint: gender (p. 275).

15.2.5 For **auias de llorar**, l.15, see **Keypoint: periphrastic verb forms** (p. 283).

Vocabulary

15.3.1 No solo . . . mas (l.21). There has been much movement in the meaning and usage of adversative conjunctions in Castilian. There are three principal words involved: *mas* < Lat. MĂGIS 'greater' → 'rather', *pero* < Lat. PER HŌC 'therefore' → 'nevertheless' and *sino* < Lat. SĪ NŌN 'if not', 'unless' → 'except'. In Old Castilian, *mas* is the most general term, encompassing many of the functions of MSp. *pero* and, as here, the contrastive function of MSp. *sino*. *Pero* was originally distinct from *mas* in that it had an exclusively restrictive adverbial meaning ('nevertheless'), though by the time of the *Celestina* it was rivalling *mas* in adversative usage, and overall is much more frequent. *Sino* originally had the meaning of 'except' and so was associated with marking exceptions to negatives; by the time of the *Celestina* it had come to rival *mas* in this usage. *Mas* in Modern Spanish is still encountered in registers which maintain archaic usage, but is obsolete in the spoken language.

15.3.2 Mora (l.6) derives from Lat. ?MŎRAT [MŎROR] 'to stop', 'remain'. OCast. **morar** had the meaning 'to dwell', which may be observed in the morphological derivative *morada*, which persists in Modern Spanish as a high register word meaning 'dwelling'. Modern Spanish does not readily discriminate the general notion of 'to live' from 'to dwell', *vivir* being used for both; this may be an example of the pruning of a semantic area rich in near synonyms.

15.3.3 There are several words of learned origin in this passage: **abominable** (l.12), **blasfemia** (l.7), **brutos** (l.27), **dignos** (l.22), **indigno** (l.18), **magno** (l.20) and **pusilanimo** (l.20). Learned influence also probably accounts for the use of **animales** (l.27); *animal* is originally from the Lat. adjectival noun ĂNĬMĀLE [ĂNĬMĂL], and is used adjectivally in Old Castilian; it resembled the Latin noun more closely than the metathesised development *alimaña* of the neuter plural ĂNĬMĀLĬA (see 11.1.6).
  Keypoints: consonant groups (p. 267); **palatalisation** (p. 280); **stress** (p. 291); **learned and popular, semilearned and semipopular** (p. 277).

15.3.4 Azemileros (l.26) is an example of a borrowing from Ar. √*zāmila* 'mule'.

15.3.5 The word **can** (l.27) < Lat. CĂNE [CĂNIS] makes satisfactory sense in the context (**brutos animales**), though it has been suggested that better sense is made of the mythological allusion to Minerva if the phrase **conel can** is read as *Vulcán*, i.e. the god Vulcan. However that may be, *can* is attested from the earliest texts, though it increasingly comes into competition with *perro*, which is of unknown origin and peculiar to Castilian. *Perro* may originally have been a popular, slang, word which was promoted in register (cf. 3.3.2, 22.3.2, 25.3.2, 29.3.1). In the Golden Age, *can* appears to have enjoyed some revival in literary register, either as a result of learned influence, its (by then) archaic nature, or its increasing association with higher registers (see Green 1953 and 1956).

15.3.6 Cuchillo (l.29) is a variant development of MSp. *cuclillo*, which is a diminutive derivative of *cuco* 'cuckoo'. Although the Latin form CŬCŬLU[S] is similar, it is likely that both the Latin word and the Spanish *cuco* are onomatopoeic creations (as English), representing the distinctive call of the cuckoo. The semantic extension of *cuclillo* to 'cuckold' is easily understood as the result of a metaphorical association with the cuckoo's laying its eggs in other birds' nests.

15.3.7 Porradas (l.31) probably belongs to colloquial register, and corresponds to the more neutral register form *necedad* (cf. **necio** < Lat. NESCĬU[S] 'ignorant' → 'stupid', l.31). The root *porra* is of unknown origin.

15.3.8 Ogaño (l.14) derives from the Latin phrase HŌC ANNŌ 'in this year'. This is one of the few instances in which the demonstrative HĪC survives in Romance, though it is unrecognisable (cf. 4.2.2). In Modern Spanish *ogaño* has been replaced by the analytic expression *este año*.
  Keypoint: adverbs (p. 262).

15.3.9 For **ante** (l.18) see 8.3.5.

VIII The Golden Age
Linguistic self-awareness

With the advent of humanism, scholars began to take an active interest in the vernacular. Writings about Castilian, in the shape of grammars, discourses and pedagogical works are of especial importance to historians of the language, since for the first time we have explicit statements about usage and variation in usage, the latter often as a result of discussion or prescription of what is represented as 'correct' or 'desirable' usage. Furthermore, some of these works formed the basis of the Spanish standard orthographical, grammatical and lexicographical traditions which continue to the present day.

16 The first grammar of Castilian. Antonio de Nebrija, *Gramática de la lengua castellana* (1492)

16.0 Antonio de Nebrija was born in Lebrija (Seville), the Roman Nebrissa Veneria, in 1441 or 1444 and died in 1522 in Alcalá de Henares. After studying in Salamanca, he spent some years at Bologna where he assimilated Italian humanism, especially the efforts of Lorenzo Valla to restore rigour in the study of Latin; the pursuit of a similar end in Spain, especially in Salamanca, was to be the motivating force of the rest of his life, beginning with the publication of the *Introductiones latinae* in 1481, which became a standard university textbook. It was far from being a peaceful academic endeavour, however, since he was in fact challenging the traditions of the university establishment of the time. It was also potentially hazardous: when Nebrija spent a brief period at the new University of Alcalá (founded by Cardinal Cisneros in 1499) working on the Polyglot Complutense Bible, his insistence, on philological grounds, that the text of the Latin Vulgate might be corrupt in parts brought him into conflict with theologians who insisted on the inviolable nature of the biblical text, and he had to leave the project.

The *Gramática de la lengua castellana* is usually reckoned as the first ever grammar of a Romance vernacular. It is partly the product of genuine humanist interest in the vernacular, but it was no doubt chiefly motivated by a desire to make potential students of Latin aware of linguistic structure, and in particular the structure of Latin, through the medium of their own language. Comparisons with Latin, as we see in the extract below, are frequent, though the grammar is broadly descriptive in nature, and there is no attempt to make Castilian closer to Latin. Although Nebrija follows the traditional strategy for writing a grammar of Latin and uses Latin grammatical terminology, he is always aware of the essentially different structure of Castilian, as the first sentence here (ll.2–3) reveals; more specifically, in his discussion of the passive, he perceptively observes that Castilian does not really have a passive inflection as Latin did, but uses a verbal paraphrase (*rodeo* or *circunloquio*) consisting of *ser* + past participle or a third person reflexive, and that, furthermore, the impersonal function of the Latin passive is rendered in Castilian by a third person plural or a reflexive.

The year of the publication of the *Gramática*, 1492, was propitious. This *annus mirabilis* opened with the fall of the Moorish kingdom of Granada to the forces of the Reyes Católicos and closed with the news of the discovery of America by a Spanish expedition under Columbus. The *Gramática* is dedicated to Queen Isabel herself, at whose request Nebrija had prepared a Castilian translation of the *Introductiones Latinae* in 1486, and the dedication, though no doubt politically motivated (royal patronage would have been important to Nebrija's personal crusade to reform the teaching of Latin), makes a number of claims which we can with hindsight see were astonishingly well motivated. First, foreigners (and in these are included *vizcaínos* and *navarros*) would be able to learn Spanish more easily with the aid of such a grammar; this is a dimension which has never been far away from the minds of many subsequent writers of grammars and dictionaries in Castilian, and effectively marks the beginning of teaching of Spanish as a foreign language; it also suggests the growing importance of Castilian as a world language. Second, in a famous phrase, Nebrija appropriately describes language as 'compañera del imperio'. The fortunes of Latin as the language of the Roman empire and its consequent dissemination through much of the western world were certainly in his thoughts; and though Nebrija probably had only the expansion of Castilian in the Iberian Peninsula in mind, we can now see how Spanish was on the threshold of undergoing a further, and much more massive, expansion in the New World in very much the same way as Latin had expanded its use in Europe through the Roman empire. Third, he refers to language as a unifying force in the nation, and again we can see how Castilian was quite shortly to become the effective standard of the new union of Castile and Aragon, with the rapid exclusion of Aragonese, Catalan and other vernaculars. Strongly centralised government and the universal imposition of Castilian have gone hand in hand at many points in Spain's subsequent history. Fourth, Nebrija points to the need to stabilise, or, as we would now say, standardise, the vernacular. He may well have had in mind here the 'degeneration' of Latin and have been keen, consistently with his agenda for Latin, to avoid a similar fate for Castilian, which he (naively, we would think today) saw as being at its zenith. But in fact linguistic standardisation is a feature of all advanced societies, where it is an advantage for education, literature and official documents to be in a standard linguistic form; latterly, the first task in re-establishing other languages of the Peninsula has similarly been the creation of standardised spellings and grammars. We must also remember that the cultural revolution to be brought about by printing was just under way, and that printing houses would increasingly seek standardised 'house styles' and criteria for spelling and usage. Lastly (and no doubt this clinched the royal seal of approval), Nebrija points out how language is the vehicle for the transmission of present glories to future ages. Indeed, the vernacular had been used for such a purpose since Alfonso X, and this may be seen as a further assertion of the status of Castilian as opposed to Latin.

Amongst Nebrija's other works are the *Diccionario latino-español* of 1492 and the *Vocabulario español-latino* of around 1495, which formed the basis for many subsequent dictionaries, including Covarrubias's *Tesoro de la lengua castellana* of 1611, and the *Reglas de orthographia en la lengua castellana* of 1517 which, building on his work in the *Gramática*, proposed an essentially phonemic spelling system for Castilian, the basic principles of which have been mantained ever since.

The text

The text is transcribed from a facsimile of the original Salamanca edition of 1492 (Marcos Marín 1993). Accentuation is totally editorial, and punctuation has been extended to conform to modern practice, following Quilis (1980:187); otherwise it is faithful to the original. Given the interest of Nebrija's proposals about Castilian spelling (see below), it is clearly very important not to change any orthographical conventions in this text.

Further reading

Bahner (1966); Quilis (1980); Rico (1978).

Delos circunloquios del verbo.

[A]ssí como en muchas cosas la lengua castellana abunda sobre el latín, assí por el contrario, la lengua latina sobra al castellano, como en esto dela conjugación. El latín tiene tres bozes: activa, verbo impersonal, passiva; el castellano no tiene sino sola el activa. El verbo impersonal   *5*
suple lo por las terceras personas del plural del verbo activo del mesmo tiempo & modo, o por las terceras personas del singular, haziendo en ellas reciprocación & retorno con este pronombre 'se'; & assí por lo que en el latín dizen 'curritur, currebatur', nos otros dezimos 'corren, corrían', o 'córrese, corríase'; & assí por todo lo restante de la conjugación. La passiva *10*
suple la por este verbo 'so, eres' & el participio del tiempo passado de la passiva mesma, assí como lo haze el latín en los tiempos que faltan en la mesma passiva; assí que por lo que el latín dize 'amor, amabar, amabor', nos otros dezimos 'io so amado, io era amado, io seré amado', por rodeo deste verbo 'so, eres' & deste participio 'amado'; & assí de todos los otros   *15*
tiempos. Dize esso mesmo las terceras personas dela boz passiva por las mesmas personas de la boz activa, haziendo retorno con este pronombre 'se', como dezíamos del verbo impersonal, diziendo 'ámasse Dios; ámanse las riquezas, por es amado Dios; son amadas las riquezas'.

Translation

As in many features the Castilian language has more [forms] than Latin, so vice versa Latin has more [forms] than Castilian in conjugation. Latin has three voices: active, impersonal verb and passive; Castilian only has the active. It replaces the impersonal verb by the third person plural of the active verb in the same tense and mood, or by the third person singular, made reflexive by the pronoun *se*; and so for Latin *curritur, currebatur* ['people run, people ran'] we say *corren, corrían*, or *córrese, corríase*, and similarly for the rest of the conjugation. It substitutes the passive by the verb *so, eres* plus the past participle of the same passive, just as Latin does in the tenses which are lacking in the passive; so where Latin says *amor, amabar, amabor* ['I am loved, I was loved, I will be loved'], we say *io so amado, io era amado, io seré amado*, by a turn of phrase consisting of the verb *so, eres* and the participle *amado*, and so on in all the other tenses. It expresses the third persons of the passive voice by the same persons of the active voice in the reflexive, as we said for the impersonal verb, saying *ámasse Dios; ámanse las riquezas*, for *es amado Dios; son amadas las riquezas*.

Phonetics and phonology

16.1.1 Nebrija uses here a first version of the spelling system he was to elaborate in more detail in the *Reglas de orthographia*. The guiding principle is 'tenemos de escrivir como pronunciamos, y pronunciar como escrivimos' (Quilis 1980: 116); he rejects etymological and logographic spellings in favour of a system which is broadly phonemic, although some letters correspond to more than one sound (e.g. *g* represents /g/ before *a*, *o* and *u* and /ʒ/ before *e* or *i*) and conversely one sound can be represented by more than one letter (e.g. /ʒ/ is represented by both *g* and *j*). None the less, as in Modern Spanish, the system is phonemic to the extent that we can deduce the phonemic system from the spelling even though the spelling is not maximally simple. He takes the step of establishing as individual letters *ç* (/ts/), *ll* (/ʎ/), *ñ* (/ɲ/) and *c̃h* (/tʃ/), and uses *x̃* (in the *Reglas* without a tilde) to represent /ʃ/; *x* is otherwise suppressed, being replaced by *s* in learned borrowings from Latin, e.g. *estender*; he eliminates the letters *q*, *k* and *y* and uses *j* (the 'long *i*') to represent /ʒ/; he distinguishes vocalic or semivocalic *u* from consonantal *v*. *H* is reserved for the aspirate result of Latin initial /f/ and is not used etymologically or in the representation of the initial group /we/.

Later practice was not to be so radical: etymological *h* and *x* were restored, as was *h* in the initial *hue-* sequence (MSp. *huevo* for Nebrija's proposed *uevo*). The custom of considering *ll* and *ch* as separate letters, however, continued until 1994, when the Asociación de las Academias de la Lengua Española agreed no longer to do so (the only practical consequence of which was in fact to cease the alphabetical ordering of *ll* after *l* and *ch* after *c*, since spelling itself was not affected), but *ñ* continues to be counted as a separate letter, and indeed has become a symbol of Spanish individuality, being adopted in the logo of the Instituto Cervantes.

16.1.2 Orthographic distinctions between *ss* and *s* and between *ç* and *z* were still made, though Nebrija does not comment on this feature of spelling (interestingly neither suppressing *ss* nor requiring that *ss* be thought of as a separate letter). Although *ss* was not generally used for /s/ at the beginning of a word or morpheme (cf. **córrese**, l.10), the spelling **ámasse** (l.18) may indicate consciousness of a continuing distinction between /s/ and /z/.
   Keypoint: the sibilants of Old Castilian (p. 290).

16.1.3 In his *Orthographia*, Nebrija insists on a distinction between *b* and *v*, though recognising that some people make the distinction neither in speech nor writing: 'algunos de los nuestros apenas las [la *b* y la *v* consonante] pueden distinguir, assí en la escriptura como en la pronunciación, siendo entre ellas tanta diferencia quanta puede ser entre cualesquier dos letras' (Alonso 1967: 23–4). Despite this strong view, we find here Nebrija himself using the spelling **boz** < Lat. VŌCE [VOX]. This raises a number of interesting questions: perhaps the distinction was not as real as Nebrija thought, or perhaps the 'mistake' in spelling was not made by Nebrija himself but by a typesetter (on this question, see also 18.1.4).

   Keypoint: the 'b/v' distinction (p. 262).

16.1.4 For **mesmo** (l.6, etc.), see **Keypoint:** *mismo* (p. 279).

Morphology and syntax

16.2.1 The passage is valuable for the equivalences it establishes between the Latin passive and the expression of this notion in Castilian. Nebrija shows a considerable independence of mind in not limiting his attention to the *ser* + past participle construction but in presenting the reflexive as a passive equivalent. However, his example **ámasse Dios** (l.18) appears odd; it would be resisted in Modern Spanish on the grounds that it could be interpreted literally as 'God loves himself' (though an indefinite subject reflexive with a personal *a* could be used unequivocally: *se ama a Dios*). In fact, the stricture against the use of a 'reflexive passive' in cases where a literal reflexive interpretation is possible may be nothing more than later purist pressure, and in colloquial Modern Spanish we find usages such as *nos vamos a matar* 'we'll all get killed' (for an earlier example from Old Castilian, see 12.2.9). Such usages are possible because pragmatically the passive interpretation is more likely than the literal reflexive interpretation, and the same is true of Nebrija's example: it is more natural to assert that people love God than that God loves himself, and so there is no risk of misinterpretation.

   In **en el latín dizen** . . . (ll.8–9) a 3rd p.pl. verb is used to express the notion of an indefinite subject, as in Nebrija's glossing of the Latin impersonal passive *curritur* by **corren** (l.9).

   Keypoints: the passive (p. 281); **the reflexive** (p. 288).

16.2.2 La lengua latina sobra al castellano (l.3). The 'personal' *a* is here used with a non-personal object, as became usual in Modern Spanish with a number of verbs of 'precedence' (*seguir, sustituir, preceder*, etc.). The motivation for this usage, which is clearly an extension from the original use of the object *a* as a marker of respect or personality, may be to make the identity of the object clearer when subject and object belong to the same semantic category, as is typically the case with these verbs.

   Keypoint: 'personal' *a* (p. 283).

16.2.3 There is left-dislocation of **el verbo impersonal**, l.5, and **la passiva**, l.10 (contrast 7.2.11) and the consequent introduction of the 'resumptive' pronouns *lo* and *la*.

16.2.4 Nebrija consistently uses **nos otros** (ll.9 and 14), written as two words, in the *Gramática* as the subject and prepositional object (i.e. the tonic) forms of the 1st p.pl. pronoun. In describing the Castilian pronouns, however, he refers to *nos* as the canonical form, and links *nosotros* and *vosotros* with such expressions as *io mesmo*, saying that they are emphatic in nature (Quilis 1980: 180). Certainly *nosotros* often, as here, had a contrastive value (Castilian speakers as opposed to Latin speakers), but the very general use of *nosotros* suggests that it was becoming the preferred form of the pronoun; we must bear in mind that in Spanish, a pro-drop language, any subject pronoun carries a degree of emphasis – cf. the plainly contrastive usage of *vos* in earlier times identified in 7.2.8. (See 17.2.1 for the continuing distinction between *vos* and *vosotros*.)
   Keypoint: personal pronouns (p. 284).

16.2.5 Some contracted forms of preposition + demonstrative continued from Old Castilian: **deste** = *de* + *este* (l.15) is such a form (see also 17.1.4).

16.2.6 For the **no … sino …** construction (l.5), see 15.3.1; for *el* used as the article preceding an initial *a-* (**el activa**, l.5), see 8.2.4 and 13.2.9.

Vocabulary

16.3.1 Nebrija consistently refers to his language as **castellano** (l.2): *español* is used only once in the *Gramática*, as an example of an adjective referring to a nation, and it is clear that *España* is construed as the union of its constituent states at this time. There was hence as yet no notion of a 'national' language, though Nebrija clearly thought that the elevation of Castilian to national standard status was desirable (see above, 16.0).

16.3.2 The first sentence (ll.2–3) expresses a direct contrast and hence uses the same verbal notion of 'to exceed'; in accordance with rhetorical practice, Nebrija avoids using the same word twice and chooses two near synonyms, **abundar** (**sobre**) (l.2) and **sobrar** (**a**) (l.3). **Sobrar** < Lat. [SŬPĔRO] 'to be above', 'to be in abundance', 'to overcome' is in Modern Spanish restricted and slightly changed in meaning to 'to be over-abundant', 'to be too much', and its former meaning of 'to overcome' is rendered by a later learned doublet development, *superar*. **Abundar** < Lat. ĂBUNDO 'to abound', while a near synonym for *sobrar* at this time in its intransitive meaning, seems not normally to be used with *sobre* in this fashion; Nebrija's need was to create a parallel to **sobrar a**.

16.3.3 There are many items of 'technical' vocabulary in this extract which are either learned borrowings or use existing words with the corresponding technical meanings of their etyma: **conjugación**, **boz**, **activa/passiva**, **impersonal**, **personas**, **singular**, **reciprocación**, **pronombre**, **participio**, **tiempo**, **modo**. **Restante** (l.10) was also a learned borrowing; the exploitation of the Latin present participle inflection *-nte* was much favoured in the fifteenth century.
   Keypoint: learned and popular, semilearned and semipopular (p. 277).

16.3.4 Rodeo (l.14) was a morphological derivative of Lat. √RŎTA 'wheel', first attested in the thirteenth century; it may be used in preference to the learned **circunloquio** of the title because it was more readily understandable (this is possibly the first attestation of **circunloquio**).

17 The 'best' Spanish? Juan de Valdés, *Diálogo de la lengua* (1535)

17.0 Juan de Valdés was born in Cuenca at the end of the fifteenth century and died in Naples in 1541. Little is known of his early life; he was in the service of the Marqués de Villena before studying at the University of Alcalá de Henares, from where he began to correspond with Erasmus, and had to leave Spain for Italy after incurring the displeasure of the Inquisition with the publication of a humanist-inspired work on Christian doctrine. He eventually settled in Naples, where he produced a number of highly regarded religious works which were only published after his death.

   The *Diálogo de la lengua* was directed towards an Italian-speaking public, though the enterprise was consistent with other humanist publications of the sixteenth century which sought to 'defend' and 'enrich' vernacular languages: for example, Pietro Bembo's *Prose della volgar lingua* of 1525, à propos of which Valdés says, in the person of Marcio, 'prueva que todos los hombres somos más obligados a ilustrar y enriquecer la lengua que nos es natural y que mamamos en las tetas de nuestras madres, que no la que nos es pegadiza y que aprendemos en libros' (Lope Blanch 1969: 44). It is a mine of information on the Spanish of the time, especially on attitudes towards different variants, Valdés consistently praising the cultured usage of Toledo (which would be eclipsed by Madrid on the removal of the court to Madrid by Philip II). Castilian was by this time irrevocably fixed as the standard language of the whole of Spain, although it had many regional variations; as Valdés tells us (Lope Blanch 1969: 62):

> Si me avéis de preguntar de las diversidades que ay en el hablar castellano entre unas tierras y otras, será nunca acabar, porque como la lengua castellana se habla no solamente por toda Castilla, pero en el reino de Aragón, en el de Murcia con toda el Andaluzía, y en Galizia, Asturias y Navarra, y esto aun hasta entre la gente vulgar, porque entre la gente noble tanto bien se habla en todo el resto de Spaña, cada provincia tiene sus vocablos propios y sus maneras de dezir, y es assí que el aragonés tiene unos vocablos propios y unas propias maneras de dezir, y el andaluz tiene otros y otras, y el navarro otros y otras, y aun ay otros y otras en tierra de Campos, que llaman Castilla la Vieja, y otros y otras en el reino de Toledo, de manera que, como digo, nunca acabaríamos.

Evidence of the pre-eminence of Castilian within Spain is that literary activity from the beginning of the sixteenth century was almost wholly in Castilian, despite the very recent union of the Castilian and Aragonese crowns under the Reyes Católicos in 1474. A telling case is that of the Catalan Boscán who was a key figure in Castilian literature of the period (see Text 20). Castilian was also beginning to enjoy great prestige throughout Europe as Spain increased in imperial might; an important symptom (or even contributory cause) of this was the attitude of Charles I (better known as the Holy Roman Emperor Charles V), who, though not a native speaker, used Castilian to utter in Italy on 17 April 1536 his famous challenge before Pope Paul III to François I of France, reputedly answering the French ambassador's complaint with the words (Lapesa 1981:297):

> 'Señor obispo, entiéndame si quiere, y no espere de mí otras palabras que de mi lengua española, la cual es tan noble que merece ser sabida y entendida de toda la gente cristiana.'

As for Italy itself, Valdés himself tells us (through Marcio) that 'ya en Italia assí entre damas como entre cavalleros se tiene por gentileza y galanía saber hablar castellano' (Lope Blanch 1969: 41), and the grammarian Jiménez Patón remarked that the Roman nobility sought Spanish tutors for their children (Pastor 1929: xxvii).

The text

Three MSS of the *Diálogo* survive, all dating from the second half of the sixteenth century. The MS belonging to the Biblioteca Nacional appears to be the source for the other two, which are in the Escorial Library and the British Library. The work was not printed until the eighteenth century, when it was included in Gregorio Mayáns y Siscar's *Orígenes de la lengua española* (1737: 1–178). The following extract is reprinted from Lope Blanch (1969: 108–10), who follows Barbolani de García (1967), Montesinos (1928) and Lapesa (1940).

Further reading

Barbolani de García (1982); Hamilton (1953); Mazzocco (1997).

Marcio: ... Y dexando esto, nos dezid de dónde viene que algunos españoles cn muchos vocablos, que por el ordinario escrivís con *z*, ellos ni la pronuncian ni la escriven.

Valdés: Esse es vicio particular de las lenguas de los tales, que no les sirven para aquella asperilla pronunciación de la *z* y ponen en su lugar la *s* y   *5* por *hazer* dicen *haser*, y por *razón*, *rasón*, y por *rezio*, *resio*, etc. ¿No os parece que podría passar adonde quiera por bachiller en romance y ganar mi vida con estas bachillerías?

Marcio: Largamente ... passemos a lo que haze al caso. Al principio dixistes que la lengua castellana, demás del *a.b.c.* latino, tiene una *j* larga que vale *10* lo que al toscano *gi*, y una *cerilla* que puesta debaxo de la *c* la haze sonar casi como *z*, y una *tilde*, que puesta sobre la *n*, vale lo que al latino y toscano *g*. Querríamos que nos dixéssedes lo que observáis acerca destas letras o señales.

Valdés: Quanto a la *j* larga me parece averos dicho todo lo que se puede   *15* dezir.

Pacheco: Assí es verdad.

Valdés: Quanto a la cerilla, que es una señaleja que ponemos en algunos
vocablos debaxo de la *c*, digo que pienso pudo ser que la *c* con la cerilla
antiguamente fuessen una *z* entera.   *20*

Marcio: Quanto que esso, no os lo sufriré. ¿Queréis dezir que el tiempo corta
las letras como las peñas?

Valdés: Donoso sois. No quiero dezir que las corta el tiempo, sino que los
hombres, por descuido, con el tiempo las cortan. Pero esto no importa;
séase como se fuere. Lo que importa es dezir que la cerilla se ha de   *25*
poner quando, juntándose la *c* con *a*, con *o* y con *u* el sonido ha de ser
espesso, diziendo *çapato, coraçon, açúcar*.

Pacheco: Y quando se junta con *e* y con *i*, para dezir *cecear* y *cimiento*, ¿no se
ha de poner la cerilla?

Valdés: No, que no se ha de poner.   *30*

Pacheco: ¿Por qué?

Valdés: Porque con cerilla o sin ella, siempre pronunciáis essos vocablos y los
semejantes a ellos de una mesma manera; pues pudiendôs ahorrar la
cerilla, indiscreción sería ponerla.

Pacheco: Tenéis muy gran razón, yo me la ahorraré de aquí adelante.   *35*

Coriolano: ¿Cómo sabré yo quándo tengo de poner essa cerilla, o como la
llamáis, debaxo dessas letras, y quándo no?

Valdés. La mesma pronunciación os lo enseñará.

Coriolano. De manera que para saber escrivir bien ¿es menester saber primero
pronunciar bien?   *40*

Valdés: ¿Quién no lo sabe esso?

Translation

M: . . . And leaving this aside, tell us how it comes about that in some words in which
they ordinarily write a *z*, some Spaniards neither pronounce nor write it.

V: That is a fault which is particular to the tongues of such people, which are
not able to make the sharp pronunciation of the *z*, and put in its place the
s, and for *hazer* say *haser*, and for *razón, rasón*, and for *rezio, resio*, etc. Don't
you think that I could pass anywhere as a *bachiller* [expert] on the vernacular and earn my living from such *bachillerías* [pearls of wisdom]?

M: Most surely . . . Let's get back to the point. At the outset you said that the
Castilian language, besides the *a, b, c* of Latin, has a long *j* which has the
same value as the Tuscan *gi*, and a *cedilla* which placed below the *c* makes
it sound almost like a *z*, and a *tilde*, which placed over the *n*, has the same
value as Latin and Tuscan *g* [because *gn* in Italian has the same phonetic
value ([ɲ]) as *ñ* in Spanish]. We would like you to give us your observations
on these letters or signs.

V: As far as the long *j* is concerned, I think I've said all there is to be said.

P: That's true.

V: As far as the cedilla is concerned, which is a sign we place under the *c* in
some words, I would say that I think it could have been that *c* with the cedilla
was formerly a whole *z*.

M: I won't grant you that. Do you mean that time can cut letters like rocks?

V: What a wit! I don't mean that time cuts them, but that with time people, through carelessness, cut them. But that's unimportant; let it stand. The important thing to say is that the cedilla must be used when the sound of the *c*, when it goes with *a, o,* or *u*, has to be thick, saying *çapato, coraçon, açúcar.*

P: And when it goes with *e* and *i*, in *cecear* and *cimiento*, don't you have to use the cedilla?

V: No, you don't have to use it.

P: Why?

V: Because with or without the cedilla, you always pronounce those and similar words in the same way; so, since you can save yourself the cedilla, it would be superfluous to use it.

P: You're absolutely right, I'll stop doing so from now on.

C: How will I know when I have to use the cedilla, or whatever you call it, under those letters, and when not?

V: The pronunciation itself will tell you.

C: So in order to write well, you must first know how to pronounce well?

V: Whoever doesn't know that?

Phonetics and phonology

17.1.1 The substitution of *z* by *s* which Marcio and Valdés discuss (ll.1–6) can be seen as indicative of incipient *seseo*, the spelling **razón** representing [radzon] and the spelling **rasón** representing [razon]. Valdés regards this, as is to be expected, as a *vicio*, for it is not a feature of the speech of Toledo; Valdés held Andalusian in low esteem, and makes disparaging remarks about Nebrija (cf. Text 16) who was an *andaluz*: 'él era de Andaluzía, donde la lengua no stá muy pura' (Lope Blanch 1969: 46).

Valdés himself still makes the orthographical distinctions corresponding to the medieval sibilant phonemes: *ss* for /s/ in **fuessen** (l.20), *s* for /z/ in **caso** (l.9), *ç* for /ts/ in **coraçon** (l.27), *z* for /dz/ in **dezid** (l.1), *x* for /ʃ/ in **dexando** (l.1), *j* for /ʒ/ in **scñaleja** (l.18).

Keypoint: the sibilants of Old Castilian (p. 290).

17.1.2 Valdés's own spelling system is rigorously worked out. He continues the principle (16.1.1) that spelling must reflect pronunciation (ll.36–41). At the same time spelling must be maximally economical: hence his statement (ll.32–4) that the *ç* should not be used where it is not 'needed' (this is the principle followed in a rather different way in modern orthography, when *z* is usually not used before a front vowel; at the same time, the use of both *c* and *ç* in Valdés to represent /ts/ and of *c* and *z* in modern Spanish to represent /θ/ goes against the 'one letter one phoneme' principle).

17.1.3 Valdés consistently represents the initial /h/ < Lat. /f/ by *h* (**hazer**, l.5) and in another passage (Lope Blanch 1969: 97) states his principle of not using *h* where it is silent (i.e., etymological spellings of words beginning with *h* in Latin) except in the verb forms *he* and *ha* and in words beginning with /we/, e.g. *huér-fano*. However, spellings such as **hombres** (l.24), as well as elsewhere *historia* and *hora*, are found in this edition, which suggest that amendments were probably made to Valdés's original version by the printer.

   Keypoint: **the f>h change** (p. 271).

17.1.4 A device used by Valdés to represent *sinalefa* is the circumflex accent (e.g. **pudiendôs**, l.33, modern *pudiéndoos*). In **dessas** (l.37) *sinalefa* is not overtly represented, though such morphological contractions are frequent at this time, as in Old Castilian (see 16.2.5).

17.1.5 Valdés himself introduces the use of an acute accent to mark stress in verb forms which might otherwise be confused, e.g. **enseñará** (l.38) versus *enseñara*. Other uses of the acute accent in this text are editorial.

Morphology and syntax

17.2.1 The pronoun **vos**, with the corresponding second person plural verb form, is used as a polite singular (9.2.1, 13.2.8), as shown by the singular adjective in **Donoso sois** (l.23). *Vosotros*, with the same verb form, is used consistently in the *Diálogo* for the plural.

   Keypoint: **personal pronouns** (p. 284).

17.2.2 Second person plural verb forms show syncope of the intervocalic /d/ in the present tense (**pronunciáis**, l.32, **tenéis**, l.35), but note the persistence of the /d/ in the proparoxytone **dixéssedes** (l.13) || MSp. *dijeseis* ≤ Lat. DĪXISSĒTIS [DĪCO] (see 7.2.6, 13.2.2, 14.2.1). **Dixistes** (l.9) || MSp. *dijisteis* ≤ Lat. DĪXISTĪ [DĪCO] does not yet have its modern analogical *-eis* ending (cf. 13.2.3).

17.2.3 Clitic pronouns still do not occur in absolute initial position. While they now regularly follow the gerund (**juntándose**, l.26; **pudiendôs**, l.33: contrast 10.2.9), they may still precede the imperative (**nos dezid**, l.1, though *dezidnos* is found regularly elsewhere in the text).

   Keypoint: **clitic pronoun position** (p. 264).

17.2.4 The expression **séase como fuere** (l.25) shows the future subjunctive form **fuere** which has survived in Modern Spanish in this idiom.

   Keypoint: **the future subjunctive** (p. 275).

17.2.5 The complementiser *que* is absent in **pienso pudo ser** ... (l.19 and cf. 12.2.3). This is a frequent feature of sixteenth-century prose (cf. 22.2.6, 23.2.4).

17.2.6 For **tener de** + infinitive (l.36) see 13.2.5.

17.2.7 **¿Quién no lo sabe esso?** (l.41) is an unusual example of the use of a 'redundant' direct object pronoun (see 24.2.5 and the observations in 33.2.5).

Vocabulary

17.3.1 Cerilla (l.18), also used by Nebrija, is a variant form of *cedilla*, a diminutive of *zeda* (< Gk. ζῆτα), 'the letter *z*'. It was used both as the name of the ç and the cedilla itself. This orthographical device, abandoned in later Spanish (22.1.1), was of Spanish origin. The phonetic change of intervocalic /d/ to /r/ is unusual, though: a well-known modern example is the *cante jondo* musical form *seguiriya* corresponding to standard *seguidilla*.

18 The etiquette of address. Gonzalo de Correas, *Arte de la lengua española castellana* (1625)

18.0 Gonzalo de Correas Iñigo was born in Jaraíz (Plasencia) in 1570 or 1571 and died in Salamanca, where he spent most of his life, first as a student and then as the holder of chairs in Greek and Hebrew, in 1631. Of all the Golden-Age writers on the vernacular, he is the most original and perceptive. He adopted a phonemic spelling system which was different from Nebrija's, and was an acute observer and recorder of dialectal, chronological, sociolinguistic and stylistic variation in Spanish, not to mention his perception of language attitudes (compare his reference to ' à su parezer cortesanos criticos' below, ll.4–5). He tells us in the *Ortografia kastellana* (1630), for instance, that *ceceo* coexists with *seseo* in Seville, and that it is found sporadically in localities which are some way apart; he also says that *ceceante* speakers are laughed at by their neighbours (Alarcos García 1954: xxvii-iii). From this we can deduce that *ceceo* was a social, as well as a geographical, variant, and that already *seseo* was held in greater esteem (as in Andalusia it still is today). At another point he observes that *cautivar* and *rescatar* are used 'pasivamente' by 'xente de gherra'; in other words, these verbs undergo a change of valency to mean, respectively, 'to be captured', 'to be rescued', but that this development is restricted to soldiers' usage (*ibid.* 322). His is by far the most detailed among the accounts of Spanish syntax that we have from this period, as the following treatment of forms of address amply shows.

This is not to say that Correas has completely separated description from prescription or personal idiosyncrasy. He calls *ceceo* a 'necedad', for instance, revealing his own subjective attitude to the phenomenon, and regards what with hindsight we can see as the newer usage of *¿te vas?* instead of *¿vaste?* as that of 'inadvertidos' (*ibid.* 189). He presents the use of the second person plural verb forms in -*ades*, -*edes* as canonical instead of what he recognises as the increasingly used -*áis*, -*éis* forms.

Generally, Correas took as the norm the language of 'la xente de mediana i menor talla, en quien mas se conserva la lengua i propiedad'; he rejected not only low-class usage ('grosero', 'tosco') but also usages which he regarded as affected or academic ('cortesano', 'estudiantado', 'de escuelas'), and, as we see in his rather limited notion of language use in the passage below (ll.6–7), he is thoroughly disapproving of the stylistic imitation of Latin or Italian. Thus for him the use of the possessive with the definite article (e.g. *la mi capa*) was more acceptable than that without (*mi capa*) because 'el pueblo' adopted the former and those who affected to be 'cortesanos' the latter (*ibid.* 144). At the same time, he was aware of variations in the norm and did not castigate local usage just because it did not conform to his own concept of the Castilian norm: he observes, for instance, that in Aragon (which was only Castilianised in the course of the sixteenth century) the use of *el aquel* rather than *aquel* was not considered 'grosero' (*ibid.* 186). He was also favourably disposed towards older literary usages, such as the word *ende*, which, while restricted to the speech of rustics and old people, he dubs 'antiguo i mui elegante' (*ibid.* 340).

The text

This extract is taken from Alarcos García (1954: 363), which is a palaeographic edition of the Biblioteca Nacional MS 18969, thought to be a copy made for the press and corrected by Correas himself, though never published until the twentieth century. The only substantial modification to the original is the regularisation of the use of capital letters.

> I quanto la orazion fuere guardando la dicha orden natural irá mas clara, propia, dulze i grave. I es mas lexitimo i propio estilo este de la lengua Castellana, que de la Latina i Griega, i mas conforme al umor Español. No entendiendo esto algunos modernos poetas, i à su parezer cortesanos criticos, enrredan de manera su lenguaxe i conzertos que hablan en 5 xerigonza, i huien de hablar Castellano claro i bueno, sino bastardeado con un poco de Latin ò Italiano que saben. La lengua para que es sino para darse à entender, i declararse?
>
> Devese tanbien mucho notar la desorden, i discordante concordia, que á introduzido el uso, ora por modestia, ora por onrra, ò adulazion. Para lo 10 qual es menester primero advertir, que se usan quatro diferenzias de hablar para quatro calidades de personas, que son: *vuestra merzed, él, vos, tu* ... De *merzed* usamos llamar à las personas à quien rrespetamos, i debemos ò queremos dar onrra, como son: xuezes, cavalleros, eclesiasticos, damas, i xente de capa negra, i es lo mas despues de *señoria. Él* usan los 15 maiores con el que no quieren darle *merzed*, ni tratarle de *vos*, que es mas baxo, i propio de amos à criados, i la xente vulgar i de aldea, que no tiene uso de hablar con *merzed*, llama de *él* al que quiere onrrar de los de su xaez. De *vos* tratamos à los criados i mozos grandes, i à los labradores, i à personas semexantes; i entre amigos adonde no ai gravedad, ni 20 cunplimiento se tratan de *vos*, i ansien rrazonamientos delante de rreies i dirixidos à ellos se habla de *vos* con devido rrespeto i uso antiguo. De *tu* se trata à los muchachos i menores de la familia, i à los que se quisieren bien: i quando nos enoxamos i rreñimos con alguno le tratamos de *él*, i de *vos* por desdén. Supuesto lo dicho, en las tres diferenzias primeras de 25 hablar de *merzed, él, vos*, se comete solezismo en la gramatica i concordanzias contra la orden natural de las tres personas, xeneros i numeros.

Translation

And the more that the sentence keeps this natural order the clearer, more proper, sweeter and more becoming it will be. And this is a more legitimate and proper style of the Castilian language than that of Latin or Greek, and conforms more to the Spanish humour. Since some modern poets, and those who think themselves courtly critics, do not understand this, they complicate their language and constructions to such an extent that they speak in jargon, and avoid speaking a good, clear Castilian, but instead a Castilian which is bastardised with the little Latin or Italian that they know. What is language for, but to make oneself understood and to express oneself?

The disorder and disconcordant concord which usage has introduced, whether through modesty, respect or adulation, should also be noted. For this it is necessary, first, to state that four different ways of speech are used for four qualities of person, namely: *vuestra merzed, él, vos, tu* . . . We usually call people we respect by *merzed*, such as judges, gentry, clergy, ladies and black cape people, and it is the highest after *señoría. Él* is used by older people for someone they do not wish either to call *merzed* or address as *vos*, which is lower, and typical of masters to servants; and common and village people, who are not accustomed to using *merzed* in their speech, address as *él* people to whom they want to show respect from their class. We call servants and grown up boys *vos*, and labourers, and such like people; and among friends where there is no gravity nor ceremony *vos* is used, and so in speeches made in front of kings and addressed to them *vos* is used with due respect and old usage. Children, younger members of the family and loved ones are called *tú*; and when we get angry and quarrel with someone we call them *él*, and *vos* to disparage them. Bearing in mind the foregoing, in the first three of speaking (*merzed, él, vos*) there are violations of grammar and agreement against the natural order of three persons, gender and number.

Phonetics and phonology

18.1.1 Correas's spelling system no longer distinguishes between /ts/ and /dz/, *z* being used consistently where Nebrija used either *z* or *ç*. Similarly, *x* corresponds to Nebrija's *x* and *j*, and reveals the merger of OCast. /ʃ/ and /ʒ/. The devoicing of the sibilants is therefore complete, and the development of their Modern Spanish phonetic values probably largely achieved.
   Keypoint: the sibilants of Old Castilian (p. 290).

18.1.2 Correas continues to represent as *h* the initial /h/ which was the result of Lat. initial /f/ and does not use etymological spellings of Latin words beginning with Lat. /h/: thus **hablan** (l.5) < Lat. ?FĀBŬLANT [FĀBŬLOR], **huien** (l.5) ≤ Lat. FŬGĬUNT [FŬGĬO], but **umor** (l.3) < Lat. HŪMŌRE(M) [HŪMOR], **onrra** (l.10) → Lat. √HŌNOR, **á** (l.9) and **ai** (l.20) ≤ Lat. HĂBET [HĂBĔO].
   Keypoint: the f>h change (p. 271).

18.1.3 Double *rr* is consistently used to represent a trill and single *r* to represent a flap, even though this distinction is not always phonological.

18.1.4 However, Correas makes a distinction between *b* and *v*, which he employs apparently arbitrarily (thus **debemos** l.14 but **devido** l.22), where in both cases the intervocalic bilabial must have been the fricative [β] since the etymology must be considered identical (Lat. intervocalic /b/ in forms of DĒBĔO). It is an interesting question as to why Correas did not apply the same rigour to this as to every other aspect of his spelling. It is true that this was an area in which etymological spellings had been very widely used previously; but Correas was not one to be hidebound by such tradition, given his independence of mind in so many other areas. Maybe he was attempting (inappropriately), as with *r* and *rr*, to represent a phonetic difference, since in this case too there were readily available orthographical signs, *b* and *v*, to represent [b] and [β]. Perhaps, on the other hand, there was a lingering phonological distinction of which he was aware, or which he himself practised. Another possibility is that he considered *b* and *v* to be advantageous in the distinction of multiple meanings of the same word, some of which have become enshrined in Modern Spanish spellings, e.g. MSp. *varón* 'man' and *barón* 'baron' which both derive from Germ. ?[BARO]): at one point in the *Arte* he insists on a distinction in meaning between *voz* 'word' and *boz* 'tone of voice' (both < Lat. VŌCE [VOX]), which in Modern Spanish at any rate are homophonous. We cannot be clear to what extent such a distinction in pronunciation in Correas's time was wishful thinking on his part, or how much there was a genuine phonetic distinction (cf. 16.1.3).

Keypoint: the 'b/v' distinction (p. 262).

18.1.5 Correas does not use *y*, and employs *i* for both the vocalic [i] (the conjunction **i**, l.1, ‖ MSp. *y*) and semivowel [j] (**huien**, l.6 ‖ MSp. *huyen*).

18.1.6 The written accents ´ and ` are used to distinguish homophones rather than to indicate stress: thus **á** 'has'/**à** 'to', **el** (article)/**él** (personal pronoun).

Morphology and syntax

18.2.1 Of prime interest here are Correas's own observations about the use of the second person address forms **vuestra merzed**, **él**, **vos** and **tú**. **Vuestra merzed** still had something of its original honorific overtones as a title, although it was coming to be construed as a pronoun: Correas links it both with **señoría**, which seems otherwise to have been the lowest rung on the ladder of honorific forms of address, and with the forms we would traditionally regard as personal pronouns. We also have the information that **vuestra merzed** was not used by 'xente vulgar i de aldea', so its use had not yet generalised. **Él** was restricted to the speech of older people and those who did not use **vuestra merzed**, but also indicates a degree of respect. Nevertheless it could also be used, presumably to indicate a degree of contempt, for someone with whom one was quarrelling. **Vos** had a very complex use: (a) as a familiar term amongst friends, (b) by masters to servants and workers, (c) by adults to older children, (d) to the king, in accordance with older usage, (e) as a term of insult (presumably for someone who would normally be addressed as **vuestra merzed**). **Tú** was used as a form of intimate address, or to young children. This is therefore a most interesting intermediate step, here amply documented, in what at first sight might appear to be quite a simple change from the OCast. *tú/vos* distinction to MSp. *tú/usted*.

Correas also remarks on the anomaly that these changes in forms of address produced in the verb system of Spanish (ll.25–7). He is referring to the fact that while **merzed** and **él** are third person and **vos** is second person plural, they refer to second person singular concepts; additionally, **merzed**, which is feminine as a noun, may refer to people of the male sex. This new situation subverts what he (and others) saw as the 'orden natural' (neatly enshrined in Latin) of person, gender and number, since *vuestra merzed* > *usted* increasingly took masculine adjective agreements, and *vos* had long taken singular adjective agreements, if semantically appropriate. There was also an impact on the verbal system, which has remained most evident in the Latin-American *voseo*, where a formerly plural verb form (e.g. *hablás* || OCast. *hablades~habláis*) is now exclusively singular in reference, as is the *vos* pronoun (see 30.2.1).

Keypoint: **personal pronouns** (p. 284).

18.2.2 Quanto ... mas (l.1). This construction ('the more ... the more'), typical of cultivated written registers, undergoes a slight change between Latin and Modern Spanish. The Latin construction is TANTŌ + comparative adjective/adverb ... QUANTŌ + comparative adjective/adverb; in Modern Spanish the usual order is *cuanto más* (+ adjective/adverb) ... *tanto más* (+ adjective/adverb), and *tanto* is usually omitted. (The sequence *tanto* ... *cuanto* ... expresses the relation 'as many ... as ...'.) In this text the first *más* is also omitted.

18.2.3 Algunos modernos poetas i à su parezer cortesanos críticos (ll.4–5). The use of the adjective before the noun here is a good example of the Spanish exploitation of this order to express a subjective point of view; the full sense (which is not easy to render economically in English) is probably 'some poets who try to be ultra-modern and critics who think themselves rather lofty'. The use of the adjective before the noun (apart from common adjectives of size and quantity, which had probably always been able to precede the noun) became more frequent in the rhetorical style of the fifteenth century (see 15.2.2) and in Modern Spanish is especially cultivated in formal prose.

18.2.4 Lo qual (ll.10–11) is a transition relative the use of which is a feature of Latinate syntax.

18.2.5 Desorden (l.9), a morphological derivative of *orden*, like **orden** at this time (see ll.1 and 27), feminine, shows a gender change from Lat. ORDĪNE [ORDO], which was masculine. (See 18.3.11.)

Keypoint: **gender** (p. 275).

18.2.6 Usamos + infinitive (l.13) shows **usar** being used an aspectual auxiliary which has the sense of 'usually to do something' (also expressed by **tener uso de** + infinitive, l.18). This paraphrase is common in the Golden Age and is formally similar to the English habitual past tense 'used to do'. The Modern Spanish paraphrase *soler* + infinitive, which corresponds to Lat. SŎLĚO + infinitive, was however also used in Old Castilian.

Keypoint: **periphrastic verb forms** (p. 283).

18.2.7 Adonde is used here in a locative sense (see 6.3.9) rather than in the allative sense of MSp. *adonde* (see 27.2.1).

18.2.8 Rreñimos con alguno (l.24). **Alguno** corresponds to MSp. *alguien*: Correas tells us that **alguno** was preferred to **alguién**, the latter being considered archaic or vulgar (cf. 21.2.10). Note the position of the stress in *alguién* < Lat. ĂLĬQUEM [ĂLĬQUIS]: the diphthong /je/ is indeed most naturally seen as the result of a placing of stress on the final syllable (Lat. ĂLĬQUEM would have been stressed on the first syllable), though analogy with *quien* may also have played a part in this development. Correas also records that some speakers moved the accent to the first syllable (**álguien**) 'por finura'. *Alguien* is indeed not common in Old Castilian, and even in Modern Spanish, such alternatives as *uno* or *una persona* are preferred in certain registers.

18.2.9 Correas employs some learned absolute constructions using the gerund and past participle: **no entendiendo esto algunos modernos poetas** . . . (l.4), **supuesto lo dicho** (l.25).

18.2.10 The future subjunctive continues to be used in two contexts here: the (hypothetical) future-referring **quanto la orazion fuere guardando** . . . (l.1) and in a relative clause with an indefinite antecedent **los que se quisieren bien** (ll.23–4).
   Keypoint: **the future subjunctive** (p. 275).

Vocabulary

18.3.1 This is a technical work on language, and we can see how Correas makes use of a technical vocabulary of learned words with very specific meanings: **orazion** 'sentence' (l.1), **concordia** (l.9) and **concordanzia** 'grammatical agreement' (ll.26–7), **solezismo** 'solecism', 'grammatical error' (l.23), **gramatica** 'grammar' (l.26), **xenero** 'gender' (l.27), **numero** 'grammatical number' (l.27).
   Keypoint: **learned and popular, semilearned and semipopular** (p. 277).

18.3.2 There are also a large number of words of learned or semilearned origin, as is to be expected in academic prose: **lexitimo** (l.2), **conforme** (l.3), **critico** (l.5), **discordante** (l.9), **modestia** (l.10), **adulazion** (l.10), **diferenzia** (l.11), **rrespetamos** (l.13) (with semipopular modification, see 15.1.1), **eclesiastico** (l.14).
   Keypoint: **learned and popular, semilearned and semipopular** (p. 277).

18.3.3 Lenguaxe (l.5). Modern Spanish has a number of words for the notion 'language': *lengua*, *idioma* and *lenguaje* are amongst them. Of these, the word of longest standing is *lengua*, the derivative of Latin LINGUA. *Lenguaje*, with its characteristic *-aje* suffix, no doubt a borrowing from Occitan, is first attested in Berceo, and has the meaning of 'a kind of language', the sense it still has today. *Idioma* is a word of Greek learned origin (Gr. ἰδιώμα 'personal characteristic') which appears during the Golden Age and first of all means a national language, rather than language in general. **Xerigonza** (l.6), which also belongs to this semantic field, may also be based on a northern French borrowing (*jergon* or *jargon*), deriving from the Latin onomatopoeic stem √GARG-, associated with the idea of 'throat', and hence 'swallowing', 'confused talk'.

18.3.4 Menester (l.11) < Lat. MĬNISTĔRĬU[M] 'service', 'assistance' coexisted for a long time with the learned word *necesidad* (< Lat. NĔCESSĬTĀTE [NĔCESSĬTĀS]), which is preferred in the modern language. **Menester** is sometimes found in a syncopated form, *mester*, in Old Castilian (see 8.0).

18.3.5 Calidad (l.12). The distinction in Modern Spanish between *calidad* and *cualidad* is quite recent, and is an interesting example of semantic differentiation between variant forms of what is arguably in origin the same word. Covarrubias gives only *calidad*, and even as late as the eighteenth century, the *Diccionario de autoridades* (see Text 23), whilst recording that 'algunos Españoles escribieron Qualidád, lo que no es tan usado', in fact uses the two words apparently indiscriminately. *Calidad* is first attested in the thirteenth century, while *cualidad*, first attested in the late fifteenth century, seems to owe its initial /kw/ to learned imitation (Cor., II, 258, and cf. 13.1.3).
  Keypoint: **learned and popular, semilearned and semipopular** (p. 276).

18.3.6 Xente de capa negra (l.15) were city dwellers or bourgeoisie, as opposed to the *gente de capa parda*, farm workers.

18.3.7 Aldea (l.17) < Ar. *ḍáy'a* 'field', 'village' is increasingly in Modern Spanish replaced by its near-synonym *pueblo* (< Lat. PŎPŬLU[S] 'people'). The long survival of *aldea* may be attributed to the fact that OCast. *pueblo* has exclusively the meaning of 'people', 'the populace'; its extension to the concrete meaning of 'village' is relatively recent.

18.3.8 Xaez (l.19) || MSp. *jaez* is from Ar. *ŷahāz*, 'equipment', 'provisions', 'accoutrements', which is still current in modern Arabic. Atypically, it does not incorporate the Arabic definite article. *Jaez* in Spanish came to have the specific meaning of 'horse's harness', which may be the basis of the borrowing from Arabic. Its assimilation into Spanish is demonstrated by the fact that it has spawned morphological derivatives formed in the Romance way, most notably *enjaezar* 'to harness', *enjaezamiento* 'harnessing'. In the Golden Age, it developed the wider meaning 'type', 'class' seen here, which may be the result of association with team colours worn by horses on festive occasions (Cor., III, 481).

18.3.9 Mozo (l.19), like *muchacho*, to which it may be related, is a word of unknown origin. Cor., IV, 172–5, associate these words with Basque *motz* 'shaven', a term probably adopted because of the custom of young boys having their hair cut short. Its meaning extends to that of 'servant'. *Mozo* is also used as an adjective meaning 'young', and in Old Castilian is regarded as an antonym of *viejo* (we must bear in mind in this connection the apparently semilearned status of *joven*, which although found throughout Old Castilian, became widely used only in the seventeenth century).

18.3.10 Rreñimos (l.24). *Reñir* derives from an analogically regularised form of the Latin deponent verb [RINGOR] 'to snarl', 'bare one's teeth'. Its meaning has weakened and generalised in Spanish to that of 'to scold', 'to quarrel'.

18.3.11 Orden (l.27) is here in the feminine gender. In Modern Spanish its many meanings have come to be discriminated to a certain extent by a gender difference, the masculine being used for 'order' in the sense of 'arrangement', 'precedence' (e.g. *orden alfabético*), and the feminine for the sense of 'command' or 'rule' (e.g. *la orden de atacar, la orden de Santiago*).

Keypoint: gender (p. 275).

IX The Golden Age

The sixteenth and early seventeenth centuries marked a high point in Spanish fortunes. The emergence of Spain as a world power under the Habsburgs and its expansion overseas corresponded with an explosion of cultural activity which has come to be known as the Siglo de Oro. The variation within Spanish was as a consequence vast, and textual evidence is abundant. In creative literature we can see authors exploiting all manner of registers, from the highly rhetorical to the extremely colloquial. The texts in this chapter have been chosen to illustrate some of this variety, though it is of course possible only to give the barest indication of the range available.

The sixteenth century is sometimes represented as being a period of rapid change in Spanish. In assessing such a claim, we have to ask ourselves once again what exactly we mean by 'the Spanish language' (see Chapter II). What is likely is that within Spain (the question of Latin America will be discussed separately in Chapter XII) there were a number of competing prestige norms: the preference of one over another could give the impression of speed of change, though it would be more accurate to construe such a development as the replacement of one norm by another rather than change within the same norm. This is almost certainly the most appropriate way to view the significance of the preference given to Madrid over Toledo as a centre of prestige when Philip II moved his capital there in 1561: Toledan usage, so much prized by Valdés (see Text 17), rapidly came to be regarded as old-fashioned compared with that of the new capital, where it seems likely that more northerly features prospered (Philip himself had spent his early years in Valladolid). Another possibility, proposed recently by Penny (forthcoming), is that the large influx of new residents into Madrid from all over Spain produced a koiné effect which may have led to a preference for the simpler variants available, and, indeed, it is quite striking how in a number of ways Spanish does seem to be 'pruned', especially on the phonological level, as the distinctions between the voiced and voiceless medieval sibilants are lost, the distinction between /b/ and ?/β/ disappears and initial /h/ eventually falls.

Another centre of prestige was Seville, which was already an important city when in 1502 the Casa de la Contratación was established to regulate trade with the overseas empire. In Text 22 we have some indication of Quevedo's perception of some of the characteristic features of the pronunciation of lower-class Seville. The speech of Andalusia must already have been distinctive in the early sixteenth century (see Text 17). Within Andalusia, cultured Sevillian speech still exercises prestige.

Further reading

Menéndez Pidal (1962a); Penny (forthcoming).

19 A model for Castilian prose. Juan de Boscán, *El cortesano* (1534)

19.0 Baldassare Castiglione's *Il Cortegiano*, published in Venice in 1528 though written much earlier, is a classic of the Renaissance which was widely admired throughout Europe. Juan de Boscán (*c.*1490–1542), whose admiration for Italian poetry led to his imitation of its metres in Castilian, a practice that was to be followed more effectively by Garcilaso de la Vega (it was Garcilaso, in fact, who sent his friend Boscán a copy of Castiglione's work from Italy), produced a Castilian translation which is remarkable both as a work of art in its own right and for the fact that Boscán, a Catalan by birth, wrote in a Castilian that was regarded as a model for sixteenth-century prose (Canellada de Zamora and Zamora Vicente 1970: 193).

Boscán's task as a translator was not eased by the very specific references to Italy and the Italian language in the original work. He sets out his policy as a translator in the dedicatory preface:

> Yo no terné fin en la traducción deste libro a ser tan estrecho que me apriete a sacalle palabra por palabra, antes, si alguna cosa en él se ofreciere, que en su lengua parezca bien y en la nuestra mal, no dexaré de mudarla o callarla
> (Castiglione 1942 [1534]: 6).

As can clearly be seen in the extract below, Boscán strikes a happy balance between fidelity to the original and freedom from word-by-word translation which would have made the Castilian unnatural. What he does glean from Castiglione's work is the concern for elegance and clarity which he clearly admired, and which is precisely the subject-matter of the discussion here, and it is this that represented the real revolution in Castilian prose. It may be that Boscán also felt a certain linguistic affinity with Castiglione: Castiglione as a Lombard and Boscán as a Catalan were both writing in a medium that was essentially foreign to them, the former in Tuscan and the latter in Castilian, and the rejection of an excessive deference to former writers in these languages was also an affirmation of what such 'new' writers as themselves had to offer. Indeed, written Castilian would from now on be shaped as effectively the national language of the whole of Spain.

This extract is taken from the part of *Il Cortegiano* in which language is discussed and is a classic exposition of the humanist view of the subject. Writing is seen as a function of speech, and as such must use words which are familiar from speech and readily understandable; archaisms and affectation are to be shunned. At the same time, writing must not be pedestrian but be appropriate to the subject: elegant, solemn or witty as the case may be. Novelty and inventiveness in language are highly prized and slavish imitation criticised. Latin is recognised as being subject to the same pressures of change as the vernacular.

The text

The text given here is transcribed from *El Cortesano tradvzido por Boscan en nvestro vulgar Castellano, nueuamente agora corregido*, Antwerp: Philippo Nucio, 1574, f.43r.-43v. This counts chronologically as the twelfth edition of the work, but it differs only in slight details from the first edition of 1534 (Barcelona: Pedro Monpezat), which was the basis of the CSIC modern edition (Castiglione 1942 [1534]). The corresponding material is to be found on pp.71–2 of this edition, which unfortunately does not give any editorial rationale and clearly makes some adjustments in favour of modern Spanish spelling. The Italian text, which is also given for interest, is from Castiglione (1972 [1528]: 73–4).

Further reading

Castiglione (1942) [1534]

Querria tambien que hablasse y escriuiesse nuestro Cortesano, de manera, que no solame*n*te tomasse los buenos vocablos de toda Ytalia, mas aunque alguna vez vsasse algunas palabras Francesas o Españolas, delas q*ue* son por nosotros en nuestro vso recebidas ..., con tal que se pudiesse esperar que auian de ser entendidos.

Seria ta*m*bien bueno, que alguna vez tomasse algunas palabras en otra significacion diferente de la propria, y transfiriendo las a su proposito las enxiriesse como vna pla*n*ta en otra mejor, por hazer las mas hermosas y por declarar con ellas y casi figurar las cosas tan à lo proprio que ya no nos paresciesse oyrlas, sino verlas y tocarlas. Desto no podria dexar de seguirse gran deleyte al que oyesse o leyesse. Y a bueltas de todo esto no ternia por malo, que se formassen algunos otros vocablos nueuos, y con nueuas figuras o terminos de hablar, sacando se por gentil arte de los Latinos, como los latinos los solian sacar de los Griegos. Assi que con esto si entre los hombres dotos y de ingenio y de juyzio que en nuestros tiempos entre nosotros se hallan vuiesse algunos que quisiessen poner diligencia en escreuir de la manera que hemos dicho, en esta

*Io vorrei che 'l nostro cortegiano parlasse
e scrivesse di tal maniera, e non solamente
pigliasse parole splendide ed eleganti
d'ogni parte della Italia, ma ancora laudarei
che talor usasse alcuni di quelli   5
termini e franzesi e spagnoli, che già sono
dalla consuetudine nostra accettati ..., pur
che sperasse esser inteso.*

*Talor vorrei que pigliasse alcune parole   10
in altra significazione che la lor propria e,
traportandole a proposito, quasi le
inserisse come rampollo d'albero in più
felice tronco, per farle più vaghe e belle, e
quasi per accostar le cose al senso degli   15
occhi proprii e, come si dice, farle toccar
con mano, con diletto di chi ode o legge.*

*Né vorrei che temesse di formarne ancor
di nove e con nove figure di dire,   20
deducendole con bel modo dai Latini,
come già i Latini le deducevano dai Greci.*

25

*Se adunque degli omini litterati e di bon
ingegno e giudicio, che oggidì tra noi si
ritrovano, fossero alcuni, li quali
ponessimo cura di scrivere del modo che
s'è detto in questa lingua cose degne   30
d'esser lette, tosto la vederessimo culta ed*

nuestra lengua cosas dinas de ser leydas,	*abundante de termini e belle figure, e*
presto la veriamos pura y elegante y	*capace che in essa si scrivesse così bene*
abu*n*dosa de gentiles terminos y figuras,	*come in qualsivoglia altra ...*
y aparejada à que en ella se escriuiesse	
tambien, como en otra qualquier.	

35

Translation (of the Spanish text)

I would also wish that our Courtier should speak and write in such a way that not only should he take good words from all over Italy, but even that sometimes he should use some French or Spanish words, from amongst those which are accepted in our usage . . ., provided that he can expect them to be understood.

It would also be good for him to take some words in a sense other than their literal one, and by transferring them to his purpose he should graft them like a plant on to another, better, one, in order to make them more beautiful, and through them to express and, as it were, represent things in a way that is so like their literal meaning that it might seem to us that we do not just hear about them, but rather see them and touch them. The consequence of this cannot be any other than to give great delight to anyone who hears or reads. And concerning all this I would not consider it a bad thing if other new words were coined, and with new figurative meanings or figures of speech, taking them over tastefully from the Latin, as Latin speakers used to take them over from the Greeks.

And so, if amongst the learned men of intellect and judgement that are alive today there were any who would take the trouble of writing things worthy of being read in our own language, in the way we have described, we would soon see it made pure and elegant and abounding in tasteful words and figures of speech, and as suitable for literature as any other.

Phonetics and phonology

19.1.1 The use of *b* and *v* is mainly etymological, though the spelling **bueltas** (1.21), with its initial *b*, (≤ VŎLŪTAS [VOLVO]) suggests the indistinguishability of the two letters in terms of pronunciation.
    Keypoint: the 'b/v' merger (p. 262).

19.1.2 *H* is generally reserved for the /h/ of sixteenth-century Spanish (**hablasse**, 1.1, < Lat. ?FĀBŪLĀVISSET [FĀBŬLOR], **hazer**, 1.15, ≤ Lat. FĂCĔRE [FĂCĬO], etc.). Forms of *haber* < Lat. HĂBĒRE [HĂBĒO] are generally written without an initial *h* (**auian**, 1.9, **vuiesse**, 1.29), although there is an etymologial spelling too (**hemos**, 1.31); **hombres** < Lat. HŎMINES [HŎMO] likewise has an etymological *h*.
    Keypoint: the f>h change (p. 271).

19.1.3 Distinctions in sibilants are still represented in spelling: **quisiessen** (1.30) exhibits both *s* [z] and *ss* [s], **recebidas** (1.8) has *c* [ts] as opposed to the *z* [dz] of **hazer** (1.15), and there is a distinction between the *x* of **dexar** (1.19) and the *j* and *g* [ʒ] of **mejor** (1.15) and **diligencia** (1.30) respectively.
    Keypoints: the sibilants of Old Castilian (p. 290); **palatalisation** (p. 280).

19.1.4 The later decisions of the Real Academia (see Text 23) regarding the variant forms of certain words of learned origin do not always tally with the variants encountered here. Thus we have **propria** for MSp. *propia* (l.12), **dotos** for MSp. *doctos* (l.27), **dinas** for MSp. *dignas* (l.32); in the first case the semipopular variant has been subsequently adopted, and in the last two cases the full 'learned' form. See also 22.1.4.

    Keypoint: learned and popular, semilearned and semipopular (p. 277).

Morphology and syntax

19.2.1 Figurar las cosas tan à lo proprio (l.17). It is not easy to gauge the exact meaning of this phrase, which is part of a circumlocution apparently introduced to explain the full meaning of the Italian original (see below 19.3.2). I take it to mean 'to represent things in their own way' i.e. 'as if they had their literal meaning'. If this is appropriate, it is a relatively early example of the *a lo* + adjective construction, e.g. *a lo español* 'in the Spanish way'.[1] The model for this construction may be the idiom *a lo menos* 'at least' (MSp. *por lo menos*), which was common in the sixteenth century. Spanish also exploits *a la* + adjective with much the same meaning.

    Keypoint: gender (p. 275).

19.2.2 One noticeable change that is made between the 1534 and the 1574 editions is in the form of infinitives with clitic pronouns. The 1534 edition regularly uses such forms as *vellas, tocallas*, in which the /r/ of the infinitive has assimilated to the /l/ of the clitic pronoun to produce the group ?/ll/ which palatalised to /ʎ/. This edition uses **verlas, tocarlas** (l.18). In general, such morphologically more transparent variants are preferred in post-Golden-Age Spanish.

19.2.3 The metathesised future stem *tern-* (**ternia**, l.21) is used here. Though this is common in the medieval language (cf. 4.2.9, 11.2.11), the modern language uses the form *tendr-* with a homorganic plosive (cf. 7.1.5).

    Keypoint: future stems (p. 274).

19.2.4 Although there are places in which Boscán follows the Italian original more or less word for word, there is always an independence which reflects the nature of Spanish. In the very first sentence, he adopts the Spanish preference for verb-first order (**que hablasse y escriuiesse nuestro Cortesano**, ll.1–2), although simple imitation of the Italian subject-first order would have been perfectly acceptable. He also seems to prefer the Spanish use of *se* to indicate an indefinite subject: thus **se pudiesse esperar que** ... (ll.8–9) contrasts with Italian *sperasse*, which continues *il cortegiano* as subject, and similarly in l.21–2 we have **no ternia por malo** ... **que se formassen** rather than *né vorrei che [il cortegiano] temesse di formarne* ...

    Keypoint: the reflexive (p. 288).

---

1   Keniston (1937: 241) dates the first occurrences of this construction to 'the last decades' of the century.

Vocabulary

19.3.1 As in syntax, Boscán does not wantonly borrow Italian words, but tries to find Spanish equivalents, even if this involves explanatory paraphrase. A striking case here is the translation of the Italian word *bello*, which appears three times (ll.13, 22, 32). It is never translated by Spanish *bello*, even though this word meant much the same thing and had been available since the thirteenth century. But Spanish *bello* was a relatively rare word at this time (it does not occur once in the *Celestina*, for instance); Boscán uses **hermosas** (l.15), **gentil** (l.24) and **gentiles** (l.34) instead.

19.3.2 Boscán seems not to want to leave anything to chance in communicating the essential and difficult information about figures of speech. It is worth examining one instance of this, lines 13–16 of the Italian text, in some detail. There are a number of practical difficulties with the translation of this passage. *Vaghe* is being used here in the sense of 'beautiful', though it also has connotations of 'fickle', a meaning which is not inappropriate here; but Spanish *vago*, first attested in the late fifteenth century, had the meaning 'wandering', without the positive meaning of the Italian word. The reference of *proprii* is not immediately clear, and the general meaning is really only supplied by the pragmatic context: 'people's own eyes'. The passive meaning of the infinitive in the construction *farle toccar con mano* 'make them able to be touched' cannot be rendered in this way in Spanish. Boscán therefore carries out a complete reorganisation of the material, proceeding to expand on it so that there can be no doubt about the meaning. The scheme below shows the phrase-by-phrase equivalents used: Boscán has begun a completely new, and fuller, sentence at (vi) in order to make the structure less complex; he expands on the notions of *accostare* (ii) and *toccare* (iv and v). At the same time all the elements of the original are there: *come si dice* is rendered by **paresciesse** (iv); *degli occhi* (iii) is implied by the use of **verlas** in (v).

i	**por hazer las mas hermosas**	*per farle più vaghe e belle*
ii	**y por declarar con ellas**	*quasi per accostar le cose*
	y casi figurar las cosas	
iii	**tan à lo proprio**	*al senso degli occhi proprii*
iv	**que ya no nos paresciesse oyrlas**	*e, come si dice,*
v	**sino verlas y tocarlas.**	*farle toccar con mano.*
vi	**Desto no podria dexar de seguirse gran**	*con diletto di chi ode o legge.*
	deleyte al que oyesse o leyesse.	

It is this concern for syntactic and semantic clarity which no doubt accounted for the admiration of his work, and the fact that, though a translation, *El Cortesano* 'reads like Spanish'.

20 Standing on ceremony. Lope de Rueda, *Eufemia* (mid-sixteenth century)

20.0 Lope de Rueda (first decade of the sixteenth century – 1565) was a gold-beater by trade, but became a fine comic actor, eventually directing his own company of players. He was much admired by Cervantes, who saw him perform in Seville. His life seems to have been the epitome of the picaresque. In his plays he followed the new Italian *commedia alla villanesca*, rejecting the learned tradition and introducing a realism into the dialogue by catching the different styles of speech around him. His plays are thus extremely interesting from the linguistic point of view; they include such characters as servants, gypsies, negros and simpletons. Although no doubt some of the features of their speech, like the characters they represent and the scenes in which they appear, are exaggerated, they provide, if interpreted judiciously, a wealth of information about sociolinguistic variation in early Golden-Age Spain.

In the following extract from *Eufemia*, probably written some time between 1542 and 1554, Vallejo and Polo are footmen and Grimaldo is a page. Vallejo considers he has been affronted by Grimaldo and has challenged him to a duel. But Vallejo is in fact all bluster, and is taken aback when Grimaldo calls his bluff. The two are now trading insults, while Polo is trying to pour oil on troubled waters.

The text

This version follows Hermenegildo (1985: 88–89), who based his reading on the 1567 Timoneda edition, with variants from the 1576 Seville edition. I have, however, restored original spellings whilst retaining editorial accents and punctuation.

Vallejo: Espérame aquí, ratonzillo.

Grimaldo: Buelue acá, cobarde.

Vallejo: Ora, pues soys porfiado, sabed que os dexara vn poco más con vida si por ella fuera. Déxeme, señor Polo, hazer a esse hombrezillo las preguntas que soy obligado por el descargo de mi conciencia.   5

Polo: ¿Qué le haueys de preguntar, dezí?

Vallejo: Déxeme vuessa merced hazer lo que debo. ¿Qué tanto ha, golondrinillo, que no te has confessado?

Grimaldo: ¿Qué parte eres tú para pedirme aquesso, cortabolsas?

Vallejo: Señor Polo, uea vuessa merced si quiere aquesse pobrete moço que le   10 digan algo a su padre, o qué missas manda que le digan por su alma.

Polo: Yo, hermano Uallejo, bien conozco a su padre y madre, quando algo sucediesse, y sé su possada.

Vallejo: ¿Y cómo se llama su padre?

Polo: ¿Qué os va en saber su nombre?   15

Vallejo: Para saber después quién me querrá pedir su muerte.

Polo: Ea, acabá ya, que es vergüença. ¿No sabeys que se llama Luys de Grimaldo? ...

Vallejo: ¿Qué me cuenta vuessa merced?

Polo: No más que aquesto.   20

Vallejo: Pues señor Polo, tomad aquesta espada y por el lado derecho apretá cuanto pudiéredes, que después que sea essecutada en mí aquesta sentencia os diré el porqué ... ¿No dezís que es esse hijo de Luys de Grimaldos, alguazil mayor de Lorca?

Polo: Y no de otro.   25

Vallejo: ¡Desuenturado de mí! ¿Quién es el que me ha librado tantas vezes de la horca sino el padre de aquesse cauallero? Señor Grimaldo, tomad vuestra daga y vos mismo abrid [a]queste pecho y sacadme el coraçón y abrilde por medio y hallareys en él escrito el nombre de vuestro padre Luys de Grimaldo ... No quisiera haueros muerto, por los sanctos de Dios, *30* por toda la soldada que me da mi amo. Uamos de aquí, que yo quiero gastar lo que de la vida me resta en servicio deste gentilhombre, en recompensa de las palabras que sin le conoscer he dicho.

Grimaldo: Dexemos aquesso, que yo quedo, hermano Vallejo, para todo lo que os cumpliere.   *35*

Translation

V: Wait here, you little mouse.

G: Come back here, you coward.

V: Well, since you're so persistent, I'll have you know that I would have left you alive for a bit longer if I'd gone back for it. [He was going back home to collect a holy relic.] Allow me, Señor Polo, to put to this young man the questions I am obliged to put in order to salve my conscience.

P: What have you got to ask, then?

V: Allow me to do what I must. How long is it, little swallow, since you went to confession?

G: What business is it of yours to ask me that, you cutpurse?

V: Señor Polo, see if this poor young boy wishes his father to be told anything, or what masses he will have said for his soul.

P: Brother Vallejo, I'm well acquainted with his father and mother, if anything should happen, and I know where he lives.

V: And what is his father's name?

P: What do you want to know his name for?

V: So I know who is going to hold me responsible for his death afterwards.

P: Come on, stop it, shame on you: don't you know that he is Luis de Grimaldo?

V: What are you saying?

P: Just that.

V: Well, Señor Polo, take this sword and plunge it as hard as you can into my right side, and when this sentence has been carried out on me I'll tell you why. Aren't you saying that this is the son of Luis de Grimaldos, the head of the watch in Lorca?

P: None other.

V: Woe is me! Who has saved me so many times from the hangman's noose but this gentleman's father? Señor Grimaldo, take your dagger and open up this breast yourself, open it down the middle and you will find written the name of your father, Luis de Grimaldo. I would not have wanted to kill you, by the saints of God, by all the wages my master gives me. Let us away from here, for I will spend what remains to me of life in the the service of this gentleman, in recompense for the words which I unwittingly spoke to him.

G: Leave off this, for I am here, brother Vallejo, for anything you wish.

Phonetics and phonology

20.1.1 The representation of sibilants still implies the distinctions represented by *ç* *(c)*, *z*, *x* and *j* in Nebrija (see 16.1.1), though the *ss* of **possada** (l.13, see 20.3.4) suggests devoicing. **Essecutada** (l.22) and the ancestor of MSp. *ejecutada* are variant developments of the learned morphological derivative of the past participle √EXSĒCŪTA of the Latin deponent verb EXSĔQUOR 'to execute', 'accomplish'; we may view both /s/ and /ʃ/ (the ancestor of MSp. /x/) as semipopular modifications of the Latin group /ks/.
    Keypoints: the sibilants of Old Castilian (p. 290); **consonant groups** (p. 267).

20.1.2 Popular words with initial /f/ in Latin are in this text uniformly represented with an initial *h*: **hazer** (l.7) < Lat. FĂCĔRE [FĂCĬO], **hijo** (l.23) < Lat. FĪLĬU[S], **horca** (l.27) < Lat. FŬRCA, **hallareys** (l.29) ← ?[(F)AFFLO] (see 11.3.2). But at the same time there are many etymological instances of initial *h* which would have had no phonetic value: **hombrezillo** (l.4) → Lat. √HŎMO and the various forms of **haber** ← Lat. [HĂBĔO]. Initial *h* is also used in **hermano** (l.34) which derived from Lat. GERMĀNU[S], the initial /g/ being lost in Castilian (cf. 5b.1.3).
    Keypoints: the f>h change (p. 271); **palatalisation** (p. 280).

20.1.3 Vuessa in **vuessa merced** (l.7, etc.) has diverged from **vuestra** (l.28), which is used in other contexts. This is evidence of the considerable phonetic erosion which was to overtake the new courtesy address formula (see 18.2.1) to produce the highly abbreviated and modified modern *usted* (Pla Cárceles 1923); see also 22.2.1.
    Keypoint: personal pronouns (p. 284).

Morphology and syntax

20.2.1 The first few lines of this passage are rich in affective suffixes which indicate disparagement. With *-illo* we have **ratonzillo** (l.1), **hombrezillo** (l.4) and **golondrinillo** (ll.7–8), and with *-ete* there is the form **pobrete** (l.10) from *pobre*. In the course of the history of the language, some combinations of noun and suffix have lexicalised: **pobrete** is now reckoned as such a word, with an individual dictionary entry and the meaning of 'poor devil', 'poor thing'.

20.2.2 One of the most interesting aspects of this text is the oscillation between the three address forms **tú**, **vos** and **vuessa merced**. **Tú** is used by Grimaldo and Vallejo in the trading of insults (cf. ll.1–2), and Vallejo takes the use of *tú* as an insult in itself; earlier in the scene he protests '¿Tal se ha de sufrir, que se ponga este desbarbadillo conmigo a tú por tú?' Vallejo, standing on his dignity, sometimes uses **vos**, as if he cannot bring himself to stoop to using **tú** (ll.3–4). When peace is eventually made, they both adopt **vos** (l. 27 onwards). Vallejo also varies between **vos** and **vuessa merced** in addressing Polo: the use of **vuessa merced** may be intended to strike a more formal and aggrieved tone in front of Grimaldo, emphasising (by contrast) the esteem in which Vallejo holds Polo (l.4). Polo does not respond in kind but uses the *vos* that was the normal form of address between equals.
    Keypoint: personal pronouns (p. 284).

20.2.3 There is variation in the form of the *vos* imperative, which appears both with and without a final *d* (**tomad** but **apretá**, l.21). The form without -*d* eventually supplies the imperative of *vos* in the modern Argentinian *voseo* (see 30.2.1) and reflects a widespread popular pronunciation of the Peninsular MSp. *vosotros* imperative.

   Keypoint: personal pronouns (p. 284).

20.2.4 The sequence of tense in the past counterfactual conditional sentence **os dexara vn poco más con vida si por ella fuera** (ll.3–4, cf. 13.2.1) is still frequently encountered in the sixteenth century (see also 23.2.2), although compound tenses were beginning to be used too at this time. The Modern Spanish equivalent is *os habría dejado . . . con vida si hubiera/hubiese ido . . .* The -*ra* form still regularly substitutes the conditional of modal auxiliary verbs in Modern Spanish: there is an example in this passage on l.30, **no quisiera haueros muerto** = *no querría . . .* (see also 28.2.8).

   Keypoints: conditional sentences (p. 265); **the pluperfects of Old Castilian** (p. 286).

20.2.5 Las preguntas que soy obligado (ll.4–5). This is an example of the 'loose' syntax of relative clauses that is typical of spoken register: the full structure in Modern Spanish would be *las preguntas que estoy obligado a hacer* or possibly *las preguntas a las que estoy obligado*. The meaning, however, is quite clear. The use of **soy** with **obligado** shows that the full trajectory of *estar* to denote resultant state with past participles has not yet been reached.

   Keypoint: *ser* and *estar* (p. 290).

20.2.6 The form of the interrogative in **¿qué tanto ha?** (l.7) 'how long?' (cf. MSp. *¿cuánto tiempo hace?*) is unusual, and may have been a colloquial feature; the construction is more analytic than *¿cuánto?* (For the use of *haber* in time expressions, see 11.2.1.)

20.2.7 Cortabolsas (l.9) illustrates the process of word creation by the compounding of a verb and noun. This device has always been popular in Spanish, and has more recently been employed in a number of calques from English, e.g. *rascacielos* 'skyscraper', *limpiaparabrisas* 'windscreen wiper'.

20.2.8 The future subjunctive is still used (**pudiéredes** l.22, **cumpliere** l.35), although the present subjunctive is also clearly used in temporal clauses referring to future time (**después que sea essecutada** . . ., l.22). This gave rise to a rather complex situation regarding the use of future and present subjunctives which was eventually simplified by the disappearance of the former.

   Keypoint: the future subjunctive (p. 275).

20.2.9 Abrilde = MSp. *abridle* (l.29) shows metathesis of the /dl/ sequence in this combination of verb and clitic pronoun. Such phonetic modification (cf. 14.2.4) was still a common variant in the sixteenth century; later the variants which retained the basic form of verb and pronoun were preferred, giving Modern Spanish a very transparent morphology in this area.

20.2.10 In **abrilde** (l.29) and **sin le conoscer** (l.33) the phenomenon of *leísmo* can be observed (see 10.2.7).
Keypoint: personal pronouns (p. 284).

20.2.11 Muerto (l.30), though formally the past participle of *morir* 'to die', here has the meaning of 'killed', and it continues to be used in this way in some registers of Modern Spanish. In the *Diccionario de autoridades*, IV, 511 (1734), it is listed as a past participle of *matar*.

20.2.12 The *haber de* + infinitive construction (**haueys de preguntar**, l.6) appears to be used here in a deontic modal sense (see 22.2.8, 24.2.3).
Keypoint: periphrastic verb forms (p. 283).

20.2.13 There is continuing use of the full forms of the demonstratives **aquesse** (l.27) and [a]**queste** (l.28).
Keypoint: demonstratives (p. 270).

Vocabulary

20.3.1 Intriguingly, words cognate with Eng. *rat* are shared by many European languages, both Romance and Germanic, although the etymology of the word is unknown. *Ratón* (**ratonzillo**, l.1), a suffixal derivative of *rata*, has in Spanish provided the word for 'mouse'. Latin appears not to have distinguished between 'rat' and 'mouse', using MŪS to cover both notions, and this semantic haziness may have been a factor in the interestingly anomalous use of the typically augmentative *-ón* suffix in *ratón* for what is in fact normally a smaller kind of rodent.

Another word whose cognates are widely shared among the Romance languages but is of unknown origin is **daga** (l.28) 'dagger'.

20.3.2 The allative **acá** (l.2) is distinct in meaning from the locative *aquí* (Latin distinguished locative HĪC, allative HŪC and elative HINC, cf. 6.3.9). This is a semantic field which seems to be very volatile, and which differs from period to period and from region to region: MSp. *acá* is very generally used in Latin America as the equivalent of Peninsular *aquí*, for instance. *Aquí* itself is an expanded form of Lat. HĪC which follows the same pattern of reinforcement by Lat. ?ACCU as the demonstratives. Possible sources for the other general locative pronouns of Spanish are *acá* < ?ACCU HĀC, *ahí* < ? Ā HĪC, *allí* < Ā ILLĪC; there is also the rarer form *acullá* < ?ACCU ILLĀC, and in Old Castilian, *aquén* 'this side' < ?ACCU HINC (see 10.2.3) is also found. The exact meaning of each of these adverbs is difficult to determine exhaustively, since they participate idiosyncratically in a large number of idiomatic constructions.
Keypoints: adverbs (p. 262); **demonstratives** (p. 270).

20.3.3 For the origin of *porfiar*, see 4.3.3. **Porfiado** (l.3) 'persistent' (= *que porfía*) is here used as an adjective with the verb *ser* with an active valency which is typical of a number of verbs used intransitively – e.g. *callado* 'quiet', *confiado* 'confident', and even of some which are used both intransitively and transitively, e.g. *empeñado* 'insistent', *cansado* 'tiring'. This is probably made possible (a) by the impossibility or unlikelihood of the interpretation of the *ser* + past participle expression as a passive and (b) by the growing availability of the *ser/estar* contrast with adjectives; with regard to the latter, contrast MSp. *es cansado* 'it is tedious' and *está cansado* 'he is tired'.

   Keypoint: *ser* **and** *estar* (p. 290).

20.3.4 Possada (l.13) 'lodging' is derived from Lat. PAUSĀTA [PAUSO] 'to stop'. The verb *posar* 'to settle', 'come to rest' has in the twentieth century extended its meanings to that of 'to pose' as a result of a calque from its French cognate *poser*, which has developed a wider range of meanings.

20.3.5 Alguazil (l.25) derives from Ar. *wazīr* 'minister'. This word has seen a number of changes in meaning, beginning in Arabic itself, when the term came to be applied in Al-Andalus to the governor of a town, and was subsequently applied to holders of a range of official duties. In the sixteenth century it has the meaning of 'bailiff' or 'constable'.

20.3.6 Soldada (l.31) is a morphological derivative of Lat. √SŎLĬDU[M] 'sum of money', 'pay' (which was itself the origin of Sp. *sueldo*). Another derivative is *soldado*, originally 'mercenary' (as distinct from a soldier who fought through feudal allegiance – the notion evolves in the course of the fifteenth century, and as a paid army became the norm the word lost its financial connotations to have its modern meaning of 'soldier').

20.3.7 Both *restar* (**resta**, l.32) and the longer-standing *quedar* (**quedo**, l.34, see 6.3.6) are used in this passage. *Restar* was infrequent in Old Castilian and may be a learned word or a borrowing from It. *restare* or Fr. *rester*, both of which have the meaning that *restar* has here of 'to remain'. In Modern Spanish this notion is rendered by *quedar*, and *restar* has developed the meaning of 'to take away', which in some respects is the converse of 'to remain', since what is not taken away remains.

20.3.8 Gentilhombre (l.32) is a calque of Fr. *gentilhomme* 'gentleman', 'member of the nobility'. It is a term of great respect.

20.3.9 For **moço** (l.10) see 18.3.10; for *suceder* (**sucediesse** l.13) see 23.3.1; for *apretar* (**apretá** l.21) see *prieto* 11.3.6.

21 Santa Teresa, Letter to Padre García de Toledo (1562)

21.0 Santa Teresa (1515–82) was a nun of the Carmelite order who at the age of 40 experienced a religious renewal which led her to found a reformed Carmelite order based on a life of prayer, in a state of poverty and complete withdrawal from the world. She left a number of writings which described the contemplative life, together with an extensive correspondence.

This text is interesting not only in its own right but for the secondary information it gives about Santa Teresa's writings. The letter, to Padre García de Toledo, was written to accompany the manuscript copy of the *Libro de la Vida*, which Santa Teresa had been rewriting, at the request of her confessors, as a continuous narrative. She had been encouraged to write as the spirit moved her, without too much care for style; thus the *Vida*, like her letters, represents in some respects a much more spontaneous style of cultured Spanish than other contemporary creative literary texts. Spontaneity must not be confused with illiteracy, however: Teresa was an educated lady whose written style is indebted to cultured sources.

The text

In the left hand column is Teresa's manuscript, which has been transcribed intact apart from the modernising of word divisions (Fuente 1873: 414–5); in the right hand column is the Salamanca *editio princeps* version of 26 years later (Artigas 1935: 544). As in the case of Text 22, it is interesting to be able to compare the two; Teresa's manuscript was prepared for publication by no less a figure than Fray Luis de León, who for his time was exemplary as an editor, but this did not mean that original spelling was respected or even that every word was left intact.

Further reading

Menéndez Pidal (1942); Poitrey (1983).

El espiritu santo sea sienpre con v.m.	*El Spiritu santo sea siempre con v.m.*
amen. no seria malo encareçer a v.m.	*Amén. No seria malo encarecer a v.m.*
este serviçio por obligarle a tener	*este seruicio, por obligarle a tener*
mucho cuydado de encomendarme a	*mucho cuydado de encomendarme a*
nuestro señor q̃ sigun lo q̃ e pasado en	*Dios, que segũ lo que he passado en* 5
verme escrita y traer a la memoria	*verme escrita, y traer a la memoria*
tantas miserias mias bien podria	*tantas miserias mias, bien podria,*
anq̃ con verdad puedo deçir q̃ e	*aunque con verdad puedo dezir, que he*
sentido mas en escrivir las mercedes q̃	*sentido mas en escriuir las mercedes que*
el señor me a echo q̃ las	*nuestro Señor me ha hecho, que las* 10
ofensas q̃ yo a su majestad/yo e	*offensas que yo a su Magestad. Yo he*
echo lo q̃ v.m. me mando en	*hecho lo que v.m. me mãdo en*
alargarme a condiçion q̃ v.m. aga lo	*alargarme a condicion, que v.m. haga lo*
q̃ me prometio en Ronper lo q̃ mal le	*que me prometio, en romper lo q̃ mal le*
pareçiere no avia/acabado de leerlo	*pareciere. No auia acabado de leerlo* 15
despues de escrito cuando v.m. enbia	*despues de escrito, quãdo v.m. embia*
por el/puede ser vayan algunas cosas	*por el: puede ser vayã algunas cosas*
mal declaradas y otras puestas dos	*mal declaradas y otras puestas dos*
veçes por q̃ a sido tan poco el tienpo	*vezes; porque ha sido tan poco el tiempo*
q̃ e tenido q̃ no podia tornar a ver	*que he tenido, que no podia tornar a ver* 20
lo q̃ escrivia suplico a v.m. lo	*lo que escriuia, suplico a v.m. lo*

enmjẽde y mande trasladar si se a de
llevar a el pᵉ maestro avila porq̃
podria ser conoçer algien la letra yo
deseo arto se de orden en como lo vea
pues con ese intento lo començe a
escrivir porq̃ como a el le parez[?]ca voy
por buen camjno q̃dare muy
consolada q̃ ya no me q̃da mas pa
açer lo q̃ es en mj/en todo aga v.m.
como le pareçiere y ve esta obligado a
qujen ansi le fia su alma/la de v.m.
encomendare yo toda mj vida a nuestro
señor por eso dese priesa a servir a su
majestad pa açerme a mj merced
pues vera v.m. por lo q̃ aquj va quan
bien se enplea en darse todo como v.m.
lo a començado a qujen tan sin tasa se
nos da sea bendito por sienpre q̃ yo
espero en su misericordia nos veremos
adonde mas claramente v.m. y yo
veamos las grandes q̃ a echo con
nosotros y pa sienpre jamas le
alabemos amen +
acabose este libro en junio año
de mdlxij.

enmiende, y mande trasladar, si se ha de
llevar al padre maestro Auila, porque
podria conocer alguno la letra. Yo
desseo harto se de orden como lo vea,   25
pues cõ esse intento lo comence a
escriuir; porque como a el le parezca voy
por buen camino, quedare muy
consolada, que ya no me queda mas para
hazer lo que es en mi. En todo haga v.m.   30
como le pareciere y vee esta obligado a
quien ansi le fia su alma: la de v.m.
encomendare yo toda mi vida al
Señor, por eso de se priessa a seruir a su
Magestad para hazerme a mi merced,   35
pues vera v.m. por lo que aquí va quã
bien se emplea en darse todo, como v.m.
lo ha començado, a quien tan sin tassa se
nos da, sea bendito por siempre, que yo
espero en su misericordia nos veremos   40
a donde mas claramente v.m. y yo
veamos las grandes que ha hecho con
nosotros, y para siempre jamas le
alabemos, Amen.
Acabose este libro en Iunio, de   45
M.D.LXII.

Translation

May the Holy Spirit be always with you, amen.

It would not be amiss to stress to you the importance of this service in order
to oblige you to take great care to commend me to Our Lord, which I might
well do in view of what I have undergone in seeing my life written down and
calling so many of my miserable deeds to mind; although I can truly say that
I have felt more in writing of the mercies the Lord has done me than I have
felt in writing of the offences I have committed against His Majesty.

I have done what you ordered by writing at length, on condition that you will
do what you promised me by cutting out anything which seems bad to you. I
had not finished reading it through after writing it, when you sent for it. It may
be that some things are badly put and that other things are said twice, because
the time I have had has been so short, that I could not look again at what I was
writing. I beg you to amend it and have it copied, if it is to be taken to Maestro
Ávila, because someone may recognise the handwriting. I sincerely wish you to
do as you see fit, since I began to write it with that intention; because if it seemed
to you that I was on the right track, I would be greatly consoled, for now I have
no more strength to represent what is in me. In everything, do as you think fit
and see that you are obliged to the one who so entrusts her soul to you.

Plate 4 Santa Teresa, Letter to Padre García de Toledo (Text 21). © Patrimonio Nacional.

For the whole of my life I will commend your (soul) to Our Lord. Therefore hurry to serve God in order to show me favour, for you will see, by what is set down here, how well one is employed in giving oneself completely – as you have begun to do – to Him who gives Himself so freely to us.

May He be blessed for ever, for I hope in His mercy that we shall see one another where you and I may more clearly see the great things He has done for us and that we shall praise Him for ever. Amen.

This book was finished in June, in the year 1562.

Phonetics and phonology

21.1.1 There is clear evidence in Teresa's text of the devoicing of the medieval sibilants: there is no distinction between *ss* and *s* corresponding to OCast. /s/ and /z/ (**pasado**, l.5, **deseo**, l.25) and *ç* rather than *z* is used in **veçes** (l.19), **açer** (l.30). The printed version continues the distinction in spelling (*passado*, *desseo*, *vezes*, *hazer*). Initial /h/ must also have fallen, since initial written *h* is completely absent (**echo**, l.10, **aga**, l.13, etc.).
   Keypoint: the sibilants of Old Castilian (p. 290); **the f>h change** (p. 271).

21.1.2 Priesa (l.34) < Lat. PRĔSSA, the past participle of PRĔMO, is an earlier form of MSp. *prisa*; the modern development illustrates the reduction of the diphthong /je/ which appears to have been favoured by a following /s/.
   Keypoint: vowels (p. 296).

21.1.3 Sigun (l.5) ‖ MSp. *según* < Lat. SECŬNDUM, corrected to *segun* in print, illustrates the variation often seen between atonic /e/ and /i/ in Old Castilian (see 9.1.7, 28.1.3).
   Keypoint: vowels (p. 296).

21.1.4 For **ansi** (l.32) see 11.1.11. Although *así* was eventually preferred in the modern standard language, *ansí* is still encountered in popular speech and is reasonably common in Latin America.

Morphology and syntax

21.2.1 The future subjunctive continues to be used in a relative clause with an indefinite antecedent (**lo q̃ mal le pareçiere**, ll.14–15) and in a semantically very similar adverbial clause (**como le pareçiere**, l.31); in both cases there is clear future reference (cf. 4.2.8, 18.2.10, 22.2.5, 28.2.4). However, we can see in this text how the present subjunctive is also used in a very similar adverbial clause (**adonde . . . veamos las grandes . . . y . . . le alabemos**, ll.41–44), and in other contexts as a future-referring form: (conditional conjunction: **a condiçion q̃ v. m. aga . . .**, l.13; indirect commands: **suplico . . . lo enmjẽde y mande trasladar . . .**, ll.21–22, and **deseo arto se de orden . . .**, l.25).
   Keypoint: the future subjunctive (p. 275).

21.2.2 Vayan mal declaradas y ... puestas dos veçes (ll.17–19). This is an example of *ir* used as an aspectually marked passive auxiliary. In Modern Spanish, *ir* + past participle has the nuance of a resultant state of affairs (like *estar* + past participle) or of a stage that is reached in a process. Spanish has developed a wide range of such usages with auxiliary verbs.

    Keypoints: the passive (p. 281); **periphrastic verb forms** (p. 283).

21.2.3 Despues de escrito (l.16). The past participle provides an economical alternative to an infinitive or full-clause after *después de* (cf. here *después de haberlo escrito*); the construction is still to be found in modern journalistic register.

21.2.4. Lo començe a escrivir (ll.26–7). This is an example of clitic-climbing (see 8.2.6).

    Keypoint: clitic pronoun position (p. 264).

21.2.5 Quan (l.36) is an apocopated form of *cuanto* < Lat. QUANTU[M], though it was QUAM that had this function in Latin. *Cuán* survives in Modern Spanish in formal written register, though in the spoken language *qué* is preferred; the notion of 'how' + adjective/adverb can also be rendered by a structure involving the 'neuter' form *lo* (here the corresponding construction would be *lo bien que se emplea*), a construction which appears to date from around this time (Keniston 1937: 159).

    Keypoint: gender (p. 275).

21.2.6 The complementiser *que* is omitted in a number of complement constructions: **puede ser vayan** ... (l.17), **suplico ... lo enmjēde** ... (ll.21–2), **deseo arto se de** ... (l.25), **parezca voy** ... (l.27), **ve esta obligado** (l.31), **espero .. . nos veremos** ... (l.40). This is a very common feature of Santa Teresa's style (see also 12.2.3, 17.2.5, 22.2.6, 23.2.4).

21.2.7 In the construction **podria ser conoçer algien la letra** (l.24) an infinitive complement is used where a full clause complement would be used in the modern language (*podría ser que alguien conociera la letra*). This is an example of what is sometimes referred to as 'nominative and infinitive' complementation; it is favoured in fifteenth- and sixteenth-century Spanish alongside the more frequent 'accusative and infinitive' complementation, which is also very common in Santa Teresa. These constructions have often been seen as the result of learned syntactic influence and were certainly used in the consciously Latinate style of several fifteenth-century authors (see 13.2.7), though their free adoption in Golden-Age prose by writers, who, like Santa Teresa, were not seeking any learned affectation, shows just how far they penetrated the language. (On the other hand, Santa Teresa's prose style is not without learned precedent: see 21.2.9.)

21.2.8 Ellipsis typical of the spoken language (see Text 25) is observable in **e sentido mas en escrivir las m*erce*des q̄ el señor me a echo q̄ [en escribir] las ofensas q̄ yo [he hecho] a su Majestad** (ll.8–11; the understood material is given in square brackets). It is the omission of *he hecho* that is most striking (a phenomenon sometimes known as 'gapping', in which a repeated verb is suppressed): whilst common in English, e.g. *John likes pears and Harry carrots*, it is less common in Spanish even in spoken registers, perhaps because of the range of information which the more highly inflected Spanish verb carries. Ellipsis of a noun is to be seen in **las grandes** (l.42), where *mercedes* is to be understood.

21.2.9 Notwithstanding the spontaneous nature of Santa Teresa's style, it is clear that she uses a number of rhetorical devices which were regularly employed in cultured prose. There is circumlocution or periphrasis in l.32 **qujen ansi le fía su alma** (i.e. Santa Teresa herself) and ll.38–9 **qujen tan sin tasa se nos da** (i.e. God). She varies anaphoric reference in l.11 by using **su majestad** rather than **el Señor**. There is a rather complex cataphoric reference of *la* to *vida* in **la de v.m. encomendar yo toda mj vida a nuestro señor** (ll.32–4). What all these devices have in common is avoiding using the same word too often.

21.2.10 For the use of **adonde** (l.41) in a locative rather than an allative sense, see 18.2.7, 27.2.1; for the use of **algien** (as opposed to the printer's *alguno*, l.24), see 18.2.8.

Vocabulary

21.3.1 *Ser* is still used with locative expressions to indicate the notion of existence: **El espiritu santo sea sienpre con v.m.** (l.1), **lo q̃ es en mi** (l.30).
  Keypoint: *ser* and *estar* (p. 290).

21.3.2 Encareçer (l.2) is a morphological derivative of Lat. √CĀRU[S] 'dear', and has the basic meaning of 'to make dearer'. By associative extension it comes to have the meaning of 'to give a high(er) value to' (as here), and hence 'to commend'.

21.3.3 Arto (l.25) (*harto*) is extensively used at this time in the sense of *mucho* (and also, with an adjective, in the sense of *muy*). *Harto* derives from Lat. FARTU[M] the past participle of FARCĬO 'to fill' and especially 'to stuff'; as an adverbially used adjective (cf. 6.2.3) it must originally have had the meaning 'fully'. The adverbial function continues in formal literary register in modern Spanish, and, more generally, in Latin America. Alongside this development it comes to have a pejorative meaning '(stuffed) full of food' which continues in the modern meaning of 'fed up', which is nowadays its usual function in the Peninsula.
  Keypoint: **adverbs** (p. 262).

21.3.4 The vocabulary of this letter contains no rare learned words; such learned words as are here are of long standing in the language and have passed into everyday usage, a selection being: **memoria** (l.6), **miserias** (l.7), **suplico** (l.21), **obligado** (l.31).
  Keypoint: **learned and popular, semilearned and semipopular** (p. 277).

22 Streetwise in Seville. Francisco de Quevedo, *El Buscón* (1626)

22.0 Francisco de Quevedo Villegas (1580–1645) was a product of the new capital of Madrid, where his family were civil servants. *El Buscón* is an early work, in the nascent picaresque genre which took as its theme a youngster living by his wits as he grows up; such works are extremely valuable linguistically because they record, albeit within the conventions of literature, the usage of many sectors of society, both the language of the *pícaro* and the petty (and not so petty) criminal classes and the language of the many people the *pícaro* meets on his travels. Quevedo was fascinated by language, and the passage studied here, from the last chapter of the novel, gives a considerable amount of information about *germanía*, or thieves' slang (Quevedo was one of very few poets to write *romances* using this jargon and is a major source of our knowledge of this sociolect) and about its contemporary pronunciation. He is also well known for his ingenuity as an author in using word-play, which often exploits the multiple meanings of the same word in different registers.

The text

The version in bold is transcribed from *Historia de la Vida del Buscón, llamado Don Pablos; exemplo de Vagamundos, y espejo de Tacaños, por Don Francisco de Quevedo Villegas* . . . (Rouen, Carlos Osmont, 1629), pp.159–61, which is derived from the *editio princeps* published in Zaragoza by Pedro Vergés three years earlier. We are fortunate in having an early seventeenth-century manuscript (known as MS B) which is generally held to represent Quevedo's intentions most faithfully. The transcription of this manuscript made by Lázaro Carreter (1980) is given in roman type. The texts are literally transcribed, even though some errors are obvious (e.g. the use of **le** for **se** in the published edition, l.23, **quietar** for **quitar**, l.17, possibly **entienden** for **entiende**, l.18).

Further reading

Two indispensable editions of *El Buscón* are Lázaro Carreter (1980) and Jauralde Pou (1990). Hill (1945) is a modern edition of Quevedo's *Jácaras* and *Bailes*, together with Juan Hidalgo's 1609 anthology of *romances* in *germanía* and Hidalgo's glossary, which is an invaluable source of reference.

Mas quiza declarando yo algunas chanzas, y modos de hablar estaran
Mas quiça declarando yo algunas chanças y modos de hablar estaran
mas auisados los ignorantes, y los que leyeron mi libro sera*n* engaña-
mas auisados los ignorantes, y los que leyeren mi libro, seran engaña-
dos por su culpa. No te fies ombre en dar tu la varaja, que te la
dos por su culpa. No te fies hombre en dar tu la varaja, que te la
trocaran al despauilar de vna vela; guarda el naype de tocamientos
trocaran al despauilar de vna vela, guarda el naype de tocamientos

raspados, o bruñidos cossa con que se conocen los azares. Y por si fueres

raspados, o bruñidos, cosa con que se conocen los azares, y por si fueres   *5*

picaro letor aduierte, que en cocinas, y cauallerizas, pican con vn

picaro (lector) aduierte, que en cozinas y caualleriças pican con vn

alfiler, v dobla*n* los azares para conocerlos por lo hendido. Si

alfiler, o doblando los açares para conocerlos por lo hendido: y si

tratares con gente onrrada guardate del naype, que desde la estampa

tratares con gente honrrada, guardate del naype, que desde la estampa

fue concebido en pecado, y que con traer atrauessado el papel dize lo

fue concebido en pecado, y que con traer atrauessado el papel dize lo

que viene. No te fies de naype lympio, que al que da vista, y reten, lo

que viene; no te fies de naype limpio, que al que da vista y retiene, lo   *10*

mas jabonado es sucio. Aduierte que a la carteta el q*ue* haze los

mas xabonado es suzio; aduierte que a la carteta, el que haze los

naypes que no doble mas arqueadas las figuras fuera de los reyes, que

naypes que no doble, más arqueadas las figuras, fuera de los Reyes, que

las de mas cartas: por que el tal doblar es por tu dinero difu*n*to. A la

las demas cartas, porque el tal doblar es por tu dinero difunto: a la

primera mira no den de arriba las que descarta el que da y procura,

primera, mira no den de arriba las que descarta el que da, y procura,

q*ue* no se pidan cartas, v por los dedos en el naype, v por las primeras

que no se pidan cartas, o por los dedos en el naype, o por las primeras   *15*

letras de las palabras. No quiero darte luz de mas cossas estas bastan

letras de las palabras. NO quiero darte luz de mas cosas, estas bastan

para saber que as de viuir con cautela: pues es cierto, que son infinitas

para saber que has de viuir con cautela, pues es cierto que son infinitas

las maulas, que te callo. Dar muerte: llaman quitar el dinero, y con

las maulas que te callo. Dar muerte llaman quietar el dinero, y con

propiedad. Reuessa llama*n* la treta contra el amigo, que de puro

propiedad: reuesa llaman la treta contra el amigo, que de puro

reuessada no la entiende. Dobles so*n* los que acarrean sencillos, para

reuessada no la entienden: dobles son los que acarrean senzillos, para   *20*

que los desuellen estos rastreros de volsas Blanco; llaman al sano de

que los desuellen estos rastreros de bolsas; blanco llaman al sano de

malicia, y bueno como el pan: Y negro al que dexa en blanco sus

malicia, y bueno como el pan; y negro al que dexa en blanco sus

diligencias. Yo pues con este lenguaje . . . llegue a Sebilla con el dinero

diligencias. Yo pues con este lenguage . . . llegue a Seuilla con el dinero

de las camaradas . . . Fuime luego a apear al meson del moro donde

de las camaradas . . . Fuyme luego a apear al Meson del Moro, donde

me topo vn condicipulo mio de Alcala, que se llamaba Mata, y agora

me topo vn condiscipulo mio de Alcala, que se llamaua Mata, y agora   *25*

se decia, por parecerle nombre de poco ruydo; Matorral . . . Dixome,

le decía, por parecerle nombre de poco ruydo, Matorral . . . dixome,

que me auia de ir a cenar con el, y otros camaradas, y que ellos me

que me auia de yr a cenar con el, y otros camaradas, y que ellos me

voluerian al meson. Fui, llegamos a su posada, y dixo, Ea quite la capa

boluerian al Meson. Fuy, llegamos a su posada, y dixo: ea quite la capa
buace y parezca ombre, que vera esta noche todos los buenos hijos de
buze y parezca hombre, que vera esta noche todos los buenos hijos de
jeuilla. Y por que no lo tengan por Maricon ahaje, esse cuello; y
Seuilla. Y por que no lo tengan por maricon ahaxe esse cuello, y   *30*
agobie de espaldas; la capa cayda; que siempre nosotros andamos de
agouie de espaldas, la capa cayda (que siempre andamos nosotros de
capa cayda. Esse hoçico de tornillo, gestos, aun lado, y a otro, y haga
capa cayda y esse ozico de tornillo, gestos a vn lado y a otro, y haga
buce de las. i. h. y de las. h. J. diga conmigo jerida, mojino, jumo,
buce de la g, h, y de la h, g, diga conmigo: gerida, mogino, gumo;
paheria, mohar, habali y harro de vino. Tomelo de memoria . . .
paheria, mohar, habali y harro de vino. Tomèlo de memoria . . .

Translation

(The translation that follows gives something of the flavour of the original whilst keeping as close to it as possible for purposes of elucidation; a more literary version could go much further in the use of English slang):

But perhaps if I tell of some tricks and turns of phrase, the ignorant will be better informed, and those who read my book will be deceived only through their own fault.

Do not trust, friend, to using your own pack of cards, because it will get swapped for you as quickly as you can snuff out a candle. Beware of any card which has marks, scratches or shine, by which the cards can be recognised. And just in case you are a vagabond, reader, know that in kitchens and stables they prick the cards with a pin or bend them in order to be able to recognise them by the crease. If you play with a better class of person, beware of a card which was conceived in sin from the printer's and has a watermark in it which says what it is. Do not trust a clean card, because to someone who has a keen eye and a trick to play (a retentive memory) even the best washed one is dirty. Watch when you are playing *carteta* that the dealer doesn't bend over the picture cards more than the other cards except for the kings, because such a bending (tolling) is for your money, which is dead. At *primera*, watch that you don't get given from the top of the pack those cards that the dealer is discarding, and make sure that the players do not ask for cards (surreptitiously) either by using their fingers on the card or the first letters of words. I do not want to enlighten you about anything else; these things are enough for you to know that you must live cautiously, because for sure the tricks that I don't mention are infinite in number. *Dar muerte* ('kill') means to take someone's money, appropriately enough. *Revesa* ('trick', 'twist', 'reversal') means deception of a friend (i.e. partner at cards), which is so thoroughly obscure (twisted) that he doesn't realise what's going on. *Dobles* ('doubles') are those who bring along *sencillos* ('simpletons') to be fleeced by these swindlers; *blanco* ('white') is what they call someone who is innocent of evildoing and thoroughly honest; and *negro* ('black') anyone who leaves his mark on a *blanco* [?].

So, with this jargon . . . I arrived in Seville with my comrades' money . . . I then went to stay at the Moor's inn, where I bumped into a fellow student from

Alcalá who was called Mata ('thicket') and because he didn't find it resonant enough, now called himself Matorral (also 'thicket') . . . He said that I should dine with him and some other comrades, and they would take me back to the inn. I went along; we arrived at his dwelling and he said:

'Hey, take off your cape and look like a man, for you'll see all the good lads of Seville tonight. And so they don't take you for a queer, lower that collar and hunch your shoulders; [wear] your cape off the shoulder, for we always wear our capes off our shoulders. That mug of yours, give it a twist; gesticulate this side and that, and turn your "i"s into "h"s and "h"s into "j"s. Say after me: *jerida (herida), mojino (mohino), jumo (humo), pahería (pajería), mohar (mojar), habalí (jabalí)* and *haro de vino (jarro de vino).*'

I took it to heart.

Phonetics and phonology

22.1.1 The variations in spelling observable between the two versions given here show how unstandardised the spelling of Spanish still was. They also show that, despite the retention of many of the features of medieval spelling, the phonemic distinctions that these imply could not possibly have been realised.

The variant spellings **cosas** and **cossas** (l.16) suggest that there is no longer a distinction between /s/ and /z/, and that it has been neutralised as /s/.

The printed version uses ç, which is infrequent in the manuscript, where *z* is used (where the manuscript does use ç, the printed version uses *z*: **hoçico/ozico**, l.29); both use *c* before a front vowel to render the sibilant, and here again there is variation between printed **suzio** and manuscript **sucio** (l.11). This suggests an absence of contrast between /dz/ and /ts/.

X and *j* vary similarly (**xabonado** in print versus **jabonado** in the manuscript, l.10), suggesting a lack of distinction between /ʃ/ and /ʒ/.

B and *v* seem to be completely interchangeable: **volsas/bolsas**, l.21, < Lat. [BŬRSA], **boluerian**, l.28, < Lat. [VOLVO], and **varaja**, l.3 (while the ultimate etymological origin of this word is uncertain, the cognate Ptg. *baralhar* may be compared).

Keypoint: the 'b/v' merger (p. 262).

Initial *h* is generally used in words which had an initial /h/ in the sixteenth century (**hablar** ← Lat. [FĀBŬLOR], l.1, **hendido** ← Lat. [FINDO], l.7, **haze** < Lat. FĂCĬT [FĂCĬO], l.11, **hijos** < Lat. FĪLĬŌS [FĪLĬUS], l.29, **haga** ≤ Lat. FĂCĬAT [FĂCĬO], l.32); however, the spelling **ozico**, l.32 (see 22.3.2 below), suggests that the *h* may not always have been articulated. Derivatives of words which had an initial /h/ in Latin show the now usual vacillation in spelling between the use and non-use of *h*: **honrada/onrrada** < Lat. HŎNŌRĀTA [HŎNŌRĀTUS], l.7, **as/has**, < Lat. [HĂBĒO], l.17. The word **desuellen** (l.21), from Lat. ?[EXFOLLO] 'to skin' (from √FOLLIS 'bellows', 'leather bag' which came to mean 'skin of an animal'), also shows weakening of an internal Latin /f/, though it seems to have undergone early loss, no doubt due to the preceding consonant which would have made articulation of such a group awkward.

Keypoint: the f>h change (p. 271).

22.1.2 A number of features of the speech of the Seville underworld are indicated here.

Matorral's instructions to Pablos on pronunciation (ll.32–4) appear to be (a) that the Madrid /h/ should be pronounced [x] and (b) that /x/ should be pronounced [h] (the variation in the text here shows that this was not easy to express using conventional orthography!). (a) probably indicates the later preservation in Andalusia of the /h/ of Golden-Age Spanish, since whatever sound is represented by *j* in all the words quoted here, it derives from Latin /f/: **jerida/gerida** (‖ MSp. *herida*) from Lat. FĔRĪTA [FĔRĬO], **jumo/gumo** ‖ (MSp. *humo*) from Lat. FŪMU[S] and **mojino/mogino**, though of uncertain origin, has a cognate *mofino* in Portuguese. Indeed, /h/ is preserved today in some of the Extremaduran and western Andalusian dialects (Zamora Vicente 1967: 298–9). (b) is a familiar feature of modern Andalusian and Latin American pronunciation, the laxing of [x] to a point where it loses its frication and is articulated as [h] (see Chapter XII, introduction). It is also likely that /h/ and /x/ had merged in Sevillian speech as /h/.

 Keypoint: the f>h change (p. 271).

22.1.3 Two spellings in particular are not easy to interpret. **Jeuilla** (l.30), in the manuscript, seems to be a deliberate attempt to represent the speech of Matorral, but it is unlikely that *j* represents [h] or [x] (unless we assume a variant development of initial /s/ to OCast. /ʃ/, see 15.1.4; another possibility is hypercorrection, see 38.1.4). **Ahaxe/ahaje** (l.30) presumably corresponds to *abaje*, though the devoicing of [β] to [ɸ] or [h] which the use of *h* appears to imply is again not usual.

22.1.4 As frequently occurs at this time, there are variant spellings of learned words which have undergone semipopular modification: **letor/lector**, l.6, **condicipulo/condiscipulo**, l.25. See also 19.1.4 and 23.1.2.

Morphology and syntax

22.2.1 Buace and **buce** (ll.29 and 33) provide evidence of the changing forms produced by the progressive reduction of the courtesy formula *vuestra merced* to MSp. *usted*. It is likely that these forms are again a particular feature of Matorral's speech, since the abbreviation *V.M.* or *V.Md.* is used in other parts of *El Buscón*. See also 20.1.3, 24.2.1.

 Keypoint: personal pronouns (p. 284).

22.2.2 Porque + subjunctive (l.30) continues to be used as a way of expressing purpose, though both *para que* and *por que* are used in this way in *El Buscón*, with a slight preference for the former.

22.2.3 Mas quiça declarando yo ... (l.1). Since the gerund has a subject (**yo**) which is different from the subject of the main verb (**los ignorantes**), it is overtly expressed: see also 23.2.6. An overt subject with a non-finite verb may also be used for clarity: **No te fies hombre en dar tu la varaja** (l.3) ('don't trust to supplying the cards yourself').

22.2.4 The now firmly-established contrast between *ser* and *estar* with past participles is neatly illustrated in the first sentence: **estaran mas auisados los ignorantes** (ll.1–2), implying 'they will have been warned' and so envisaging the result of that warning, as opposed to **seran engañados por su culpa** (ll.2–3) 'they will be deceived' (on particular occasions, that is to say, people will deceive them). The first is what we may call a stative passive, the second a dynamic passive.

   Keypoints: *ser* **and** *estar* (p. 290); **the passive** (p. 281).

22.2.5 The future subjunctive continues to be used in the protases of future-referring conditional sentences (**si tratares con gente honrada**, ll.7–8, cf. 28.2.4) and with **por si** (l.5), and with indefinite antecedents in future-referring relative clauses (**los que leyeren mi libro**, l.2, cf. 4.2.8, 18.2.10, 28.2.4).

   Keypoints: **conditional sentences** (p. 265); **the future subjunctive** (p. 275).

22.2.6 The complementiser *que* is omitted in the construction **mira no den de arriba** . . . (l.14), though it is used elsewhere (**procura que no se pidan** . . ., ll.14–15). See also 12.2.3, 17.2.5, 23.2.4.

22.2.7 The notion of an indefinite subject is expressed by the third person plural (**te la trocaran**, ll.3–4, **no den de arriba** . . ., l.14, **llaman**, ll.18 and 21) or by the passive reflexive (**no se pidan cartas** . . ., l.15, cf. 19.2.4).

   Keypoint: **the passive** (p. 281); **the reflexive** (p. 288).

22.2.8 The *haber de* + infinitive paraphrase is here used in a deontic modal sense (**has de viuir con cautela** 'you should live cautiously', l.17; **que me auia de yr a cenar con el** 'that I should go and dine with him', ll.27).

   Keypoint: **periphrastic verb forms** (p. 283).

Vocabulary

22.3.1 Camarada (l.24) is a derivative of √*cámara*, and originally refers to a group of soldiers sharing the same quarters – as such it is attested in the sixteenth century, and Covarrubias refers to it as having a primarily military application. From this meaning it particularises to the meaning of 'comrade' (the English word is a borrowing from Fr. *camerade* which in turn is a borrowing from the Spanish). It is used in this passage in both the feminine (l.24) and the masculine (l.27) gender; in origin, as a collective noun, it would have been feminine, though subsequently as a count noun its gender changes in accordance with its male reference (cf. such words as *guardia, policía*). The evidence of the feminine gender in a count use here suggests that for a time it may have functioned as a member of the very small class of nouns in Spanish which, while feminine, can refer to either sex (e.g. *persona, víctima*).

   Keypoint: **gender** (p. 275).

22.3.2 Quevedo obligingly glosses several expressions from the language of the *germanía*. Some of the types of semantic change exemplified in the course of the history of Spanish are also in evidence in the development of the specialised meaning of *germanía* words.

Dar muerte (l.18) for **quitar el dinero** is an example of hyperbole, though Quevedo plays on the literal meaning, since ruin may imply starvation, by adding **y con propiedad**.

Metaphor and the traditional pragmatic association of goodness with the colour white and evil with the colour black are responsible for the meanings here of **blanco** and **negro** (ll.21–2).

Reuesa 'double-cross' (l.19) is a morphological derivative of the verb **reuesar** (cf. *habla* from *hablar*). Covarrubias 1977 [1611] gives this verb in the sense of 'to vomit' (cf. MSp. *devolver*), but its most common form seems to be the past participle **reues(s)ada**, on which Quevedo plays in l.20, and which, as *enrevesado*, still survives in the sense of 'entangled'. Covarrubias gives it the specific meaning of 'obscure', which is also the meaning in this text. (*Revés*, and possibly **reuesar**, are based on Lat. √RĒVERSU[M], the supine of RĒVERTOR; *reverso* is of more recent date – Covarrubias considers it 'más italiano que español'.)

Reten (l.10), which is 'corrected' to **retiene** in printed versions, is in fact a *germanía* word recorded by Hidalgo (see Hill 1945: 121) as meaning 'tener el naype quando el fullero juega, que se suele dezir saluar: y ellos dizen Salua tierra'. **Reten** must presumably be a noun formed from the imperative of *retener*. A play on this slang meaning of the word and its more generally accepted meaning of 'to retain (in the mind)' is no doubt intended.

Hoçico (l.32), *lit.* 'snout', is a morphological derivative of *hozar* 'to root (as of pigs)', which comes ultimately from Lat. ?FŎDIĀRE, itself a derivative of Lat. FŎDIO 'to dig'. Its use as a slang equivalent for *nariz* 'nose' is an example of incipient amelioration through self-deprecation. See also 3.3.2, 15.3.5, 25.3.2, 29.3.1.

22.3.3 Picaro (l.6) is of uncertain origin, but seems to have a connection with the verb *picar* 'to prick', which had various metaphorical meanings. Hidalgo (see Hill 1945: 120) defines *picador* as 'ladrón de ganzúa', i.e. a thief who makes use of a hook to carry out robberies and pickpocketing, and this is an obvious synecdochic association.

22.3.4 Mata and **Matorral** (ll.25 and 26) are close synonyms; the preference for the latter is reminiscent of many changes to vocabulary brought about by phonetic reinforcement of short words (see, for example, 6.3.9, 10.2.12).

22.3.5 Chanza (l.1) is a borrowing from It. *ciancia* 'trick'. This is one of its earliest attestations in Spanish.

22.3.6 Maulas (l.18) appears to be a morphological derivative of *maullar*, the onomatopoeic word for the mewing of a cat; the meaning of 'tricks' is presumably due to association with the animal.

22.3.7 Treta (l.19), is a borrowing from Fr. *traite*, a term used in fencing.

22.3.8 Rastreros (l.21) were so called because they worked the *Rastro* area of Madrid (formerly the abattoir, now the famous flea-market); there may also be a phonetic association with *rastrillo* 'rake' and *rastillo*, the *germanía* word for 'hand'.

22.3.9 *Topar* (**topo**, l.25) is a morphological derivative of the onomatopoeic expression *¡top!*

22.3.10 Maricon (l.30) is a derivative by affective suffixation of the proper name *María*, also rendered by *marica* and *mariquita*. From the original meaning of *marica* as 'effeminate man', these words evolved in popular usage to the meaning of 'homosexual'.

22.3.11 Agouie [**agobiar**] (l.31), derives from Lat. √GIBBU[S] 'hunch'; *agobiado* was originally used especially in the meaning of 'weighed down by a load on one's back'. The verb has since broadened in meaning to mean 'to oppress'.

22.3.12 Doblando (l.7) < Lat. [DŬPLO] 'to double' underwent a remarkable number of associational changes of meaning without losing its Latin meaning: in Modern Spanish, its meanings include 'to fold', 'to toll (of a bell)', 'to turn (a corner)' and most recently 'to dub (a film)'. Quevedo exploits its polysemy to make his pun.

22.3.13 For **estampa** (l.8), see 23.3.2; for **lenguage** (l.23), see 18.3.3.

X   The Enlightenment

The eighteenth century in Spain brought many political and social changes through the implantation of the Bourbon dynasty beginning with Philip V, which was a consequence of the death of the last of the Habsburgs, the childless Charles II. Government became more centralised, and France became a model to be imitated; the ideas of the Enlightenment were also cultivated and reforms carried out, especially in the reign of Charles III (1758–88), although Spain continued to suffer from the deadweight of many of its ancient customs and institutions. It is an extremely important time in the history of Spanish because of the work of the Real Academia Española, founded in 1713 along the lines of the Académie Française, which had been created by Richelieu in 1634. In the course of the century the RAE produced its dictionary, the so-called *Diccionario de autoridades* (1726–39), the first edition of a standard orthography of Spanish (1741) and its first Grammar (1771: see Sarmiento 1984). These have been regularly revised ever since: at the turn of the twentieth century the dictionary was in its twenty-first edition and effectively fixes the official spelling of the language, though updates are issued through the *Boletín de la Real Academia Española*, which is published at bi-monthly intervals and on the Internet. The most recent Grammar is Alarcos Llorach (1994). A distinctive feature of the Academia is the number of professional academic linguists amongst its members, which ensures the prestige of such work.

23 A policy for linguistic standardisation, from the *Diccionario de autoridades* (1726)

23.0 The constituent members of the RAE were faced with a situation in which, despite a growing consensus about many aspects of usage through the accessibility of printed literature and the pronouncements of a number of commentators on language in the fifteenth and sixteenth centuries (see Texts 16, 17 and 18), Spanish still remained essentially unstandardised, with a large number of variant forms.

  The Academia built its dictionary on the work of those whom they considered to be the best authors (hence the name commonly given to this Dictionary, the *Diccionario de autoridades*), though this policy was generously interpreted, and other authors were cited when necessary. Since a clear aim was enabling a reading of these authors by both Spaniards and foreigners, some words which were obsolete were included, as well as some regional words which were not commonly used in Castilian and words characterised as *jerigonza* or *germanía*. Taboo words, however, are excluded, as are proper nouns and 'technical' words from science and the arts. Amongst previous works to which a debt was owed, the authors acknowledged the great early seventeenth-century dictionary of Covarrubias and the third edition of the Italian *Vocabolario della Crusca*, published in 1691, though they showed considerable independence of mind, not following Covarrubias in a concern with etymology and insisting that their project was the more ambitious one of a dictionary which might include obsolete words rather than being just a simple vocabulary.

Of course, in the end many decisions must have been arbitrary, and the dictionary resolves much of the variation between Latinate and more popular spellings of learned words, generally opting for the former (so, for example, *efecto* is preferred to *efeto*) unless an awkward consonant group was involved (thus *sustancia* is preferred to *substancia*); it can be seen that these preferences have shaped modern standard usage to a considerable degree.

The text

The text is taken from the *Diccionario de autoridades*, I, p.ii.

Further reading

Fries (1989); Lázaro Carreter (1949).

Como basa y fundamento de este Diccionario, se han puesto los Autóres
que ha parecido à la Académia han tratado la Léngua Española con la
mayor propriedád y elegáncia: conociendose por ellos su buen juício,
claridád y proporción, con cuyas autoridades están afianzadas las voces, y
aun algunas, que por no practicadas se ignóra la notícia de ellas, y las   5
que no están en uso, pues aunque son próprias de la Léngua Española, el
olvido y mudanza de térmnos y voces, con la variedád de los tiempos, las
ha hecho yá incultas y despreciables: como igualmente ha sucedido en las
Lénguas Toscana y Francesa, que cada dia se han pulido y perficionado
mas: contribuyendo mucho para ello los Diccionarios y Vocabularios, que   10
de estos Idiómas se han dado à la estampa, y en lo que han trabajado
tantas doctas Académias: sobre lo que es bien reparable, que haviendo
sido Don Sebastian de Covarrubias el priméro que se dedicó à este
nobilissimo estúdio, en que los extrangéros siguiendole se han adelantado
con tanta diligéncia y esmero, sea la Nación Española la última à la   15
perfección del Diccionario de su Léngua: y sin duda no pudiera llegar à
un fin tan grande à no tener un fomento tan elevado como el de su
Augusto Monarcha.

Translation

As the basis and foundation of this Dictionary there have been set those authors who in the opinion of the Academy have treated the Spanish language with the greatest propriety and elegance, and through whom its good judgement, clarity and proportion are realised. The words are accredited by such authorities, and even some words for which there is no information, since they are not current, and those which are not in use, since although they belong to the Spanish language, some terms and words are forgotten and change with the changing times, and this renders them uncultured and despicable, just as has happened in the Tuscan and French languages, which each day are ever more polished and perfected. To this there have contributed the Dictionaries and Vocabularies of these languages which have been given to the press and on which so many learned Academies have laboured. Concerning this, it is noteworthy that though Don Sebastián de Covarrubias was the first to devote himself to this most noble study, in which those foreigners who have followed him have progressed with such diligence and care, the Spanish Nation is the last to achieve a Dictionary of its language. And no doubt it would not have achieved so lofty a goal without an encouragement as elevated as that of its august Monarch.

Phonetics and phonology

23.1.1 The reform of Spanish spelling begun in the *Diccionario* and continued in the 1741 and 1763 *Ortografías* marked the definitive end of the spelling customs which had continued in Spain since the time of Alfonso X (see Text 10) and which had now become totally unsatisfactory because of the considerable changes in the consonant system which had taken place during the sixteenth and seventeenth centuries (see **palatalisation** (p. 280)). The Academia broadly affirmed the principle of a phonemic system of spelling:

- *u* was used only for /u/ and *v* for /b/ (so **Covarrubias**, l.13).
- *ç* was suppressed and replaced by *c* or *z* according to context (see below).
- The distinction between *s* and *ss* was eventually abandoned in the 1763 *Ortografía*, though it is still used in the *Diccionario* (**nobilissimo**, l.14).

However, there was not a one-to-one match between phoneme and letter:

- /θ/ was represented by *c* before a front vowel (*e, i*: **voces**, l.4, **Diccionario**, l.1) but by *z* before a back vowel (*a, o, u*: **afianzadas**, l.4).
- /x/ was generally represented by *g* before a front vowel (**extrangéros**, l.14) but by *j* before a back vowel (**juício**, l.3).
- A distinction was made between some occurrences of [j] and [i], though these could be considered to belong to the same phoneme /i/ in just the same way as [u] and [w] belong to the same phoneme /u/: *i* was used to represent the vowel [i] except in the conjunction *y* 'and' and in some words deriving from Greek, and it represented [j] in diphthongs, provided that [j] was neither initial nor intervocalic, when it was represented by *y* (so **tiempos**, l.7, but **contribuyendo**, l.10).

Etymological spellings were used in a number of cases:

- Both *b* and *v* were used to represent the phoneme /b/, though it was explicitly recognised that there was no distinction in pronunciation. An etymological principle was followed, and in doubtful cases *b* was used (this is how such spellings as *bermejo* < Lat. VERMĬCŬLU[S] come about); so uncertain was this principle, however, that in the Prologue to the *Diccionario* users are enjoined to look words up under both the *b* and *v* spellings. The reason for this maintenance (or rather reintroduction) of an obsolete distinction may lie in the Academia's view in the Prologue that Spanish speakers confuse *v* and *b* 'por la poca advertencia' (i.e., carelessness).

Keypoint: the 'b/v' merger (p. 262).

- The etymological spelling of Latin words beginning with *h* was supported, thus introducing a spurious letter which had not been generally represented in medieval spelling: thus **ha** < Lat. HĂBET [HĂBĔO] (l.2). Similarly, the initial /h/ of Golden-Age Spanish, which also by the eighteenth century had ceased to be pronounced in the standard language, is represented by *h*: thus **hecho** < sixteenth-century /hetʃo/ < Lat. FACTU[M] [FĂCĬO] (l.8).
- Despite the avoidance of complex consonantal groups, *x* is used in a number of words (**extrangéros**, l.14), though in speech /ks/ would no doubt frequently have been reduced to /s/, as today, when *extranjero* is normally pronounced [estraŋxero].
- Many words of Greek origin represented Greek *theta* (θ) by *th*, *chi* (χ) by *ch* and *phi* (φ) by *ph*: here we have **Monarcha** (Gr. μόναρχος (l.16). This principle was abandoned in the 1763 *Ortografía* (observable in the very change of the title from the 1741 *Orthographía*).
- *Qu* continued to be used for /kw/; the modern convention of using *cu* was not adopted until the 1815 *Ortografía*.

Accents were used for two purposes: (a) to indicate word stress, especially in words of more than two syllables (e.g. **Académia**, l.2, **última**, l.15), although **Léngua** (l.2) also receives an accent; (b) perhaps to distinguish homonyms (the preposition **à** is hence written with a grave accent, and indeed *a* continued to be written with an accent until the twentieth century). Although the principles of accentuation have changed (and continue to change – minor alterations were prescribed in the *Nuevas normas* of 1959 and subsequently), the general principle of representing word stress through spelling has remained a constant. This practice, which might be regarded as totally redundant for native speakers, who know where the stress falls, is of course particularly helpful to foreigners, a concern always held in mind by the Academia.

Keypoints: the 'b/v' merger (p. 262), **the f>h change** (p. 271).

23.1.2 The choice of variant in learned words sometimes does not correspond to the form that was eventually adopted in modern Spanish: **propriedád** (l.3) for MSp. *propiedad*, semipopular **perficionado** (l.9) for MSp. *perfeccionado* (cf. 15.1.1).

Perfeccionar is also given in the *Diccionario* itself as a variant, though obviously not yet preferred, form. The same process is evident in the semipopular *afición*, which survived alongside learned *afección*, though in this case the two words developed slightly different meanings.

   Keypoints: consonant groups (p. 267); **learned and popular, semilearned and semipopular** (p. 277).

Morphology and syntax

23.2.1 Nobilissimo (l.14). The *-ísimo* suffix (the semantic equivalent of *muy*) was introduced into Spanish as a result of learned or, perhaps more likely, Italian influence (it increases in frequency in the sixteenth century when Italian influence makes itself most felt). It clearly remained a high register usage for a long time, though in modern Spanish there is some evidence of its increased popularity in the spoken language, maybe as a result of wider education and awareness of the literary language (Lorenzo 1971: 196, 200). It is a phenomenon which is traced in the secondary literature: Nebrija (1492) states baldly that Castilian does not have a 'superlativo' in this form; Valdés (1535), on the other hand, records and exemplifies the category, while Correas (Alarcos García 1954: 200) still regards it as uncommon at the beginning of the seventeenth century. While the suffix has become fairly productive in Spanish, simply attaching to existing adjectives, a number of adjectives have special forms which are clear learned borrowings, of which **nobilissimo** is one. There is a good deal of variation evident in the modern language; for example, for *pobre* a learned *paupérrimo* and a derived *pobrísimo* are both attested, and for *bueno* there is the 'learned' *óptimo* as well as the derived *bonísimo* and *buenísimo*.

   Keypoint: learned and popular, semilearned and semipopular (p. 277).

23.2.2 No pudiera llegar à un fin tan grande . . . (ll.16–17). The *-ra* form is here the equivalent of a conditional perfect, *no habría podido llegar* . . . The strong association of the *-ra* form with conditional sentence use has meant that even after its adoption as a subjunctive it continues to have conditional force, particularly with modal verbs (20.2.4, 28.2.8).

   Keypoints: conditional sentences (p. 265); **the pluperfects of Old Castilian** (p. 286).

23.2.3 À no tener un fomento tan elevado . . . (l.16). This is the equivalent of a conditional protasis, MSp. *si no hubiera tenido* . . . The use of the infinitive with a preposition is a Romance development (in Latin the gerund could be used with a preposition, though only with a limited range), and such usages as *a* + infinitive with conditional force in Spanish are relatively recent creations (*de* is also used with the infinitive in the same function, and *al* + infinitive has come to be a very common way of rendering a range of temporal and other adverbial functions). Such constructions clearly have the advantage of economy over their more cumbersome full-clause equivalents.

   Keypoint: conditional sentences (p. 265).

23.2.4 The syntax of the text is complex and convoluted. The text consists of a single long sentence which cannot easily be subdivided: even where colons appear in the punctuation they are followed by a subordinate structure such as a gerund or a relative element which requires that the sentence continues. The change of topic required by the sense does not always correspond well to the syntax: thus **autóres** (l.1) gives way to **voces** (l.4), then successively to **las Lénguas Toscana y Francesa** (l.9), **los Diccionarios y Vocabularios** (l.10), **Covarrubias** (l.13), **la Nación Española** (l.15).

The complementiser *que* is omitted in **los Autóres que ha parecido à la Académia [que] han tratado la Léngua Española con la mayor propriedád** ... (ll.1–2, see also 12.2.3, 17.2.5, 21.2.6, 22.2.6). The presence of the complementiser would in fact in modern Spanish yield an unacceptably complex sentence; the antecedent of the relative clause (**los Autóres**) is the subject of the verb **han tratado**, and is here separated from it by the verb **ha parecido** ...

23.2.5 The Spanish relative adjective *cuyo* (= *de quien*, *del que*, etc.) is a reanalysed form of the genitive form of the Latin relative pronoun CUIŬS [QUĪ] 'of which', 'of whom'. It had a function both as a relative (*aquellos cuyo es el pleito* 'those whose lawsuit it is') and interrogative pronoun (*¿cúyo es?* 'whose is it?') until recent times. **Cuyas** (l.4) is not here used in the genitive sense of 'whose', but as what is sometimes called a transition relative, the equivalent of 'the aforementioned' (compare the obsolete English usage 'with which [= these] authorities'). This usage, which is still to be found in very formal register in modern Spanish, probably originated in imitation of Latin syntax, where relatives could be used in something of the same way (cf. 18.2.4).
Keypoint: relatives (p. 289).

23.2.6 The gerund is extensively used here in a number of functions.
One interpretation of **los extrangéros siguiendole** (l.14) is that the gerund is the equivalent of an adverbial clause of manner, 'by following him', and this is the sense that a modern reader would instinctively give it; but the general sense seems to suggest that it is functioning as an adjectival clause (compare the translation 'those foreigners who have followed him'). The latter function is heavily castigated in modern Spanish and generally considered to be a Gallicism (in the nineteenth century) or an Anglicism (today); it was, however, reasonably favoured in the eighteenth century, and can still be found in modern Spanish, especially in journalistic prose (cf. 26.2.3).[1]
In **conociendose por ellos su buen juício** ... (l.3), **haviendo sido Don S. de C. el priméro** ... (ll.12–13) and **contribuyendo mucho para ello los Diccionarios** ... (l.10), the gerund participates in an absolute construction.

23.2.7 The past participle is also exploited in the interests of constructing economical subordinate structures: **por no practicadas** (l.5) is the equivalent of *porque no han sido practicadas*. Again it is striking how such constructions are used for the sake of economy in modern journalistic register (see Text 26).

1   For further discussion, see Pountain 1998a.

Vocabulary

23.3.1 There are many words of learned origin, showing how firmly formal register has become associated with such words; a selection are: **Diccionario** itself (l.1), **Académia** (l.2), **elegáncia** (l.3), **proporción** (l.4), **practicadas** (l.5, rather than *usadas* or *empleadas*), **ignóra** (l.5), **sucedido** (l.8, popular words for 'to happen' were *acontecer* and *pasar*, making this an area rich in near synonyms), **doctas** (l.12), **Nación** (l.15, a loftier notion than the popular *pueblo*), **última** (l.15; 'last' was formerly expressed by *postrer* or *postrimer*), **fomento** (l.17), **augusto** (l.18), **Monarcha** (l.18, a higher register word than *rey*).

   Keypoint: learned and popular, semilearned and semipopular (p. 277).

23.3.2 Estampa (l.11) is possibly a borrowing from Fr. √*estamper*, originally 'to crush' (cognate with Eng. *stamp*); *prensa* was also used for the notion of 'printing press'. *Estampa*, while it can still used in this sense, is in modern Spanish more usually associated with the idea of a 'print', i.e., a mechanically prepared picture.

XI Modern Peninsular Spanish

As we proceed towards the present day, the range of available texts becomes steadily greater. In particular, different types of text show a good deal of register and stylistic, as well as dialectal, variation. The texts in this chapter reveal some of this.

24 Renting a flat in nineteenth-century Madrid. Ramón de Mesonero Romanos, *Escenas matritenses* (1837)

24.0 Ramón de Mesonero Romanos (1803–82), who wrote under the *nom de plume* of El Curioso Parlante, was the son of a well-to-do Madrid businessman who at the age of 16 had to take charge of the family's affairs on the death of his father and simultaneously pursued a business and literary career, both with success. He was very actively engaged in the social, artistic and political life of Madrid, founding the Ateneo and the Liceo, becoming an elected councillor and city librarian (he sold his books to the city to form the first municipal library). He is best known for his *costumbrista* writings on life in the capital, which are widely regarded as a model for the genre. His articles capture vividly the characteristic detail of everyday existence, and though there is inevitably exaggeration for the purpose of literary effect and social comment, his representation of dialogue is valuable evidence of the usage of the time.

The text

The passage below first appeared in the *Semanario Pintoresco Español* of 27 August 1837, and was subsequently published in *Escenas Matritenses*. The version here, which is taken from the the modern edition by Rubio Cremades (1993: 289–91) follows the 1851 edition (Madrid: Imprenta y Litografía de Gaspar Roig).

–Entre usted, señora.
–Beso a usted la mano.
–Y yo a usted los pies.
–Yo soy una señora viuda de un capitán de fragata.
–Muy señora mía; mal hizo el capitán en dejarla a usted tan joven y sin 5
arrimo en este mundo pecador.

–Sí señor, el pobrecito marchó de Cádiz para dar la vuelta al mundo, y sin duda hubo de darla por el otro, porque no ha vuelto.

–Todavía no es tarde ... ¿y usted, señora mía, trata de esperarle en Madrid por lo visto?   *10*

–Si señor; aquí tengo varios parientes de distinción, que no podrían menos de ser conocidos de usted ...

–¿Y el precio, señora, qué le ha parecido a mi señora la marquesa? El precio será el que usted guste, por eso no hemos de regañar.

–Supongo que usted, señora, no llevará a mal que la entere, como   *15* forastera, de los usos de la corte.

–Nada de eso, no señor; yo me presto a todo ... a todo lo que se use en la corte.

–Pues señora, en casos tales, cuando uno no tiene el honor de conocer a las personas con quien habla, suele exigirse una fianza y ...   *20*

–¿Habla usted de veras? ¿Y para qué? ¿para una fruslería como quien dice, para una habitacioncilla de seis al cuarto que cabe en el palomar de mi casa de campo de Chiclana? ...

–Pues señora, si usted, a Dios gracias, se halla colocada en tan elevada esfera, ¿qué trabajo puede costarla el hacer que cualquiera de esos señores *25* parientes salga por usted?

–Ninguno, y a decir verdad no desearían más que poder hacerme el favor; pero ...

–Pues bien, señora, propóngalo usted y verá cómo no lo extrañan, y por lo demás, supuesto que usted es una señora sola ...   *30*

–Sola, absolutamente; pero si usted gusta de hacer el recibo a nombre del caballero que vendrá a hablarle, que es hermano de mi difunto, y suele vivir en mi casa las temporadas que está su regimiento de guarnición ...

–¡Ay, señora! pues entonces me parece que la casa no la conviene, porque como no hay habitaciones independientes ... luego tantos criados ...   *35*

–Diré a usted; los criados pienso repartirlos entre mis parientes, y quedarme sólo con una niña de doce años.

–Pues entonces ya es demasiado la casa, y aun paréceme, señora, que la conversación también.

Translation

'Come in, madam.'

'(*lit.*) I kiss your hand.'

'(*lit.*) and I your feet.'

'I am the widow of a frigate captain.'

'My dear lady; it was too bad of the captain to leave you so young and unprotected in this sinful world.'

'Yes, sir, the poor fellow left Cadiz to sail round the world, and doubtless he was destined to sail round the next, for he has not returned.'

'It is still not too late ... And you, my lady, plan to await him in Madrid, it seems?'

'Yes, sir; here I have several distinguished relatives who cannot but be known to you.'

'And the price, madam; how did that strike my lady the Marchioness?'

'The price can be what you like, we won't argue about that.'

'I suppose, madam, that you will not take it amiss if I acquaint you, since you are a stranger here, with the procedures of the capital.'

'Not at all, no, sir; I am ready for any . . . for any of the capital's procedures.'

'Well, madam, in cases such as this, when one does not have the honour of knowing the people one is talking to, one usually asks for a reference and . . .'

'Are you serious? For what? For a mere trifle, as one might say, for a miserable little six-by-four apartment which would fit in the dovecote of my country house in Chiclana?'

'Well, madam, if by the grace of God you are placed in such high circles, what trouble could it be to you to have one of these noble relatives come forward on your behalf?'

'None, and, to tell you the truth, they would desire nothing more than to oblige me; but . . .'

'Well, madam, you propose it and you will see how they will not find it odd, and, moreover, assuming you are a lady on her own . . .'

'On my own, absolutely; but if you would care to put the account in the name of the gentleman who will come and deal with you, who is the brother of my dead husband, and usually lives in my house when his regiment is stationed . . .'

'Oh, madam! Then I think the house will not suit you, because as there are no independent rooms . . . and so many servants . . .'

'I'll tell you what; I intend to distribute the servants amongst my relatives and stay on my own with my twelve-year old girl.'

'Then the house is too much for you, and I think, madam, that this conversation is too.'

Morphology and syntax

24.2.1 Usted (l.1 and throughout) is now completely lexicalised as the polite second person pronoun. It is used disjunctively with *a* as an indirect object (**diré a usted**, l.36) whereas today *le digo* or *le digo a usted* (see below 24.2.5) would be preferred; such disjunctive use may be indicative of its continuing twilight status between full noun and pronoun.

Keypoint: personal pronouns (p. 284).

24.2.2 Le is used as both direct and indirect object pronoun when referring to male persons: **esperarle** (l.9, direct object), **hablarle** (l.32, indirect object); **lo** is used as the direct object pronoun when referring to things (or people who are not 'personalised', as in **los criados pienso repartirlos**, l.36 – note the corresponding absence of the personal *a* with **los criados**) or to the 'neuter' (**propóngalo**, l.29). **La** is used as both direct and indirect object pronoun when referring to females: **la entere** (l.15), direct object; **costarla** (l.25) and **la conviene** (l.34), indirect objects. The use of *la* as a feminine indirect object pronoun (*laísmo*), puristically castigated, is today particularly associated with Madrid, though it is also found regionally throughout Castile and León. The usage, however, is completely absent from Andalusia and Latin America (and hence from the majority of the Spanish-speaking world). *Laísmo* dates back to at least the early seventeenth century, when it was described by Correas (see Text 18), who considered it normal (Alvar and Pottier 1983: 128).

24.2.3 Haber de + infinitive is used frequently, usually with a deontic modal nuance: **hubo de darla** (l.8) 'was (destined to) . . .', **no hemos de regañar** (l.14) 'we won't argue'. See also 22.2.8.
   Keypoint: **periphrastic verb forms** (p. 283).

24.2.4 Conocidos de usted (l.12): **de** rather than *por* is used as the agentive preposition. *Por* has today replaced *de* for the most part, though *de* is still normal with stative past participles, e.g. *acompañado de su mujer* (cf. 7.2.3).

24.2.5 ¿Qué le ha parecido a mi señora la marquesa? (l.13) illustrates the so-called 'redundant' indirect object pronoun construction, which is a typically Spanish phenomenon. There is both a full noun phrase as indirect object here (**mi señora la marquesa**) and a personal pronoun (**le**). In Modern Spanish, the usage of such a 'redundant' pronoun is apparently syntactically optional when an indirect object full noun follows the verb (*Les di un regalo a mis sobrinos/Di un regalo a mis sobrinos*). There is, however, a perceivable semantic difference between these last two possibilities: the use of the 'redundant' pronoun is often thought of as showing a greater 'personalisation' of the indirect object.
   Keypoint: **personal pronouns** (p. 284).

24.2.6 Las personas con quien habla (l.20). The plural form *quienes* would be used in Modern Spanish. However, *quienes*, the analogical plural of *quien* (see 6.2.7, 7.2.4), made a relatively late appearance in Spanish and was slow to diffuse: Correas records *quienes* as being not so frequently used and not so old as *quien*.
   Keypoint: **relatives** (p. 289).

24.2.7 Clitic pronouns do not yet always follow the modern rule of placement according to the morphological form; variation is observable between **pues entonces me parece** (l.34) and **aun paréceme** (l.38). Postposing the clitic pronoun to a finite verb has persisted systematically with imperatives and in some quasi-idiomatic expressions. *Dícese* was regularly used in written register until the early twentieth century; *érase una vez* 'once upon a time' continues in the restricted context of children's stories.
   Keypoint: **clitic pronoun position** (p. 264).

Vocabulary

24.3.1 Gustar has a different valency from its most usual modern usage, which is the equivalent of English 'to be pleasing' (so *me gustan las peras* 'pears are pleasing to me = I like pears', *me gusta cantar* 'singing is pleasing to me = I like singing'). Here **gustar** is used with a direct object and with an infinitive complement introduced by **de**: **el que usted guste** (l.14), **si usted gusta de hacer el recibo** (l.31).

24.3.2 There are two examples of affective suffixes in this text: **pobrecito** (l.7), used affectionately, **habitacioncilla** (l.22) used pejoratively.

24.3.3 Fruslería (l.21) has an interestingly complex associational history. The Latin √FŪSĬLIS 'melted', 'liquid' yielded the sixteenth-century *fuslera* or, by metathesis, *fruslera*, which was the name given to thin strips of brass worked together which reduced to a small volume when molten. Figurative associations for this notion were natural: Covarrubias equates the notion with academic sophistry, and under the form *fruslería* the word has come down to the modern language in the meaning of 'trifle', having lost all derivational associations.

24.3.4 Extrañan (l.29) derives from Lat. √EXTRĀNĔU[S] 'not belonging', 'foreign', 'external'. *Extraño* develops the related meaning of 'strange', 'unusual' while the notion 'foreign' eventually comes to be expressed by *extranjero*, a borrowing from OFr. *estrangier* (which also derives from √EXTRĀNĔU[S], though the two words coexisted for some time in the meaning of 'foreign'. The verb *extrañar* has had a varied semantic trajectory. Its original meaning was most probably 'to make strange' and hence 'to banish'; in the Golden Age it has the meaning 'to find strange', 'not to know', which is close to the meaning in this text. The verb also takes on a causative valency in the meaning of 'to surprise', and with this double valency it is used in the Peninsula today (both *(ella) extraña la falta de agua/(a ella) le extraña la falta de agua* '(s)he is surprised by the lack of water'/'the lack of water surprises her'), as well as a reflexive function (*se extraña de la falta de agua*). In Latin America, *extrañar* has developed the sense of 'to miss', 'to yearn for' (Peninsula *echar de menos*), presumably via the stages 'to wonder at' → 'to feel the novelty of' → 'to feel the lack of'.

24.3.5 There are a number of polite formulae in this conversational exchange. The initial greetings **beso a usted la mano** (l.2) and **y yo [beso] a usted los pies** (l.3) are excessively polite, though not unusual: *que besa sus pies* and *que besa sus manos*, abbreviated to *q.b.s.p.* and *q.b.s.m.* were used in formal letter writing until this century. **Señor** and **señora** (sometimes reinforced to **señora mía**, l.9, **muy señora mía**, l.5) are liberally employed both in direct address and in deferential reference to others, e.g. **mi señora la marquesa** (l.13), **esos señores parientes** (ll.25–6). Expression is often convoluted: **Supongo que usted, señora, no llevará a mal que la entere, como forastera** . . . (ll.15–16) introduces the request for references, which is framed as a general principle using **uno** (l.19) and the reflexive **suele exigirse** (l.20) rather than as a direct command.

25 A busy housewife. The spoken Spanish of Madrid (1970)

25.0 Although a number of the texts examined so far have purported to be examples of spoken Spanish, it is only in the twentieth century that the linguist has had access to literal transcripts of actual speech. This has been facilitated chiefly by the advent of the tape recorder, which makes transcription of speech at natural speed a much more feasible task. It can immediately be seen that real speech is quite different in nature from representations of speech in literature. Real speech usually involves repetition of material, elision, false starts or modification of a structure in the course of its utterance. A particular feature, which will be examined in detail in 25.2.8, is that speakers begin with the topic (what they are talking about) and then add comments to it, and that syntax is often subservient to this pragmatic motivation of order. Complex subordination is also avoided in favour of more paratactic structure.

The examination of such texts is particularly important in the context of the history of language. It will be remembered that Latin evolved into the Romance languages primarily as a result of the oral transmission from generation to generation of everyday spoken language, that is to say, of the kind of language that is represented here. While written texts of an official or recreational nature are related to the spoken language because they are the work of some its speakers, they are not necessarily typical of it, and, indeed, written registers are at times cultivated specifically so as to be different from everyday spoken usage. By observing the increasingly well-documented differences in modern Spanish between spoken and written language, we can begin to suspect the nature of similar differences in other periods.

This text

The text is taken from Esgueva and Cantarero (1981: 199–200).

Further reading

Steel (1976); Vigara Tauste (1992).

–¿Cómo son cada uno de ellos, sobre todo los mayores?
–Los mayores, ¡ah! los mayores ya la de ... la mayor que tiene quince años; el otro que tiene trece, el mayor de los pilaristas, pues, lógicamente ya están formaditos, ya ... en fin ya los chiquillos, ya tienen una inclinación ... tienen sus aficiones ya más formadas y demás. Los otros, son   5
pequeños todavía.
–Y ¿a qué se dedican aparte de estudiar, en cuestión de deportes?
–Sí, sí, sí. Bueno todo lo que ... lo que se puede brindar en tan poco tiempo como les queda libre de los estudios, pues, sí son aficionados; sobre todo, el fútbol; allí se pasan la vida metidos en el colegio dándole   10
al ... al ... a la punta de los zapatos, porque vamos a dejar a un lado las botas; vamos a poner la de los zapatos de vez en cuando también. Y la mayor, pues, también es aficionada a ... al deporte, le gusta sobre todo en verano, la natación y todo eso, claro, además tiene eso, tiene más lugar, más tiempo para poderlo practicar en la playa, todo el verano, que da   15
mucho de sí; así que siempre que el tiempo no lo impida. Y ... después la ... los pequeños, pues, claro, nada: ésos, a jugar; fuera de las horas de colegio, jugar, porque ahora ya sabe usted, ahora no se estudia, ya no hay deberes en casa. Y son buenos en general, ¿eh? En líneas generales, pues, son buenos, son ... bastante dóciles. Yo soy, desde luego, el látigo casero.   20

Yo aquí, soy la que dispongo y dirijo el cotarro, porque lógicamente el marido, pues, para poco en casa. Así, que me toca a mí ese numerito y ... los pequeños, pues en fin, nada, la, únicamente la, pequeña es la que es más traviesilla. Que ahora tengo que tener un cuidado enorme con el recién nacido, porque, claro, se ha creído que le venía un muñeco para Reyes. Ha sido un poco antes de Reyes, pero ... pero es que el muñeco es de carne y hueso, y tengo que tener muchísimo cuidado, no me vaya a encontrar un día al muñeco debajo de la cama ¿eh? y a otro de los verdaderos muñecos metido en la cuna todo preparado. Así, que tengo que tener un cuidado ¡ay Dios mío! horrible.   *30*

25

Translation

'What are they like, especially the older children?'

'The older ones, oh, the older ones: well, there's the eldest girl who's fifteen, the other, the boy, who's thirteen, the eldest of the ones at the boys' school – of course, they're more or less grown up, the young folk; well, they've got their own ideas, they know what they like, and so on. The others are still little.'

'And what do they spend their time doing in the way of sport?'

'OK; well, anything on offer in the little time they have free from studying; yes, they like it, football in particular; they spend their time in school scuffing the toes of their shoes – never mind their boots – because they also play in their shoes sometimes. And the eldest girl, well, she likes sport as well, especially in summer, swimming and so on, she's got more space, more time then, she can do it all summer on the beach, she spends a lot of time doing that, if the weather doesn't prevent it. And then, the little ones, well, outside school hours they just play, they just play, because they don't study now, you know, there's no home-work set any more. And on the whole they're good kids. In general, they're good, very quiet. Naturally I'm the one who keeps them in order; of course I'm the one who's in charge of the household, because my husband, well, he's not at home much. So that's my little lot and the little ones, well, they're not a lot of trouble, it's just the little girl who's the naughtiest. At the moment I've got to be very careful with the baby, because, of course, the little girl thought she was getting a doll for Reyes [Epiphany, 6 January, when Christmas presents were traditionally given to children in Spain]. It was a bit before Reyes in fact, but, the "doll" was real flesh and blood, and I've got to be very careful in case I find the "doll" under the bed one day and one of her dolls all dressed up in the cot instead! So, goodness me, I've got to be terribly careful.'

Morphology and syntax

25.2.1 Diminutive suffixes may be associated with the literal idea of smallness (**chiquillos**, l.4, **traviesilla**, l.24) but are also used affectively to express a number of nuances. **Formaditos** (l.4) suggests that the older boys' preferences are now firmly fixed, and the suffix has a broadly intensifying meaning while at the same time suggesting youth and therefore the idea of recentness: it would be inappropriate to use the suffix in relation to an old person who was set in their ways. **Numerito** (l.22) has an ironic sense: the 'little' job of running the household is of course not little at all.

25.2.2 The suffix *-ista* is used productively in **pilaristas** (l.3), formed from the name of the boys' school dedicated to the Virgen del Pilar.

25.2.3 Tengo que tener muchísimo cuidado, no me vaya a encontrar . . . (l.24). This construction seems to be typical of the spoken language and renders the idea of *para que . . . no* (English 'lest').[1] In fact, written register would probably use *para* with the infinitive here (*tengo que tener cuidado para no encontrar . . .*) or a conditional structure (*tengo que tener mucho cuidado si no voy a encontrar . . .*). Such features illustrate how different the characteristics of spoken and written register can be.

25.2.4 Sentences in this register contain functional categories which are not encountered so frequently, if at all, in written usage. Interjections express attitudes (**¡ah!**, l.2, **¡ay Dios mío!**, l.30) or seek to engage the ongoing attention of the interlocutor (**¿eh?**, ll.19, 28, **ya sabe usted**, l.18). Fillers are used by a speaker to hesitate and play for time: **en fin** (l.4), **bueno** (l.8), **pues** (ll.9, 13, etc.), **pues (en fin) nada** (ll.17, 23), **claro** (l.17), **desde luego** (l.20). Another device for lengthening a declarative sentence is the use of an introductory **es que** (l.26). Using such strategies to gain time in formulating a response to a question is very important in the spoken language. It can be done also by the introduction of essentially extraneous material or repetition of what has already been said, as in the beginning of the reply on l.8. The question is a simple one: what sports do the children play? The answer begins with an acknowledgement that a question has been asked (**Sí, sí, sí. Bueno** . . .) and then essentially repeats the question in different words (**todo lo que . . . se puede brindar en tan poco tiempo como les queda libre de los estudios** – the only new information here is that the children do not have very much free time) before leading round, again with hesitation, to the crucial first part of the answer, **fútbol**.

25.2.5 There is ellipsis of a main verb (most likely *van*) in the sentence **los pequeños . . . a jugar** (l.17). A preposition (*a*) or other material is missing in **son aficionados; sobre todo, el fútbol** (ll.9–10). In both cases the ellipsis in no way compromises meaning; pragmatically the relation between **pequeños** and **jugar** and **aficionados** and **fútbol** is completely clear, and it is in such cases that such omissions are tolerated in spoken register. Another means of effecting economy is by the use of expressions with vague reference, such as **y demás** (l.5) and **y todo eso** (l.14), the meaning of which has to be pragmatically inferred by the hearer (in the first case it seems to cover all the consequences of young people having formed their own preferences, and in the second, all aspects of swimming). Cf. 28.2.5.

---

1   The history of this construction is not very well documented. Keniston (1937: 386–7), records some sixteenth-century examples and points to its equivalence with Lat. NE + subjunctive, from which, with a change in the form of the negative element, it may be a descendant.

25.2.6 Que is frequently used to introduce a clause in the spoken language. Sometimes it appears to substitute for a causal conjunction such as *porque* or *ya que*, as in l.15; in l.24 it seems simply to signal the beginning of a new sentence. (*Si*, not illustrated here, has a similar kind of usage in spoken register, where it expresses a broadly contrastive nuance, and is often used in combination with *pero*.)

25.2.7 A change of mind in mid-sentence is often reflected in hesitation and correction, and this is particularly noticeable in Spanish with number and gender agreements between article and noun; the speaker begins with one noun in mind but then continues with another: **Los mayores . . . la mayor** (l.2), **al . . . al . . . a la punta de los zapatos** (l.11), **y . . . los pequeños . . . la pequeña . . .** (l.23).

25.2.8 The speaker orders her thoughts more or less as they occur to her, as in the sentence which begins on l.12 with the simple proposition that **la mayor es aficionada al deporte**. This is then refined to a particular kind of sport, **natación** (l.14), and there follows further more specific information about the time (**todo el verano**, l.15), the manner (**da mucho de sí**, ll.15–16) and the place (**en la playa**, l.15), followed by the proviso introduced by the **siempre que** clause. The structure thus follows the mental processes of the speaker, who moves from a simple statement towards increasing definition and refinement. In written style it might have been possible to construct a syntactically more tightly-knit and 'elegant' sentence by the use of greater subordination, and by the placing of subordinate clauses before the main verb, as follows: *A la mayor le gusta sobre todo la natación, que, dando mucho de sí, y siempre que el tiempo no lo impida, practica todo el verano, que es cuando tiene más tiempo, y en la playa, que es donde tiene más lugar.*

25.2.9 The use of the subject pronoun **yo** (ll.20 and 21) and the 'redundant' pronoun construction (**me toca a mí**, l.22) are devices which allow contrastive stress to be placed on the first person notion.

25.2.10 The extent of the 'nuance' use of the reflexive in Modern Spanish, which is a particular feature of the spoken language, can be seen in such examples as **se ha creído que le venía un muñeco** (l.25) 'she was quite convinced that she was getting a doll' and **no me vaya a encontrar . . . al muñeco** (ll.27–8), which expresses the personal concern of the mother in such a potential disaster.
  Keypoint: the reflexive (p. 288).

Vocabulary

25.3.1 Ya (< Lat. IAM 'now', 'already') is a very frequently used adverb and has a range of functions. In **ya tienen una inclinación** (ll.4–5) and **ya no hay deberes** (ll.18–19) it retains its full lexical meaning of 'already' and 'now' respectively; but in the formula **ya sabe usted** (l.18) it has become little more than a verbal reinforcement.
  Keypoint: adverbs (p. 262).

25.3.2 This passage does not contain a large amount of specifically colloquial vocabulary. The word **cotarro** (l.21) is one such word, however, meaning 'house', 'affair'. Historically, it is an augmented form of *coto*, and is first encountered in the early seventeenth century in the meaning of 'doss-house'. It is thus an example of semantic evolution by amelioration through self-deprecation (cf. 3.3.2, 9.3.6, 15.3.5, 22.3.2. 29.3.1).

25.3.3 We have the opportunity here to see something of the etymological complexion of everyday modern Spanish vocabulary, though the passage is too short to be of any serious statistical significance. The number of words of learned origin that have passed into common usage is impressively high: **lógicamente** (**lógico**) (l.3), **inclinación** (ll.4–5), **aficiones** (l.5, see 23.1.2), **cuestión** (l.7), **natación** (l.14), **colegio** (l.18), **general** (l.19), **líneas** (l.19), **dóciles** (l.20), **numerito** (**número**) (l.22), **únicamente** (**único**) (l.23), **horrible** (l.30). As it happens, there is not one word of Arabic origin here. **Muñeco** (l.25), the analogical masculine form of *muñeca*, is ultimately of pre-Roman (and rather uncertain) origin; the feminine is first encountered in the meaning of 'boundary stone' and from there by a complex series of associations comes to mean 'protuberance', especially the protuberance characteristic of the wrist, and 'round bundle', which also specialises in meaning to that of 'doll'. **Látigo** (l.20) is of unknown origin. Modern borrowings from English are apparent in the ubiquitous **fútbol** (l.10) and, less obviously, in **deportes** (l.7, etc.); this word, a morphological derivative of a now obsolete verb *deportarse* 'to enjoy oneself', 'to rest', was rescued from oblivion in the twentieth century in order to form a calqued native equivalent of English *sport*.

   Keypoint: learned and popular, semilearned and semipopular (p. 277).

26 King Hassan of Morocco arrives in Spain. A newspaper article (1989)

26.0 The language of journalism (I am referring here primarily to the reporting of current affairs, since it is clear that essays, satirical articles, and so on will all have their different styles) responds to two sometimes conflicting pressures: the need to be concise and the need to attract the reader's attention. Both these pressures are evident in the text that follows: concision is probably a motivating factor in such features as adjective placement (26.2.1) and use of the gerund (26.2.3) and the generally more rarefied vocabulary (26.3.1) and use of paraphrase (26.3.2) create an impression of importance.

   Journalistic usage is likely to depart from the standard as reporters write at speed and seek striking effects; in foreign news they are often working on foreign-language sources, especially English. The language of journalism is therefore particularly prone to neologism and especially the use of Anglicisms (some of which are ephemeral). The high public profile of the press and the rapid dissemination of journalistic material to a large reading public means that this language can be exceedingly influential, and it is notable that there have been considerable attempts by the quality press to regulate the language of their reporters and sub-editors, the general policy being to encourage the avoidance of excessive numbers of calques from English and new usages of Spanish words.

The text

This text is taken from *El País Internacional* of 25 September 1989.

Further reading

Agencia Efe (1985); Alcoba (1987).

La tantas veces rumoreada e incluso anunciada visita oficial del rey Hassan
II a España se inició por fin el domingo 24, cuando las tradicionalmente
tensas relaciones entre ambos países se han desdramatizado hasta el punto
de ser prácticamente amistosas. Hassan tomó tierra en Sevilla y dio
comienzo así la parte privada de su estancia, que con el desplazamiento el 5
lunes 25 a Madrid se convirtió en oficial.

La pompa de este esperado viaje ha quedado un poco mermada por el
aparente cansancio del monarca alauí, de 60 años de edad, que le ha
incitado a acortar en más de 24 horas la parte privada de su visita,
renunciando, por ejemplo, a la espectacular llegada a Cádiz en su lujoso 10
paquebote *Marraquech*. Por el mismo motivo, ninguno de los actos de su
estancia en Madrid, ni la ofrenda floral en la plaza de la Lealtad ni la
visita al Ayuntamiento, empezarán antes de las doce de la mañana.

Estas circunstancias y la versatilidad de la Administración marroquí han
complicado la organización de un viaje que el ministro de Exteriores, 15
Francisco Fernández Ordóñez, califica, no obstante, de 'histórico' por el
hecho de que se celebre.

Translation

The official visit to Spain of King Hassan, which had been so often rumoured
and even announced, began at last on Sunday 24th, when the traditional tension
in the relations between the two countries was reduced almost to the point of
friendship. Hassan landed in Seville and so the private phase of his visit began,
which became official when on the 25th he moved on to Madrid.

The pomp of this long-expected journey was a little tempered by the apparent
fatigue of the Moroccan king, who is 60 years old, a factor which forced him to
to reduce the private phase of his visit by 24 hours, so omitting, for example, his
spectacular arrival in Cadiz on board the luxurious yacht *Marrakesh*. For the same
reason, none of the events of his stay in Madrid, neither the presentation of a
floral tribute in the Plaza de la Lealtad nor his visit to the Town Hall, will begin
before noon.

These circumstances and the changeability of the Moroccan administration
have complicated the organisation of a visit which the Minister of Foreign Affairs,
Francisco Fernández Ordóñez, described as 'historic' on account of the very fact
that it was taking place at all.

Morphology and syntax

26.2.1 There is a high incidence of adjectives placed before the noun in this text, e.g., **este esperado viaje** (l.7), **la espectacular llegada a Cádiz** (l.10). Preposed adjectives may be adverbially qualified: **las tradicionalmente tensas relaciones** (ll.2–3) and the very complex **la tantas veces rumoreada e incluso anunciada visita** (l.1). The preposing of adjectives is associated with rhetorical style and historically was particularly favoured by authors who imitated Latin syntax (see 15.2.2, 18.2.3), and so it is a feature which elevates the tone of prose. It also has a practical advantage in journalism since it permits the inclusion of subordinate information without recourse to lengthy relative clauses: this is especially noticeable in the example on l.1 where such recasting would be quite long-winded because of the complex nature of the noun phrase (perhaps *la visita oficial, tantas veces rumoreada e incluso anunciada, que iba a hacer el rey Hassan II a España . . .* or *la visita oficial del rey Hassan II a España, que tantas veces ha sido rumoreada e incluso anunciada . . .*; compare the difficulties of translation into English). However, the basic principles of adjective placement in modern Spanish are not broken: the adjective follows the noun if it represents a distinguishing or defining property of the noun (e.g. **la ofrenda floral**, l.11, specifies the precise kind of tribute; **la parte privada de su estancia**, l.5, contrasts the private part of his visit with **la . . . visita oficial**, l.1) and precedes if it is not distinguishing, but is a known or expected attribute of the noun (e.g. the luxuriousness of the royal yacht in **su lujoso paquebote**, ll.10–11; *su paquebote lujoso* could be the king's <u>luxurious</u> yacht as opposed to some other). Adjectives which follow the noun may also typically communicate new information about the noun, so while the implication of **la espectacular llegada a Cádiz**, l.10, is 'his arrival in Cadiz (as is only to be expected) would have been spectacular' while *la llegada espectacular a Cádiz* could have implied 'his arrival in Cadiz (we understand from information received) would have been spectacular'. Thus, by using adjectives before the noun, the journalist is also able to give the impression that (s)he is familiar with the circumstances of the king's visit, and pays the reader the compliment of being so too. As can be seen, then, adjective position is an extremely versatile stylistic device in modern Spanish.

26.2.2 There is a preference in this style of Spanish for nominalisation, that is to say, the use of a noun which is a morphological derivative of a verb to denote an action or state rather than a full clause. For example, **que con el desplazamiento el lunes 25 a Madrid se convirtió en oficial** (ll.5–6), uses **desplazamiento**, a nominalisation of the verb *desplazarse*, rather than a structure such as *que se convirtió en oficial cuando se desplazó el lunes 25 a Madrid*. Other examples of such nominalisations are **cansancio** (l.8), **llegada** (l.10), **estancia** (l.12), **ofrenda** (l.12) and **visita** (l.13). This again contributes to concision in journalistic writing. By increasing the incidence of abstract nouns, it also elevates the tone of the discourse.

26.2.3 The gerund, the use of which can obviate the need for a full clause or new sentence, is frequent in journalistic register. While the normative view in modern Spanish is that the gerund should have the same understood subject as that of the main clause in which it appears, unless it forms part of an absolute construction, this rule is frequently broken in journalism and 'officialese'. The subject of **renunciando** (l.10) is **el monarca alauí** (l.8); but **el monarca alauí** is not the subject of any of the other clauses in the sentence that runs from l.7 to l.11. There is no problem of comprehension, however, because *renunciar* must have a human subject, and the king is therefore the only candidate as the understood subject: pragmatic considerations therefore ensure the correct interpretation.

26.2.4 El hecho de que (ll.16–17) is followed by a subjunctive, **se celebre**. This feature of modern Spanish seems to be the complete antithesis of the longstanding association of the subjunctive with clauses which do not assert facts but rather give value judgements and emotional reactions or express hypothetical, non-existent or future situations of one kind or another. The extension of the subjunctive to this context may be due to constructions such as *El hecho de que sea así me extraña*, where an emotional attitude is being expressed with regard to the clause beginning with *el hecho de que*; it is a near equivalent of *Me extraña que sea así*, where the use of the subjunctive is obligatory. The example in this text is not of this type, however, and shows a clear association of the subjunctive with *el hecho de que* as such.

Vocabulary

26.3.1 Several items of vocabulary are uncommon in colloquial usage. **Mermada** (l.7) is used instead of the more usual *disminuida* or *rebajada*, **incitado** (l.9) instead of the more general *hecho* or in this context the more usual *inducido*. **Paquebote** (l.11) is a rather old-fashioned word for *yate* or the more general *barco*. **Actos** (l.11) is in this context more likely to be rendered in speech by a paraphrase such as *lo que vas a hacer* and **floral** (l.12) by *de flores*. The journalist not only heightens the tone of the passage by using these rather more rarefied words but achieves variation. Sometimes, however, such words can become clichés of journalistic usage, such as **calificar de** (l.16) 'to describe as'.

26.3.2 Going against the demand for concision is the use in some cases of periphrastic expressions. **Tomó tierra** (l.4) is a way of expressing the idea of *se desembarcó*; **dio comienzo** (ll.4–5) could be rendered by the simple use of *comenzó*. The subconscious intention here is probably that of investing rather pedestrian activities with a greater significance, and it is akin to the historical semantic processes of hyperbole and phonetic strengthening.

26.3.3 Desdramatizado (l.3) is a neologism, but one which fits well into the lexical structure of Spanish as another morphological derivative of root *drama*. *Dramatizar* is of long standing in Spanish with the meaning of 'to dramatise', 'to turn into a play', but more recently *drama* has by metaphorical extension come to be associated not simply with theatrical performances but with major incidents involving tension; hence the verb comes to mean 'build up into a tense situation' and an antonym, *desdramatizar* (which would have little sense in a theatrical context) is coined with the meaning 'to lower the tension'. These words may also be a calque of the English journalistic terms *escalate* and *de-escalate*.

27 An Andalusian maid bemoans her lot. Carlos Arniches, *Gazpacho andaluz* (1902)

27.0 Carlos Arniches (1866–1943) was a prolific writer of plays and *zarzuela* (comic opera) libretti for the Madrid stage at the turn of the nineteenth and twentieth centuries. He was an acute observer of popular speech, and is best known for the plays he wrote in the everyday language of the capital. *Gazpacho andaluz*, however, is written entirely in the language of Andalusia, and captures, albeit in somewhat caricatured form, many of the general features of the speech of the region.

The text

The text is taken from Arniches (1915: 7–8).

Further reading

Alvar (1955); Alvar *et al.* (1961–73); Seco (1970).

MARIA VIRTUDES

(Muy tímida y revelando en sus palabras un genio apocado y una cortedad y sosería exageradas.) ¿Yo? ... Yo no he *inventao* la pórvora ... ¡no señó! ¡ni muchísimo meno! Y que soy un arma é cántaro ... también lo sé. Me soplan ... fú ..., ú ... ú ... *(Sopla.)* y vuelo y aonde m'agarro ... ayí me queo, hasta que fú ..., ú ... ú ... *(Sopla otra vez.)* me vuerven a soplá. Por 5
eso, aunque no hase más que dos meses que me he casao, ya me paso la metá é las noches hasiendo solitarios. Mi marío, asín de que anochese, fú ... uú ... *(Soplando)* vuela. Y no hase falta que lo soplen ... no; sopla él por su cuenta. Sabe que soy mu sufría y mu cayá y abusa de las dos cosas ... del vino y del aguardiente. Y yo rabio y yoro, porque es lo que yo 10
digo: argo paraíta sí soy ... ¡y hasta pué que fea!; pero tanto como para *pasáme* las noches hasiendo solitarios ... yo creo que no. Y digo yo, si esto de pasá las noches sola ¿no será una desgracia de familia? Porque mi agüela se casó con un sonámbulo ... dormío y tóo se iba a la taberna. Mi mare se casó con un sereno, como que yo nasí de resultas de una 15
sesantía! Y a mí me ha tocao un borracho. ¡Dios mío, y qué lástima que mi Curro sea asín! ... porque quitándole er vino ... güeno, es como un baúl, se saca *dél* lo que se quiere. Pero esto no pué seguí asín. ¡No, no y no! Vaya, de ninguna manera! Porque si voy a pasá muchas noches como esta ... ¿pa qué hemos comporao er *somier*? ¡Si yo no fuá tan sosa! ¡Pero, 20
sí ... yo tengo que hasé argo! ¡Argo pa que ese arrastrao no se ría de mí, ni me deje sola! ¿Y qué haría yo, Dios mío, qué haría yo? ... ¡Ah, ya sé! ... Yo voy a hasé una cosa. Yo voy a barré ... *(Coge la escoba.)* a esperá a mi comare, pa que eya me aconseje, y hasé lo que mande, sea lo que sea. Porque yo quiero haselo tóo, tóo, tóo ... menos solitarios. ¿Aonde habrá 25
pasao la noche er muy ...? iba a yamale perro, Dios me perdone ...

Translation

(Very shy and showing in her words a timid disposition and an exaggerated shyness and insipidness.) Me? . . . I haven't invented dust . . . no indeed, nothing like that! And I'm a dimwit . . . I know that too. People blow me away *(she blows)* and I fly away, and wherever I manage to hang on . . . there I stay, until *(she blows again)* they blow me away again. That's why, although I've only been married two months, I spend half my nights playing patience. My husband, as soon as it gets dark, *(blowing)* flies away. And there's no need for people to blow him away . . . no; he blows himself of his own accord. He knows that I am very long-suffering and very quiet and he abuses both . . . wine and cheap brandy. And I get cross and cry, because it's as I say: yes, I am a bit dull . . . and even unattractive! . . . but enough to be spending my nights on my own playing patience . . . I don't think so. And I ask myself if spending nights on my own isn't a family failing? Because my grandmother married a sleepwalker . . . he went down to the pub in his sleep. My mother married a nightwatchman, so I was born as a result of his being laid off! And I've got a drunkard. Oh dear, what a pity my Curro is like that! . . . because without wine . . . well, he's like a trunk, you can get anything you want out of him. But things can't go on like this. No, no, no! By no means! Because if I'm going to spend many nights like this . . . why have we bought the mattress? If only I wasn't so very stupid! But, yes, I've got to do something! Something to make this good-for-nothing stop laughing at me or leaving me on my own! And what should I do, oh dear, what should I do? . . . Oh, I know! I'm going to do something. I'm going to do the sweeping . . . *(She takes up the broom.)* and wait for my friend, so she can give some advice, and do what she says, whatever it is. Because I want to do everything, everything . . . except play patience. Where can he have spent the night, that . . .? I was going to say dog, God forgive me.

Phonetics and phonology

It is in this area that the main interest of the passage lies, since the spelling used by Arniches reflects, as it was intended to, for the benefit of actors, the rather exaggerated Andalusian pronunciation he required on stage. In actual closely transcribed examples of modern Andalusian speech, few of these features would in fact be so thoroughgoing, and it is worth bearing this in mind as we approach other literary texts which purport to represent regional pronunciations.

27.1.1 *Seseo* (the absence of an opposition between /s/ and /θ/, here realised as /s/) is consistently represented by such spellings as **hase** (l.6), **anochese** (l.7), etc. There is of course no precise phonetic information about the nature of the /s/, which is generally coronal in Andalusia, by contrast with the apico-alveolar [ş] of standard Spanish, though in some areas a dorsal [ş] is heard.
  Keypoint: the sibilants of Old Castilian (p. 290).

27.1.2 *Yeísmo* (the absence of an opposition between /j/ and /ʎ/, here realised as [j]) is similarly reflected by **yoro** (l.10), **yamale** (l.26), etc.

27.1.3 Intervocalic [d] is represented here as having been completely lost. Thus we find not only such examples as **inventao** for standard *inventado* (l.2), but in past participles generally (the feminine **cayá** = standard *callada* and the *-ido/a* form **dormío** = standard *dormido*, l.14, **sufría** = standard *sufrida*) and indeed in words of all categories (**aonde** corresponding to standard *adonde*, l.4, **marío** = standard *marido*, l.7, **pué** = standard *puede*, l.11). There is also loss across word-boundaries, though this seems to be restricted to the initial [d] of the preposition *de*: **arma é cántaro** = standard *alma de cántaro* (l.3), **la metá é las noches** = standard *la mitad de las noches* (ll.6–7). These features may be compared with those observed for Chilean Spanish in 30.1.3. Even in standard Peninsular Spanish, [d] is regularly omitted in a final /ado/ sequence, especially in past participles, though it is not considered 'correct'; but it is retained in most other environments.
  Keypoint: lenition (p. 278).

27.1.4 There is general loss of final /r/: **señó** = standard *señor* (l.2, etc.), **soplá** = standard *soplar* (l.5), etc., and sporadic loss of intervocalic /ɾ/ in **pa** = standard *para* (l.20) (but note also **para**, l.11). The loss of the final /r/ of the infinitive extends even to contexts where a clitic pronoun follows the infinitive, as in **pasáme** = standard *pasarme* (l.12).

27.1.5 Implosive /r/ and /l/ are neutralised, apparently as [ɾ]: **arma** = standard *alma* (l.3), **vuerven** = standard *vuelven* (l.5), **er vino** = standard *el vino* (l.17), etc. This is a very common feature of Andalusian speech, though the precise phonetic realisation of the merger varies very considerably; it is often a sound somewhere between [ɾ] and [l], which Spanish phoneticians represent by notations such as [ɺ].

27.1.6 Final /s/, which tends to be aspirated (pronounced as [h]) or lost very widely in Andalusia, is here represented (perhaps for purposes of aiding comprehension) except in the case of **meno** (l.3).

27.1.7 The group /bw/ is here represented as /gw/ (**agüela** for standard *abuela*, l.14, **güeno** for standard *bueno*, l.17). This is a very common non-standard feature of modern Spanish, and is discussed in 29.1.3.

27.1.8 Several complex consonant groups are simplified. The /mn/ group of the learned word *somnámbulo* has undergone semipopular reduction to /n/ (**sonámbulo**, l.14) in a way that resembles the simplifications of a number of learned words in the sixteenth and seventeenth centuries, some of which became standard in the eighteenth century (see 23.1.2). /dr/ is reduced to /r/ in **mare** = standard *madre* (l.15) and **comare** = standard *comadre* (l.24). Another method of simplifying a consonantal group can be seen in the epenthesis of a vowel in **comporao** = standard *comprado* (l.20).
  Keypoint: consonant groups (p. 267).

27.1.9 Some diphthongs are monophthongised. Standard *muy* [mwi] is here **mu** [mu]; this is a well-known feature of Andalusian speech, and is probably encouraged by the fact that *muy* is usually unstressed and quickly articulated.

27.1.10 The combination of the reduction of the /we/ diphthong and the elision of intervocalic /r/ leads to the form **fuá** for standard *fuera* (l.20).

Morphology and syntax

27.2.1 Aonde (l.4 and 25) is used in the locative sense of standard *donde* rather than in the allative sense of standard *adonde* (see also 6.3.9, 18.2.7, 21.2.10, 30.2.6).

27.2.2 The standard Spanish conjunction *así que* in the sense of 'as soon as' here has the preposition *de* added: **asín de que** (l.7). There is much analogical addition of *de* to *que* in modern Spanish, the patterns for such analogical extension being the complements of nouns (*la idea de que*, etc.), and some complex conjunctions (*antes de que*, *después de que*, etc.); in particular there is a tendency to use *de* with *que* after verbs (e.g. *pienso de que . . .*), a phenomenon referred to as *dequeísmo* and puristically castigated.

27.2.3 Some of the strategies observed in colloquial usage (see also Text 25) can also be seen here in this representation of direct speech: the abbreviatory devices **y tóo** (l.14), cf. 25.2.5, and the interjections ¡**Dios mío**! (l.16, etc.), ¡**Vaya**! (l.19), cf. 25.2.4.

27.2.4 Er . . . muy perro (l.26) shows the use of *muy* with a noun which denotes a quality and hence is being used in an adjectival way (cf. English 'very much a').

Vocabulary

27.3.1 Asín (l.7, see also 11.1.1) was one of a number of variant Old Castilian forms of the now standard *así*, and is still found in a number of present-day varieties of Spanish.

27.3.2 Señó (l.2) is used as an intensifier with **no**, most likely motivated by the need to strengthen phonetically a rather insubstantial word.

27.3.3 A diminutive suffix used affectively can be seen in **paraíta** = standard *paradita* (l.11); its effect here is to intensify the adjective 'so very stupid'.

27.3.4 Sereno (l.15) was a nightwatchman employed to watch over a street at night and to keep the keys of the main entrances to apartment blocks. This use of the word is due to the custom of the nightwatchman calling out the time during the night, followed by the phrase *y sereno* 'all's well'. Such a complex associational history can only be understood if the social circumstances which produced it are known, and this is why some semantic histories prove difficult to establish.

27.3.5 Sesantía = standard *cesantía* (l.16) is first encountered in the nineteenth century and is a nominal derivative of the verb *cesar*, in the specialised meaning of a worker's temporary redundancy.

XII Latin America

The discovery of the New World was to open up a vast overseas empire for Spain and ultimately to turn Spanish into one of the most widely spoken languages in the world. At the turn of the twentieth century, Spanish stood second only to Mandarin Chinese, and slightly ahead of English, in terms of numbers of native speakers, the vast majority of which are in the Americas (Grimes 1999). The spread of Spanish led to its further dialectalisation, although the Spanish-speaking world has preserved a remarkable homogeneity despite regional differences.

Although the term 'Latin-American Spanish' is often used in contrast to 'Peninsular Spanish', many of the commonest phonological and morphological features of Latin-American Spanish are also found in Peninsular regional varieties, and it is in vocabulary and idiomatic expressions, especially in colloquial register, that the most striking differences are to be found; at this level, local usages within Latin America can vary as much with one another as with Peninsular colloquial usage. Overall, Latin-American Spanish is characterised by the following phonological and morphological features, most of which are also found in Andalusian varieties of Peninsular Spanish; such similarities with Andalusian have encouraged the 'Andalusian hypothesis', according to which Latin-American Spanish can be seen as a continuation of Andalusian Spanish.

- Seseo: the absence of distinction between /s/ and /θ/ (only /s/ is used, articulated as a coronal [s]).
- Yeísmo: the absence of distinction between /j/ and /ʎ/ (realised as [j] or [(d)ʒ] and many degrees of fricativisation in between: the prepalatal quality of this phoneme is referred to as *rehilamiento*).
- /x/ is frequently weakened to be realised as [h].
- /f/ is frequently weakened to be realised as [ɸ].
- /s/ in implosive position is in many areas weakened to [h] or not articulated at all.
- The second person plural pronoun *vosotros/as* and its verb forms are not used: *ustedes* with a third person plural verb is the only second person plural form.
- In some areas *vos* is used for the familiar second person singular *tú*, a phenomenon known as *voseo*. *Vos* takes a variety of verb forms according to area (see 30.2.1).
- The *-ra* form of the past subjunctive is strongly preferred to the *-se* form. It is also used as a pluperfect, even in cultured written register.

	Vos or tu	Weakening of /x/ to [h]	Weakening of implosive /s/	Distinction between /j/ and /ʎ/maintained	Assibilation of /r/	Pronunciation of initial /f/
I	*tú*	[h]	[h] or nothing	no	no	[f]
II	*tú*	[x]	[s] maintained	no	no	[f]
III	*vos*	[h]	[h] or nothing	no	yes	[Φ]
IV	*vos or tú*	[h]	[s] maintained	yes	yes	[f]
V	*vos or tú*	[h]	[h] or nothing	no	no	[Φ]
VI	*tú*	[h]	[h] or nothing	no	no	[f]
VII	*vos or tú*	[x]	[s] maintained	yes	yes	[f]
VIII	*vos or tú*	[x]	[h] or nothing	no	yes	[Φ]
IX	*vos*	[x]	[h] or nothing	no	no	[Φ]

Map 3 Some linguistic features of Latin America (expansion of a suggestion by Zamora Munné and Guitart 1982)

- *Lo(s)* and *la(s)* are used only as direct object pronouns, a phenomenon often referred to as *loísmo*.

On the other hand, the importance of local variation must not be underestimated. One notable development which is not shared with Andalusia is the assibilation of /r/ (a pronunciation halfway between [ɹ] and [z], which is particularly associated with Chilean Spanish). As more data from colloquial registers of Latin-American Spanish are charted, it seems likely that a number of local features may have been encouraged by the autochthonous Amerindian languages, especially in those areas where a high degree of bilingualism developed. A particularly interesting area in this respect is Paraguay, where Guaraní is in fact a co-official language with Spanish.

A problematic issue in the study of Latin-American Spanish is the identification of dialect areas. In the Peninsula, isoglosses can relatively easily be drawn because linguistic features are shared by a number of neighbouring areas; we can also clearly see the importance of geographical factors and of the history of the *Reconquista* in the shaping of the modern linguistic map. In Latin America, the picture is much less coherent. It seems that the same feature may occur in areas which are separated by thousands of miles, and there are few major isoglosses to be drawn. Sometimes geography seems to be of importance: thus the *altiplano* shares a number of features which differentiate highland speech from that of the lowland coastal areas. Sometimes it is possible to associate particular linguistic features with patterns of settlement or Amerindian language areas: thus the Yucatán peninsula in Mexico, the speech of which shows a number of idiosyncrasies, had no easy means of communication with the capital for hundreds of years and also had a large number of Maya speakers (Lipski 1994: 281–2). In fact it is likely that a number of cross-currents have conspired to produce the patchwork of linguistic features which make up the dialect map of Latin America (see Map 3, p. 192).

Further reading

Lipski (1994); Rosenblat (1977); Zamora Munné and Guitarte (1982); Fontanella de Weinberg (1992).

28 A love letter from Mexico (1689)

28.0 A source of extremely interesting texts from the linguistic point of view is the correspondence and official archival material from the Archivo de Indias in Seville. Letters written spontaneously for practical purposes and with little care for style, such as the one reproduced here, are probably as close to the speech of the time as we are likely to get, and from the spellings used in them we can deduce much information about the chronology of sound changes: it is now clear, for instance, that some changes must have taken place in ordinary speech considerably earlier than had been previously thought (Boyd-Bowman 1975). The letter below, dating from 1689, is from one Agustín to Mariana, a girl with whom he is in love and

whom he is trying to abduct from a convent. It is the first of a series of similar letters, in the course of which Mariana appears to hesitate over the abduction; but
in the end Agustín's efforts are successful, and he is denounced to the authorities
– hence the survival of the documents.

The text

The text is document 144 of Company Company (1994).

Further reading

Boyd-Bowman (1975) gives a detailed analysis of three similarly interesting documents from over a century earlier which hail from Veracruz in Mexico.
Boyd-Bowman is able to show evidence from these texts of *seseo*, the passage of
/ʃ/ and /ʒ/ to /x/ (probably realised as [h]), *yeísmo*, merger of implosive /l/
and /r/, loss of syllable- or word-final /s/, nasalisation of vowels followed by
/n/ and the loss or weakening of voiced intervocalic fricatives [ð] and [ɣ].

> **Regalo y bien de mis ojos, no sé cómo ponderátelos. Deseo de berte, q**ue
> **lla me parese q**ue **me muro sin berte, y q**ue **los dias son años para mí y**
> **silglos. Mi bien, todos los dias estoy moliendo a estos clergos de santa**
> **Catalina y a Parsero, y lo lleban muy a la larga todo, y me mulen mucho.**
> **Yo estoy dispuesto a sacarte, como te lo enbié a desir el otro dia, entre**   5
> **las dose y la una de la noche, q**ue **son lindas para el efeto. Lo que te**
> **encargo es q**ue **cuando salgas al coredor del primer patio, q**ue **tosas para**
> **qu**ellos **te conoscan por la tos y te digan el nobre de Juana Peres. Y, por**
> **bida tulla, q**ue **no ayga falta; porq**ue **si ellos ben q**ue **los engañan, an de**
> **entrá adentro y te an de buscar para sacarte pestos allo. Y lo que te**   10
> **encargo, el retrato contigo. Y los papeles q**ue **tubires mios, q**ue **los quemes;**
> **no deges memoria mia allá, q**ue **con eso estamos seguros; y no te dé**
> **cuydo de nada. Y si puedes sacar a la biuda, aslo; porq**ue **con eso no se**
> **acata quién lo yso, pero no le abises asta q**ue **sea ora del efeto. Si no,**
> **sarcalla por engaños, como q**ue **le dises: '¿si ara ubira qu**en **nos sacara por**   15
> **la sotea, salieras?'. En disiendo q**ue **sí, dile: 'pues bamos'. Y no se te olbide**
> **el toser y la seña de 'Ju**an**a Peres' qu**ellos **an de disir asi q**ue **bean q**ue
> **toses. Y en todo caso, tú por delante. Y mira q**ue **si no fure esta noche,**
> **porta respuesta q**ue **bine tarde. De lo q**ue **dises, no dejes de salir, porq**ue
> **enter esta noche y mañana en la noche, as de salir, como tú no faltes a**   20
> **las ora referidas. Tu esclabo y negrito, sienpre.**

Translation

Gift and good of my eyes, I cannot praise them too highly. I have a desire to
see you, for I think I shall die without seeing you, and the days are years and
centuries for me. My treasure, every day I keep on pressing these clergy of Santa
Catalina and Parsero, and they take such a long time over everything, and they
are wearing me down. I am prepared to get you out, as I sent a message to you

to say the other day, between twelve and one at night, which are good for the purpose. What I would charge you is that when you come out on to the corridor of the first courtyard, that you cough, so that they may recognise you by the cough, and say to you the name of Juana Pérez. And, on your life, do not default; because if they see that they are being deceived, they will go in and look for you in order to get you out once they have set about the task (?). And I also charge you to bring the picture with you. Any papers of mine that you have, burn them; do not leave any record of me there, so that then we are safe, and do not worry about anything. And if you can get the widow out, do so; because then they will not know who did it; but do not tell her until it is time for the deed. If not, get her out by deception, such as by saying to her, 'If at this moment there were someone who would get us out across the roof, would you come?' If she says yes, say to her, 'Well, we're going.' And do not forget to cough and the password 'Juana Pérez' which will be said to you, so that they can see you coughing. And in any case, you go first. And look, if it cannot be tonight, carry a reply that I came late. From what you say, do not fail to come out, because between tonight and tomorrow night, you will come out, if you do not default at the times mentioned. Your servant and slave, always.

Phonetics and phonology

28.1.1 The spelling reflects a number of phonemic mergers, and is reminiscent of uneducated spelling in the Spanish-speaking world today. Because Spanish spelling is phonemic rather than logographic, Spanish-speakers learn to spell by transcribing syllables (*silabear*), and follow pronunciation; ironically, because the orthographic system has a number of redundant letters and because in many varieties of Spanish some phonemic distinctions assumed in the standard language are not made, there is much room for error. Reading such a text aloud usually soon resolves any difficulties of interpretation, however.

B and *v* are not distinctive, and the writer appears simply not to use *v*; thus we have the spellings **berte** = *verte* (1.1), **lleban** = *llevan* (1.4), **bida** = *vida* (1.9). etc.
Keypoint: the 'b/v' merger (p. 262).

Both *j* and *g* are used to represent /x/ before a front vowel: **deges** (1.12) and **dejes** (1.19). (Choice of the modern spelling was not definitively fixed by the Real Academia Española until much later: see 23.1.1.)

Ll is used to represent both standard /ʎ/ and /j/: **lla** = *ya* (1.1), **lleban** = *llevan* (1.4), **tulla** = *tuya* (1.9), etc. This is good evidence that the writer is *yeísta*, though it is impossible to be precise about the exact phonetic value of these words. *Yeísmo* is a common development in Andalusian and Latin-American Spanish (and is in fact nowadays the majority situation within the Spanish-speaking world).

s is used to represent both standard /s/ and /θ/: **parese** = *parece* (1.2), **desir** = *decir* (1.5), **dose** = *doce* (1.6), **aslo** = *hazlo* (1.13), **yso** = *hizo* (1.14), etc. This provides evidence of *seseo*, which is virtually universal in Latin America.
Keypoint: the sibilants of Old Castilian (p. 290).

28.1.2 Other features of the spelling reflect tendencies which are less general, but which are familiar from some present-day varieties of Spanish.

The diphthongs /we/ and /je/ are sometimes represented by a single vowel: **muro** = *muero* (l.2), **mulen** = *muelen* (l.4), **tubires** = *tuvieres* (l.11), **ubira** = *hubiera* (l.15), **quen** = *quien* (l.15), **fure** = *fuere* (l.18). While this may indicate a tendency towards the reduction of diphthongs which can be observed in very rapid speech even in the standard language (compare the widespread pronunciation of *¡hasta luego!* as [talwo], and cf. 31.1.1, 32a.1.5), it may simply be a feature of semi-literate spelling (cf. 4.1.5).

Final /r/ is occasionally not represented, suggesting its loss (cf. 27.1.4): **ponderátelos** = *ponderártelos* (l.1), **entrá** = *entrar* (l.10).

Final /s/ is not represented in the sequence **las ora referidas** = *las horas referidas* (l.21): the loss of /s/ before /r/ is in fact an assimilation which takes place even in the present-day standard language when spoken at a normal pace: thus *las ratas* is pronounced [laratas].

Sinalefa is represented in the spelling of **la sotea** = *la azotea* (l.16) and **quellos** = *que ellos* (l.17).

28.1.3 Finally, there are a number of idiosyncrasies; it is difficult in some cases to decide whether these are simply spelling 'mistakes' or whether they reflect features of the writer's language.

silglos = *siglos* (l.3) apparently shows epenthesis of /l/ (compare 11.1.11).

clergos = *clérigos* (l.3) seems to show reduction of the proparoxytone, which would tend to happen in any case in rapid speech. This may be compared with the earlier process which systematically affected Latin proparoxytones.
Keypoint: stress (p. 291).

coredor = *corredor* (l.7) lacks a second *r*; however, while the absence of the distinction between intervocalic /r/ and /ɾ/ is a feature of creoles (see Chapter XVI), it is not generally absent in mainstream Spanish varieties.

sarcalla = *sacarla* (l.15). The spelling *ll* seems to suggest the common assimilation of /r/ and /l/ to /ʎ/ (here probably pronounced as [j], see 28.1.1) which took place in combinations of an infinitive and a clitic pronoun. The *r* may be a simple error caused by a memory of the full infinitive form *sacar* or it may be a kind of metathesis (cf. 14.2.4, 20.2.9).

disir = *decir* (l.17). The spelling of the first vowel with *i* may be indicative of the neutralisation of the opposition between /i/ and /e/ in unstressed syllables, which is a common feature of many Spanish varieties, especially in Latin America. (This phenomenon is suggested by the spellings of a number of Old Castilian texts: see 9.1.7, 13.1.5 and cf. 21.1.3.)

enter esta = *entre esta* (l.20) may be a simple inversion of the order of the letters or may reflect the epenthesis of an /e/ to ease the complex consonantal group /ntr/ which would otherwise result.
Keypoint: consonant groups (p. 267).

Morphology and syntax

28.2.1 Deseo de berte (l.1). The use of prepositions with infinitive complements is a Romance development (cf. 23.2.3). Although it is possible to see some general patterns in preposition choice, such as the association of the derivatives of Latin

AD (> MSp. *a*) with verbs of beginning and motion, and the derivatives of Latin DE (> MSp. *de*) with verbs of stopping and generally 'negative' meaning, the choice of preposition, and indeed the presence or absence of a preposition at all, varies between the Romance languages and from period to period in the history of the languages (compare MSp. *comenzar a* + infinitive with MFr. *commencer de* + infinitive). In Modern Spanish transitive verbs which take dependent infinitives tend not to take a preposition before the infinitive, however: *desear* is such a verb, and the modern structure is *deseo verte*.

28.2.2 Ayga = *haya* (l.9). *Haiga*, with an epenthetic /g/ in its first person singular stem and hence throughout the present subjunctive, is still sometimes found in popular speech as a variant form of *haya*. The form is analogically created on the basis of several other irregular but frequently occurring first person present stems, most obviously *caigo*, *traigo* and *oigo* (see also 30.2.2). There are a number of common verbs in standard Spanish which have a /g/ in their 1st p.sg. stems with no obvious etymological source: *caigo* ⩽ Lat. CĂDO, *oigo* ⩽ Lat. AUDĬO, *traigo* ⩽ Lat. TRĂHO (see also 7.2.13). Even *hago* ⩽ Lat. FĂCĬO is irregular in its development. This strongly suggests an analogical process for which the model may have been the regular Lat. DĪCO > *digo*. /g/ is also found in 1st p.sg. stems deriving from Latin /nj/ and /lj/ groups: Lat. TĔNĔO ⩾ *tengo*, Lat. VĔNĬO ⩾ *vengo*, Lat.VĂLĔO ⩾ *valgo* and Lat. SĂLĬO ⩾ *salgo*; note also Lat. ?PŌNĔO (the Classical Latin form was PŌNO) ⩾ *pongo*. This is a development which creates a good deal of irregularity in the Spanish verb system; it may be compared with the history of irregular preterites (see 8.2.1).

28.2.3 There are several examples of tonic possessive adjectives in this text. In **por bida tulla** = *por vida tuya* (ll.8–9) the value of the adjective seems to be emphatic; this usage in modern Spanish is restricted to formal literary register, though the tonic forms are regularly used in address formulae, e.g. *vida mía* 'my dear', *¡Dios mío!* 'Good God!', *muy señor mío*, 'Dear Sir', etc. In **memoria mia** (l.12), the meaning is 'memory (trace) of me', a function which continues in the modern language.
   Keypoint: possessives (p. 287).

28.2.4 The future subjunctive is used in the two contexts in which it held on most tenaciously: future-referring relative clauses with an indefinite antecedent (**los papeles que tubires mios**, l.11) and the protasis of a future-referring conditional sentence (**si no fure esta noche**, l.18). Otherwise, the present subjunctive is used to refer to the future in temporal clauses (**cuando salgas al coredor**, l.7) and in conditional sentences which involve a conjunction other than *si* (**como tú no faltes**, l.20).
   Keypoints: the future subjunctive (p. 275); **conditional sentences** (p. 265).

28.2.5 There are a number of syntactic features which are typical of the colloquial nature of this text:
   Elliptical constructions: **Y lo que te encargo, el retrato contigo** = *te encargo de [traer] el retrato contigo* (ll.10–11); **tú por delante** = *tú [has de ir] por delante* (l.18, cf. 25.2.5).
   Use of topicalisation: **los papeles que tubires mios** [topic], **que los quemes** (l.11). Closely associated with this is the use of clefting: **Lo que te encargo (es)**

... (ll.6–7 and ll.10–11).

The sentences are relatively short, and although there is no avoidance of subordinate constructions such as conditional sentences and indirect commands, the syntax tends to be paratactic in nature (note the absence of a relative clause in the sentence that runs from ll.3–4, and the frequency of the conjunction *y*). The conjunction *que* is used, as in modern spoken Spanish, as a general conjunction: **no deges memoria mia allá, que con eso estamos seguros** (l.12); cf. 25.2.6, 36.2.4.

28.2.6 The verbal paraphrase *haber de* + infinitive is used extensively in this text to refer to the future without marked modal value: **an de entrá adentro** (ll.9–10), **te an de buscar** (l.10), **quellos an de disir** (l.17), **as de salir** (l.20). This form is still widely used in Latin-American Spanish in much the same way.

    Keypoints: future and conditional (p. 274); **periphrastic verb forms** (p. 283).

28.2.7 En disiendo que sí (l.16). The gerund is here used with the preposition *en*, and has the function of a conditional protasis ('if she says yes'); see Mozos Mocha (1973). In the modern language the use of *en* with the gerund is obsolete.

28.2.8 ¿Si ara ubira quen nos sacara por la sotea, salieras? (ll.15–16). The *-ra* form is used in both the protasis (**ubira**) and the apodosis (**salieras**) of this counterfactual conditional sentence (contrast the earlier use of this sequence to indicate past counterfactuality, cf. 13.2.1, 20.2.4, 23.2.2). This apodosis use of the *-ra* form accounts for its ability to replace the conditional (20.2.4), a phenomenon which seems to be much more general in Latin America (Kany 1951: 182–3 and see also 31.2.7) than in the Peninsula. The *-ra* form is also used here as a subjunctive in a past-referring relative clause with an indefinite antecedent (**sacara**).

    Keypoint: conditional sentences (p. 265).

Vocabulary

28.3.1 Ponderátelos (l.1). *Ponderar* is a word of learned origin from Lat. [PONDĔRO] 'to weigh', 'to evaluate', which by metonymic association has come to have also the meaning of 'to praise', 'to exalt'. The first sentence of this letter is a conventional higher register compliment to the lady.

28.3.2 Moliendo (l.3), **mulen** (l.4). *Moler* has the literal meaning of 'to grind', from Lat. [MŎLO], and undergoes metaphorical extension of meaning to that of 'to worry', 'to pester', 'to bore'.

28.3.3 Lindas (l.6). *Lindo* is a word of very general favourable meaning (cf. Eng. *nice*, *cute*, etc.) which is particularly favoured in Latin-American Spanish today (Peninsular speakers prefer *bonito* or *majo*, see 36.3.7). Like many such words with a 'debased' meaning, it has undergone considerable semantic evolution: deriving by a rather complicated phonetic route from Lat. LĒGĬTĬMU[S] 'real', 'genuine', it reaches the general meaning of 'good' in the fourteenth century and in the Peninsula further develops to that of 'pretty'.

28.3.4 Efeto (l.6). This learned word, driving from Lat. EFFECTU[M], the past participle of EFFĬCĬO 'to produce an effect', became very widely diffused in Spanish and developed the semipopular form with the /kt/ group reduced to /t/ that we see evidence of here. However, the learned form *efecto* was the variant eventually preferred by the Real Academia Española (see 23.0).

  Keypoints: **consonant groups** (p. 267), **learned and popular, semilearned and semipopular** (p. 277).

28.3.5 Negrito (l.21) is not to be interpreted literally as 'negro', but as 'slave', slavery being associated with the African negros imported into the Americas for this purpose. (The word **esclabo**, which has cognates in many languages, has a similar history, in fact, deriving from the word designating the Slav peoples, who were similarly subject to slavery in Eastern Europe in the Middle Ages.)

29 The gaucho conscript. José Hernández, *Martín Fierro* (1872, Argentina)

29.0 This famous poem has become something of a symbol of Argentininian identity, although it relates only to the *pampas* area of the country and the life of its white/Indian *mestizo* inhabitants, the *gauchos*. The poem exposed the unjust way in which the *gauchos* were treated by the government in the Indian wars, when many were conscripted and compelled to serve in the army in brutal conditions. Forgotten and unpaid in remote outposts, they were nevertheless treated as deserters if they attempted to return to their normal way of life as itinerant cattlemen. Hernández's poem is of epic proportions and elevates the *gauchos'* characteristic language, turns of phrase and imagery, to an original art-form. Accordingly it is an extremely important text linguistically, since it contains much valuable data about the *gauchos'* way of speech, even adopting an individual spelling system which we may assume captures some of the phonological features of this variety of Spanish.

The text

The extract below, which recounts Martín Fierro's departure after conscription and the conditions of the frontier fort to which he is sent, is taken from the first edition (dated 1872), as reproduced in facsimile in Carrino *et al.* (1974: 16–17). The spelling, accentuation and punctuation are as they appear in the original.

Further reading

Castro (1957); Tiscornia (1925–30).

> Yo llevé un moro de número,
> Sobresaliente el matucho!
> Con él gané en Ayacucho
> Mas plata que agua bendita–
> Siempre el gaucho necesita
> Un pingo pa fiarle un pucho–

5

Y cargué sin dar mas güeltas
Con las prendas que tenía,
Gergas, poncho, cuanto habia
En casa, tuito lo alcé–   *10*
A mi china la dejé
Media desnuda ese dia.

No me faltaba una guasca,
Esa ocasion eché el resto:
Bozal, maniador, cabresto,   *15*
Lazo, bolas y manea ...
¡El que hoy tan pobre me vea
Tal vez no crerá todo esto!!

Ansi en mi moro escarciando
Enderesé á la frontera;   *20*
Aparcero! si usté viera
Lo que se llama Canton ...
Ni envidia tengo al raton
En aquella ratonera–

...

En la lista de la tarde   *25*
El Gefe nos cantó el punto,
Diciendo: "quinientos juntos
"Llevará el que se resierte,
"Lo haremos pitar del juerte
"Mas bien dese por dijunto."   *30*

A naides le dieron armas
Pues toditas las que habia
El Coronel las tenia
Segun dijo esa ocasion
Pa repartirlas el dia   *35*
En que hubiera una invasion

Translation

I took a fine dark roan horse – a brilliant beast! In Ayacucho I won with him more money than holy water. A gaucho always needs a good horse to rely on.

  And without further ado I loaded up everything I had: saddle-blankets, a poncho, all there was at home, I took it all; I left my woman half-naked that day.

  There wasn't a single piece of crude leather missing [= I took absolutely everything]; on that occasion I put everything in: halter, tether, leading-rein, lasso, bolas and hobble ... Anyone who sees me so poor today perhaps will not believe all this!

So, on my roan, his head tossing, I headed for the frontier. Friend, if you could see the place they call a fort . . .! I don't envy a mouse in that mousehole.
. . .

At the evening roll-call, the boss laid it on the line: 'Anyone who deserts will get five hundred lashes on the trot; we'll give him the works; he might as well give himself up for dead.'

They didn't give anyone weapons because the colonel kept all that there were (as he said at the time) to hand out the day there was an attack.

Phonetics and phonology

29.1.1 Hernández's spellings show some attempt to represent the phonological system of Argentine *gaucho* Spanish. Amongst the features he captures are: *seseo*, represented in **enderesé** (l.20) (standard *enderecê*); the loss of final [d] in **usté** (l.21) (standard *usted*); the reduced form of *para* as **pa** (ll.6 and 35); the avoidance of hiatus by (i) the conversion of a front vowel to [j], represented by **maniador** (l.15) for standard *maneador* and **escarciando** (l.19) for *escarceando*, and (ii) the reduction of an /ee/ sequence to a single /e/ as in **crerá** (l.17) for standard *creerá*.
Keypoint: the sibilants of Old Castilian (p. 290).

29.1.2 The aspirate nature of initial /f/ is represented in **juerte** (l.29) (standard *fuerte*) and **dijunto** (l.30) (standard *difunto*), which may be taken to represent pronunciations such as [hweɾte], [dihunto].
Keypoint: the f>h change (p. 271).

29.1.3 The spelling **güeltas** (l.7) represents the pronunciation [gweltas]; words which in the standard language begin with [bwe] (here *vueltas*) or [we] (e.g. *huerto*) show this development in several regional varieties of Spanish (cf. 27.1.7, 30.1.6). We may imagine that this situation is brought about by (i) weak articulation of initial /b/ (which would in any case be realised as [β] when intervocalic: in the standard language the unstressed Old Castilian pronoun *vos* was weakened to *os*, see 11.2.2) and (ii) the reinforcement of an initial back semivowel /w/ by the corresponding velar consonant /g/ ([ɣ] when intervocalic).

29.1.4 The use of *g* rather than *j* before a front vowel to represent /x/ (**Gergas**, l.9; **Gefe**, l.26) was a spelling custom much favoured in Latin America in the late nineteenth and early twentieth centuries, though as such it does not represent a distinctive pronunciation.

29.1.5 The form **cabresto** (l.15) for standard *cabestro* shows metathesis of the /ɾ/, which as a liquid consonant, is particularly prone to such movement (cf. 11.1.6).

29.1.6 Tuito (l.10) (= standard *todito*, see also 29.2.2) is produced by the elision of intervocalic /d/ (cf. 30.1.3) and the avoidance of the resulting hiatus by the realisation of the back vowel /o/ as [w].

29.1.7 Naides (l.31). Many variant developments of the now standard *nadie* are found in the Spanish dialects. *Nadie* may be derived from an ellipsis of Lat. HŎMĬNES NĀTI [HŎMO NĀTUS] ('people alive') or it may have been a more spontaneous movement within Old Castilian as a means of distinguishing personal reference from the non-personal *nada* (see 4.3.2). OCast. *otro* had a similar set of variant forms (*otri, otre, otrie(n)*) which suggests an analogical development (Alvar and Pottier 1983: 146–8).

Morphology and syntax

29.2.1 Enderesé (l.20) corresponds to standard *me enderecé*. Regional varieties of Spanish often display such differences from the standard as regards the valency of verbs, though in Latin-American Spanish the reverse situation is more common, i.e. intransitive verbs which are non-reflexive in standard Peninsular usage are reflexive (Kany 1951: 186–97 gives examples of *adelantar, amanecer, aparecer, atrasar, cambiar, crecer, demorar, devolver* in the sense of *volver(se), dilatar, enfermar, huir, importar, recordar, regresar, soñar (con), tardar* and *venir* used in this way).
   Keypoint: the reflexive (p. 288).

29.2.2 Tuito (l.10) and **toditas** (l.32) are typical examples of the use of an affective diminutive, *-ito* being the preferred form in Latin America; here it conveys the intensive meaning of 'every single thing', 'every single one'.

29.2.3 Esa ocasión (l.34). *En* is often omitted with *ocasión, momento, instante* and similar words in popular speech. This may be by analogy with expressions involving *vez, (una vez, varias veces*, etc.) which have become set adverbial expressions (Kany 1951: 366–7).

Vocabulary

29.3.1 The semantic field of 'horse' is, as to be expected in a society where horses are all-important, well discriminated: in the first stanza **moro** 'a black and white horse', **matucho** 'an old, worn-out horse' and **pingo** 'fast, lively horse' are used. The ironical use of **matucho**, which here reflects the fondness of the gaucho for his horse, recalls the process of amelioration through self-deprecation by which Latin CĂBALLU[S] 'old nag' became the standard word for 'horse' (Sp. *caballo*) in many Romance languages (see 9.3.6).

29.3.2 Similarly, there is a wealth of vocabulary relating to horses and riding equipment: **gergas** (l.9), **bozal, maniador, cabresto** (l.15), **manea** (l.16). Some of these are not standard in form or meaning, and presumably reflect the individual development of a remote and self-contained society. Thus **jerga**, which in standard usage has the meaning of 'serge', 'coarse cloth' (not to be confused with its homonym meaning 'jargon'), here has the more restricted meaning of a blanket (of coarse cloth) which is placed beneath the saddle; **maneador** is a strap of worn leather, no doubt a derivative of √*mano*; similarly, **manea** is a hobble, i.e. a fetter which restricts the front legs (*manos*) of the horse (in standard usage *maniota*). **Lazo**

and **bolas** (l.16) have the specific meanings, respectively, of 'lasso' (the English word *lasso* is in fact a borrowing from Sp. *lazo*) and the gaucho weapon consisting of a series of metal balls attached to ropes, used for bringing down animals.

29.3.3 Other words or usages particular to Latin America are:

Plata (l.4), the normal word for 'money' (Peninsular *dinero*), an associative extension of its original meaning of 'silver' (the same process is evident in Fr. *argent* deriving from Lat. ARGENTU[M] 'silver').

China (l.11), originally meaning 'Indian woman' (by association with the Orient) but subsequently used as a term of endearment and generally used by gauchos to denote their partner (formal marriage being uncommon in this community).

Aparcero (l.21) is a morphological derivative of Lat. PARTĬĀRĬU[S] 'participant' and comes to have the meaning of 'co-owner' and, by implication therefore, 'business partner'. It then widens in meaning to become, as here, a general form of friendly address: compare the use of Eng. *partner* among cattlemen in the US.

29.3.4 Some expressions are presumably local within Argentina. Tiscornia (1925: 33) noted that neither **cantar el punto** (l.26) nor **hacer pitar del juerte** (l.29) appeared in dictionaries of Argentinian Spanish. The latter expression is apparently an image based on reference to black Brazilian tobacco which few people could tolerate.

29.3.5 Pucho (l.6) 'a little' and **guasca** (l.13) 'strip of crude leather' are borrowings from Quechua, and **poncho** (l.9) is from Araucanian.

30 Caring for the wounded. Marta Brunet, *Montaña adentro* (1923, Chile)

30.0 The period immediately following the First World War saw a desire on the part of many Latin-American writers to represent the distinctive way of life and linguistic usage of America in their writings, and this naturally provides the linguist with a wealth of material that otherwise would not be easily accessible: this was one of the spurs to Charles E. Kany in producing his three monumental works on Latin-American syntax and vocabulary. The text below is such a work, first published in the 1920s, by the Chilean author Marta Brunet (1901–67), dealing with the hard life and times of inhabitants of the rural Chilean south.

The text

The text is taken from Brunet (1962: 374–5).

Further reading

Lenz (1940); Oroz (1966).

—¡Ay! ¡Señorcito! Si es Juan Oses —gritó Cata adelantándose.

De rodillas junto al hombre, trató de levantarlo: pesaba el cuerpo lacio y fueron vanos sus esfuerzos.

—Aguárdese, mamita, déjeme sacarme el manto. —Tomó entonces a Juan cuerpo a cuerpo, y, alzándolo, consiguió, ayudada por doña Clara, dejarlo *5* boca arriba.

—¡Ay mamacita Virgen! ¡Ay Señorcito! ¡Ayayay! —clamaba horrorizada la vieja.

—Menos mal qu'está vivo —gimió resignada Cata ...

—Mi Diosito! Cómo lo'ejaron esos condenaos ..., hecho una pura lástima y *10* la ropita hecha güiras ... ¡Ay mi Diosito!

—Vaya a buscar un pichicho di'agua al río, mamita.

—En qué te la traigo, m'hijita quería ...

—Tome, en la chupalla. Algo puee que llegue.

Sujetándose a las quilas logró la vieja bajar el talud resbaladizo; la ascen- *15* sión fue más penosa y lenta.

—Aquí está.

—Vaiga agora onde la Margara pa ver si lo llevamos pa su puebla d'ella, mientras podimos llevarlo pa la rancha.

—¿Vos querís llevarlo pa la puebla e nosotras? *20*

—No lo vamos a ejar aquí, botao como un quiltro sarnoso, con too lo qu'hizo por Aladino.

—¿Y qué va'icir la gente? Vos sabís lo reparones que son.

—A mí no se me da na ... Ejelos qui'hablen.

—Pero el cuento es que vos no te vayái a enrear con él ... Vos sos muy *25* bien retemplá.

—¿Hasta cuándo le voy a icir qu'éste no es como l'otro?

—Güeno ... Vos sabrís lo que vai'hacer ... Pero cuidaíto, ¿no?

—Ya está. Camine ligero.

Translation

'Lord, it's Juan Oses!' shouted Cata, moving forward.

Kneeling down by the man, she tried to raise him: his limp body was heavy and her efforts were useless.

'Wait, Ma, let me take off my shawl.' She then took Juan bodily, and, raising him up, managed, with Doña Clara's help, to put him on his back.

'Oh Virgin Mother! Oh Lord! Ah!' the old woman cried out, horrified.

'At least he's alive,' Cata sighed resignedly ...

'My God! How those bastards have left him ..., in a pitiful state and all his clothes in shreds. Oh, my God!'

'Go and get a drop of water from the river, Ma.'

'What shall I put it in, my dear daughter?'

'Here, in the hat. Perhaps some will get here.'

Holding on to the *quila* trees, the old woman succeeded in getting down the slippery slope; getting back up was more troublesome and slower.

'Here it is.'

'Now go to Margara's place and see if we can take him to her to her *puebla*; meanwhile we'll take him to the *rancha*.'

'You want to take him to our *puebla*?'

'We're not going to leave him here, abandoned like a mangy dog, after all he's done for Aladino.'

'And what will folks say? You know how they're always finding fault.'

'I don't care. Let them talk.'

'But the fact of the matter is that you shouldn't get mixed up with him . . . You're very keen on him.'

'How many more times do I have to tell you that he's not like the last one?'

'Well . . . You know your own business . . . But be careful, OK?'

'There we are. Go easy.'

Phonetics and phonology

30.1 The use of conventional spelling gives only an approximate phonetic representation, and does not explicitly represent all features of pronunciation (e.g. *seseo* is not shown). To do so would in fact mean making the text visually incomprehensible to a reader. The intention is clearly to incorporate local colour through the use of adjusted spellings which will not interfere with comprehension, and the text must be approached in this way.

30.1.1 *Sinalefa* of identical vowels is frequently represented, suggesting that its result is here identical with the articulation of a single vowel: **qu'está** = *que está* (l.9), **m'hijita** = *mi hijita* (l.13), **d'ella** (l.18), **va'icir** = *va a decir* (l.23), **vai'hacer** = *vai(s) a hacer* (l.28). Cf. 28.1.2.

30.1.2 Atonic /e/ closes to [j] before a following back vowel: **di'agua** = *de agua* (l.12), **qui'hablen** = *que hablen* (l.24). Although most noticeable in such a context, there is a widespread tendency for atonic /e/ and /o/ to close when in hiatus (cf. 29.1.1).
   Keypoint: vowels (p. 296).

30.1.3 Intervocalic /d/ is elided in many instances, not only word-internally (**condenaos** = *condenados*, l.10, **puee** = *puede*, l.14, **quería** = *querida*, l.13, **botao** = *botado* and **too** = *todo*, l.21, **na** = *nada*, l.24, **enrear** = *enredar*, l.25, **retemplá** = *retemplada*, l.26, **cuidaíto** = *cuidadito*, l.28) but also across a word boundary (**lo'ejaron** = *lo dejaron*, l.10, **la puebla e nosotros** = *la puebla de nosotros*, l.20, **vamos a ejar** = *vamos a dejar*, l.21, **va'icir** = *va a decir*, l.23, **na** . . . **Ejelos** . . . = *nada. Déjelos* . . ., l.24, **voy a icir** = *voy a decir*, l.27). Cf. 27.1.3, 29.1.6.
   Keypoint: lenition (p. 278).

30.1.4 Intervocalic /ɾ/ is elided in **pa** = *para* (l.18, etc.), though [pa] is a common realisation of this word throughout the Spanish-speaking world, even in the Peninsula (cf. 27.1.4).

30.1.5 A well-known characteristic of much lowland Latin-American Spanish is the tendency to aspirate or to completely elide implosive /s/ (so that, for example, *este* is articulated as [eʰte]. /s/ here is generally represented, though the tell-tale spellings of **vayái** = *vayáis* (l.25) and **vai'hacer** = *vais a hacer* (l.28) suggest a more general loss (cf. 27.1.6).

30.1.6 For **güeno** see 27.1.7, 29.1.3. **Güiras** (l.11) may be an instance of the same phenomenon (see below 30.3.1).

Morphology and syntax

30.2.1 Very noticeable in this conversation are the forms of *voseo* and the use of second person forms of address. Beginning with the latter, it is striking that while the mother addresses her daughter as **vos**, the daughter addresses her mother as **usted**; there is a very great deal of variation in present-day Latin America in this respect, and in Chile affectionate uses of *usted* and an absence of 'symmetry' in the use of second person forms of address are common. Thus the use of **usted** in this passage should not be taken as implying any abnormal respect or distance on the part of the daughter. The social acceptability of *voseo* in Chile has varied a good deal, even in recent times. Kany (1951: 67) speaks of it being 'to a large extent eradicated' in cultured usage while Lipski (1994: 201–2) reports the growing use of the *voseo* verb-forms among the younger middle- and upper-classes, though with *tú* as the (optional) subject pronoun.

As regards the *voseo* forms, **vos** is the subject pronoun and **te** is the corresponding object clitic. The verb forms attested here are the present and future tense of *-er* verbs, which have an *-ís* ending by contrast with the Argentinian *-és* (see 13.2.2), **querís** (l.20), **sabís** (l.23), **sabrís** (l.28); the present tense of the verb *ser*, **sos** (l.25), which is the same as in Argentina, and the present subjunctive **vayái(s)** (l.25), in which the elision of final /s/ (see 30.1.5) is most noticeable, which contrasts with the *vayás* of Argentina.

Keypoint: personal pronouns (p. 284).

30.2.2 The verb-form **vaiga** = standard *vaya* (l.18) is an analogical development (compare the /g/ of *haiga* = standard *haya* discussed in 28.2.2); note, however, the inconsistency of **vaya** (l.12), which may be genuine variation or simply that the author has omitted to use the distinctive dialectal form. **Vaiga** is also found in Andalusia and in Judeo-Spanish.

30.2.3 The same identity between *-er* and *-ir* verbs we have observed in the *voseo* verb-forms in 30.2.1 can also be seen in the first person plural of the present tense in **podimos** (l.19). For regular verbs, the *-er* and *-ir* conjugations are already identical in the standard language in all but a few forms (the first and second persons plural of the present tense, the infinitive and the plural imperative), and so such further analogical merger as is evidenced here is not a surprising development.

30.2.4 There is extensive use of the affective diminutive suffix **-ito/a** in this text. It appears to be added as a matter of course to affectionate forms of address (**mamita**, l.4, **mamacita**, l.7, **Señorcito**, l.1, etc., **Diosito**, l.11, **hijita**, l.13); in **ropita** (l.11) it expresses a feeling of sympathy, rather like English 'poor', and in

cuidaíto (l.28) it has the value of an intensifier ('be very careful'). The *-ito/a* suffix is very commonly used in such ways throughout Latin America, cf. 29.2.2.

30.2.5 Another intensifying device is the prefix *re-* in **retemplá** (l.26). This device is fairly general in popular speech throughout the Spanish-speaking world, and has the variant forms *rete-* and *requete-*. (See also 31.2.5.)

30.2.6 Onde = standard *donde* (l.18) is used in a prepositional sense in the meaning of *a casa de*. Such variants as *adonde* and *aonde* and *ande* are also widely encountered in popular speech, and in fact the puristic distinction between *donde* and *adonde* seems to be observed only in educated standard usage. The use of *donde* as a preposition is very widespread in colloquial register throughout the Spanish-speaking world. A similar development is that of *cuando*, which can mean *en tiempo de*, e.g. *cuando la guerra*. It is perhaps to be expected that such fundamental spatial and temporal notions should come to be expressed synthetically rather than analytically. Perhaps also the existence of elliptical usages such as *cuando (yo era) niño* contributed to the development of *cuando* in this way and *donde* followed suit because of its related meaning (Kany 1951: 363).

30.2.7 Su puebla d'ella (l.18), **la puebla e nosotras** (l.20). The use of *de +* personal pronoun phrase is more common in Latin America than in the Peninsula (see Kany 1951: 47–8), though it is probably motivated here by the need to express a clear contrast.

    Keypoint: possessives (p. 287).

Vocabulary

30.3.1 Some words in this passage have a very local reference (and as a result are not easily translatable).

    Güiras (l.11). This word exists in a number of forms and meanings through Latin America (the citation form in the DRAE is *huira*). In origin it is the name of a tree (*Crecentia cujete*) in Arawak, and the oldest forms attested in Spanish are *hibuera* or *higüera*; it has then become associated with the fruit of the tree, its sap, and its bark, which are all used for different purposes. As the fruit of the tree, it has undergone associational extension to the meaning of 'calabash' (to which the original fruit bore a resemblance), and metaphorical extension to provide a slang word for 'head' in some areas. A masculine form, *güiro*, presumably created to distinguish two sizes of similar objects in the same way as such gender pairs as *jarra* and *jarro* (see 3.3.5) is the name of a kind of gourd, which is also used as a musical instrument, and as a word for 'head' and 'small baby' in the Caribbean area. In its meaning of the bark of the tree, *güira* was originally associated with the strips of bark used to make ropes, and has come to mean 'strip' in general – it is that meaning we see here in the meaning of 'strips (of clothing)', 'tatters'. As such, it also participates in the idiomatic expression *dar güira* 'to whip'. In short, this is a fascinating example of semantic change taking place in relatively recent times (since the sixteenth century); it also reveals the huge variations of usage between different areas of Latin America which are of necessity only partially described in standard reference works.

Keypoint: gender (p. 000).

Chupalla (l.14), of Quechua origin, is more localised, but has a similar history to **güira**. It is the name of a plant (*Puya pyramidata*) whose leaves are used for hat-making; accordingly, the word undergoes associational extension to the meaning of 'hat', as here.

Quila (l.15), of Araucanian origin, is the name of a bamboo-like plant.

Quiltro (l.21), another word of Araucanian origin, is the name of a small dog; here, it is used in the more general but pejorative sense of 'stray dog'.

Puebla (ll.18 and 20) and **rancha** (l.19), both more usual in their masculine forms *pueblo* 'village' and *rancho* (various meanings), here have special meanings within the context of rural southern Chile. **Puebla**, which can also be 'town', 'settlement' (cf. the placename in Mexico) is here a dwelling on an estate (British English 'tied cottage') and is often used in a way which is a near-synonym of *casa*. **Rancha** is so specific in meaning that Brunet defines it for the benefit of her readers earlier in the novel:

> Más allá aún estaba ese horror que en los campos sureños se llama la rancha: tablas apoyadas en un extremo unas contra otras, formando con el suelo un triángulo y todas ellas una especie de tienda de campaña donde duermen hacinados los peones fuerinos, es decir: aquellos que están de paso en la hacienda trabajando a jornal o a tarea durante los meses de excesivo trabajo.

Both these words are examples of how gender continues to be exploited in Spanish to render semantic distinctions in common nouns which do not correlate with sex.
Keypoint: gender (p. 275).

30.3.2 Botar (**botao**, l.21) is in origin a borrowing from OFr. *boter*, which in turn is of Frankish origin, from a source cognate with Eng. *beat*, and meant 'to throw'. In colloquial use in Peninsular Spanish, it means, as here, 'to throw out'; otherwise in the Peninsula it tends to be restricted to the specialised nautical usage of 'to turn (a boat)' and to the intransitive meaning of 'to bounce'. In Latin America, however, it has a more general application, being preferred to Peninsular *echar* in the meaning of 'to throw out'.

30.3.3 Pichicho (l.12), also used adjectivally, appears to be a spontaneous creation by a process very similar in nature to the one we must imagine for the creation of such Romance terms as Sp. *pequeño* and Fr. *petit* (see 7.3.4).

30.3.4 Condenao (‖ standard *condenado*, l.10) is in general use in spoken Spanish as a term of disparagement and, as an adjective, the expression of a hostile attitude, rather like English *damn*, *goddam*.

30.3.5 Retemplá (‖ standard *retemplada*, l.26). The verb *templar* < Lat. [TĔMPĔRO] 'to be temperate', 'to control' has undergone substantial semantic evolution in Spanish whilst also retaining this original meaning. In its basic meaning of 'to make mild' it was applied not only to the cooling of hot substances but also to the warming up of cold (thus *agua templada* is 'lukewarm water'). The latter process has subsequently been exaggerated in Andalusian and Latin-American usage to mean 'to heat up', and has thus become associated there with the idea of drunkenness, as well as developing sexual connotations (cf. English 'on heat'), so, ironically enough, reversing its original meaning completely.

31 On the streets of Mexico City. Luis Buñuel, *Los olvidados* (1951, Mexico)

31.0 Luis Buñuel's film *Los olvidados*, shot on location in Mexico City in 1951, highlights the plight of street children in Mexico. Buñuel toured the slums of the city in shabby clothes for several weeks in order to research his theme, and in the film used local amateurs as the actors. The result is a script which abounds in the language of the Mexico City lower classes.

It is at this level that the differences among varieties of Spanish are at their most pronounced: the first few lines of this scene are in fact opaque to many Peninsular speakers. Local idiomatic usages, and multiple developments of the same word through associational and metaphorical extension and transfer, conspire to produce this differentiation.

The text

The text is taken from Buñuel (1980: 23–4).

Voces: ¡Quiobo, Tejocote! ¡Quióbole, mano!
Jaibo: Quiobo, Tejocote ... Pues, como les decía, allí en la Correccional si te aplomas te traen todos de su puerquito. Yo llegué y me tuve que sonar con una bola.
Pedro: ¿Y son montoneros?   5
Jaibo: No, hasta eso, de uno en uno ... No le hace que pierdas ¿ves?, pero que vean que eres macho, y te respetan.
Pedro: Y tú no eres de los que se dejan así nomás.
Bola: ¿Y qué tal es la de adentro en la Corre? ¿Suave?
Jaibo: Pos la comida no estaba tan pior, a más que yo agarré la mejor cama,   10
pero pos siempre es mejor la calle. Por eso me puse abusado, nomás se descuidaron tantito y me pelé.
Pelón: ¿Y no te dio miedo? Porque si te agarran hubiera sido pior.
Cacarizo: ¡Qué miedo, ni qué miedo! Éste es retemacho y no le tiene miedo a nadie.   15
Golfo: ¿Es cierto que te encajonaron por culpa del Julián?
Jaibo: Sí ... rajón maldito. ¿Quién tiene un cigarrito?
Golfo: Yo no.
Golfo II: Y yo tampoco, mano.
Jaibo: ¿Traes tú, Pedro?   20
Pedro: Pus ahora andamos re pránganas.
Cacarizo: Ni cigarros, ni quinto, mano.

Jaibo: Uuy, cómo se conoce que andaba yo encajonado. Pero ora van a ver ...
  He aprendido mucho allá, y si hacen lo que yo les digo, a ninguno le
  faltarán sus centavos.   *25*
Muchachos: ¡Hijo, mano! Seguro, Jaibo. Haremos lo que tú quieras.

Translation

VOICES: Hi, 'hardhead'! Hi, chum!

JAIBO: Hi, 'hardhead' ... So, as I was saying, in the Detention Centre if you
  don't stand up for yourself they'll wipe the floor with you. I got there and
  had to fight a whole crowd.

PEDRO: So they're hooligans?

JAIBO: No, not that, taken one by one ... They don't care if you lose, right?,
  but if they see you're a man, they respect you.

PEDRO: And you're not one to let things go.

BOLA: And what's it like in the Centre? Cool?

JAIBO: Well, the food wasn't so bad, and I grabbed the best bed; but being out
  on the streets is better. So I watched for my chance, and as soon as their
  backs were turned for a moment, I was off.

PELÓN: And weren't you scared? 'Cos if they catch you it'd be a lot worse.

CACARIZO: Scared, my foot! He's a real man and he's not scared of anyone.

STREETBOY: Is it right that they banged you up because of Julián?

JAIBO: Yes ... the goddam squealer. Anyone got a fag?

STREETBOY: Not me.

STREETBOY 2: Me neither, chum.

JAIBO: Have you got one, Pedro?

PEDRO: At the moment we're stony broke.

CACARIZO: Not a fag, not a dime, chum.

JAIBO: Wow, you can tell I was in jail. But now you'll see ... I've learnt a lot
  inside, and if you do what I tell you, no one will be short of cash.

BOYS: OK, chum! Sure, Jaibo. We'll do whatever you want.

Phonetics and phonology

Only the merest indication is given of pronunciation: the intention is not to give
a 'silent' reader local colour but to provide a mnemonic script for actors.

31.1.1 The forms **pos** (l.10) and **pus** (l.21) show the tendency for the diphthong
[we] to reduce in the rapid spoken articulation of this short, common connective; cf. 28.1.2 and 32a.1.5.

31.1.2 The closing of /e/ to [i] before a following vowel, seen in the greeting
¡Quiobo! (ll.1 and 2) < standard *¿qué hubo?* and **pior** (ll.10 and 13) < standard
peor, with the consequent avoidance of hiatus, is a common feature of Mexican
speech (cf. 30.1.2).

31.1.3 Mano (l.1, etc.) is a truncated form of *hermano*.

Morphology and syntax

31.2.1 The system of Mexican second person usage is apparent in this text. While the boys address each other as **tú** in the singular, also using the standard second person singular verb and pronouns (**tú no eres**, l.8, **te encajonaron**, l.16.), they use *ustedes* in the plural (**si hacen lo que yo les digo**, l.24.). *Tú* is also used, as in colloquial Peninsular usage, with general reference, a particularly useful device when the verb in question is reflexive, as in **si te aplomas** (ll.2–3), where using a *se* construction would not be possible with the already reflexive verb.

　Keypoint: personal pronouns (p. 284).

31.2.2 Hasta (l.6) is often used in the sense of *no hasta* in Latin American speech, e.g. *hasta las tres iré* 'I won't go until three o'clock' (Kany 1951: 370). Here **hasta eso** has the meaning of 'it didn't come to that'. Kany suggests that the reason for this development was originally the avoidance of the pleonastic *no* which is sometimes used with *hasta que*; he traces the rise in the non-use of the negative with *hasta* to as recently as the eighteenth and nineteenth centuries.

31.2.3 Nomás (ll.8 and 11) is widely used in Latin American speech, and has a number of functions. In l.8 it means 'only', 'just', and is closest to its original literal meaning of *no más* 'not more', which was used in Golden-Age Spanish in this sense but has now been replaced in the Peninsula by *nada más*. Its usage has extended in Latin America to be a general replacement for *solamente* and to the meaning of 'exactly', 'precisely', in which function it acts as an intensifier for adjectives, adverbs and verbs. Thus *ahora no más* means 'right now', *siga no más* means 'carry right on'. It can also have the function of a temporal conjunction, 'as soon as' (*no más llegó* 'no sooner than (s)he had arrived', **no más descuidaron** (l.11) 'as soon as they were careless', and especially, with the same meaning, in infinitive constructions like *al no más llegar* (again, cf. Peninsular *nada más llegar*).

31.2.4 Pior (l.10) is used apparently in the non-comparative meaning of 'bad', since it is qualified by **tan**. (See also 33.2.6.)

31.2.5 Re- (**re pránganas**, l.21) and **rete-** (**retemacho**, l.14) are used as intensifying prefixes (see also 30.2.5).

31.2.6 The affective suffix **-ito** is very common throughout Latin America. It is used here with nouns (**cigarrito**, l.17 – see 31.3.1 below, and **puerquito**, l.3 – though this is part of an idiomatic expression) and with the adverb *tanto* in **tantito** (l.12).

31.2.7 Si te agarran hubiera sido pior (l.13). The pluperfect is used in Latin American speech, usually with present time-reference, to indicate a modality of surprise: *¡había sido usted!* 'so it's you!' (Kany 1951: 166). We may interpret **hubiera sido** here, then, as the equivalent of standard *sería*, the *-ra* form being the equivalent of the standard conditional (cf. 28.2.8).

31.2.8 Though not specifically a Latin-American feature, the use of **andar** as a copular verb with an adjectival complement can be observed here. Although in some usages *andar* appears to retain something of its meaning as a verb of motion (e.g. *andar enamorado* 'to be (go around) in love'), in **andaba yo encajonado** (l.23), it seems to be simply the equivalent of *estar*, perhaps with some nuance of duration: 'I spent time in jail' (see Alonso 1951).

Vocabulary

This text is rich in words which are specific to Latin America, and especially to the Mexican lower classes.

31.3.1 A number of words here, though also found in Peninsular usage, have different meanings in Latin America.

Agarrar (ll.10 and 13) is used very generally in many parts of Latin America in the sense of Peninsular *coger*, which in America has the taboo meaning of 'to screw', 'fuck', and is for that reason avoided (indeed, even compounds of *coger* are avoided in these areas). **Agarrar** in standard usage has the meaning of 'to grasp', 'seize', and this shift is therefore also an example of hyperbole, or the use of a more semantically distinctive word.

Suave (l.9) is a specifically Mexican slang alternative to *bien*; in some other parts of Latin America it has the meaning of 'large'. This is a widening of meaning from its more specific Peninsular and older meaning of 'smooth'.

Aplomarse (ll.2–3), a near synonym of *desplomarse*, which is more favoured in the Peninsula, with the meaning of 'to collapse', has developed here the metaphorical moral meaning of 'to show weakness'. In some other parts of Latin America it has the meaning of 'to get embarrassed'.

Abusado (l.11) has, specifically in Mexico, the meaning of 'careful', 'watchful', and is also used as an interjection in the sense of 'look out!' The link with *abusar* is not totally clear; it may be that it is an associational extension of *abusado* in the meaning of 'taken advantage of' to the converse meaning of 'being careful not to be taken advantage of'.

In the Peninsula, *cigarrillo* is preferred to **cigarro** (l.22) in the meaning of 'cigarette'.

31.3.2 A number of words show remarkable histories of widening of meaning and participate in idiomatic expressions which vary considerably from area to area.

The metaphorical extension of **encajonar** (ll.16, 23) from its standard meaning of 'to put in a box' to the meaning here of 'to put in jail', is easy to envisage.

Me pelé (l.12). **Pelar**, in origin 'to remove hair' < Lat. [PĬLO], first comes to mean 'to remove skin', and so applied to fruit, for instance, in the sense of 'to peel'; these meanings are general within the Spanish-speaking world. It subsequently underwent many metaphorical extensions of these meanings. They are usually to do with robbery ('to fleece') or damage ('to beat', 'to slander'). The reflexive (often with *la* or *las*) adds metaphorical moral meanings such as 'to crave for'. Here the idea is once again removal (of oneself).

Another verb with a similarly complex history is **sonar** (l.3), originally 'to sound', deriving from an analogically regularised form of Lat. [SŎNO], extending in areas of Latin America to such meanings as 'to fail', 'to lose', 'to die'. *Hacer sonar* comes to mean 'to thrash' (cf. *hacer pitar*, 29.3.4), and it is this causative meaning that the simple verb seems to have taken on in the usage here.

Bola (l.4) (ultimately ≤ Lat. BŬLLA 'bubble', possibly via Occitan) is a natural candidate for metaphorical extension to anything resembling a ball. In Mexico the expression *una bola de gente* has the meaning of 'a crowd of people', and it is in that meaning that **bola** is used here, though without the qualifying prepositional phrase.

Rajón (l.17) is a morphological derivative of the verb *rajar*, originally and still in standard Spanish 'to tear', 'to split', whence it develops the associated metaphorical meanings of 'to defeat', 'to pester', 'to annoy'. As an intransitive verb it is found with the meanings of 'to brag', and 'to chatter', the common idea here being that of going beyond what is normally acceptable. **Rajón** is similarly found with the meanings of 'braggart' and (as here) 'tell-tale', as well as 'free-spending', 'generous' and 'cowardly', 'unreliable'. In Mexico the pejorative meanings seem to prevail.

31.3.3 Pránganas, of unknown origin, is used in some areas, mainly the Caribbean, to mean 'broke', 'having no money'.

31.3.4 Quinto (l.22), literally 'a fifth', is a five *centavo* piece, i.e. a coin of little value.

XIII   US Spanish

Spanish is indubitably the most widely-spoken language in the United States apart from English, and is probably the only language likely to challenge English significantly (as reflected by the Federal and State rulings in the mid-1990s that deemed English to be the official language). The exact number of Spanish speakers is difficult to ascertain (one current figure is 22 million, Grimes 1999) not only because an unknown number of Hispanics have the status of illegal immigrants, but also because the degree of use of Spanish among the Hispanic population is very variable. Several different groups of speakers can be identified: the *chicanos* of the South West, Puerto Ricans (who are especially dominant in New York), Cubans (particularly concentrated in Miami) and Canary Islands immigrants (particularly in Louisiana), not to mention a number of speakers of Judeo-Spanish (see Texts 33 and 34). However, some communities have an interesting mix of features, cf. Hart González (1985) on Washington DC.

The names given to the varieties of Spanish spoken in the US South West are numerous. *Chicano* is the most favoured term and tends to be applied to literature emanating from the Hispanic communities. 'Spanglish', 'Tex-Mex' and 'pocho' are widely used to refer to those varieties of *chicano* which involve a large number of English loanwords or exhibit code-switching, or movement between the two languages. 'Spanglish' in particular has been the subject of many press articles, from both the English- and Spanish-speaking worlds, which highlight anecdotally some of the more striking adaptations of English words into *chicano*. 'Pachuco' and 'caló' (see also Texts 35 and 36) often refer to the special language of underworld or criminal groups.

Chicano

32.0 Historically, the Spanish of the US South West is most closely related to the Spanish spoken in the north of Mexico, although it has a large number of English loanwords (a distinction, not always straightforward, must be made between English words which have been fully incorporated into this variety of Spanish from code-switching to and from English). Rather like Judeo-Spanish, though over a much shorter period of time and in different social circumstances, its speakers have become separated from any reference to a standard language, since it has been a domestic vernacular rather than a literary language or a language of public education. This situation is now changing in a number of ways. Standard Mexican

Spanish is the language of public education in Spanish, and the language of the professional class (in situations which do not require English); however, there has been a considerable awakening of consciousness of a *chicano* identity (which is not entirely related to the use of Spanish), and a sizeable literature in *chicano* now exists (some written entirely in Spanish, some in English and some in parallel Spanish and English versions: code-switching has also been effectively employed in *chicano* poetry). Another potentially complicating factor with reference to a standard is the Academia Norteamericana de la Lengua Española, founded in the 1970s, which in principle is a sister of the *academias* which exist in all countries of the Spanish-speaking world, and seeks to register distinctively North-American Spanish usage.

The texts

Text 32a is taken from Penfield and Ornstein-Galicia (1985: 10–11). It is an imaginary conversation between two speakers of South-West Spanish; although therefore not strictly authentic, it has the advantage for present purposes of showing a number of features within a short space (rather like some representations of colloquial language in works of literature). I have not italicised the portions considered by the authors to be 'distinctively SW Sp.', as they do, in order that readers may approach it with a more open mind, and I have corrected some errors in the 'standard' spellings.

Text 32b, taken from Sánchez (1982: 15), illustrates the phenomenon of code-switching between Spanish and English. I have deliberately not indicated which language is meant to be which here. Recent investigation of this phenomenon (see below 32b.2) suggests that code-switching is not as random as it might seem at first sight.

Further reading

Amastae, Jon and Lucía Elías-Olivares (1982); Craddock (1973); Hart-González (1985); Hernández Chávez *et al.* (1975); Ornstein-Galicia (1981); Penfield and Ornstein-Galicia (1985).

32a A helpful daughter. US Spanish of the twentieth century

Rosa: '**Áma, déjame ayudarle con la limpia de la casa ahora.**
La Mama: Qué bueno, m'hijita. Eres una hija muy buena. Munchas hijas de
    tan flojas no hacen na' pa' ayudar.
Rosa: ¿Quiere Ud. que use primero la mapa? ¿Puedo hacer el try?
La Mama: No, m'hijita. Primero hace falta que límpienos toda la casa, barrién-   *5*
    dola con la escova. 'Ta muncho polvo y hasta arena. Ay válgame Dios, aquí
    andan unas cucarachas. Válgame se echó el cereal – la crema de trigo.
Rosa: Quizá puedo llamar mi cuata Enriqueta que nos ayude tamién ... pos'
    tanto que hacer.
La Mama: Por Dios, no lo vayas a hacer, m'hijita. Entre más personas, más   *10*
    ruido. Semos capaces de hacer la lucha. ¿Que no?
Rosa: Sí, 'áma, sí. De'pues tenemos que sacudir los muebles – el sofa [sic], las
    sías, tamién el tívi.

Rosa: Y espérate ... tamién chainiar el espejo en la recámara y cambiar las sábanas. Fíjese, 'áma, tamién en la cocina. Ya hace tiempo no hemos ... como   *15* se dice ... soltado el agua del fridge. Es decir defrost.

Translation

R: Mum, let me help you with the house cleaning now.

M: Fine, dear. You're a very good girl. Many girls are so lazy that they do nothing to help.

R: Do you want me to use the mop first? Can I give it a try?

M: No, dear. First we need to clean the whole house, sweeping it with the broom. There's a lot of dust and even sand. Oh, gracious, here are some cockroaches. Gracious, the cereal's spilt – cream of wheat.

R: Perhaps I can phone my best friend Enriqueta to help us too . . . since there's so much to do.

M: For goodness' sake, don't do that, dear. The more people there are, the more noise there is. We're capable of doing the job ourselves, aren't we?

R: Yes, Mum, yes. Then we have to dust the furniture – the sofa, the chairs, the TV as well.

R: And wait . . . also polish the mirror in the bedroom and change the sheets. Hey, Mum, look in the kitchen as well. It's a long time since we . . . how do you say . . . drained the water from the fridge. That is, defrost.

Phonetics and phonology

32a.1.1 There is a good deal of phonetic erosion of the kind found very widely in popular speech, and it can be seen how commonly occurring words are the most obviously affected by this process. The weakening of intervocalic /d/ and /ɾ/ to the point of elision has led to the reduction of *nada* to **na'** (cf. 30.1.3) and *para* to **pa'** (l.3, cf. 29.1.1, 30.1.4). In **m'hijita** (l.2, etc.), a common term of endearment, the *sinalefa* of /mi-i-xi-ta/ has given way to complete assimilation (/mi-xi-ta/, cf. 28.1.2, 30.1.1). The reduction of *mamá* to /ama/ (**'áma**, l.1, etc.) is also common in Central American popular speech. Another common reduction is standard *está* to **'ta** (l.6).
   Keypoint: lenition (p. 278).

32a.1.2 The spellings **munchas** (l.2) and **muncho** (l.6) show epenthesis of /n/.

32a.1.3 Sías (l.13) suggests the total disappearance of [j] after the front vowel [i], that is to say, an advanced stage of *yeísmo*; cf. 27.1.2 and 28.1.1.

32a.1.4 Tamién (l.13) shows reduction of the /mb/ group of standard *también* to /m/. Historically, the Latin /mb/ group underwent the same change to /m/ in Castilian, e.g. Lat. LUMBU[S] 'loin' > Sp. *lomo* 'back' (although there are one or two exceptions which are sometimes attributed to learned influence, such as Lat. AMBŌ 'two together' → ?AMBŌS > Sp. *ambos* 'both' and Lat. [CAMBĬO] > Sp. *cambiar* – both *amos* and *camiar* are also attested in Old Castilian).
   Keypoint: consonant groups (p. 267)

32a.1.5 For **pos'** (l.8) see 31.1.1; for the loss of implosive /s/ in **de'pues** (l.13), see 30.1.5.

Morphology and syntax

32a.2.1 Two verb forms which differ from the standard are of interest. **Límpienos** (l.5) is apparently used for standard *limpiemos*; the change of *-mos* to *-nos* by analogy with the personal pronoun is quite common in non-standard varieties, though the change of stress is less so. **Semos** (l.11) for standard *somos* (the latter < Lat. SŬMUS [SUM]) is widely attested as a popular form in the Spanish-speaking world; it may derive independently from a Latin form ?SEDĒMUS or ?SĬMUS (Alvar and Pottier 1983: 226), or by later analogy with *-er* verbs and future tenses which form their 1st p.pl. in *-emus*.

32a.2.2 The mother addresses her daughter as *tú* (**Eres una hija muy buena**, l.2), whereas the daughter addresses her mother as *usted* (**¿Quiere usted que use** . . .**?**, l.4) – see also 30.2.1.
   Keypoint: personal pronouns (p. 284).

32a.2.3 The 'personal' *a* is absent in **llamar mi cuata** (l.8). It is possible that this is a result of the influence of English *call my buddy*.
   Keypoint: 'personal' *a* (p. 283).

32a.2.4 Hace tiempo no hemos soltado . . . (ll.15–16): in the standard language *que* is used in this construction (*Hace tiempo que* . . .).

Vocabulary

32a.3.1 Cuata (l.8) is an example of the hypercharacterisation of gender by the addition of a feminine *-a* ending to the noun *cuate*, which originally meant 'twin' and has now also come to mean 'buddy'. The word is typical of Central American Spanish usage, and is a borrowing from Nahuatl *coatl*.
   Keypoint: gender (p. 275).

32a.3.2 Recámara (l.14) is widely used in the sense of 'bedroom' in Spanish America, while in the Peninsula it has the meaning of 'dressing room'.

32a.3.3 There are a number of patent borrowings from English which are not in general use in the Spanish-speaking world. Some appear, however, to have been fully assimilated into the structural patterns of Spanish, and are not, therefore examples of code-switching. **Hacer el try** (l.4) is clearly modelled on Eng. *to give something a try*, but the use of a different verb and the definite article turn it into a peculiarly Spanish idiom. **Mapa** (l.4) is an adaptation of *mop*, reflecting the American-English pronunciation [mɑp]. It becomes, perhaps rather unusually for a loanword, feminine; this could be due to analogy with *escoba*, but significantly it creates a gender opposition with the already existing el *mapa* 'map'. **Chainiar** (l.14), adapted from Eng. *shine*, has been given the characteristic morphology of a Spanish *-ar* verb.
   Keypoint: gender (p. 275).

32a.3.4 In other cases, however, it appears that an English word is used with no adaptation: **sofa** (l.12) (with the stress on the first syllable, as in English *sofa*), **tívi** (l.13), **fridge** (l.16), and **defrost** (l.16).

32b Music and boys. The Spanish of US teenagers (late twentieth century)

Hey, Mary, ¿por qué no vienes pa mi casa? Tengo un magazine nuevo that I got this morning nel drugstore. Tiene todas las new songs, muy suaves, de los ... cómo se llaman ... You know ... los que cantan ésa que tocaron ... ahí nel jukebox, when we were at the store. No, hombre, not that one, the other one, la que le gustó much a Joe. I like it too porque   5
tiene muy suave rhythm y las words también, muy suaves ... yeah ... what? Really!!! ... te llamó? OOOOhhhh, Mary. Ese está de aquellotas.

Translation

Hey, Mary, why don't you come round to my place? I've got a new magazine that I got this morning down at the drugstore. It's got all the new songs, really great, by ... what are their names? You know, those who sing that one they played ... on the jukebox, when we were at the store. No, no, not that one, the other one, the one Joe liked a lot. I like it too, 'cos it has a really great rhythm and the words too are really great ... yeah ... what? really!!! he called you? Wow, Mary. He's something else.

32b.1 In some cases the English words in this text appear within a predominantly Spanish discourse and can be thought of as borrowings in the same way as those discussed in 32a.3.4 (**magazine**, l.1; **drugstore**, l.2; **songs**, l.2, **jukebox**, l.4, **rhythm**, l.6, **words**, l.6). These are all words which relate to things typical of the English-speaking world (bearing in mind that the songs in question are no doubt in English). In some cases, however, the feminine gender of the word is revealing, since it is the gender of the corresponding Spanish word, and it is as if the Spanish word is being thought of simultaneously (**las songs** = *las canciones*, **las words** = *las palabras*).

32b.2 Additionally here, however, there are complete phrases and clauses in English which show that the speaker is in fact code-switching between the two languages. It is far from easy to see (and especially in an extract as short as this) what might motivate such switching, or whether it is random. One study of the phenomenon (Gumperz 1970) has suggested that Spanish tends to be associated with personal reference or the expression of emotions whereas English is used for more general, detached statements, though this is not immediately apparent here.

XIV Judeo-Spanish

The most inglorious aspect of Spain's *annus mirabilis* of 1492 was the wholesale expulsion on 31 March of Jews who refused to convert to Christianity. It is important to realise that the Spanish Jews were very far from being a fringe community in medieval Spain; in fact, it has been argued that in some respects they were the linchpin of the Spanish economy and their expulsion represented a grave political, not to mention moral, error, which irretrievably damaged Spanish life. The Sephardic Jews certainly considered themselves to be Spanish, and, as Text 34, shows, arguably still do. They were monolingual speakers of Romance, and, while there must be doubt on this issue, it has been plausibly argued that there was essentially no difference between their speech and that of the community at large (Penny 1996; Sephiha 1986: 23–4). They took their language with them, and, although the vicissitudes of emigration and war have vastly reduced the numbers of speakers and even whole dialect areas, there are still some surviving Sephardic communities which speak a language now generally known as *djudeo-espanyol*, but also sometimes as *ladino*.[1] However, the researches of scholars before the Second World War (see Text 33) are the only testimony of the speech of a number of now disappeared communities. In recent years Israel has provided a focus for Judeo-Spanish: there are radio broadcasts in the language and since 1997 a review, *Aki Yerushalayim* (see Text 34), has been published. The advent of the Internet has allowed readier exchange amongst Sephardic communities, which are now dispersed all over the world. The aspiration to unite Sefarad through Judeo-Spanish has brought the familiar problem of the need for standardisation, though different publications still adopt different spelling systems. As recently as 1996 the Autoridad Nasionala del Ladino i su Kultura was created by the Israeli government. Another significant factor in the history of Judeo-Spanish is that in the twentieth century it came back into contact with the Spanish-speaking world from which it was in effect separated for nearly five centuries. Not only is there a warmer attitude towards the Sephardic Jews within Spain (academic interest has been firmly established by the periodical *Sefarad*, and there are now some relatively small Jewish communities in Spain) but there has also been contact with Spanish through emigration to Latin America and the USA. The effect of

---

1 Sephiha (1986) vigorously opposes the use of the term *ladino*, which he reserves for the language represented by medieval Jewish translations of the Bible which set out to gloss the Hebrew text as literally as possible; however, the fact remains that Judeo-Spanish is often known as such.

this is that standard Spanish can be used a source of borrowing, especially in the abstract and technical areas of the lexicon.

Apart from its intrinsic interest, Judeo-Spanish throws light on the history of mainstream Spanish in a number of important ways. First of all, it has developed completely independently of the speech-community of Spain and its empire. It preserves some features of late fifteenth-century Castilian in a way which no other variety of Spanish does, most obviously the system of sibilant consonants, which have not undergone the process of devoicing or the characteristic Castilian movement of position of articulation in the merger of /ʃ/ and /ʒ/ to /x/ (see **Keypoint: the sibilants of Old Castilian**, p. 290), the preservation of an opposition between /b/ and /β/ and the initial ?/ɸ/ of Old Castilian, usually realised as [f]. (At the same time, it is possible to overrate the 'archaic' aspects of Judeo-Spanish: as will be clear, considerable innovation has also taken place, especially in morphology and word-formation.) Second, Judeo-Spanish has not been subject to the same contact pressures as mainstream Spanish: thus, we would not expect to find so many words of learned origin, indigenous American words, Gallicisms, Italianisms and Anglicisms as in the standard language. Instead, there will be borrowings from languages with which its speakers came into contact (and with which they were often bilingual), such as Arabic, Turkish, Greek, Romanian and other Balkan languages, with which mainstream Spanish had little if any contact. Third, since Judeo-Spanish has largely been a domestic, spoken language, it did not have the vast corpus of creative and technical literature that is available in a national standard language such as Spanish. This means in particular that it did not have such a rich passive vocabulary (as, for example, is enshrined in the *Diccionario de autoridades* and its successors, see Text 23) or the complexity of syntax that is encouraged by a written medium. It is now having to acquire some of these features in its relatively new written forms.

Further reading

Besso (1964); Harris (1994); Luria (1930); Penny (1996); Sephiha (1986).

33 The love of three oranges. The Judeo-Spanish of pre-war Macedonia (early twentieth century)

The text

This text is taken from Crews (1935: 85), converted into standard International Phonetic Alphabet symbols, though with conventional punctuation, and with all word-stress supplied. It records the speech of one Esther Cohen, who at seventy years of age had been a lifelong inhabitant of Monastir, speaking only Judeo-Spanish. This is an extract from one of the folk-tales she tells, the traditional story of the Love of Three Oranges.

> [si fwe al kam'inu.
> no la βo paɾ'tiɾ an este na'ɾanʒe, me βo a'ji, 'ondi βo fa'ʒaɾ 'aɣwes 'mutʃes.
> kami'nandu, kami'nandu, fa'ʒo in un lu'ɣwaɾ, ki 'toðu 'fwentis, 'podʒus aj.
> i la'βɾo la na'ɾandʒe i sa'ljo 'otɾa 'noβje, maz mi'ʒoɾ 'destaz dos. li 'ðiʃu:

'mire, mi 'fiʒe, 'kwandu ti βa fa'zer si'kuɾe, a'baʃa ðil ka'βaju i 'beβi 'aɣwe. **5**
ān'sine fa'zije, si fweɾun.

'ondi fa'jaßen, a'ji bi'βijen aɣwe.

a las 'faldaz di biðaha'im, a'ji es 'seɾka ði su 'kaze, li 'ðiʃu:

ti βo ði'ʃar a'ki ki no ez mi u'zānsa ðe ti ji'βar jo kon mi 'manu. βo ðar
ha'beɾ a mi 'paðɾi i ja mi 'maðɾi ki ti 'tomin kun u'noɾ. **10**

'bwenu, a'ma ti βaz a alβu'ðaɾ di mi, ti βa bi'zar tu 'paðɾi i tu 'maðɾi i ti βaz
alβu'ðaɾ di mi.

no mil'βuðu, no mi 'ðeʃu bi'zar.

e ma'ðam ke ez ān'sine, 'kiteti il na'niju i 'ðamilu a mi puɾ ni'ʃan.

i si lu ki'to il na'niju i si lu ðjo en 'eje. i si fwe.] **15**

Translation

He went on his way.

'I will not break open this orange; I will go where I will find a lot of water.'

On and on he went, and found a place that was all springs and wells.

And he opened the orange and another bride came out, better than the first two. He said to her: 'Look, my girl, when you are thirsty, get down from the horse and drink some water.'

So she did, and they went on.

Wherever they found water, they drank.

At the foot of Bidaha'im, which was near his house, he said to her: 'I am going to leave you here, for it is not my custom to lead you in by my hand (= myself?). I will give the news to my father and my mother so that they can receive you with honour.'

'Fine, but you will forget me; your father and mother will talk to you and you will forget me.'

'I will not forget you; I won't let them talk to me.'

'In that case (*lit.* as it is so), take off your ring and give it to me as a sign.'

And hc took off his ring and gave it to her. And off he went.

Phonetics and phonology

33.1.1 In this variety of Judeo-Spanish, medieval /s/ and /ts/ have merged to /s/ and medieval /ʒ/ and /dz/ have merged to /ʒ/:

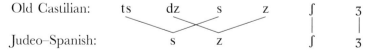

Examples are:

/s/: no intervocalic examples, but
  ['seɾka] (l.8) (cf. OSp. [tseɾka]) > MSp. [θeɾka] (*cerca*)
  [si'kuɾe] (l.5) (cf. OSp. √[seko]) > MSp. [seko] (*seco*)

/z/:

    [faˈzeɾ] (l.5) (cf. OSp. [fadzeɾ]) > MSp. [aθeɾ] (*hacer*)

    [ˈkaze] (l.8) (cf. OSp. [kaza]) > MSp. [kasa] (*casa*)

/ʃ/:

    [ðiˈʃaɾ] (l.9) (cf. OSp. [deʃaɾ]) > MSp. [dexaɾ] (*dejar*)

/ʒ/:

    [miˈʒoɾ] (l.4) (cf. OSp. [meʒoɾ]) > MSp. [mexoɾ] (*mejor*)

This development is essentially the same as took place in a number of neighbouring Romance varieties, most obviously Portuguese. The merger of /ts/ with /s/ and /dz/ with /z/ is also the process that produces the *seseo* of Andalusia and Latin America, although in these areas there has also been the expected loss between the voiced and voiceless phonemes, the result of the merger of all four medieval phonemes /ts/, /dz/, /s/ and /z/ being /s/.

Final /s/ is also sometimes voiced to [z] in this text between vowels ([βaz a ulβuˈðar], l.11, and regularly becomes [z] before a voiced consonant as a result of assimilation ([ˈdestaz dos], l.4). The former process never occurs in Castilian, though the latter can be observed occasionally within words such as *mismo* [mizmo] and *desde* [dezde]. But both processes regularly occur in Portuguese: *os outros* [uz owtɾuʃ], *os mesmos* [uʒ meʒmuʃ].

Keypoint: the sibilants of Old Castilian (p. 290).

33.1.2 There is a distinction between initial /b/ and /β/ (cf. 34.1.2): hence [βo] (l.2) (‖ MSp. *voy*) ≤ Lat. VĀDO but [beβi] (l.5) (‖ MSp. *bebe* < Lat. BĪBE [BĪBO], [bwenu] (l.11) (‖ MSp. *bueno*) < Lat. BŎNU[S].

Keypoint: the 'b/v' merger (p. 262).

33.1.3 [ˈpodʒus] (l.3), cognate with standard modern /poθos/ *pozos* < Lat. PŬTĔOS [PŬTĔUS] is a surprising result; either [posus] or [pozos] would be the expected development in the light of the correspondences given in 33.1.1.

33.1.4 The initial /f/ of Old Castilian is preserved in all contexts, apparently with a labiodental articulation; thus [faˈjo] (l.3) (‖ MSp. [aʎo], *halló*), [ˈfiʒe] (l.5) (‖ MSp. [ixa], *hija*), etc.

Keypoint: the f>h change (p. 271).

33.1.5 Judeo-Spanish is uniformly *yeísta*: [faˈjaɾ] (l.2) (‖ MSp. [aʎaɾ], *hallar*), [kaˈβaju] (l.5), (‖ MSp. [kaβaʎo], *caballo*), etc.

33.1.6 The vowel-system of this language is essentially the same as that of standard Castilian, except that there is a systematic tendency for final atonic vowels to close, so that [a] becomes [e], [e] becomes [i] and [o] becomes [u]: examples are [ˈfiʒe] (‖ MSp. [ixa]), l.5, [ˈpaðɾi] (‖ MSp. [paðɾe] *padre*), l.11, [kaˈminu] (‖ MSp. [kaminu] *camino*), l.1. The closure of [o] to [u] is a feature of many varieties of Castilian; that of [e] to [i] is less common, though it is sporadically encountered (see 30.1.2, for example); but the closure of [a] to [e] is decidedly less usual (it is a feature of feminine plural morphology in *bable*, the (non-Castilian)

dialect of Asturias, where paradigms such as [bwenu], [bwena], [bwenus], [bwenes] are found, and the feature can consequently be heard in the speech of some Asturian speakers of Castilian).
Keypoint: vowels (p. 296).

33.1.7 Hiatus is avoided by the insertion of a semivowel: [fa'zije] (|| MSp. [aθia] *hacía*), l.6, [i ja] (|| MSp. *y a*), l.10.

33.1.8 There is variation between [u] and [a] in the first vowel of the verb [ulβu'ðaɾ], l.11, and [alβu'ðaɾ], l.12 (|| MSp. *olvidar*); the [i] of [mil'βuðu], l.13, is presumably the result of the assimilation of [u] to the [i] of [mi]. Such minor variation is typical of speech. Taking [ulβu'ðaɾ] as the base form would allow us to see the development of [u] in the second syllable as the result of assimilation with [u] in the first syllable.

33.1.9 [lu'ɣwaɾ], l.3 (|| MSp. *lugar*). Velar and labial consonants sometimes add [w] before /a/ in Judeo-Spanish.

33.1.10 [na'niju], l.15, has an initial [n] by comparison with standard Spanish *anillo* which is the consequence of reanalysis of the sequence [un aniju], the final /n/ of the indefinite article being construed as the initial phoneme of the noun. (The reverse process accounts for the borrowing of Sp. *naranja* into French as *orange*.)

Morphology and syntax

33.2.1 The paraphrase *ir* + infinitive (not with the preposition *a* as in standard Spanish) is extensively used in this passage. It functions as a future tense ([no la βo paɾ'tiɾ], l.2) and also corresponds to the Modern Spanish present subjunctive in future-referring temporal clauses (['kwandu ti βa fa'ʒeɾ si'kuɾe], l.5, standard *cuando tengas sed*).
Keypoint: periphrastic verb forms (p. 283).

33.2.2 The form [βo] (l.2), the equivalent of MSp. *voy*, is maintained. *Vo* and *voy* were variants in the medieval language (see 7.2.5).
Keypoint: monosyllabic verb forms (p. 280).

33.2.3 [a'βro] (l.4), corresponding to MSp. *abrió*, shows the analogical extension of the simple *-ó* third person preterite inflection. Such analogical developments in the verb paradigm are frequent in Judeo-Spanish.

33.2.4 The preposition *a* of MSp. is represented by [**an**] or [**en**] before a vowel: [paɾ'tiɾ an 'este na'ranʒe] (l.2) || MSp. *partir/cortar esta naranja*, [si lu ðjo en eje] (l.15) || standard *se lo dio a ella*. As can be seen from these examples, the use of the 'personal', or direct object, *a* is not identical in Judeo-Spanish to that of standard modern Spanish: here it seems to be used also before an inanimate noun (though one with clear animate associations). Divergence in use would not be surprising given that late fifteenth-century usage was not identical with that of the present-day (see 12.2.4). [faˈjo in un luˈɣwaɾ], l.3, may be another example of this phenomenon.

Keypoint: 'personal' *a* (p. 283).

33.2.5 The direct object is expressed by a 'redundant' pronoun, e.g. [si lu̱ kiˈto il naˈniju] (l.15) ‖ MSp. *se quitó el anillo*. The use of such a 'redundant' pronoun is a characteristic feature of standard Castilian with indirect objects (see 24.2.5), but the modern standard language does not permit direct objects to be reduplicated in this way; however, instances can be found in colloquial usage both in Spain and Latin America (Kany 1951: 116; Lipski 1994: 82–90; see also 17.2.7).

Keypoint: personal pronouns (p. 284).

33.2.6 [maz miˈʒoɾ] (l.4) shows extension of the irregular comparative *mejor* to form an analogical analytic comparative in the same way as the majority of other adjectives. The expression should not necessarily be thought of as tautologous (cf. 31.2.4).

33.2.7 The repetition of the gerund [kamiˈnandu] (l.3) is a common intensifying device in many varieties of Spanish.

Vocabulary

33.3.1 Contact of Judeo-Spanish speakers with local languages is revealed here in a number of words which have been borrowed from Turkish. [haˈber] (l.10), [niˈʃan] (l.14) and, perhaps most intriguingly, [maˈðam ke] (l.14) < Turkish *mademki* 'as', 'although', are all examples of this process. It is striking that such a 'grammatical' word as a conjunction has been borrowed (compare the borrowing of *hasta* from Arabic, see 8.3.11), and perhaps no accident that it is in the semantic area of concession, in the expression of which there was much variation in the medieval language (see 8.3.7, 11.3.14).

33.3.2 The text shows the expected preservation of some archaisms. [ˈondi], l.2, is a variant of *donde* in Old Castilian, perhaps reinforced by Portuguese *onde* (it must be remembered that many Sephardic Jews went first to Portugal on their expulsion from Spain – though those who refused to convert to Christianity were in due course expelled from Portugal too): see 6.3.9. [ãnˈsine] (ll.6 and 14) is one of the many medieval variants of MSp. *así* (see 11.1.11). [aˈbaʃa] (l.5) is infrequently attested in Old Castilian (Nebrija's Latin-Castilian dictionary has the form *abaxamiento*), though *abajar* is used in Latin America.

33.3.3 The new formation [siˈkuɾe] in the expression [faˈzer siˈkuɾe] (l.5) is a morphological derivative of the adjective *seco*, which is unknown in standard modern Spanish, where *sequedad* < Lat. SICCĬTĀTE [SICCĬTĀS] is used.

34 Judeo-Spanish as a worldwide language. *Aki Yerushalayim* (late twentieth century)

The text

The text below is taken from the magazine *Aki Yerushalayim*, 50.

El eskritor espanyol Miguel de Unamuno definio el lenguaje komo "la sangre de muestra alma". Ke mijor modo de deskrivir la intima relasion de los sefaradis kon sus lengua, el djudeo-espanyol? Uno es sinonimo del otro: no puedes ser sefaradi si tus parientes o tus avuelos no avlaron en muestra amada lengua. **5**

Mizmo si pedrites el uzo del djudeo-espanyol tienes dainda en tu korason, en tu alma, el eskarinyo por este atadijo ke te izo parte de la nasion sefaradi.

Puede ser ke pedrites la kapachidad de guadrar esta lengua kuando tus avuelos se fueron a Portugal i de ayi se dispersaron por el Sud-Oeste de **10** la Fransia, Holanda, Inglitiera i el kontinente amerikano ...

Ma onde kere ke sea, mizmo si te kazates kon alguno ke no es de "los muestros" i si no podias ambezar a tus kriaturas las pokas palavras de djudeo-espanyol ke te avias d'akodrar, en el fondo de tu alma guadrates el eskarinyo de esta lengua ke tomimos kon mozotros kuando salimos de **15** Espanya en 1492. En verdad era una de las muy pokas kozas ke podiamos tomar kon mozotros!

Translation

The Spanish writer Miguel de Unamuno defined language as 'the blood of our soul'. What better way of describing the intimate relation of the Sefardis to their language, Judeo-Spanish? The one is synonymous with the other: you cannot be a Sefardi if your parents or grandparents did not speak in our beloved language.

Even if you lost the use of Judeo-Spanish you still have in your heart, in your soul, the love of this gift which made you a part of the Sefardic nation.

It may be that you lost the ability to keep this language when your ancestors went to Portugal and from there dispersed through the south-west of France, Holland, England and the American continent...

But wherever you are, even if you married someone who is not one of 'our people', and if you could not teach your children the few words of Judeo-Spanish that you were to remember, in the depths of your soul you will keep the love of this language which we took with us when we left Spain in 1492. Truly, it was one of the few things we could take with us!

In the following commentary, features described in connection with Text 33 are not recapitulated in detail.

Phonetics and phonology

34.1.1 The same sibilant system as in Text 33 is in evidence here, though an unexpected [tʃ] is present in **kapachidad** (l.9). There is also *yeísmo*.

34.1.2 A distinction is made in orthography between initial *b* and *v* (cf. 33.1.2); *v* represents the sound [β]. Intervocalically, [β] is the result of Latin intervocalic /b/ (**deskrivir**, l.2, ‖ MSp. *describir* < Lat. [DESCRĪBO] and /w/ **avuelos**, l.10, ‖ MSp. *abuelos* < Lat. ?AVĬŎLOS [√ĂVUS]); it also occurs in the group [βɾ] in **palavras** (l.13) ‖ MSp. *palabras* < Lat. [PĂRĂBŎLA], and (though this is not illustrated in this text) implosively in such words as *sibdat* (‖ MSp. *ciudad*) < Lat. CĪVĬTĀTE [CĪVĬTĀS] where standard Spanish has vocalised the consonant to /u/ (cf. 13.1.3).

   Keypoint: the 'b/v' merger (p. 262).

34.1.3 Metathesis of /rd/ to /dr/ quite regularly occurs: **pedrites** (MSp. *perdiste*), l.9, **guadrar** (MSp. *guardar*), l.9, **akodrar** (MSp. *acordar*), l.14.

Morphology and syntax

34.2.1 Forms relating to the first person plural change initial /n/ to /m/ by analogy with the /m/ of the characteristic verbal ending -*mos*: **muestra** (‖ MSp. *nuestra*), l.2, **mozotros** (‖ MSp. *nosotros*), l.15. This process is also common, often with varying results, in spoken varieties of Andalusian Spanish.

34.2.2 The second person singular of the preterite (**kazates**, l.12, **pedrites**, l.6) has added, probably analogically with other second person singular forms, a final /s/, but lost the implosive /s/ (MSp. *casaste, perdiste*; which like the corresponding Latin forms, end in /ste/).

Vocabulary

34.3.1 As in Text 33, we find a number of archaisms preserved. **Ma** (see also 15.3.1) is from the conjunction *mas*, which is still sometimes used in literary language in modern Spanish, though it has been replaced in normal spoken usage by *pero*. **Ambezar** 'to teach' (l.13) is equatable with OCast. *abezar* (restricted in the modern language to the meaning of 'to accustom', though Covarrubias defines it as 'enseñar y acostumbrar').

34.3.2 Dainda (l.6), cognate with Portuguese and Galician *ainda*, is not attested in Old Castilian. The presence of such non-Castilian forms in Judeo-Spanish may be a result of the heterogeneous composition of emigrating Jews.

34.3.3 Independent morphological derivation is observable in **eskarinyo** (l.15) (standard *cariño*).

34.3.4 The adoption of abstract vocabulary from modern Spanish is clearly visible in **dispersar** (l.10), which is first attested in Spanish only in the nineteenth century and **sinonimo** (l.3), seventeenth century. Such words can be easily incorporated into Judeo-Spanish, and may tend to bring about a rapprochement with the standard language. The process is comparable with learned borrowing.

XV   Caló

The terms *caló* and *germanía* have often been used interchangeably as general pejorative designations for the language of the criminal underworld (see in this connection Chapter XIII introduction and 22.0). However, I will use the term *caló* in its more 'proper' (and certainly not pejorative) sense of the language of the Spanish gypsies, reserving the term *germanía* for underworld jargon (see Text 22). *Caló* and *germanía* are both extremely interesting as linguistic phenomena, though they have often been marginalised from mainstream studies of the history of Spanish as effectively as their speakers have been marginalised from society. They share the striking feature of possessing a large amount of non-standard lexis which is grafted on to Spanish morphology and syntax. While *caló* uses Romani words, *germanía* uses lexical resources which emanate from within Spanish itself, typically euphemism (e.g. *enano* 'dwarf' for standard *puñal* 'dagger', *comadreja* 'weasel' for 'thief adept at burglary', *cierta* 'the certain (thing)' for standard *muerte* 'death'), metaphor (e.g. *culebra* 'snake' for standard *lima* 'file', the image being something that is passed between bars) and oblique association (e.g. *cofradía* '(religious) brotherhood' for standard *muchedumbre* 'crowd'). Since the seventeenth century, however, there has clearly been much interchange between *caló* and *germanía*. Many words of Romani origin have passed into the usage of non-gypsies and some of these have even found quite wide acceptance in the spoken language, e.g. *parné* 'money' from the *caló* word *parné* 'white or silver money', *parno* being 'white', though there were relatively few such words in Hidalgo's seventeenth-century glossary of *germanía*. It is, in fact, such lexical interchange that has led to some confusion concerning the difference between *caló* and *germanía*, which is otherwise clear conceptually.

Both *caló* and *germanía* share the feature of being cryptolectic languages, that is, restricted codes of communication that are intended to be in part opaque to an outsider. In *caló* this has probably been responsible for the preservation of Romani words which might otherwise have been lost, and in *germanía* the desire to confuse has probably accelerated changes of meaning: another feature of *germanía* is the selection of a less frequent Spanish word in substitution for a more common word, such as *columbrar* for *mirar* and *bramar* for *gritar*. There is also evidence in *caló* of apparently deliberate obfuscations of Spanish words. A well-known example is the word for the month of March, Spanish *marzo*. In *caló* this is *loriazo*: *loria* is the Romani word for 'sea' (Sp. *mar*) which replaces the (semantically completely unrelated) *mar* syllable of *marzo*; such a process of macaronic word-formation would produce a form that was intelligible only to the Romani community (see also 36.3.1).

In modern times, the Romani element in *caló* is becoming progressively weaker, and so the rather scanty textual evidence from former periods is of crucial importance in establishing the history of this very individual variety of Spanish. The present-day aspirations of the Barcelona-based Unión Romaní, an organisation which is intent on recovering the cultural heritage of the Spanish gypsies, are directed towards the adoption of a reconstructed Romani ('Romanó-Kaló') which will facilitate communication with gypsies worldwide rather than towards any cultivation of *caló* as such; in fact, *caló* is despised by gypsy purists because of its 'foreign' (i.e. Spanish) syntactic structure. But 'Romanó-Kaló' is not native to any present-day Spanish gypsy speakers.

The question of the genesis of *caló* is much discussed. Gypsies have certainly been present in the Iberian Peninsula since the fifteenth century. An early seventeenth-century account reports that the Spanish gypsies no longer spoke Romani, and the work of the nineteenth-century writer George Borrow (1843, see Text 35), with his more concrete and extensive linguistic evidence, confirms this. The conclusion must be, then, that *caló* dates from relatively soon after the gypsies' arrival in the Peninsula. Within immigrant groups, neither the quick adoption of a host language nor the maintenance of a native language would be surprising (compare the tenacious use of Judeo-Spanish, Texts 33 and 34); but *caló* raises the question as to how, if loss of Romani was so swift, so many Romani words remained in use. From a structural point of view, it is much more likely that *caló* represents a grafting of Romani lexis on to Spanish morphology and syntax than the converse, i.e., the grafting of Spanish grammar on to Romani, since lexical borrowing, even on this scale, is easier to achieve than syntactic borrowing. Assuming that this is so, the answer to the question of the scale of lexical borrowing seems to lie not in the supposition of a lengthy period of bilingualism so much as in the special nature of gypsy society. The motivation for the gypsies to adopt Spanish must have been strong, since the gypsies, whilst not a fully integrated part of Spanish society, were nevertheless in constant contact with it and depended on it economically. The use of Romani words, however, served both the function of bonding within the gypsy community and as a defence against outside intrusion.

Further reading

Besses (1906); Bakker (1997); Borrow (1843).

35 The *caló* Apostles' Creed. George Borrow, *The Zincali* (1843)

35.0 An extreme form of *caló* is represented in this text, which is a version of the Apostles' Creed recorded by George Borrow in his book *The Zincali*. Borrow, who was a prodigious linguist, had a lifelong interest in Romani which began in England, and the amount of information he was able to collect on the language of the Spanish gypsies while he was an agent for the British and Foreign Bible Society in Spain was remarkable. The circumstances of the production of this text, which is from the mid-nineteenth-century *caló* of Cordoba, are singular, and Borrow's own description (Borrow 1843: 240–2) is worth quoting in full:

After the Gitanos had discussed several jockey plans, and settled some private bargains amongst themselves, we all gathered round a huge brasero of flaming charcoal, and began conversing SOBRE LAS COSAS DE EGYPTO, when I proposed that, as we had no better means of amusing ourselves, we should endeavour to turn into the Calo language some pieces of devotion, that we might see whether this language, the gradual decay of which I had frequently heard them lament, was capable of expressing any other matters than those which related to horses, mules, and Gypsy traffic. It was in this cautious manner that I first endeavoured to divert the attention of these singular people to matters of eternal importance. My suggestion was received with acclamations, and we forthwith proceeded to the translation of the Apostles' creed. I first recited in Spanish, in the usual manner and without pausing, this noble confession, and then repeated it again, sentence by sentence, the Gitanos translating as I proceeded. They exhibited the greatest eagerness and interest in their unwonted occupation, and frequently broke into loud disputes as to the best rendering – many being offered at the same time. In the meanwhile, I wrote down from their dictation; and at the conclusion I read aloud the translation, the result of the united wisdom of the assembly, whereupon they all raised a shout of exultation, and appeared not a little proud of the composition.

Thus what follows is a somewhat artificial piece and not the usual register of *caló* to which speakers were accustomed: it is more than likely that their delight was in the sheer concentration of *caló* elements that they had achieved. Some of the translation is circumlocutory (*vivos* is translated as **los que no lo sinélan**, l.7, 'those who are not [dead]') and some may not be quite natural (the use of **debajo de**, l.4, rather than *bajo*). None the less it is an extremely valuable document, since at the very least it shows which words were still understood by some speakers at the time. Borrow's account also shows that *caló* speakers were also perfectly well able to operate in Spanish, and that *caló* is most appropriately seen as a special language used for particular purposes, especially for dealing in horses.

The text

The text is taken from Borrow 1843: II, *128; Borrow's spelling and accentuation have been preserved, though there are some obvious inconsistencies: **Un-debel** (l.1) and **Un-debél** (l.2), **barreá** (l.7) and **baréa** (l.8).

> **Pachabélo en Un-debel batu tosaro-baro, que ha querdi el char y la chiqué; y en Un-debél chinoró su unico chaboró eraño de amangue, que chaló en el trupo de la Majarí por el Duquende Majoró, y abió del veo de la Majarí; guilló curádo debájo de la sila de Pontio Pilato el chínobaró; guilló mulo y garabado; se chalá á las jacháris; al trin chibé se ha sicobádo de los mulés al char; sinéla bejádo á las baste de Un-debél barreá; y de oté abiará a juzgar á los mulés y á los que no lo sinélan; pachabélo en el Majaró; la Cangrí Majarí baréa; el jalar de los Majaries; lo mecó de los grécos; la resureccion de la maas, y la ochi que no maréla.**

5

Borrow's literal translation into English

I believe in God the Father all-great, who has made the heaven and the earth; and in God the young, his only Son, the Lord of us, who went into the body of the blessed (maid) by (means of) the Holy Ghost, and came out of the womb of the blessed; he was tormented beneath the power of Pontius Pilate, the great Alguazil; was dead and buried; he went (down) to the fires; on the third day he raised himself from the dead unto the heaven; he is seated at the major hand of God; and from thence he shall come to judge the dead and those who are not (dead). I believe in the blessed one; in the church holy and great; the banquet of the saints; the remission of sins; the resurrection of the flesh, and the life which does not die.

Phonetics and phonology

35.1.1 The sound-pattern of *caló* is entirely consistent with that of Spanish. The only difference is in the frequency of certain sounds in certain positions. Initial /tʃ/ is significantly more frequent than in Spanish, and is the consequence of the fusion of Romani initial /tʃ/, /ts/, /tʃʰ/ and /tʰ/ as /tʃ/ in *caló* (Bakker 1997: 130). Final /i/ occurs more frequently, chiefly because it is the characteristic feminine gender inflection in words of Romani origin (see 36.2.2).

Morphology and syntax

It can quickly be seen that while the vast majority of lexical stems here are Romani, the inflectional morphology, syntax and 'grammatical' words (article, conjunctions, most prepositions and pronouns) are Spanish.

35.2.1 The verbal morphology is entirely Spanish: examples are **pachabélo** (l.1), 1st p.sg. present tense; **chaló** (l.3), 3rd p.sg. preterite tense; the reflexive 3rd p.sg. perfect tense **se ha sicobádo** (ll.5–6), **abiará** (l.7), 3rd p.sg. future tense. Romani verbs are all adapted regularly into the *-ar* conjugation of Spanish, and in this respect the form **querdi** (l.1), the irregular past participle of *querar* 'to do', 'make', is unusual.

35.2.2 The verb *chalar* 'to go' (**chaló**, l.3) is fully adapted as a Spanish reflexive, just like its Spanish parallel *irse*: **se chalá á las jacháris** = *se fue a los fuegos (al Infierno)* (l.5).

35.2.3 One extremely interesting feature of verbal morphology is the continuing use of the infixed morpheme *-el-*, here evident in the verb-forms **pachabélo** (ll.1 and 8), **sinéla(n)** (ll.6 and 7) and **maréla** (l.9). In Borrow's glossary the forms *sinar* 'to be' and *marar* 'to kill' are also given, as are *bejelar* 'to sit' (compare the past participle **bejádo**, l.6) and *abillelar* 'to come' (compare **abió**, l.3, **abiará**, l.7). (See also 35.3.1 below concerning *currar/currelar*.) In Romani this is the third person ending of the verb, but in *caló* it is fully incorporated into the verb stem to produce pairs of verbs which seem to differ in aspectual value, those with *-el-* expressing a more intensive action.

35.2.4 Nouns are masculine or feminine, as in Spanish, and it is striking how in most cases the gender of the *caló* noun is the same as that of the corresponding Spanish noun (cf. 32b.1): **el char** (l.1) = *el cielo*; **la chiqué** (l.2) = *la tierra*; **el trupo** (l.3) = *el cuerpo*, etc. The case inflections which must have been present in older Romani and are vestigially evidenced in some Catalan *caló* sources from the Iberian Peninsula are totally absent. The Romani gender markers are apparent in some words: masculine *-ó* in **chinoró** (l.2) 'young', **los grécos** (l.9) 'sins'; feminine *-i* in **la Majarí** (l.3) 'the Virgin', **la Cangrí** (l.8) 'the Church', **la ochí** (l.9) 'life'. Plurals are formed by the addition of /s/, again as in Spanish, although a remnant of the Romani plural marker for nominalised masculine adjectives, *-e*, can also be seen in **los mulés** (l.7) 'the dead', the plural of **mulo** (l.5) 'dead'. Thus while some of the morphological features of Romani remain 'frozen' in *caló*, they have been overlaid by Spanish.

35.2.5 The diminutive suffix *-oró* is evident in **chinoró** (l.2) and **chaboró** (l.2).

35.2.6 Word order is identical to that of Spanish (though it must be borne in mind that this text is a word-by-word translation of a Spanish original).

35.2.7 The personal *a* is clearly taken over wholesale from Spanish: **juzgar a los mulés y á los que no lo sinélan** (l.7) = *juzgar a los muertos y a los que no lo están (a los vivos)*.
  Keypoint: 'personal' *a* (p. 283).

Vocabulary

35.3.1 It is beyond the scope of this book to look in detail at the sources of all the Romani words here. Particularly interesting are those which have found acceptance more widely in Spanish, at least in colloquial usage. **Chaboró** (l.2) 'boy', 'son' is from the same root (*chav-*) as Sp. *chaval*, which is derived from *chavale*, the old vocative plural of Romani *chavó* 'boy'. *Guillar* (**guilló**, l.4, *lit.* 'he went') has passed into Spanish as *guillarse* 'to go' → 'to go crazy (about something or someone)' and the idiom *guillárselas* 'to run off', 'to beat it'. The verb *curar* (**curádo**, l.4) 'to work', 'to beat', has yielded Sp. *currar* with the same meaning, and also *currelar* (see 35.2.3) 'to slog away', as well as derived forms *currante* 'worker', *curre* or *curro*, *currele*, *currelo* 'work'. **Mulo** (l.5) 'dead' is visible in the idiom *dar mulé* 'to kill', 'bump off'. **Cangrí** (l.8) 'church', originally 'tower', has undergone metaphorical extension in underworld jargon to the meaning of 'prison'. The verb *jalar* (**jalar**, l.8, 'banquet') exists in Spanish as *jalar* or *jamar* 'to eat'.

36 A shady business. Ramón del Valle-Inclán, *El ruedo ibérico: Viva mi dueño* (1928)

Perhaps because of its cryptolectic nature, *caló* has exercised a great fascination for outsiders. Borrow in *The Zincali* relates how a number of non-gypsies in Andalusia cultivated an 'afición' for compositions in what purported to be *caló*, and such texts cannot be taken at face-value as evidence of the nature of *caló*. Ramón del Valle-Inclán (1866–1936) was fascinated in *caló* for another reason: for him it was a part of the degradation of Spanish society which he sought to portray in his novel-cycle *El ruedo ibérico*. He includes a number of dialogues between gypsies in his novel *Viva mi dueño* which are probably deliberately cryptolectic (they are certainly extremely difficult to understand, and I can offer only a tentative translation). Yet, contrived though they probably are, like many novelistic representations of popular speech (see Texts 22, 24 and 30), they offer interesting evidence of a *caló* which still contains a fairly high proportion of Romani words. We must bear in mind, however, that Valle-Inclán was a consummate artist with words, and had an amazingly rich vocabulary which is evident in the narrative passages in standard Spanish in this extract; it is likely that this same pursuit of lexical variation, coupled with a desire to be deliberately obscure, increased the range and frequency of *caló* words in the dialogue.

The text

The text comes from Valle-Inclán (1971: 179–80).

Further reading

Sinclair (1977:88–103).

Saltó avispada una de las mozuelas:
—Benaldio, ¿te han dicho por un senigual alguna mala gachapla esos dos?
—Undevel, que sí me lo han dicho!
—Me extraña, porque no hay dos más callados en todo el charnín.
... El viejo advirtió, disimulado: 5
—Ostelinda, deja el rebridaque, que el planoró se trae su bulipen.
Saltó la otra mozuela:
—¡Aromali! Ése tiene más letra que el jabicote de la Misa.
El caballejo y el pollino, con los jaeces bailones, tornaban a la angosta
sombra del tapiado. Remataba un sartal la otra mozuela, y, preso en dos   10
dedos, lo bailó al sol:
—¡Benaldillo, míralo qué majo! ¿No tienes tú una chaví para quien me lo
mercar, resalao? ¿Tú tan presumido de ligero, cómo no te alcuentras en la
capea?
—Estoy bizmado.   15
Cercioró el viejo:
—A las ferias se viene a ganar un chulí, no a dejarlo.
—Ésa es la chachipé.
Con nuevo varazo espantó el cuatrero la pareja de rocín y jumento.
Recalcó el vejete con sorna: 20
—Anda a modo, que si se espantan, a la sangre que tienen, arman una
revolución en el charní.
—Tío Ronquete, cállese usted esa palabra condenada, que es peor que
mentar la filimicha. Un espanto apareja muchas ruinas.

–Pues no sería raro, que hay siempre muchos chories con el ojo en eso.   **25**
–¿Del Errate?
–Caloré y busné.

Translation

One of the lasses chipped in brightly, 'Benaldio, have those two made a rude *copla* about you [by any unlucky chance?]?'

'My God, they certainly have!'

'I'm surprised, because in all the fair there aren't two quieter lads.'

... Feigning igorance, the old man warned her, 'Leave off the flattery, my beauty, because our brother has brought along his trickery.'

The other lass chirped up, 'For sure, that has more words than the Mass book.'

The old nag and the young donkey, their harnesses dancing, went back to the narrow shadow of the walled area. The other girl was finishing off a string of beads and, holding it between two fingers, she jangled it in the sunlight:

'Bernaldillo, look how lovely it is! Haven't you got a girlfriend I can sell it you for, darling? You who pride yourself on being so nimble, how is it you're not in the bullfight (a *capea* is a bullfight for novices)?'

'I'm [being cautious? (*lit.* 'I've got a poultice applied')].'

The old man elucidated: 'You go to horse-fairs to earn a *duro*, not to leave it behind.'

'That's right.'

The rustler scared the nag and the donkey with another thwack with his stick. The old man insisted sarcastically: 'Take it easy; if they take fright, with their blood, they'll cause a major upset at the fair.'

'*Tío* Ronquete, don't use that goddam word; it's worse than talking about the gallows. When horses take fright, a lot of people are ruined.'

'Well it wouldn't be surprising; there are always a lot of thieves on the lookout.'

'Gypsy thieves?'

'Both gypsies and non-gypsies.'

Phonetics and phonology

36.1.1 In the spelling there are sporadic indications of the phonetic erosion typical of Andalusian Spanish. **Resalao** (l.13) for standard *resalado* shows the complete elision of intervocalic /d/ which was especially associated with Andalusia, though it has now extended far beyond (27.1.3).

36.1.2 The forms **Benaldio** (l.2) and **Benaldillo** (l.12) for standard *Bernardillo* may indicate (a) the neutralisation of the opposition between /r/ and /l/ in implosive position (see 27.1.5), (b) the loss of /r~l/ altogether in the first syllable, perhaps as a result of dissimilation (the avoidance of successive syllables ending in an implosive /r~l/), and (c) *yeísmo* (the variant spelling suggests the suffix is pronounced [ijo]).

Morphology and syntax

As in Text 35, the syntax and morphology are entirely Spanish.

36.2.1 Bulipen (l.6) shows the Romani suffix *-pen* which was used to form abstract nouns from adjectives; the word is based on *bulo* 'false piece of news'. Although there are a number of such words in *caló*, it is doubtful if the suffix is still productive at this time, however.

36.2.2 Chaví (l.12) 'girl' has the typical Romani feminine inflection *-í* (compare *chavó* 'boy', 35.3.1).

36.2.3 The syntax of spontaneous speech is reflected in a number of elliptical structures, e.g. ¡**míralo qué majo**! (l.12) = *¡míra lo majo que es!*; **Tú tan presumido de ligero** ... (l.13) = *Tú que eres tan presumido de ligero* ~ *Tú que presumes de ligero* ~ *Ya que tú eres tan presumido de ligero* ... (cf. 25.2.5).

36.2.4 Another common feature of spoken register is that the connective **que** is extensively used (ll.1, 6, 21, 23, 25), with a broadly causal meaning (cf. 25.2.6, 28.2.5).

Vocabulary

As in the commentary on Text 35, there is not an exhaustive commentary on all the *caló* words which appear here.

36.3.1 Rebridaque (l.6) is an example of a process of word-formation, common in *caló*, by which part of a Spanish word is given a Romani equivalent and the other part left as Spanish. Here the Spanish model is *requiebro*, analysed as containing the elements *re-* and *quiebro*. To the latter in its meaning of 'breaking' (it is a nominal formation from *quebrar* 'to break', *requebrado* originally meaning 'broken (by love)') corresponds the *caló* word *bridaque*, which is similarly the nominal corresponding to *bridaquelar* 'to break'.

36.3.2 The stem of **planoró** (l.6) 'brother', which has the affective suffix *-ró* (cf. 35.3.1), is cognate with the English Romani word which was the origin of Eng. *pal*.

36.3.3 Jabicote (l.8) 'book', is usually cited as *gabicote*. It seems to have added a Spanish augmentative suffix *-ote*, though its origin is obscure (Borrow relates it, not totally convincingly, to Ar. *k-t-b* 'book').

36.3.4 Chachipé(n) (l.18) 'truth' has passed into modern colloquial usage as the noun *la chipén*, as the adjective *chachi* or *chanchi* with the meaning of 'great', 'cool', 'terrific', and as the expression *de chipe* (also *de chipén, chipendi*) with similar meaning.

36.3.5 Chorí (l.25) 'thief'. A number of forms of this word, based on the root *chor-*, are known. The word *choro* has passed into popular Peninsular Spanish with the meaning of 'pickpocket'.

36.3.6 From *germanía*, we have **cuatrero** (l.19) 'rustler', 'horse-thief', now a standard Spanish word. It is derived from a *germanía* word for 'horse', *cuatro* (the association being that of a four-legged animal). In Latin America *cuatrero* has broadened it meaning to that of 'rogue' in general.

36.3.7 Majo (l.12) is widely used in modern spoken Spanish in the general sense of 'nice', 'pretty', which is the sense it has here, though Valle no doubt incorporates it because it was particularly associated with Andalusian usage. In the eighteenth century it had a very particular application, referring to aspirations of noble elegance and gallantry by members of the lower classes (this is the sense in which Goya used the word), and so was rather pejorative in tone. Its etymological origins are obscure.

XVI The African connection

The language of the large numbers of African slaves transported to Spanish America constitutes a significant chapter in the history of Spanish. Indeed, it is sometimes argued that the 'African' contribution to Latin-American Spanish is substantial. Detailed discussion of this rather contentious issue is beyond the scope of this book, though we may briefly observe that, setting patent lexical borrowings aside, there seems to be no really convincing case of any widespread feature of modern Latin-American Spanish that is attributable solely to African influence: the neutralisation of the opposition between /l/ and /r/, for example, though frequent in *bozal* and creole, is also widely attested in Andalusian Spanish (27.1.5). At the same time, this is not to deny the localised survival of 'African' features in areas of Latin America which had large African populations, most notably, perhaps, the neutralisation of intervocalic /d/ and /r/ on the Pacific coast of Colombia and Ecuador and in the Dominican Republic.

Today a number of different types of 'African' Spanish can be identified:

1   Creoles which were probably originally based on Portuguese. Into this category fall Papiamentu and Palenquero (see Text 39).
2   Partially creolised Spanish, a surviving example of which is the black *choteño* speech of Ecuador. The exact history of this language is uncertain, as is its creole status. The black population seems to have been the product not only of the importation of slaves between the sixteenth and eighteenth centuries but also of settlements by black Colombians and Jamaicans in the nineteenth century. The language, whilst not exhibiting creole features as normally understood (there is no creole verb system comparable to that of Papiamentu, for instance), nevertheless shows some ignoring of gender and number agreement which is atypical of the Spanish-speaking world as a whole.
3   More recent adoption of Spanish as a second language by speakers of African languages, the most significant example of which is the Spanish of Equatorial Guinea (see Text 38).

Further reading

Granda (1978b: 185–233); Lipski (1994: 93–135).

37 Two negros praise the Virgin. Sor Juana Inés de la Cruz (1676)

37.0 Sor Juana Inés de la Cruz (1651–95) wrote a number of *villancicos* in popular vein for use at major religious festivals. The extract below is taken from a *villancico* written for the Feast of the Assumption as celebrated in the cathedral of Mexico City in 1676. In her *villancicos* Sor Juana represents the styles of speech of negros, Indians, Biscayans and scholars (often, it has to be pointed out, for humorous effect, although there is also the serious purpose of creating a devotional genre that is accessible to a wide range of people). In this extract we have one of a number of respresentations of *bozal*, the speech of negros. Despite Sor Juana's undoubted linguistic virtuosity (she was even able to write short continuous passages in Portuguese, Latin and Nahuatl), we must remember that the representation of *bozal* had a lengthy tradition in Spanish literature – Lope de Rueda (see Text 20), Lope de Vega, Góngora, Quevedo (see Text 22) and Calderón were amongst those who introduced such a style into the mouths of their negro characters in their works – and that such representation was probably somewhat conventionalised. Even so, such documents are valuable as evidence of what were popularly considered to be the chief features of negro speech of the time. Significantly, they are much closer to later manifestations of *bozal* speech than they are to Portuguese/Spanish creoles such as Papiamentu (see Text 39). They are often described as 'inaccurate' Spanish – 'infantil medialengua', writes Méndez Plancarte, from whose pioneering edition (see below) the text is taken – but they are consistently characterised by many of the same interchanges, neutralisations and loss of phonemes and the same lack of number and gender concord that we observe in modern *bozal*.

The text

The text is taken from Méndez Plancarte (1952: 15–16). I have supplied a standard modern Spanish parallel version. Two negros discuss the Assumption, one lamenting it and one praising it.

Further reading

Ríos de Torres (1991).

1 Cantemo, Pilico,	Cantemos, Perico,
que se va las Reina,	que se va la Reina,
y dalemu turo	y daremos todos
una noche buena.	una noche buena.

2 Iguale yolale,	Igual [es] llorar	**5**
Flacico, de pena,	Francisco, de pena:	
que nos deja ascula	que nos deja a oscuras	
a turo las Negla.	a todos los Negros.	

1 Si las Cielo va	Si a los Cielos [se] va
y Dioso la lleva,	y Dios la lleva, *10*
¿pala qué yolá,	¿para qué llorar,
si Eya sa cuntenta?	si Ella está contenta?
Sará muy galana,	Estará muy linda
vitita ri tela,	vestida de tela,
milando la Sole,	mirando el Sol, *15*
pisando la Streya.	pisando la[s] Estrella[s].
2 Déjame yolá,	Déjame llorar,
Flacico, pol Eya,	Francisco, por Ella:
que se va, y nosotlo	que se va, y [a] nosotros
la Oblaje nos deja.	al Obraje nos deja. *20*
1 Caya, que sa siempre	Calla, que está siempre
milando la Iglesia;	mirando [a] la Iglesia!
mila las Pañola,	Mira [a] la[s] española[s] [*or* los
	españoles],
que se quela plieta.	que se queda[n] prieta[s] [*or* prietos].
2 Bien dici, Flacico:	Bien dices, Francisco: *25*
tura sa suspensa;	toda está suspensa:
si tú quiele, demo	si tú quieres, demos
unas cantaleta.	una[s] cantaleta[s].
1 ¡Nomble de mi Dioso,	¡Nombre de mi Dios,
que sa cosa buena!	que es cosa buena! *30*
Aola, Pilico,	¡Ahora, Perico,
que nos mila atenta ...	que nos mira atenta!
Estribillo	
¡Ah, ah, ah,	¡Ah, ah, ah,
que la Reina se nos va!	que la Reina se nos va!
¡Uh, uh, uh,	¡Uh, uh, uh, *35*
que non blanca como tú,	que no [es] blanca como tú,
nin Paño que no sa buena,	ni española que no es buena;
que Eya dici: So molena	que Ella dice: Soy morena
con las Sole que mirá!	con el Sol que me ha mirado!
¡Ah, ah, ah,	¡Ah, ah, ah, *40*
que la Reina se nos va!	que la Reina se nos va!

Translation

'Let's sing, Perico, for the Queen is going away, and we'll all give her goodnight.'

'We might just as well weep for sorrow, Francisco, since she's leaving all us Negros in darkness.'

'If she's going to Heaven and God is taking her, what reason is there to weep, if She is happy? She'll be fine dressed in [fine] cloth, looking at the Sun and treading on stars.'

'Let me weep for Her, Francisco. She's going away and she's leaving us to the cloth factory.'

'Hush, for she is always looking at the Church; she's always looking at the Spanish [people] who are black.'

'Well said, Francisco: she is standing over us; if you like, let's give her a song [some songs].'

'Name of God, that's a fine thing! Now, Perico, she is looking at us attentively . . .'

'Ah, ah, ah, the Queen is going from us! Uh, uh, uh, she isn't white like you, nor a Spanish girl who is not good, for She says: 'I am Black because the Sun has looked at me!' Ah, ah, ah, the Queen is going from us!'

Phonetics and phonology

37.1.1 Syllable-final /s/ has consistently fallen (**cantemo** for *cantemos*, l.1, **ascula**, l.7, for *a oscuras*, **turo**, l.8, for *todos*, **vitita**, l.14, for *vestida*, etc.), as has /r/ (**yolá**, l.11, for *llorar*).

37.1.2 There is interchange between intervocalic /r/, /l/ and /d/, neutralisation in favour of /l/ being in fact the most common result: **pilico** (l.1) for *Perico*, **turo** (l.3) for *todos*, **ri** (l.14) for *de*, **quela** (l.24) for *queda*. This also extends to some postconsonantal contexts: **Negla** (l.8) for *Negras*, **nosotlo** (l.19) for *nosotros*, **plieta** (l.24) for *prieta*. While the neutralisation of the opposition between /l/ and /r/ is found in many areas of Andalusia and Latin America, the inclusion of /d/ in this phenomenon is rare, and may be taken to be a hallmark of *bozal*.

37.1.3 *Yeísmo* is evidenced in **yolale** (l.5) for *llorarla*, **Streya** (l.16) for *estrella*, **caya** (l.21) for *calla*, etc.

37.1.4 There is some evidence of the closing of atonic /e/ and /o/: **vitita** (l.14) for *vestida*, **dalemu** (l.3) for *daremos*, **cuntenta** (l.12) for *contenta*.
   Keypoint: vowels (p. 296).

37.1.5 Apheresis of the initial *es-* sequence is apparent in **Streya** (l.16) for *estrella* and **Pañola** (l.23) for *española* (note that the syllable-final /s/ would tend to disappear in any case – see 37.1.1).

37.1.6 There is sporadic use of a paragogic final /e/ (**Sole**, l.15, for standard *sol*, and probably **iguale** and **yolale**, l.5, for standard *igual*, *llorar*). This has the effect of creating a consonant + vowel syllable structure.

Morphology and syntax

37.2.1 The absence of final /s/ often obscures the difference between singular and plural. While in a number of cases the /s/ remains in the article (**las Negla**, l.8, **las Pañola**, l.23), there are cases where the sense seems to require an interpretation which is apparently not overtly indicated (**las Reina**, l.2, for *la Reina*; **la Streya**, l.16, for *las estrellas*; **las Sole**, l.39, for *el Sol*), suggesting that gender is in any case not rigorously distinguished. It is hence difficult to know, for instance, whether **las Cielo** (l.9) is the equivalent of *el Cielo* or *los cielos* or **unas cantaleta** (l.28) the equivalent of *una cantaleta* or *unas cantaletas*. The provisional conclusion must be that number is simply not distinguished.

37.2.2 There are many apparent departures from standard gender, which similarly suggests that gender is not rigorously distinguished either (a feature of creole, cf. Papiamentu, Text 39). Thus **las Cielo** (l.9), **la Sole** (l.15), **la Oblaje** (l.20). For this reason it is not impossible to interpret **las Pañola** (l.23) as *los españoles*.
   Keypoint: gender (p. 275).

37.2.3 There is an example of hypercharacterisation of gender, however, in **Dioso** (l.10), where the *-o* inflection is in accordance with the masculine gender of *Dios*.

37.2.4 Verb forms generally have their standard Spanish inflections, if the fall of final /s/ is allowed for (thus **dici**, l.25, for *dices*, **quiele**, l.27, for *quieres*). The infinitive, which regularly loses its final /r/ (see 37.1.1), is extensively used: **¿pala qué yolá?** (l.11) for *¿para qué llorar?*, **con las Sole que mirá** (l.39) for *con mirar el sol* [?].

37.2.5 There is apparently no distinction between *ser* and *estar* (**sará muy galana/vitita ri tela**, ll.13–14; **sa . . . milando**, ll.21–2). The forms of *ser* seem to be those chiefly employed, though there are a number of differences from standard usage: the 1st p.sg. of the present tense is **so** (l.38) rather than *soy*, which was a common form in Old Castilian (see 7.2.5), the 3rd p.sg. of the present tense is **sa** (l.12) and the future stem is *sar-* (**sará**, l.13). This suggests a regularised paradigm based on an infinitive *?sar*, which may be a hybrid of *ser* and *estar*; such a verb is indeed encountered in some modern creoles (Lipski 1994: 99).
   Keypoint: *ser* and *estar* (p. 290).

37.2.6 There is variation in the choice of direct object clitic pronoun. In l.5 we find **yola<u>le</u>** (in Sor Juana's own usage, setting the scene a few lines earlier, she says 'Heráclito uno, <u>la</u> llora') and in l.10 **<u>la</u> lleva**.
   Keypoint: personal pronouns (p. 284).

37.2.7 Syntactic structures are in general very simple (though this is also favoured by the short hexasyllabic lines). **Que** is used frequently as a causal conjunction (ll.2, 7, 21, 36, 38); cf. 25.2.6.

37.2.8 Topicalisation of the direct object can be seen in **nosotlo / la Oblaje nos deja** (ll.19–20); cf. 28.2.5.

Vocabulary

37.3.1 There are two words for 'black': **plieta** (*prieto*) (l.24) and **molena** (*moreno*) (l.38). *Prieto* is common in Old Castilian (see 11.3.6); *moreno* is in origin a morphological derivative of *moro*. (The reference to the black Virgin is reminiscent of the *Song of Solomon* I.5, 'I am black but lovely, daughters of Jerusalem', a text which naturally had great appeal for black Catholics.)

37.3.2 Oblaje (*obraje*) (l.20), a morphological derivative of *obra*, here has the specific meaning of the workshop or factory where cloth was produced by slave labour; it continues with similar meanings ('sawmill' in the River Plate area, 'butcher's shop' in Mexico) in various parts of Latin America.

38 Spanish in Equatorial Guinea (late twentieth century)

38.0 Equatorial Guinea is centred on the island of Bioko, formerly the slaving station Fernando Poo, which passed from Portugal to Spain in 1778 and was only colonised by Spain in the nineteenth century. The situation of Spanish here has been brought to attention only relatively recently, particularly through the work of Germán de Granda and John M. Lipski (see below). Spanish is the official language of Equatorial Guinea, yet it is the true native language of very few of the inhabitants, who speak a range of African languages; such a situation, which is common in the English-speaking world in many African and Asian countries which were formerly part of the British empire, is unique in the Spanish-speaking world, and as such is of great linguistic interest. Guinean Spanish was brought about historically by a rather different kind of relation with the standard Peninsular language from that observed in Latin America: Spanish colonisation was relatively late and also relatively enlightened, with the introduction of a good educational system based on the Spanish language, and the maintenance of continuous contact with Spain itself (apart from the 11 years of the xenophobic Macías dictatorship, 1968–79). This continuous contact with the standard, plus the fact that it has never undergone pidginisation, also makes Guinean Spanish very different in nature from creoles such as Papiamentu (see Text 39). (A Portuguese creole is in fact spoken on the island of Annobon.)

Guinean Spanish has many of the characteristics of the Spanish spoken by foreigners: it does not have the same creative dimension as a native language; it appears not to have undergone significant regional dialectalisation, and its speakers give the impression of making morphological and syntactic 'mistakes' (indeed, a fundamental question is to what extent Guinean Spanish is a uniform language at all, given its apparently random variation in a number of aspects). Yet it has a number of characteristic features which make it a recognisably individual variety of Spanish: the plosive quality of /b/, /d/ and /g/ (that is to say, the sounds [β], [ð] and [ɣ] are absent), the neutralisation of the opposition between /ɾ/ and /r/ and the 'English' (alveolar) pronunciation of /t/ and /d/ may be seen as 'progressive' features; whereas the preservation of implosive /s/, the alveolar pronunciation of final /n/ and the maintenance of the opposition between /l/

and /r/ are 'conservative' (i.e. more like the Peninsular standard) compared with many other Peninsular and Latin-American varieties.

The text

This text is taken from Lipski (1985: 105). The transcription made by Lipski uses conventional Spanish orthography and so does not explicitly represent all the features noted above.

Further reading

Granda (1991: 237–84 and 1994: 470–6).

> –Los muchachos, cuando van a la escuela, ¿ya hablan español?
> –Bueno, lo aprenden en escuela, pero antes no, no ocurió de eso ... ante
> ... ante la independencia no ... sesenta y ocho la gentes ... o sea un
> chico ... mayor ... donde se nace ... desde la cuna ... de allá empieza
> hablar si lengua vernácula ... y el español.   *5*
> –¿El español se habla en las casas, entonces?
> –Se hablaba ... sí, sí, sí, hombre ... y más, entre lo bubi los combe los
> bubekas ... annobonese incluiro, no ... habla ... o sea, se hablaban más
> ... más el español que la lengua de ellos ... hasta incluso ... en las
> famiyas ... se hablaba el españó bastante.   *10*
> –Pues ahora parece que no se habla tanto entre familia, ¿no es cierto?
> –Por eso prejisamente le dió que depué de senta y ocho ... esto se fue en
> una manera ... se fue reduciéndose poco a poco, no ... de que antes no
> ocuría ... eh que la pesoa se ... conversaba en español ante eso, no ... y
> ahora ... pero ahora ... yo creo que eso es un ... un eró ... porque esto *15*
> eh lo que ... aquí solamente quedó ... nosotro el clase, o sea podemo
> dividir el clase porque ... dominano muy poco ... el casteano.

Translation (it is clearly difficult to render this fragmentary discourse adequately):

'When children go to school do they already speak Spanish?'
  'Well, they learn it at school, but before that, no, it doesn't happen. Before independence, no ... [19]78 ... people, that is to say, an older child ... where you are born ... from the cradle you begin to speak your vernacular language and Spanish.'
  'Is Spanish spoken at home, then?'
  'It used to be spoken, yes, indeed ... and more among the Bubi, the Combe, the Bubeka, even the Annobonese, they don't ... or rather they used to ... speak Spanish more than their own language, even in families, they spoke Spanish a lot.'
  'So now it seems that it's not so much spoken within the family, does it?'
  'That's exactly why I told you that after sixty-eight ... it disappeared in a way ... it reduced gradually, something which didn't happen before ... people talked in Spanish before that, and now. ... but now ... I think that's not correct, because that is what ... here we only kept it in class, we can divide the class because ... we're not very good at Castilian.'

Phonetics and phonology

38.1.1 Liquid consonants are particularly prone to merger and weakening.

Reduction of the standard distinction between intervocalic /ɾ/ and /r/ is shown by such instances as **ocurió** for standard *ocurrió* (l.2), **ocuría** for standard *ocurría* (l.14), **eró** for standard *error* (l.15). Such a neutralisation is very restricted in the Spanish-speaking world (see, however, Granda 1978a who argues that it is more widespread than might be thought): apart from Judeo-Spanish, it occurs only in varieties which have had close contact with West African languages, being evidenced in Papiamentu (see Text 39, although there are no obvious examples of the phenomenon in those particular extracts).

Incluiro for standard *incluido* (l.8) is evidence of the neutralisation in intervocalic position of /d/ and /ɾ/, which is also a feature strongly associated with speakers of black African origin and also found in Papiamentu (39.1.2).

Final and implosive /r/ is lost in some instances (**eró** for *error*, l.15; **pesoa** for *persona*, l.14), as also is final /l/ (**españó** for standard *español*, l.10, though note also **español**, l.9). Although such weakening can be related to the general difficulties with liquids noted above, partial neutralisation between /l/ and /r/ can be observed in a number of Andalusian and Latin American varieties (see 27.1.5, 36.1.2), as can loss of final /r/ (27.1.4, 28.1.2), which is also very common generally in Romance (final /r/ has been lost extensively in Catalan and French, for instance).

38.1.2 /s/ is frequently lost altogether in implosive or final position, e.g., **depué** for *después* (l.12), **nosotro** for *nosotros* (l.16). This is a phenomenon which is common to a very large number of Spanish varieties in Andalusia and Latin America (see 27.1.5).

38.1.3 *Yeísmo* is evidenced in **famiyas** for standard *familias* (l.10), **casteano** for standard *castellano* (l.17).

38.1.4 Prejisamente (l.12) may be a hypercorrection made to distinguish standard /θ/ and /s/ (/preθisamente/, see also 22.1.3). *Seseo* is sporadic in Guinean Spanish in the sense that there is a great deal of variation between /θ/ and /s/ (even to the extent that the same word can be pronounced in different ways by the same speaker).

38.1.5 Si (l.5) corresponding to standard *su* shows variation in the use of vowels of a kind which is frequent in Guinean Spanish.

Morphology and syntax

38.2.1 The fragmentary nature of the discourse precludes extensive detailed commentary, but reveals (as indeed does the substance of what is being said) that for many speakers of Guinean Spanish it is in fact a second and imperfectly learnt language, typically spoken slowly and with some difficulty.

38.2.2 A number of morphological and syntactic 'mistakes' can be discerned by comparison with the standard, though it is not easy to know whether these are simple non-native errors, 'performance' errors (i.e., the hesitations and inconsistencies which characterise spontaneous speech – see Text 28), or, indeed, regular features of Guinean Spanish.

Some prepositional usages diverge from the standard: **no ocurió de eso** = *eso no ocurrió* (l.2), **ante** (or **ante[s]**?) **la independencia** = *antes de la independencia* (l.3) and **ante eso** = *antes de eso* (l.14), **empieza hablar** = *empieza a hablar* (ll.4–5) – though this may be simply *sinalefa* of /empiesa_a/, **en una manera** = *de una manera* (or *en cierta manera*) (ll.12–13).

Le dió (l.12) seems to indicate that the speaker is addressing the interviewer as *usted*, though earlier in the interview (not reproduced here) he had said *Háblame de tú* and later asks *¿Tú ere de dónde?* Guinean speakers shift apparently at random between *tú* and *usted* forms and even have anomalous combinations of subject pronoun and verb (e.g. *usted quieres*). Such variation may be due to the particular sociological circumstances of Guinea: in colonial times, Spaniards addressed Guineans as *tú* and Guineans, through imitation, used *tú* in return, though in schools the more normatively appropriate *usted* was the form which was preferred; since independence, the situation has reversed, with Spanish nationals typically using *usted* to Guineans, as they would to strangers (and also to avoid any manifestation of what might be taken as a patronising or demeaning attitude), but with the increased use of *tú* spreading from Spain amongst younger generations (Lipski 1985: 20).

> **Keypoint: personal pronouns** (p. 284).

What morphological form the verb **dió** (l.12) represents is not entirely clear. Using the 'wrong' form of a verb is not uncommon in Guinean Spanish, but this could be equated with either a present tense *digo* or a preterite *dijo*, in either case with a movement of stress.

In **se fue reduciéndose** (l.13), *se* is repeated (standard *se fue reduciendo* or *fue reduciéndose*).

La pesoa se . . . conversaba en español (l.14). It is difficult to know whether this is genuinely singular syntactically, or whether it is the result of elisions (**la[s] pe[r]sona[s] se conversaba[n]** . . .). Lipski's (1985: 39–40) observation that the elision of final /n/ is extremely rare would lead us to suppose the former, in which case this seems to be anomalous by comparison with the standard language. The standard possibilities would be: an impersonal *se* construction (*se conversaba* . . .) or the use of a full lexical subject with indefinite reference (*la gente conversaba/las personas conversaban* . . .).

> **Keypoint: the reflexive** (p. 288)

El clase (l.16) is masculine instead of feminine gender (standard *la clase*).

XVII   Creoles and contact vernaculars

There has been a great deal of debate as to whether creole languages count as varieties of standard languages. The debate takes us back to the questions raised in Chapter 1 about the nature of languages and language names (see p. 3) and need not detain us further than one or two general observations. It is almost certainly the case that the so-called Spanish creoles and contact vernaculars do not derive exclusively from Spanish, and indeed, Papiamentu (see Text 39) was probably mainly Portuguese in origin, while Ermitaño (see Text 40) also owes a good deal to Portuguese. Some linguists are of the opinion that all creoles derive from a common ancestor, possibly a Portuguese pidgin used along the African coast where slaves were assembled for exportation (the monogenesis hypothesis). The relation between these creoles and Spanish is therefore not a straightforward genealogical one so much as a relation which consists of the extensive incorporation of Spanish words into a stripped-down Romance structural framework. It is also apparent that both Papiamentu and Ermitaño are in some respects typologically quite different from Spanish, especially with regard to their basic morphological characteristics.

Nevertheless, Spanish creoles and contact vernaculars are an important part of the study of the history of Spanish for a number of reasons. First of all, contact with Spanish plays an important part in their history, and while structurally different from Spanish in many respects, they do at the same time resemble Spanish in their vocabulary and basic syntax more than they resemble any other language. Second, creoles are an important element in the linguistic composition of a number of areas of the former Spanish empire. Lastly, and perhaps most intriguingly, it may be that the formation of creoles has something to teach us about the evolution of language in general: the bioprogramme hypothesis, developed especially by Bickerton (1981), attributes the strikingly similar developments in creoles to natural, universal evolutionary processes in language, which take place at a faster rate in the development of a creole (see also 39.1.3).

39 Papiamentu (1928)

39.0.1 Curaçao, off the Venezuelan coast, was discovered in 1499 and incorporated into the Spanish empire, the entire Indian native population being deported to Hispaniola in 1515. It was a refuge for Sephardic Jews following their expulsion from Portugal at the end of the fifteenth century. It was of great strategic importance as a port: in 1634 it was conquered by the Dutch, who imported African negro slaves from 1648 onwards, and the island was in fact to become the centre of the Portuguese slave trade. It changed hands during the Napoleonic Wars, but eventually reverted to Holland. The linguistic situation is complex: Dutch is the official language, though Papiamentu is the common language of communication and has been enouraged by the Roman Catholic Church, and education is in Dutch or Spanish. Curaçao's importance as a port near the Panama Canal and its growing tourist industry mean that it is open to many influences.

39.0.2 Papiamentu is probably most accurately described as being in origin a Portuguese creole, and Portuguese features will be very apparent in Text 39 (e.g. the form **na** < Ptg. *na* ‖ Sp. *en la*). This is the consequence of the development by African slaves, whose native languages were mutually incomprehensible, of a Portuguese pidgin as a system of communication between themselves; this pidgin was then learnt by succeeding generations and became the native language of the negro community, and it is at this point that we can speak of its becoming a creole. Dutch, the official language, has provided a number of loanwords (e.g. **fervónder** < Du. *verwonderd* ‘astonished’), as has Spanish, the language of the nearby South American mainland (see 39.3.2 below). Since the beginning of the nineteenth century, Spanish has increasingly been used as a model, especially to supply higher register vocabulary, and a process of decreolisation is therefore occurring, with Papiamentu increasingly resembling Spanish in certain respects. It is important to remember in this connection that most speakers of Papiamentu are in fact polyglot, speaking at least Spanish and Dutch as well.

39.0.3 Papiamentu has the reputation of being a ‘simple’ language. We must be wary of such a label, though it reflects a number of very interesting features of creole languages which may be relevant to our study of the linguistic evolution in general. On the one hand, by ‘simplicity’, we may mean absence of structural complexity. As we shall see in the commentaries on the two texts below, it does often seem as if Papiamentu has shorn away some of the distinctions made in Spanish and Portuguese: syllable structure is simpler (39.1.3), inflectional morphology is almost totally absent (39.2.1, 39.2.2, 39.2.4) and even semantic fields may be less well discriminated (39.3.5). An interesting reflection here is whether it is the redundant features of lexicalising languages that are abandoned in creoles: this is particularly apparent in the case of morphological gender, for instance (39.2.1) and even vocabulary. Furthermore, we may ask ourselves whether creoles carry out in an accelerated way the same kinds of simplification that we often see in language change (the Romance languages reduce dramatically the inflectional morphology of Latin, for instance). By ‘simplicity’ we might also have in mind, however, the notion of ‘restricted code’. Papiamentu began its existence no doubt as a kind of common language in which only the necessities of life were expressed; certainly we may imagine that for many years it was a language which only served the needs of everyday oral communication. This is essentially the same situation in which the Romance languages may have existed before their use in written texts of various kinds. We may suppose that as Papiamentu was used for more sophisticated purposes, and especially when it came to be used as a written language and for the expression of written creative literature, its vocabulary and structures extended, especially through imitation of foreign models. This process is reminiscent of what happened in Castilian as it was used for literary and official purposes (see especially Text 10).

The text

The text below is taken from the pioneering 1928 study of the great Chilean linguist Rodolfo (Rudolf) Lenz (Lenz 1928: 264–5). The establishing of the text makes an interesting story. Lenz was travelling by boat from Chile, where he had settled, to his native Germany. The ship put in at Curaçao, and Lenz was naturally fascinated by the phenomenon of Papiamentu. The second cook on board, Natividad Sillie, was a literate native speaker, and on the onward journey Lenz persuaded him to write down letters, songs and stories in Papiamentu. Sillie also spoke Spanish and English, and had been educated in Spanish, which he also wrote. Lenz then converted the text Sillie had given him into a kind of phonetic representation based on Spanish orthography, checking back pronunciations and meanings with the cook. Text 39 is the beginning of the first of two folk-tales. This, then, is the representation of a language which at the time had no written tradition, rather like thirteenth-century Castilian. However, unlike the twelfth- to thirteenth-century texts we have examined, this text is the work of a professional linguist with a linguistic purpose in mind.

Further reading

Bickerton and Escalante (1970); Green (1988); Holm (1988–9); Lenz (1928); Whinnom (1956).

39 A funny thing happened on the way to the fish market. Papiamentu (early twentieth century)

Un dia tabatin un mama ku su yiú; pero nan tabata mashâ pobër. Pero e tata tabata piskadó, i tur dia ku e tata [a] bini fôr di lamâr, e mama ta manda e yiú bai bende piská.

(Enfin ku) un dia e yiú ta pasa ku su bâki di piská i e ta tende un hende ta yam'é. I na ora ku el a hisa su kara na lária, tabata un laréina.   5

(Enfin ku) laréina tabatin un grandi sempatia pa es mucha bendedô di piská; i na e mês tempu laréina a present'é dyes morokóta.

I laréina disi kun-e: «Mira, bon mucha, pa kiku bo ta bende piská?– Tur dia mi ta tendé-bo, ta pasa ku piská, ta grita riba kaya. Hasí-mi fabor di bisa bo mâma i bo pâpa ku mi no kier mirá-bo mas riba kaya ta bende   10 piská; pa motibu ku bo ta un bunita mucha i ku mi mês ta gustá-bo pa mi kâsa kú bo».

(Enfin ku) Yan a bai na su kas i el a bisa su mama i su tata i nan a kit'é fôr di riba kaya. (Enfin ku) despues ku e mama ku e tata a tende lareina, (i) nan no a manda Yan mas na kaya bai bende piská.   15

(Enfin ku) despúes di algún dia laréin'a manda puntra e tata ku e mama pa kâsa ku Yan, e mama i e tata a keda mashâ ferwónder di mira kon la reina por a haya tantu amor pa nan yiú.

Equivalent using standard Spanish forms

Un día había una madre y su hijo; pero eran muy pobres. Pero el padre era pescador, y todos los días que el padre venía fuera de la mar, la madre mandaba al hijo ir a vender pescado.

Un día el hijo pasaba con su cesta de pescado y el oyó (quien) le llamaba. Y ahora que él levantó su cara en el aire, (allí) estaba una reina.

La reina tenía mucha simpatía para el muchacho vendedor de pescado, y en seguida (en el mismo tiempo) la reina le dio diez morocotos.

Y la reina le dijo (habló con él): «Mira, buen muchacho, ¿por qué vendes pescado? Todos los días yo te oigo pasando con pescado, gritando por la calle. Hazme el favor de avisar a tu madre y a tu padre que yo no quiero verte más por la calle vendiendo pescado, porque (por el motivo que) tú eres un bonito muchacho y (yo misma) me gusta mucho casar(me) contigo.»

Yan se fue a su casa y avisó a su madre y a su padre y ellos lo llevaron (quitaron fuera) a (de arriba) la calle. Después que la madre y el padre oyeron a la reina, ellos no mandaron más a Yan a la calle a vender pescado.

Después de algun tiempo (algunos días) la reina mandó a pedir (preguntar) a (con) la madre para casar(se) con Yan; la madre y el padre quedaron muy atónitos de ver (mirar) como la reina podía tener (haber) tanto amor por su hijo.

Translation

Once upon a time there was a mother and son, but they were very poor. The father was a fisherman, and every day when the father came home from the sea, the mother sent her son out to sell the fish.

One day, the son was going along with his basket of fish when he heard someone calling him. And when he looked up, there was a queen.

The queen liked the boy who sold fish very much, and immediately gave him ten morocotos.

And the queen said, 'Look, my fine lad, why are you selling fish? Every day I hear you passing by with the fish, shouting along the street. Please tell your parents that I do not want to see you in the street selling fish any more, because you are a handsome boy and I would like to marry you.'

Yan went home and told his mother and father, and they took him out into the street. When the mother and father heard the queen, they did not send Yan into the street to sell fish any more.

After a time, the queen sent to ask the mother permission to marry Yan, and the mother and father were astonished to see how the queen could love their son so much.

Phonetics and phonology

39.1.1 All tonic vowels tend to be long: Lenz signified length by the circumflex accent only in extreme cases (**lamâr**, 1.2). More recent treatments of Papiamentu generally characterise the language as having a wider range of vowels than Spanish, but it is not clear how many of these represent true phonemic contrasts: **kâsa** (1.12) may be seen as a more emphatic pronunciation for [kasɐ].

Nasalisation of vowels takes place before a nasal consonant: this feature, which is very characteristic of Portuguese, is not explicitly shown in Lenz's representation, though he observes that it occurs regularly; thus we may assume the pronunciations [tẽ(n)de] for **tende** (l.4), [hẽ(n)de] for **hende**, (l.5), etc.

All atonic vowels tend to close, so in this position *a* represents [ɐ], *o* and *u* represent [u] and *e* and *i* represent [ɪ], leading to neutralisation atonically of the oppositions between /o/ and /u/ and between /i/ and /e/, a feature observable in many Latin-American Spanish varieties (see 28.1.3 and 30.1.2). Final vowels are very weakly articulated indeed, so **motibu** (l.11) could be [mᵘtibᵘ]. Lenz uses the letter *ë* to represent [ə], which occurs before final /r/ or /l/, e.g. **pobër** [pobəɾ] (l.1). The final -*a* of a verb is regularly lost altogether when followed by a vowel: thus **yam'é** (l.5) for *yama é*, **larein'a** (l.16) for *lareina a*.

39.1.2 Papiamentu shares with Latin-American Spanish (and with Portuguese) the phenomenon of *seseo* (**disi**, l.8, < Ptg. *dizer*, corresponding to Sp. *decir*; **dyes**, l.7, corresponding to Sp. *diez*) and *yeísmo* (**yam'é**, l.5, corresponding to standard Sp. [ʎam . . .] *llama(r) él*; **kaya**, l.9, corresponding to standard Sp. [kaʎe] *calle*.

/s/ palatalises to [ʃ] before a non-back vowel: thus **mashâ** [maʃa] corresponds to Sp. *(de)masia(do)* (l.1).

Final /n/ is velarised to [ŋ]; as in the case of nasalisation (39.1.1), this is such a regular phenomenon that Lenz's orthography does not represent it explicitly.

/x/ has the weakened pronunciation [h] (**hende**, l.4 || standard Sp. *gente* [xente]); this feature is shared with many areas of Latin-American Spanish (see Chapter XII introduction).

The absence of a distinction between /b/ and /β/ or /v/ is a feature which is shared with Spanish. This may seem unremarkable until we recall the strong Portuguese element in Papiamentu (Portuguese preserves a distinction between /b/ and /v/); Papiamentu has characteristically opted for the 'simpler' phonemic situation.

Keypoint: the 'b/v' merger (p. 262).

Tur (l.2) || standard Sp. *todo* is evidence of the neutralisation of the opposition between /d/ and /ɾ/ in intervocalic position. This is a feature strongly associated with speakers of black African origin and is present in *palenquero* and early examples of negro speech (37.1.2), as well as in present-day Guinean Spanish (see 38.1.1); it is probably due to the absence of alveolar trills and flaps in several West African languages, though we must also bear in mind that intervocalic /d/ and /ɾ/ undergo weakening in many varieties of Spanish.

39.1.3 The preferred syllable structure is Consonant + Vowel (bear in mind that syllables which are orthographically shown as ending in a nasal consonant in fact have a nasal vowel, see 39.1.2). This feature, which is characteristic of many creole languages, is often related to the preference for such a syllable structure in African languages of the Bantu family. This feature may have led to the fall of final /r/ in Papiamentu (**bendedô**, l.6 = Sp. *vendedor*), though this is a loss which has taken place quite extensively elsewhere (see 27.1.4, 28.1.2 and 38.1.1).

There is a tendency to reduce the number of syllables in words to no more than two, as can be seen in the following equivalences:

Papiamentu	Spanish
tende (l.4)	*entender*
mucha (l.6)	*muchacho*
riba (l.9)	*arriba*
puntra (l.15)	*preguntar* (or Ptg. *perguntar*)

However, there are at the same time a number of longer words which more closely correspond to their source: **piskadó** (l.2) || Sp. *pescador*, **sempatia** (l.6) || Sp. *simpatía*, **bunita** (l.11) || Sp. *bonito/a*, **ferwónder** (l.17) || Du. *verwonderd*. Such words may be taken to have been introduced at a more recent stage in the history of Papiamentu, and increase in frequency in higher register (literary) texts. This process is very reminiscent of the borrowing from Latin of learned words by Castilian.

Morphology and syntax

39.2.1 In contrast to the Romance languages, there is no gender distinction in nouns and adjectives in Papiamentu; the singular definite and indefinite articles (*e* and *un* respectively) are also invariable. Thus **un mama** (l.1) || Sp. *una madre*, **un hende** (ll.4–5) || Sp. *una gente* (i.e. *una persona*), **un laréina** (l.5) || Sp. *una reina*, etc.

39.2.2 Plurality is marked by the postposed particle **nan** (see 39.2.5) only where it is not implicit from the context. There is no example of the use of the plural marker in this text since the context is always clear: in **dyes morokóta** (l.7) the numeral conveys plurality and in **tur dia** (ll.8–9) the quantifier **tur**.

39.2.3 The invariable definite article **e** (**e tata**, l.1) alternates with the invariable demonstrative **es** (**es mucha bendedô**, l.6); both are considered to derive from the Ptg. demonstrative *esse* (= Sp. *ese*), bearing in mind that the Portuguese definite article is *o/a*. The exploitation of a shortened form of the demonstrative as a definite article recalls the process by which the definite article category was created in Romance (see 1.2.3), although Papiamentu clearly parallels the structure of Portuguese/Spanish in which the definite article already existed. Apparent instances of the Spanish definite article in **lamâr** (l.2), **laréina** (l.5) and **lária** (l.5) have in fact been lexicalised as part of the noun, a process that occurred extensively with Arabic loanwords in Spanish (see 14.3.1).

The invariable indefinite article is **un**; the form **algún** (**algún dia**, l.16, 'few days') has an exclusively plural meaning.

In summary, the article 'system' of Papiamentu is quite different from that of Spanish:

	Spanish		Papiamentu	
Definite article	*el/la*	*los/las*	**e**	**(-nan)**
Indefinite article	*un/una*	*(unos/unas)*	**un**	**algún**

39.2.4 The Papiamentu verb is invariable, again in contrast to the Romance verb, which is highly inflected for person, tense/aspect and mood. Verbs are stressed on the stem, e.g. **bénde** (= *vender*), **yáma** (= *yamar*), and so resemble the third person singular present of the corresponding Spanish verb, which is arguably the most basic form available. In Papiamentu, person is indicated by nouns or pronouns (see 39.2.5); mood is not distinguished at all. Tense/aspect distinctions are one of the most intriguing features of creole languages, since it appears that a completely new system has emerged from recognisable Romance roots. For Papiamentu, there is a system of verbal prefixes which can be represented as follows:

		Aspect			
		Perfective	*Neutral*	*Imperfective*	*Prospective*
Tense	Non-past	**a kaba**	–	**ta**	**lo**
	Past	**a**	**a**	**taba ta**	**lo a**

The elements in this scheme can be related to Romance as follows:

- **a** derives from the perfect auxiliary *ha*, which was common to Spanish and older Portuguese.
- **kaba** derives from *acaba*, common to both languages (the aspectual value is connected with the periphrastic use of *acabar de* + infinitive).
- **ta** derives from Ptg./Sp. *está*.
- **lo** derives from Ptg. *logo* (cognate with Sp. *luego*), 'then'.

39.2.5 The personal pronouns of Papiamentu have the forms

	Singular	*Plural*
1st person	**mi**	**nos**
2nd person	**bo**	**boso(nan)**
3rd person	**el** (invariable)	**nan** (invariable)

The plural marker **nan**, which we have already encountered in 39.2.2, is of African origin; otherwise the Romance sources of the pronouns are fairly obvious. Since **bo** (< *vos*) is used as a singular, Papiamentu resembles the *voseante* varieties of Latin-American Spanish, though it differs from Spanish in not having a polite/familiar distinction. (*Tú* is used in Papiamentu, but only in a vocative function.)

In contrast to Romance, there are no case or tonic/atonic distinctions made: thus *mi* is both subject (**mi ta tendé-bo**, l.9) and (atonic) object (**hasí-mi**, l.9). 'Subject' pronouns appear to be obligatory in the absence of a full noun or when the verb is coordinate with another verb which has an overt subject, so Papiamentu, unlike both Spanish and Portuguese, is not a pro-drop language; this state of affairs may plausibly be seen as being related to the non-inflectional nature of the verb. Subject and object functions are distinguished by position with respect to the verb, the subject preceding and the object(s) following, as in

English, and so the phenomenon of pronoun cliticisation, which is wellnigh universal in Romance, is absent in Papiamentu.

Keypoint: personal pronouns (p. 284).

39.2.6 The existential verb in Papiamentu is **tin** (< Ptg. *tem*, cognate with Sp. *tiene*); **tabatin** is used in both an existential (l.1) and a possessive sense (l.6), and contrasts with the copula, which in the past is **tabata** (e.g. **tabata . . . pobër** 'they were poor', l.1). A verb of possession is widely used in Romance to form the existential (cf. Ptg. *há*, Sp. *hay* (see 11.2.1), Fr. *il y a*, all deriving from Lat. [HĂBĔO]), though Ptg. *ter* and Sp. *tener*, which came to replace the derivatives of HĂBĔO as the verb of possession, are not generally used in this way. Interestingly, then, the development in Papiamentu restores the earlier situation in which the same lexical item expressed both notions. (The same phenomenon occurs in the Philippines contact vernaculars, though it is unfortunately not exemplified in Text 40.)

39.2.7 Although the prepositions of Papiamentu are recognisably derived from Portuguese/Spanish sources, their functions are often slightly different.

A has been completely lost. Direction is expressed by **pa** (< *para*) or **na** (< Ptg. *na*, see below). The 'personal' *a* of Spanish is totally absent, and so is the use of *a* as an indirect object marker (thus **puntra e tata ku e mama** 'pedir al padre y a la madre'). This suggests that the marking of such case-functions is possibly redundant, and that the appropriate interpretation in fact follows pragmatic likelihood. In complex verbal constructions *pa* is often used: **ta gustá-bo pa mi kâsa kú bo** (ll.11–12).

Ku (< Ptg. *com*, cognate with Sp. *con*) is used as a conjunction (Ptg. *e*, Sp. *y*).

Fôr di (< Ptg. *fora de*, cognate with Sp. *fuera de*) has a weaker meaning, and is often simply the equivalent of Sp./Ptg. *de*.

Na (< Ptg. *na*, a contraction of *em* + *a*, cognate with Sp. *en* + *la*) has the function of Ptg. *em*, Sp. *en* and, as we have seen above, of Ptg./Sp. directional *a*. It has been suggested that this particular form was adopted because of reinforcement by Du. *naar* 'towards' and *na* 'near', 'towards'.

Pa, presumably from Ptg./Sp. *para*, corresponds to both Ptg./Sp. *para* (l.8) and *por* (**pa nan yiú** = *para su hijo*, l.18).

Riba (< *arriba*, which in Spanish atypically follows the noun, e.g. *calle arriba* 'up the street') is used in the sense of *por* (**riba kaya** = *por la calle*, l.9).

39.2.8. Complex verbal constructions often involve simple collocation of verbs, with no complementising preposition. Thus **ta manda . . . bai bende** (ll.2–3) 'sent . . . to go and sell'; **kier mirá . . . ta bende** (l.10) 'want to see . . . selling'. Conversely, however, there is one example where the syntax of Papiamentu is more complex than the corresponding Romance structure: **mi . . . ta gustá-bo pa mi kâsa kú bo** (ll.11–12) (in Spanish, lit. *yo te gusto para yo casar contigo*, i.e. *me gustaría casarme contigo*).

Vocabulary

39.3.1 The Portuguese base of Papiamentu is clear from such words as **fôr** (l.2) < Ptg. *fora* rather than Sp. *fuera*, **bon** (l.8) < Ptg. *bom* rather than Sp. *bueno*, **tempu** (l.7) < Ptg. *tempo* rather than Sp. *tiempo*.

39.3.2 Yet there are also many basic words which must derive from Spanish: **hende** < Sp. *gente* [ˈxente] rather than Ptg. *gente* [ʒẽ(n)tə], **yama** < Sp. *llama* [ˈʎama] rather than Ptg. *chama* [ˈʃɐmɐ], **kier** < Sp. *quier(e)* rather than Ptg. *quer(e)*, **dyes** (l.7) < Sp. *diez* rather than Ptg. *dez*. **Piská** is more likely to derive from Sp. *pescado* since Portuguese does not distinguish, as does Spanish, between *pez* 'live fish' and *pescado* 'caught fish', but uses *peixe* for both; **keda** (l.17) is more likely to derive from Sp. *queda*, which is more commonly used in Spanish, Portuguese preferring *ficar*; **kaya** is from Sp. *calle* (Portuguese uses *rua*). The source of **yiú** is difficult to determine: while the vocalic sequence suggests a *yeísta* development of the [ʎ] of Ptg. *filho* [fiˈʎu], the absence of the initial /f/ suggests an origin in Sp. *hijo* [ˈixo], with weakening of the [x]; this word is also one of the few that have undergone a change in stress.

39.3.3 There are also Dutch loanwords: **bâki** (l.4) < Du. *bakje* 'cup', **ferwónder** < Du. *verwonderd* 'astonished'.

39.3.4 The provenance of **hisa** (l.5) is difficult to trace exactly. Sp. *izar* 'to hoist (a flag)' is a possible candidate; but the word is borrowed in the sixteenth century from Fr. *hisser*, which in its turn is borrowed from Du. *hyssen*. All are used more specifically than Papiamentu **hisa**, which has the general sense of 'to raise', but the adoption of such an 'international' word with its clear nautical currency is not surprising. The origin of **lária** (l.5), though it clearly corresponds to Sp. *aire*, Ptg. *ar*, Fr. *air* and even more exactly to It. *aria*, is similarly difficult to pinpoint.

39.3.5 Some words have undergone slight modification of their meaning by comparison with the lexicalising languages. **Mashâ** < Sp./Ptg. *(de)masia(do)* (l.1, etc.) is used in the sense of 'very' rather than in its original sense of 'too much'. **Presenta** (l.7) appears to have the general meaning of 'to give' or 'to give (as a present)' rather than the specialised meaning of 'to present'; **bisa** (l.13) 'to tell' is similarly different from its source, Sp. *avisar*. **Puntra** (l.16) is here used in the sense of 'to ask for', i.e., as Sp. *pedir* (the distinction between *preguntar* and *pedir* is not made).

40 A Filipina's dream. A Spanish contact vernacular of the Philippines: Ermitaño (1917)

40.0 The situation of Spanish in the Philippines is and was quite different from any other area of the Spanish-speaking world. Though brought under Spanish control in the late sixteenth century, the Philippines were geographically Spain's remotest colony; furthermore, treaties prevented Spain from establishing direct trade routes via the Indian Ocean and so the main contact was indirect, via Acapulco on the Pacific coast of America. As a result, Spanish settlement was never very extensive; the situation was very different from that of the American colonies, where there was from the first a powerful Spanish-speaking presence. Even the Spanish missionaries who preached Catholicism did not propagate Spanish, since their preaching was usually through the medium of the native languages (the Philippines have a great number of native languages, all of the Malayo-Polynesian family – seventy-five was the official number given as recently as 1960 – the most important of which are 'Visayan', which denotes a group of three closely-related languages, and Tagalog). Spain only really began to take an interest in the Philippines after the secession of the American colonies in the early nineteenth century, but by this time, with the greater prosperity brought by the opening of Manila to international trade and with the beginnings of a European-educated middle class, the Philippines had increasing aspirations towards independence of their own. Public education was introduced in the 1860s, but it is estimated that under 20 per cent of the school population could read and write Spanish, and the numbers able to speak it with anything approaching native competence must have been much less. Thus Spanish was much less effectively imposed in the Philippines than latterly in Equatorial Guinea (see Text 38), though the need for a common language was just as great. The Philippines took advantage of the war between Spain and the United States to make a bid for independence, but in 1898, as a result of the war, in which Spain lost all its remaining colonies, it was ceded to the United States. The implantation of a full educational system by the US led to the rapid adoption of English; by 1939 27 per cent of the population could speak English, and the scene was set for English, rather than Spanish, becoming the common language. Since full independence in 1946, despite an early bid by the Spanish-speaking minority to establish Spanish, a form of Tagalog, known as Pilipino, is now in place as the official national language, and this is now spoken as a first or second language by around 50 per cent of the population. But English has continued to expand: it too is spoken by around 50 per cent of the population, and is the language of commerce, politics, government statistics and the media. Today, Spanish is spoken only by a small upper-class group which constitutes less than 3 per cent of the population; it was finally abolished in 1968 as a compulsory school subject.

So far we have been discussing 'Spanish' in the sense of its being a recognisable variety of the standard language; indeed, Manila Spanish is essentially a 'second-stage', nineteenth-century import based on the Peninsular standard. There were in the Philippines, however, a number of localised derivatives of a much earlier Spanish, termed 'contact vernaculars' by Whinnom (1956), which exhibit many of the creole features we can observe in Papiamentu (see Text 39). Two are recorded as still being in existence today, those of Zamboanga and Cavite (see Map 4, p. 255); both are referred to as *chabacano*, though there are differences between them. Although they have their enthusiastic proponents, they are probably doomed to eventual extinction. As in the case of Papiamentu, their origins and history are difficult to establish. There are few written texts available, since they are primarily spoken languages, and the ravages of the war have destroyed even some twentieth-century evidence (most lamentably, the entire files of the Zamboanga City newspaper *El Imparcial*, which ran a daily column in *chabacano*).

Whinnom proposes that the four contact vernaculars he identifies and studies in his 1956 book all stem from an early language of the same kind spoken on the island of Ternate which arose through contact between semi-literate Spanish garrison troops and the native community, who perhaps spoke a Portuguese-Malay pidgin, of whose exact characteristics we cannot be sure (there may be a residue of this in the use of **na** as a preposition, see 40.2.1 below). In the seventeenth century, 200 families from Ternate were evacuated first to the Ermita district of Manila and then to Cavite. Zamboanga probably owes its *chabacano* to

Map 4 The location of Spanish contact vernaculars in the Philippines

Ermitaño or Caviteño troops who provided the garrison there in the seventeenth and early eighteenth century. Davaueño, also known as Abakay Spanish, the fourth contact vernacular, is a version of Zamboangueño spoken by settlers who arrived from Zamboanga in the early twentieth century.

Ermitaño was spoken by some 12,000 people in 1942, but the war destroyed the district, and, effectively, the linguistic community. Textual evidence is therefore all that remains of this particular language, which Whinnom regards as being the closest to the original postulated 'Ternateño'.

The text

The following text, taken from Whinnom (1956: 25 and 117), is from a novel, *Na Maldito Arena*, published in 1917, by Jesús Balmori, one of a number of Filipino writers in Spanish who also cultivated Ermitaño. The phonetic version represents a modern reading by a Manila speaker. There are clearly a good many limitations in using such text as linguistic evidence, though they are ones which will be familiar, and must apply in the same way to literary documents from any period. Balmori cultivates a literary register which presumably was not typical of everyday speech; in particular, his need to express complex concepts may lead him into original constructions which were unknown in speech (see 40.2.6). The phonetic version, similarly, is a reading of a written text rather than spontaneous speech, by a speaker displaced from her linguistic community, and at a distance of 40 years from the date of the written text. Nevertheless, this imperfect evidence of Ermitaño is the only kind of evidence that remains.

Further reading

Whinnom (1954, 1956).

Cuando ya quedá acostao Pelisa, ya rezá ele puelteng-puelte con Dios nuestro Señor ...	['kwando ja ke'ða kɔs'taðo pɛ'lisa, ja rɛ'sa 'pwɛɫtɛŋ 'pwɛɫte kɔn ðjɔs 'nwɛstro sɛ'jnɔʔ
–Señor, Señor Dios mío, no consentí vos con este pobre esclava de vos el aprenta del vida ansina. Llevá vos conmigo, Señor; más ya suprí pol causa de mi culpa el que vos de ordená con mi alma que de suprí ...	sɛ'jnɔr, sɛ'jnɔr djɔs 'mio, no kɔnsɛn'ti βos kɔn 'este 'pobre ɛs'klaβa **5** ðe βos ɛl a'prɛnta ðɛɫ 'βiða n'sina. ʎe'βa βos kɔn'miɣo sɛ'jnɔʔ 'maske su'pri jo pɔχ kawsa ðe mi 'kuɫpa ɛɫ ke βos ðe ɔrðe'na kɔn mi 'aɫma ke ðe su'pri. **10**
Ya quedá ele dolmido aluego. Y ya soñá ele ansina.	ja ke'ða ɛll ðɔɫ'miðº a'lweɣo. i ja sɔ'jna ɛɫ an'sina.
Ele raw ta caminá na olas y el olas no ta sumí con ele.	ɛle raw ta kami'na na 'ɔlas, j ɛl 'ɔlas nɔ ta su'mi kɔn 'ɛle.
–Dónde tú de andá, Pelisa? ... ya gritá con ele su tata.	'ðɔnðe tu ðe an'ða, pɛ'lisa, ja **15** gri'ta kɔn ɛll su 'tata.
Y ele raw ya replicá:	i ɛle raw ja rɛpli'kaʔ
–De salí ya yo con ustedes, tay, polque ese gente de allí con nisós masiao malo el boca, ta pretujá mi corazón como sípit de alimásag na su lengua, ta destrozá el nisós honra.	ðe sa'li ja jo kɔn us'teðes, taj, poɫke 'ese 'hɛnnte ðe a'ʎi kɔni'sos ma'sjaŭ malº ɛɫ 'boka, ta prɛtu'ha mi **20** kɔra'sɔn komo 'sipiᵗ de ali'masaɣ na su 'lɛŋgwa, ta dɛstro'sa ɛɫ 'nisos 'ɔnra.
Y ya agarrá su tay un bolo y ya pelseguí con todo ilós, con todo el gente que si cosa-cosa el que ta visá ... Pero ele, Pelisa, ya proseguí su caminada sobre el olas, distante,	i ja aga'ra su taj um boɫo i ja pɛlsɛ'gi kɔn i'los, kɔn 'toðo ɛɫ 'hɛnnte ke si 'kosa-'kosa ɛɫ ke ta βi'sa ... **25** pɛro 'ele, pɛ'lisa, ja prɔsɛ'gi su kami'nada sɔbr ɛl 'olas, ði'stannte, ði'stannte,

distante, hasta que ya topá su cara na	asta ke ja to'pa su 'kara na
pondo del nubes que ta sostené el mar.	'pɔnnðo ðɛɫ 'nubes ke ta sɔstɛ'ne ɫ maʔ.
Y ya sentí ele na sus ojos un	i ja sɛn'ti 'ɛɫe na sus 'ohos um
puelte resplandor; ta abrí ele bueno	'pwɛɫte resplan'ðɔr, ja a'bri 'ɛɫe bwɛnᵒ
el ojos; ya despertá ele de un vez.	ɛl 'ɔhos, ja dɛspɛr'ta ð um bɛs.]

30

Translation

When Pelisa went to bed, she prayed very fervently to God our Lord . . .

'Lord, Lord my God, do not allow this your poor servant the insult of such a life. Take me, Lord; I have suffered for my mistake more than you would have my soul suffer . . .'

Then she fell asleep. And she dreamt in this way.

She (according to the story) was walking on the waves and the waves were not drowning her.

'Where are you going, Pelisa?' her father called to her.

And she (according to the story) replied:

'I should have gone with you (pl.), Dad, because the people there say very evil things about us; my heart is oppressed as if by a crab's pincers in their tongues; our honour is being destroyed . . .'

And her Dad took a knife and went after them all, anybody at all that he saw . . . But she, Pelisa, went on her way over the waves, far, far away, until her face touched the bottom of the clouds which are upheld by the sea.

And she felt in her eyes a strong bright light; she was opening her eyes fully; she suddenly woke up.

Phonetics and phonology

40.1.1 Ermitaño has a number of features which are not shared with mainstream Spanish varieties.

The standard Spanish fricative [ð] is generally rendered as [d] in the contact vernaculars, and the reading as [ð] here ([ke'ða], l.1) can be attributed to Spanish influence – in fact, the use of [ð] in initial position, where it would not be used in standard Spanish (['ðɔnde], l.15), is probably a hypercorrection. The only exception to this is the past participle ending -*ado*, which is variously pronounced as [aᵟo] or [aw]; here, despite the spelling **acostao** (l.1), the reading given is [(a)kɔs'taðo]. Similar remarks may be made about the fricatives [ɣ] and [β]: compare [kɔn'miɣo] (l.7) (though [aga'ra], l.23, [pɛlsɛ'gi], l.24) and [es'klaβa] (l.5).

Spanish /f/ is rendered in Ermitaño as [p]: **puelte** (l.2) < Sp. *fuerte*, **aprenta** (l.6) < Sp. *afrenta*, **suprí** (l.8) < Sp. *sufrir*, **pondo** (l.29) < Sp. *fondo*. Tagalog did not originally have /f/, and so we may presume that [p] was the nearest equivalent for Tagalog speakers, with the consequence that this feature of their pronunciation was taken over into the contact vernacular. In Zamboangueño, in fact, the bilabial sound [ɸ] is sometimes found. The fate of /f/ in these languages is particularly interesting in the light of the earlier history in Castilian of the changes which affected Latin initial /f/ and the Basque substrate hypothesis.

Keypoint: the f>h change (p. 271).

There is no distinction between /r/ and /ɾ/, a feature which is shared with Judeo-Spanish, Papiamentu and Guinean Spanish (38.1.1), and is similarly absent in Tagalog. Thus the initial /r/ of **rezá** (l.2) is articulated as a flap [ɾ] (represented in this phonetic transcription by [r]) like the /ɾ/ of **cara** (l.28). Final /r/ is variously realised here as [ɾ] (**resplandor** [resplanˈðɔr], l.31) or, more often, as the glottal stop [ʔ] (**mar** [maʔ], l.29); the former may be an imitation of Spanish, since it occurs in the 'literary' word **resplandor** and in the prayer **Señor, Señor Dios mío** (l.4) which syntactically appears to be a Spanish formula (see 40.2.3). The glottal stop also appears in the base verb form (see 40.2.1) **replicá** [repliˈkaʔ], l.17; this need not be interpreted as an /r/, however, since there is a very general tendency to add a glottal stop to any final vowel. In implosive position, the opposition between /r/ and /l/ is often neutralised, as happens widely in Andalusian (27.1.5) and Latin-American Spanish: **puelte** (< Sp. *fuerte*), l.2, **dolmido** (< Sp. *dormido*), l.11, **polque** (< Sp. *porque*), l.19, etc.

40.1.2 Some features are shared with Andalusian or Latin-American varieties of Spanish.

Seseo is evident here in the pronunciation of **corazón** as [koraˈsɔn] (l.20) and **destrozá** as [dɛstroˈsa] (l.22).

Very noticeable here is the pronunciation of implosive /l/ as the 'dark' (velar) [ł]. This may be due to English influence.

The [x] of Spanish is, as in many varieties, weakened to [h]: **gente** [ˈhɛnnte] (l.19), **pretujá** [pretuˈha] (l.20).

A contrast with most modern varieties of Spanish, however, is the absence of *yeísmo*: thus [ʎ] is articulated as in the most conservative forms of modern Peninsular Spanish in **llevá** [ʎeˈβa] (l.7), **allí** [aˈʎi] (l.19).

40.1.3 The lengthening of some consonants (**gente** [ˈhɛnnte], l.19, **distante** [ðisˈtannte], l.27) presumably reflects a deliberate manner of speech.

40.1.4 By contrast with Papiamentu (39.1.3), there is no significant simplification of syllable types.

Morphology and syntax

40.2.1 Ermitaño exhibits a number of grammatical features which are familiar in type from Papiamentu (Text 39) and apparently typical of creole languages in general.

There are no gender distinctions: **este . . . esclava** (l.5), **el vida** (l.6), etc. This effectively means that determiners and adjectives are invariable for gender, so **el** is the definite article, **un** the unique indefinite article, etc. The third person singular pronoun **ele** corresponds to both Sp. *él* and *ella* (**ya despertá ele** 'she woke up', ll.31–2) and the plural **ilós** to both Sp. *ellos* and *ellas*.

The definite article is also invariable for number: **el olas** (l.13). The possessive adjective does, however, agree in number (**sus ojos**, l.31): this is a distinctive feature of Ermitaño by comparison with the other Philippine Spanish contact vernaculars.

There is no distinctive adverbial inflection (Spanish *-mente*), adjectives being used as adverbs. Neither is there a distinctive adverbial form corresponding to Sp. *bien*, the adjective **bueno** (l.31) being used in this function.

Keypoint: adverbs (p. 262).

There is no distinction between the notions of 'very (much)' and 'too'. Here **masiao** (l.19) (< Sp. *(de)masiado*) has the meaning 'very'; cf. 39.3.5.

The verb system of Ermitaño is completely different from that of standard Spanish, and makes the same kind of aspectual distinctions as does Tagalog. At the same time, it is very striking how a system of much the same kind, and similarly different from standard Spanish, is used in Papiamentu (and, indeed, in many other Romance creoles). The verb is uninflected and is used in a base form which would appear to be the infinitive without the final /r/: **quedá** < Sp. *quedar* (l.1), **sostené** < Sp. *sostener* (l.29), **suprí** < Sp. *sufrir* (l.8). A series of obligatory preposed particles (the verb does not normally stand on its own) express aspect, and, to a certain extent, the Spanish notions of tense and mood. These are **ta** (durative aspect), **ya** (perfective or punctual aspect, closely associated with past tense) and **de** (prospective or contingent aspect, closely associated with future tense and, in Spanish, some uses of the subjunctive). Some examples from the text are:

Ta: this expresses durativity in any tense, so in the present **ta pretujá mi corazón** *lit.* 'my heart is being squeezed' (l.20), and in the past **ta abrí ele bueno el ojos** 'she opened (was opening) her eyes fully' (l.31).

Ya: **ya quedá ele dolmido aluego** 'then she fell asleep' (l.11). This corresponds to the past punctual notion ('what happened next') of the Spanish preterite (*entonces se durmió*).

De: this may be the equivalent of a future notion, as in **dónde tú de andá?** (note that neither English 'where are you going?' nor Spanish '¿Adónde vas? marks the future morphologically). It also expresses a hypothetical notion, as in the complex construction (see 40.2.6) **más ... el que vos de ordená con mi alma que de suprí** 'more than you could have ordered my soul to suffer', and so fulfils here the same role as the Spanish subjunctive: *más de lo que hubieras mandado que sufriera mi alma*.

Ya can also be used postverbally: thus **de salí ya yo con ustedes** (l.18), which appears to mean 'I should have gone with you', i.e. future perfective action.

The etymological origins of these three particles are not difficult to guess. **Ta**, like Papiamentu *ta* (see 39.2.4), must derive from Spanish *está(r)*; **ya** is the adverb *ya* (interestingly used in much the same way as a perfective marker in standard Spanish, though of course with inflected verb-forms, cf. 25.3.1), and **de** presumably derives from the future paraphrase *haber de* + infinitive, which was common in this function in Old Castilian (15.2.5) and continues to have currency in Latin America.

Keypoint: periphrastic verb forms (p. 283).

The prepositional system of Ermitaño makes extensive use of **de** and **na**. The latter, which recalls the *na* of Papiamentu (39.2.7) possibly also derives from Portuguese contraction of *em* and the feminine definite article to *na*; significantly, perhaps, a definite article never follows it in Ermitaño, as if the article were still

felt as part of the prepositional form. **A** has disappeared altogether in prepositional usage with nouns, so **pol causa de** (l.8) has substituted *a causa de*.

   Con is used in Ermitaño as an object marker, rather like the Spanish 'personal
a' (contrast **ya pelseguí con todo ilós**, ll.23–4 and **ya proseguí su caminada**,
ll.26–7). What in standard Spanish is considered an indirect object is also marked
by **con**: **ya gritá con ele su tata** (ll.15–16).

40.2.2 Personal pronouns are relatively simple morphologically, the subject
forms being **yo**, **tú**, **vos**, **ele** (see 40.2.1), **nisós**, **ustedes** and **ilós** (see 40.1.4).
The change of stress in **ilós** and **nisós** is attributable to the influence of
Tagalog, which has many Spanish loanwords in which the stress is changed to
the last syllable in the same way. Like Papiamentu, Ermitaño is not a pro-
drop language, a subject pronoun being obligatory if there is no other subject
present, even in the imperative (**no consentí vos**, ll.4–5); note how the reader
actually inserts a pronoun where it is (probably erroneously) missing in the printed
text (**más ya suprí** but ['maske su'pri jo]. Also like Papiamentu, there is no
cliticisation, the object pronouns being the subject forms preceded by the
objective preposition (see 40.2.1) **con** (**conmigo** and **contigo** survive from Spanish
as the forms corresponding to **yo** and **tú**): thus **llevá vos conmigo** (‖ Sp.
(tú) llévame), ll.6–7. Despite the presence of **tú** and **vos** in the singular, there is
in fact no systematic distinction of formality, and it seems that these two
pronouns (plus **usted**) are used indiscriminately, rather as **tú** and **usted** in
Guinean Spanish (see 38.2.2): in this passage Pelisa addresses God as **vos**, l.5,
while her father addresses her as **tú**, l.15. The plural shows no such distinctions,
however compare the situation in Latin America, where **ustedes** is the unique
plural form.

   Keypoint: personal pronouns (p. 284).

40.2.3 Distinctive possessive adjectives **mi** and **su** exist, and these, like **tu**, have
plurals in **mis**, **tus** and **sus**, but otherwise the personal pronoun form is used:
thus, for example, **nisós** is adjectival in **el nisós honra**, l.22. This example also
shows the use of the definite article, as in older Spanish and several of the
Romance languages (most significantly, perhaps, Portuguese), though such a usage
is not at all common in the contact vernaculars and must be regarded as suspect.
Another way of expressing possession is exemplified in **este pobre esclava de
vos** (ll.5–6). The phrases **Dios nuestro Señor** and **Señor Dios mío** (ll.2–4) are
standard Spanish formulae and to a certain extent may be regarded as an example
of code-switching in the context of prayer.

   Keypoint: possessives (p. 287).

40.2.4 The device of reduplication is observable in **puelteng-puelte** (l.2) and in
cosa-cosa (l.25). In both cases the nuance is one of intensification: 'very fervently'
and 'anything at all' respectively. Though a systematic feature of Tagalog, reduplication is also common in spoken standard Spanish (see also 33.2.7 and Steel
1976: 185). After a high vowel (/i/ or /e/), /ŋ/ is added to the first element of
such reduplication, as is shown by ['pwɛlteŋ 'pwɛlte].

40.2.5 Word order shows a syntactic flexibility similar to that of standard Spanish, with a high incidence of verb-first order in this text, e.g. **Y ya agarrá** (verb) **su tay** (subject) **un bolo** (object) (l.23). The order in the question **Dónde tú de andá?** (l.15) is different from that of standard Spanish, though it is also found in some Caribbean varieties of Spanish (Kany 1951: 125).

40.2.6 The complex comparative construction **más ya suprí pol causa de mi culpa el que vos de ordená con mi alma que de suprí** (ll.7–9) is not typical of a contact vernacular, and may represent a struggle by a literate Spanish-speaking author to represent a complex idea in a spoken medium which would normally avoid such expression or resort to circumlocution. Such examples, are, however, extremely interesting to the historian of the language, since they recall precisely the problems encountered in the early stages of literature in the standard language.

Vocabulary

40.3.1 As is to be expected, there are some Tagalog loanwords in Ermitaño: **sípit** and **alimásag** (l.21) have the same form and meaning in Tagalog. **Tata** (l.16) and the familiar **tay** (l.18) appear to be taken straight from Tagalog *tatay* and *tay*; but at the same time, *tata* is widely used as a familiar word for 'father' in Latin America, and similar forms exist in a number of languages. **Raw** (ll.13 and 17), which appears to be a Tagalog adverb meaning 'it is said', is difficult to render exactly; it seems to be a way of stressing that this is a story.

40.3.2 For **ansina** (ll.6 and 12), see 11.1.11, 33.3.2.

40.3.3 Aluego (l.11) || standard *luego* has a prefixed *a-*, perhaps created by analogy with such adverbs as *afuera* and *abajo*.

40.3.4 The contact vernacular sometimes appears to use the more distinctive term of a set of near synonyms. Here **ordená** (l.9) is used in preference to *mandar*, **agarrá** (l.23) for *coger* (though note the taboo resistance to *coger* in much of Latin America and its widespread substitution there by *agarrar*, see 31.3.1), **visá** (l.25) (possibly < Sp. *divisar*, though *avisar* is also found in this sense in *germanía*, see Chapter XV, introduction) for *ver*.

40.3.5 Bolo (l.23) is of unknown origin.

Keypoints

adverbs

In Classical Latin adverbs of manner were formed from adjective stems synthetically by the addition of a suffix -Ē: thus LENTUS 'slow' → LENTĒ 'slowly'. (Adverbs of time and place were idiosyncratic in their form, e.g. IAM 'already', TUNC 'then', MOX 'soon', HĔRĪ 'yesterday', HĪC 'here', etc.) In Romance the -Ē ending ceased to be used (2.11, 2.13), and it is likely that adjectives were used as manner adverbials without modification – this is still the case systematically in Romanian and partially in spoken registers of other Romance languages, including Spanish (6.2.3, 13.3.5, 21.3.3, 40.2.1). However, synthetic adverb formation is also available in Spanish, and is attested from the earliest texts: in Modern Spanish the suffix -*mente* (often -*mientre* in Old Castilian, see 8.2.8) is added to the feminine form of the adjective. This device derives from the analytic construction provided by the ablative absolute usage of adjective + MENTĒ 'mind' in Latin (Lat. °FĒLĪCĒ MENTĒ *lit.* 'with a happy mind' > Sp. *felizmente* 'in a happy way'). In Old Castilian, a number of adverbs end in -*s* (2.5, 2.8, 4.2.14, 6.3.8, 8.3.5) or in -*re* (8.2.8, 11.1.9); these may be thought of as semiproductive adverbial markers. Modern Spanish also has other analytic adverbial devices available which are semantically akin to Lat. adjective + MENTĒ, such as *de manera* + adjective, *de forma* + adjective (4.3.5).

Temporal and locative adverbs continue to be idiosyncratic and often simply continue the Latin forms (10.2.12, 20.3.2, 25.3.1); a number are the product of synthesised Latin phrases (4.2.2, 9.3.8, 15.3.8), though several have subsequently been replaced by analytic expressions.

the 'b/v' merger

Latin distinguished between /b/ and what may be regarded either as a phoneme /w/ in its own right or as a consonantal allophone [w] of the vocalic phoneme /u/, e.g. ĀMĀBIT /amābit/ '(s)he will love' / ĀMĀVIT /amāwit/ '(s)he has loved'. A number of phonetic changes were to have an impact on this state of affairs:

- The lenition of intervocalic /b/ and /p/ yielded the fricative [β] in Castilian (e.g. FĂBA > *haba* [aβa], CĂPILLOS [CĂPILLUS] > *cabellos* [kaβeʎos]).
- Intervocalic /w/ also became [β]: LĂVAT [LĂVO] > Sp. *lava* [laβa].

- Initial /b/ remained as [b] (BŬCCA > Sp. *boca* [boka]) after a pause or a nasal, and it is to be assumed that this was the case in Old Castilian too.
- Initial /w/ developed in the same way as intervocalic /w/, except that in Modern Spanish it has become indistinguishable from the results of [b] (e.g. VACCA > *vaca* [baka] and *la vaca* [la βaka]).

Since [b] and [β] are in complementary distribution in Modern Spanish, they constitute allophones of a single phoneme /b/. However, as is well known, Spanish orthography makes a distinction between *b* and *v* which is usually based on etymology (thus *viene* [bjene] < VĔNIT [VĔNIO] but *bien* [bjen] < BĚNĔ: see 23.1.1). (This is why we often speak of the 'b/v' merger, though it must be noted that it is unnecessary to assume that the pronunciation [v] was a feature of Old Castilian.)[1]

The question remains as to when exactly these mergers took place. Orthographical distinctions are certainly made in Old Castilian texts, and their interpretation is a matter of great delicacy. Alonso (1949 and 1962) detected some consistency in the use of *b* for the result of intervocalic Lat. /p/ and of *u* or *v* for the result of Lat. /w/ and intervocalic /b/ (see 10.2.1), which suggested the maintenance of a phonemic opposition as late as the fifteenth century; but, as can be seen (1.1.6, 2.8, 3.1.3, 7.1.6, 12.1.1), this is far from being an infallible principle, especially in the pre-Alfonsine period. On the other hand, if there was a phonemic contrast between two such similar elements as /b/ and ?/β/, especially when [β] is likely also to have been an allophone of /b/, some variation in scribal practice is understandable.

Further reading

Alonso (1962); Martínez Gil (1998); Penny (1976).

the case-system of Latin

The main cases distinguished in Latin, and their principal functions, were:

Nominative: the case of the subject of the verb and the complement of copular verbs.

Accusative: the case of the direct object of the verb. It also carried the meaning of 'motion towards' (allative) with certain appropriate nouns, such as placenames.

Genitive: the case which indicated possession or some other associative feature of another noun. It also expressed a partitive notion (GRĀNUM SĂLIS 'a grain of salt') and participated in many kinds of nominalisation (e.g. ĂMOR PATRĬAE 'love of the fatherland').

Dative: the case of the indirect object of the verb, with roughly the same range of functions as are expressed by the indirect object in Spanish, such as 'possession' and 'interest'.

Ablative: the case of the agent of a passive verb (see **Keypoint: the passive**), the case denoting an 'instrument' and the case used after many prepositions. It was

---

1 This indeed may now be taken as the 'standard' view, though powerful arguments in favour of the presence of [v] as the development of Lat. /w/ are given in Martínez Gil (1998).

also used in a construction known as the ablative absolute, which expressed a wide range of adverbial notions, e.g. CAESĀRĒ PRŌFECTŌ 'Caesar having set out'/'when Caesar had set out'.

Not all five cases were formally distinguished for every noun, though they were distinguished across the noun system taken as a whole.[2] There were also two other cases which were more sporadically distinguished, but which are usually identified in Latin grammar: the vocative (regularly distinguished only in second declension masculine singular nouns), which was the case of address, and the locative (distinguished only in a very few nouns denoting place).

In Romance texts from the Iberian Peninsula we have no unequivocal evidence of the survival of any of these case-distinctions in nouns (see 3.2.2).

Castilian nouns and adjectives have often been assumed to derive from the Latin accusative form, and this is particularly convincing in the case of the plural, where we can make obvious direct derivations such as *tierras* < TERRĀS and *dueños* < DŎMĬNŌS (though *noches* derives from NOCTĒS, which was both nominative and accusative). As far as the singular is concerned, however, it is probably more accurate to say that the Castilian noun derives from a 'minimum' generalised form of the noun stem plus a 'theme' vowel (/a/ for the typically feminine first declension, /u/~/o/ for the typically masculine/neuter second declension and /e/ for the mixed gender third declension): thus *tierra* < TĔRRA, *dueño* < DŎMĬNU/O and *noche* < NOCTE. It is such forms, at any rate, that are assumed for Latin source nouns in this book, though the usual citation form given in dictionaries of Classical Latin (i.e., the nominative) is also indicated in square brackets to facilitate their consultation, thus TERRA, DŎMĬNU[S], NOCTE [NOX].

clitic pronoun position

The Romance languages have developed a set of personal pronouns which are verbal clitics, i.e., they cannot be used independently but must stand with a verb. In standard Modern Spanish the rule for the placement of clitic pronouns is morphologically determined and depends on the kind of verb that is involved: clitics precede a finite verb but follow a non-finite verb or a positive imperative: thus *me vio*, but *verme, viéndome, ¡véame!* (but see 24.2.7). In some finite verb + infinitive or gerund constructions a clitic which pertains to the infinitive or gerund may be moved to accompany the finite verb, a phenomenon sometimes called clitic-climbing, but the basic rule still holds: thus *quería verme* or *me quería ver*, but not **queríame ver*: for examples in Old Castilian see 8.2.6, 21.2.3. The rule for Old Castilian, which must be worked out from a study of textual data, appears to have been more syntactically determined. Before the fifteenth century, clitics never appear in initial position (within this we may include not only sentence-initial position but also initial position after a coordinating conjunction, an intonational break, or, in verse, a caesura). But they may precede a finite verb if other material also precedes it, such as a subject, a negative element or an adverb: thus °*Fuese el conde*, but °*El conde se*

---

2   Five declensions are usually distinguished in traditional Latin grammar; since the fifth declension is small in membership and essentially 'irregular', it is not given here. For the neuters of the 2nd, 3rd and 4th declensions, see **Keypoint: gender**.

fue, °*No se fue el conde*, °*Entonces se fue el conde*. This rule also broadly holds for the gerund (10.2.9, 17.2.3), the infinitive and the imperative (9.2.9, 17.2.3). The future and conditional behave in principle exactly like any other finite verb form with respect to clitics, except that when a clitic follows a future or conditional it is usually placed between the infinitive stem and the inflection (2.6.1, 4.2.15, 6.2.5, 7.2.7, 8.2.11, 9.2.9): thus °*Verme ha mañana* but °*No me verá mañana*, °*Mañana me verá*.[3]

Related Keypoint: future and conditional.

A frequent phenomenon observable in Old Castilian texts is the intercalation of a 'short' adverb between preposed clitic and verb, which is impossible in standard Modern Spanish (see 9.2.10, 10.2.5, 11.2.3).

The order of clitic pronouns vis-à-vis one another appears to undergo little change from the earliest texts.

Further reading

Ramsden (1963).

conditional sentences

Syntactically, conditional sentences consist of two clauses: the protasis, or *if*-clause, which expresses the hypothesis or condition, and the apodosis, which expresses the consequence of the hypothesis or condition. Conditional sentences may be categorised according to their time-reference (past, present or future) and according to whether they are counterfactual (when it is implied that the hypothesis or condition envisaged is not true) or open (when there is no such implication, and the hypothesis or condition may be true or false). The distinction between counterfactual and open is very clear in the present and past; future conditions, by the very nature of the future, cannot be strictly counterfactual, but a distinction is made in the future between conditions which imply that they are unlikely to be true and those which carry no such implication, and for the sake of simplicity we will call the former counterfactual future conditions and the latter open future conditions.

Latin had the following conditional sentence types:

	Future	Present	Past
Open	SĪ HOC SCIT [present], TIBI HOC DĪCET [future] 'If he knows (he may or may not), he will tell you'	SĪ HOC SCIT [present], TIBI HOC DĪCIT [present] 'If he knows (he may or may not), he tells you'	SĪ HOC SCIĒBAT [imperfect], TIBI HOC DĪCEBAT [imperfect] 'If he knew (he may or may not have known), he told you'

---

3 Company Company (1985) argues that this is an over-simplified account of the data.

	Future	*Present*	*Past*
	SĪ HOC FĒCERIT [future perfect]> TIBI HOC DĪCET [future] 'If he does it, he will tell you' (cf. 9.2.2)		
Counterfactual	SĪ HOC SCĬAT [present subjunctive]> TIBI HOC DĪCAT [present subjunctive] 'If he knew (but he won't), he would tell you (e.g. tomorrow)'	SĪ HOC SCIRET [imperfect subjunctive]> TIBI HOC DĪCERET [imperfect subjunctive] 'If he knew (but he doesn't), he would tell you'	SĪ HOC SCI̅SSET [pluperfect subjunctive]> TIBI HOC DĪXISSET [pluperfect subjunctive] 'If he had known (but he didn't), he would have told you'

Spanish undergoes many changes in the sequence of tense in conditional sentences, the main tendencies observable being:

- Symmetry between protasis and apodosis verb-form is generally lost. While a subjunctive is used in counterfactual protases, the apodosis verb is increasingly the new conditional verb-form (see **Keypoint: future and conditional**), and in the course of time, an analogical conditional perfect tense is also formed (it is still rare in the sixteenth century). However, from time to time we can see some restoration of symmetry: in Old Castilian the pattern of using the *-ra* verb form (see **Keypoint: the pluperfects of Old Castilian**) in both the protasis and apodosis of past counterfactual conditionals is attested (20.2.4). This may have been the cause of the reanalysis of the *-ra* form as a subjunctive, in fact.
- The formal distinction between counterfactual present and future conditional sentences is lost. As in Latin, the present tense is used in the protases of both open present and future conditionals. However, in Old Castilian, and later in formal registers, the future subjunctive, the descendant of the Latin future perfect indicative (see **Keypoint: the future subjunctive**), is used in conditional protases with exclusively future reference. It is not easy to say what the exact nuance of meaning of the future subjunctive was, but it is not obviously counterfactual (Pountain 1983: 160–1); the 'counterfactual' future was most clearly expressed by the *-se* subjunctive in the protasis (11.2.12) and later by the *-ra* subjunctive too (28.2.8).
- The imperfect subjunctive in *-se* is used at first in past, present and future counterfactual protases. The *-ra* form then begins to be used in both present and past counterfactual protases. Only as late as the sixteenth century do the analytic pluperfect forms make an appearance, thus formally distinguishing past time-reference on the one hand from present/future on the other.

So great is the variation observable in the expression of counterfactual hypotheses throughout the course of the history of Spanish that it is not possible to give a simple schematic account, but the following table gives an idea of what the system *may* have looked like in the fourteenth century:

	Future	*Present*	*Past*
Open	°*Si lo faze*[present], *contártelo ha*[future] or °*Si lo fiziere*[future subjunctive], *contártelo ha*[future] 'If he does it, he will tell you'	°*Si lo sabe*[present], *cuéntatelo*[present] 'If he knows (he may or may not), he tells you'	°*Si lo sabía/sabié*[imperfect], *contábatelo*[imperfect] 'If he knew (he may or may not have known), he told you'
Counterfactual	°*Si lo supiese*[imperfect subjunctive], *contártelo ía*[conditional] (cf. 11.2.12) 'If he knew (but he won't), he would tell you (e.g. tomorrow)' (but see also 14.2.5)	°*Si lo supiese*[imperfect subjunctive], *contártelo ía*[conditional] 'If he knew (but he doesn't), he would tell you'	°*Si lo supiese*[imperfect subjunctive], *contártelo ía*[conditional] or °*Si lo supiera*[-ra form], *contáratelo*[-ra form] 'If he had known (but he didn't), he would have told you' (cf. 13.2.1)

The modern standard scheme is:

	Future	*Present*	*Past*
Open	*Si lo hace*[present], *te lo contará*[future] 'If he does it, he will tell you'	*Si lo sabe*[present], *te lo cuenta*[present] 'If he knows (he may or may not), he tells you'	*Si lo sabía*[imperfect], *te lo contaba*[imperfect] 'If he knew (he may or may not have known), he told you'
Counterfactual	°*Si lo supiera/supiese*[imperfect subjunctive], *te lo contaría*[conditional] 'If he knew (but he won't), he would tell you (e.g. tomorrow)'	°*Si lo supiera/supiese*[imperfect subjunctive], *te lo contaría*[conditional] 'If he knew (but he doesn't), he would tell you'	°*Si lo hubiera/hubiese sabido*[imperfect subjunctive], *te lo habría contado*[conditional] 'If he had known (but he didn't), he would have told you'

Related keypoints: the future subjunctive; the pluperfects of Old Castilian

consonant groups

Consonant groups were particularly susceptible to assimilation and palatalisation. We must distinguish between primary groups which existed in Latin and secondary groups which were produced by the later syncope of syllables, principally as a result of the reduction of proparoxytones (see **Keypoint: stress**). (Secondary groups are shown with an apostrophe between the consonants to represent the vowel that has undergone syncope.) The main groups affected, and their developments in Castilian, were:

Primary groups:

Initial:

> /pl/-, /kl/-, /fl/- palatalised to /ʎ/- (PLĒNU[S] > *lleno*; CLĀVE [CLĀVIS] > *llave*; FLAMMA > *llama* - but see 10.1.5). For /gl/-, see 13.1.2.
>
> /sk/-, /sp/-, /st/- added a prothetic /e/ (SCŪTU[M] > *escudo*, SPĂTŬLA > *espalda*, STĀRE [STO] > *estar*, cf. 3.1.2).
>
> /kw/- generally becomes /k/- (QUIĒTU[S] > *quedo*), though it survives as /kw/- before /a/ (QUANDO > *cuando*, see 1.1.1).

Intervocalic:

> Geminate consonants were simplified:
>
> -/nn/- palatalises to -/ɲ/- (ANNU[S] > *año*).
>
> -/gn/- (4.1.6, 15.3.3) and -/mn/- (3.1.7, 7.1.4) also follow this pattern, presumably assimilating to ?-/nn/- first: COGNĀTU[S] > *cuñado*, AUTUMNU[S] > *otoño*.
>
> -/ll/- palatalises to -/ʎ/- (CĂBALLU[S] > *caballo*).
>
> -/ss/- simplifies to -/s/- (ĀMĀVISSET [ĂMO] > *amase*) (see also **Keypoint: lenition**).(-/ps/- and -/rs/- presumably assimilate to ?-/ss/- first: ŬRSU[S] > *oso*, ĬPSE > *ese*.)
>
> -/tt/- simplifies to -/t/- (GŬTTA > *gota*).
>
> (-/pt/- presumably assimilates to ?-/t/- first: SĔPTE(M) > *siete*, but see also 13.1.3.)
>
> -/kw/- simplifies to ?-/k/-, and voices (see also **Keypoint: lenition**) to -/g/- (ĂQUĬLA > *águila*), except before /a/, when the group /gw/ is retained (ĂQUA > *agua*).

Palatalisations (see also **Keypoint: palatalisation**):

-/kt/- > -/tʃ/- (NOCTE [NOX] > *noche*).
-/lt/- > -/tʃ/- (after /u/, only a very few instances: MULTU[S] > *mucho*).

Assimilations:

Lenition (see **Keypoint: lenition**):
A voiceless plosive followed by a liquid consonant became voiced, e.g. -/kr/- > -/gr/- (MĂCRU [MĂCER] > *magro*).

A voiced plosive followed by a liquid consonant was sometimes lost, e.g. -/gr/- > -/r/- (PĬGRĬTĬA > *pereza* , though NĬGRU [NĬGER] > *negro*).

Leading to simplification:
-/ns/- presumably assimilates to ?-/s-, which then voices (see **Keypoint: lenition**) to /z/, and subsequently devoices (see **Keypoint: the sibilants of Old Castilian**) to -/s/- (MENSA > *mesa*): see 2.14.8, 3.1.6.
–/mb/– > -/m/- (LUMBU[S] > *lomo*): see 32a.1.4.

Secondary groups:
The group may simply be retained (NĔBŬLA > ?/nɛbla/ > *niebla*) or treated in the same way as the primary groups mentioned above (ŎPĔRA [ŎPUS]> *obra*). However, this is an extremely complex area of change, in which, because of the relatively small numbers of similar examples, 'rules' are often difficult to discern. Only the main types of change observable are given below.

Palatalisations:
-/k'l/- (but see 2.15), -/t'l/- and -/g'l/- became -/ʒ/- and subsequently -/x/- (ŎCŬLU[S] > *ojo*, VĔTŬLU[S] > *viejo*, TĒGŬLA > *teja*) (see **Keypoint: the sibilants of Old Castilian**).

Introduction of a homorganic plosive:
In groups consisting of /m/ or /n/ + a liquid consonant (/l/ or /r/), a homorganic plosive was often introduced between the consonants, presumably to ease the articulation of the group. /m/ was followed by /b/ and /n/ by /d/ (thus HŬMĔRU[S] > *hombro*, ĬNGĔNĔRO > *engendro*, cf. 7.1.5).
In the group -/m'n/- dissimilation of /n/ to /r/ also took place (NŌMĬNE [NŌMEN] > *nombre*): see 4.1.1, 6.1.3, 6.1.4, 7.1.4, 9.1.2, 14.1.1; but also 3.1.7.

Assimilation:
Voiceless plosives became voiced (DĒLĬCĀTU[S] > *delgado*, DŬŎDĔCĬM > ?/doddze/ > OCast. /dodze/ > MSp. *doce*, PLĂCĬTU[S] > ?/pladzdo/ simplified to OCast. /pladzo/ > MSp. *plazo*): cf. 2.15, 3.1.5, 6.1.1.

Some secondary groups were further simplified in modern Spanish. In Old Castilian groups consisting of /b/ or /p/ + plosive, the /b/ or /p/ vocalised to /u/, with varying results, according to the possibility of the creation of a diphthong with the preceding vowel: DĒBĬTA > OCast. /debda/ > MSp. *deuda*, CŬBĬTU[M] > OCast. /kobdo/ > MSp. *codo* (cf. 13.1.3).
Metathesis can be observed as an alternative way of simplifying the articulation of a number of secondary groups, e.g. GĔNĔRU [GĔNER] > *yerno*.
Some of the Latin groups which had been modified by the phonetic changes described above were reintroduced into Castilian via learned borrowings: /gn/ (15.3.3), /kt/, /pt/; they sometimes underwent subsequent semipopular modification (15.1.3, 23.1.2, 28.3.4).
Related keypoints: learned and popular, semilearned and semipopular; lenition; the sibilants of Old Castilian; palatalisation.

the definite article

Like English, all the modern Romance languages have a grammatical category which is usually termed the definite article (Sp. *el, la, los, las*). Its functions vary slightly from language to language, but in every Romance language it is used anaphorically and, especially with an adjective or a relative clause, in a defining function; these are probably its earliest functions (see 1.2.3, 3.2.1).

Latin did not distinguish in the same way between a definite article and the demonstratives. The Romance definite article derives from forms of either ILLE or IPSE, Castilian ultimately preferring the ILLE-based series (see 3.2.1). The anaphoric and defining functions of the Romance article identified above were expressed in Latin by the demonstratives themselves; the anaphoric function is especially associated with the demonstrative IS, which leaves no trace as such in Romance. The Romance definite article is therefore appropriately seen in origin as a 'weak' demonstrative which came to be formally distinguished from the 'full' demonstratives, though the rise in frequency of its usage is less easy to explain; perhaps the increased usage is a consequence of the pursuit of clarity or exaggerated expression in everyday speech.

Related keypoint: demonstratives.

demonstratives

Latin distinguished three demonstratives, used pronominally and adjectivally, which corresponded, very generally speaking, to the first, second and third persons respectively, and are often so designated. Semantically, both Old Castilian and Modern Spanish make a similar three-way distinction, though with forms that look rather different from those of Latin.

We can understand this development as follows. The relatively short Latin demonstratives came to be reinforced by a prefix based on Lat. ECCE 'behold' (the combination of ECCE + ISTE is attested as early as Plautus – see Chapter II) and there was a structural shift of ISTE to 'first person' demonstrative function, the 'second person' demonstrative function being rendered by IPSE, a pronoun which in Latin carried the emphatic meaning of '-self'. HIC, the shortest of the demonstrative forms, may have been replaced by ISTE because of phonetic weakness.

The particular prefix found in Hispano-Romance, *aqu-*, which suggests an intermediate form ?ACCU, has sometimes been explained as deriving from ?ACCE + HU(M), ACCE being a variant form of ECCE and HU(M) a popular form of HUNC, the masculine accusative singular of HĪC. In Old Castilian we can often find evidence of variation between the 'full' forms with *aqu-* and the 'reduced' forms *este* and *ese* (4.2.1, 7.2.2); although the 'full' forms survive until the sixteenth century (20.2.13), it is the 'reduced' forms that eventually become standard in Modern Spanish. *Aquel* is never reduced, however, no doubt because of the by then distinctive role of the definite article *el*, etc., with which it would have coincided.

	'this' (near me)	'that' (of yours, near you)	'that' (pertaining to neither you or me)
Latin	HIC	ISTE	ILLE
	?ACCU ISTE	?ACCU IPSE	?ACCU ILLE
OCast	*(aqu)este*, etc.	*(aqu)ese*, etc.	*aquel*, etc.
MSp	*este*, etc.	*ese*, etc.	*aquel*, etc

Related keypoints: the definite article; gender; *mismo*.

the f>h change

The term 'f>h change' is often used to denote a process which is in fact rather complex. Putting it in the simplest possible way, we may say that Latin initial /f/ is progressively weakened and eventually lost in standard Castilian in popular words, unless the /f/ is followed by a liquid consonant or a back semivowel (/w/). This eventually produces a phoneme split, creating for a time /h/ in addition to /f/, until /h/ is eventually lost. Thus:

Lat.	*MSp.*	
FURNU[S]	*horno* [orno]	
FĂBA	*haba* [aβa]	
but		
FRĀTRE [FRĀTER]	*fraile* [frajle]	(before a liquid consonant)
FLŌRE [FLŌS]	*flor* [flor]	(before a liquid consonant)
FŎCU[S]	*fuego* [fweɣo]	(before [w])
FĂCĬLE [FĂCĬLIS]	*fácil* [faθil]	(learned borrowing)

Statistically, it is difficult to know what the 'rule' is when a /j/ follows the /f/: for example, we have *hiel* [jel] < Lat. FĔL and *hierro* [jero] < Lat. FĔRRU[M] as against *fiesta* [fjesta] < Lat. FĔSTA and *fiero* [fjero] < Lat. FĔRU[S]. The change sometimes also affected /f/ in internal consonant groups, e.g.

SUBFŌMĀRE [SUBFŪMO]	*sahumar* [saumar] (see 14.1.3)
DĒFENSA	*dehesa* [deesa] (see 3.1.6)

The change has many problematic aspects and has aroused much discussion.

Phonetic detail

We cannot be sure of the phonetic detail of the movement of [f] via [h] to zero, but the most obvious assumption is that the labiodental [f] of Latin, if such it was, became first a labial fricative [ɸ], then an aspiration [h] and then disappeared. We can be reasonably sure about the last two stages of the process, since Nebrija's system of spelling, widely adopted in the Golden Age, differentiates between reflexes of the /f/ which was preserved as [f] and the /f/ which was eventually to be dropped altogether: the former generally being spelt as *f* and the latter as *h*.

Moreover, [h] is still preserved in some dialects, notably those of the southwest of Andalusia. However, the reconstruction of earlier stages in the process is problematic. Old Castilian texts generally spell all reflexes of /f/ as *f* (the sporadic use of *h* increasing with time), which gives us little clue as to the actual phonetic value of *f*. We cannot be sure, either, of the exact dating of these changes; it has been persuasively argued (Penny 1990) that there was a distinction between /f/ and /h/ (or ?/ɸ/) even when both were spelt with *f*, and it is certain that by the time of the regular Golden-Age orthographic distinction between *f* and *h*, the *h* was no longer pronounced at all by speakers of the emerging Madrid norm.

How 'regular' is the rule?

There are many apparent exceptions to the rule as stated above, the vast majority of which constitute a failure of the rule to apply in one of the expected contexts, e.g. Lat. FOEDU[S] > *feo*, Lat. FIXU[S] > *fijo*. It is sometimes possible realistically to appeal to 'semilearned influence' to explain those exceptions whose Latin parallels might have remained familiar, such as Lat. FĔSTA > *fiesta*, Lat. FĔBRŬĀRĬU[S] > *febrero*, especially since there are also cases of apparently popular/semilearned doublet developments, such as Lat. FORMA > *horma* 'shoe-last'/*forma* 'form', Lat. FACTA [FĂCĬO] > *hecha* 'done'/*fecha* 'date'; however, not all such explanations are convincing. It may also be that the inconsistent outcome of the rule is due to variation among speakers, weakening being more typical of rural speech.

Why did the change occur?

The f>h change is well known as an example of the explanation of change by appeal to the influence on the development of Latin of a substrate language, in this case Basque (it must be remembered that the Castilian homeland, roughly present-day Cantabria, bordered the Basque country, see Map 1, p. 21). There are indeed, a number of quite persuasive arguments in favour of this. First, there is evidence that Basque in the early Middle Ages had no /f/ phoneme: it may reasonably be assumed, then, that [f] would be a sound that was unfamiliar to Basque learners of Latin and would be likely to be modified, perhaps initially to [ɸ]. Second, there is a similar f>h change in Gascon, a Romance dialect area which bordered the Basque country to the north, where the change is more thoroughgoing and applies in all phonetic contexts. But there are also counter arguments. When Basque speakers adapted Latin words beginning with /f/ as loanwords into their own language, they did not use [ɸ] or [h] but rather a bilabial plosive, e.g. Lat. FĔSTA > Basque *besta*, Lat. FĀGU[S] > Basque *pago*. When, later, they borrowed Castilian words, they succeeded in introducing /f/. Indeed, the supposed difficulties with /f/ are called into question by the survival of /f/ in Castilian at all (we must remember that the f>h change in Castilian is a conditioned, not a thoroughgoing, sound-change). In fact, the movement of [f] to [h] is not an unusual change: it is evidenced in a number of southern Italian dialects (Rohlfs 1966: 206–7) and is widespread in Andalusia and Latin America. It can easily be seen as an example of articulatory weakening which could have happened quite independently and so needs no appeal to substrate influence at all.

Was [f] 'restored'?

The assumption of an intermediate step of [ɸ] in the movement from [f] to [h] is widely accepted by both substratists and non-substratists alike, but if this is so, how is it that [f] exists in modern Spanish? It has been suggested that adstrate influence may be responsible in the shape of the many influential French and Provençal speakers who came to Castile in the twelfth and thirteenth centuries. These speakers, who settled in the towns, would have had difficulty in articulating the unfamiliar [ɸ] sound and might have adapted it to [f], especially in the 'difficult' environments before consonants and the back semivowel [w]. It was in the towns as well that words of learned origin would have found first acceptance in the spoken Castilian of educated speakers (Penny 1972). Perhaps more significantly, French clerics brought to Castile a new way of reading Latin aloud (the system of 'litterae', see Wright 1982: 208–20) through which the labiodental [f] may have become familiar. Such circumstances might have favoured the adoption of [f] more generally, and would plausibly explain the many 'exceptions' to the f>h rule.

Further reading

Jungemann (1955); Martinet (1955: 304–11); Malmberg (1971) [1958]; Penny (1972, 1990).

final *-e*

The final /e/ which we must assume as having been present in a large number of words deriving from Latin, and which continues to be represented in some very early Hispano-Romance texts (cf. 2.6.3, 2.14.5, 5b.1.4) has been very generally lost in Spanish when it was preceded by a single alveolar or dental consonant, e.g. SĀLE [SĀLIS] > *sal*, PĀCE [PAX] > *paz*.

An intriguing feature of the spelling of some early Castilian texts is that final /e/ is sometimes not represented, even in cases where it has survived into the modern language. This is particularly noticeable in the thirteenth century (see 10.1.1); in texts of this period we can observe such forms as:

PARTE [PARS]	*part* (MSp. *parte*)
HOSTE [HOSTIS]	*huest* (MSp. *hueste*)

Such spellings give the impression that final /e/ was lost at this time after a wide range of consonants and consonant clusters, only to be 'restored' at a later date. It is likely that we are seeing here evidence of one variety of Castilian being eventually eclipsed by another, in which the dropping of /e/ was more restricted. In this connection, it is also worth bearing in mind that more extensive /e/-dropping is a feature of the eastern Peninsular dialects (cf. such developments as Cat. *munt, part, host, dolç* and *nit* corresponding to some of the words above).

Further reading

Lapesa (1951 and 1975).

future and conditional

The Latin synthetic future survives nowhere in Romance. Reference to the future can be made in various ways: in Modern Spanish, use of the present tense is one possibility (*Esta noche cenamos a las nueve*); there are also the periphrastic constructions *ir a* + infinitive (*¿Qué me vas a contar?*) and in Latin America *haber de* + infinitive (see **Keypoint: periphrastic verb forms**). Spanish also has a form which, though traditionally called the 'future' tense, is in fact not very frequent in spoken registers of the language except with a modal meaning, especially the epistemic modality of supposition: *Paco lo sabrá* 'Paco will (= must) know.' This has its origin in a periphrastic construction of Latin consisting of the infinitive plus the present tense of the verb HĂBĔO (considerably eroded phonetically): thus SĂPĒRE + HĂBET > *sabrá*. It is likely that this form was always associated with a range of modal meanings, in fact, both deontic and epistemic, although it has usually been seen as the replacement *par excellence* for the Latin synthetic future. A feature of Old Castilian is that a clitic pronoun may in some circumstances be placed between the infinitive and the future or conditional inflection, e.g. *partir nos hemos* (7.2.7) (see **Keypoint: clitic pronoun position**); it is a matter of debate as to whether this is simply a fully synthetic future with a rather oddly infixed pronoun or whether Old Castilian preserved vestiges of an analytic future (Company Company 1985).

The pattern of infinitive + HĂBĔO appears to have provided a model for the creation of the conditional: thus SĂPĒRE + HĂBĒBAT is the origin of the conditional form *sabría*. It is easy enough to see in formal terms how the conditional came into existence; but why was it needed? The conditional is used in two principal syntactic contexts in Spanish: (a) in reported speech to refer to the future in past time and (b) in the apodoses of counterfactual conditional sentences. These were differently constructed in Latin: in reported statements, the accusative and infinitive construction was used, and in reported questions, the subjunctive was obligatory in the subordinate clause; counterfactual conditional sentences employed a subjunctive sequence of tense. The creation of the conditional is thus indissolubly linked to these syntactic changes.

Related keypoints: clitic pronoun position; **conditional sentences**; **future stems**; **periphrastic verb forms**.

future stems

Some variety in future stems is frequently observable in Old Castilian, especially the stems of very common verbs with disyllabic infinitives, which tend to be syncopated in the formation of the future by the loss of the vowel of the infinitive ending. Two principal strategies are employed:

- A resultant consonant group is formed, e.g. MSp. *saber* + *á* → *sabrá* (8.2.5, 11.2.11).
- A new consonant has to be inserted to make the consonant group acceptable, e.g. MSp. *poner* + *á* → *pondrá*; the /d/ is an instance of a homorganic plosive, since, like the preceding /n/, it is an alveolar (19.2.3).

In Old Castilian a third strategy of metathesis is common (*tener* + *á* → *terná*, see 4.2.9, 11.2.11, 19.2.3). In Modern Spanish, perhaps through normative pressure, a number of future stems which were irregular in one of these ways in Old Castilian have been regularised, and are thus more transparent in morphological structure, most notably *deber (deberá)*, which was usually *debrá* in medieval and Golden-Age texts, and is today the only common modal auxiliary verb to be regular in its future.

Related keypoints: clitic pronoun position; future and conditional.

the future subjunctive

The future subjunctive of Old Castilian derived from the future perfect indicative of Latin:

FĒCERŌ	fiziere
FĒCERIS	fizieres
FĒCERIT	fiziere
FĒCERIMUS	fiziéremos
FĒCERITIS	fiziéredes
FĒCERINT	fizieren

Latin made no distinction between present and future in the subjunctive, so the use of a future subjunctive in Castilian poses interesting questions, especially as to how a future perfect indicative came to function as a future subjunctive. The key lies in the use of the future perfect indicative of Latin in the future-referring protases of conditional sentences, e.g. °SĪ HOC FĒCERIT TIBI HOC DĪCET 'If he does it he will tell you' (see **Keypoint: conditional sentences**), which would have been paralleled in Old Castilian by °*Si lo fiziere, dezir te lo ha* (cf. 9.2.2, 22.2.5, 28.2.4). It will be noted that these patterns are in fact associated with open conditionals whereas other subjunctives, both in Latin and Spanish, are associated with counterfactual conditionals; the designation 'subjunctive' is therefore probably inappropriate (though Nebrija, see Text 16, designated it as such). However, in Spanish and Portuguese the conditional protasis usage seems to have encouraged further uses in a number of other subordinate clause types, chiefly future-referring temporal clauses (20.2.8) and future-referring relative clauses (4.2.8, 18.2.10, 21.2.1, 22.2.5, 28.2.4): in Modern Spanish these functions are rendered by the present subjunctive.

Related keypoint: conditional sentences.

gender

Latin distinguished three genders: masculine, feminine and neuter. Neuter nouns had the characteristic of having identical nominative and accusative forms in both the singular and plural, and the nominative and accusative plural ended in /a/; otherwise they were not formally distinct from masculine nouns.

In the evolution of Latin to Castilian, the number of declension types was reduced and a neuter gender ceased to be formally distinguished. Second and fourth declension neuters were generally assimilated to the masculine, e.g. VĪNU[M] (n.) > *vino* (m.), cf. 2.14.7. Third declension neuters were assimilated to either masculine or feminine, and we can even observe ongoing variation in some cases (see below). Some neuter plurals in -A are reanalysed as feminine singulars: thus LIGNA [LIGNUM] > *leña*; a number of such cases produce new semantic oppositions between masculine and feminine, the feminine representing a collective and the masculine an individual notion (*leña* '(fire)wood' as opposed to *leño* 'log').

There are some interesting examples of the further exploitation of gender oppositions in the history of Spanish. The characteristic feminine inflection -*a* is sometimes added to a stem to signal uniquely female reference (hypercharacterisation of gender, see 32a.3.1). Some masculine/feminine pairs seem to be based on relative size, e.g. *rama* 'bough', 'large branch'/*ramo* 'branch' (see in this connection 3.3.5, and, of relatively recent date, 30.3.1). Gender oppositions sometimes seem to arise by chance, however, and there is no regular relation in meaning between masculine and feminine: a well-known example is *moral*, which as a feminine noun means 'morals' and as a masculine means 'mulberry tree' (see also 32a.3.3).

While most words in Spanish remain constant in their gender, some show variation. *Mar* is normally masculine, but is feminine in many set expressions (such as *alta mar*) and is often feminine in the speech of people who depend on the sea for a living. Sometimes semantic discrimination is achieved through gender variation: *orden* (masculine) is 'order' in the sense of 'arrangement' (*orden alfabético*) but *orden* (feminine) is used for 'order' in the sense of 'command' or 'religious order' (see 18.2.5 and 18.3.11).

The Spanish neuter

Within the demonstrative system (including the definite article), Spanish distinguishes not only masculine and feminine but also what is traditionally called a 'neuter' form, thus:

	Masculine	Feminine	Neuter
Definite article	*el*	*la*	*lo*
Demonstratives	*este, ese, aquel*	*esta, esa, aquella*	*esto, eso, aquello*

'Neuter' is in some ways an inappropriate designation: Spanish does not have a neuter category of nouns in this sense. The definite article *lo* is used only with adjectives with a special sense, e.g. *lo interesante* 'what is interesting'; 'the interesting thing about it', and the demonstratives *esto*, etc., never refer to nouns but to ideas or propositions. The phenomenon seems to be present from the earliest Castilian texts (see 2.4.2, 3.2.1, 11.2.8, 15.2.4). *Lo* has also developed the function of an adverb of degree (see 21.2.5).

The development by Spanish of such a limited 'neuter' category poses some interesting questions because such a category is found neither in Latin nor in many other Romance languages.

Related keypoint: the case-system of Latin.

the imperfect endings of Old Castilian

The imperfect endings of Spanish (which are also involved in the formation of the conditional, which was formed from the imperfect of HĂBĔO) derive by a reasonably clear series of phonetic changes from those of Latin. However, in Old Castilian, there is abundant textual evidence of a variant development in *-er/-ir* verbs and the conditional based on the sequence /ié/ (10.2.13), which seems to have had its heyday in the thirteenth century. The development of the /ié/ ending presents a number of intriguing problems:

- What could the source of the /ié/ sequence be?
- The /ié/ sequence is not normally found in the 1st p.sg. (but see 12.2.1), which is always /ía/, making the full paradigm highly irregular.
- The /ié/ ending appears to trigger metaphony in the 3rd p.sg. and pl. of *-ir* verbs in the same way as the preterite endings (thus *durmié(n)* is found in parallel with *durmió*, *durmieron*).

There has been much speculation about these questions: see Penny (1991: 167–9), Lloyd (1987: 361–4) and Malkiel (1959).

learned and popular, semilearned and semipopular

Popular words are those which have been inherited directly from Latin, whereas learned words are those which have been borrowed at a later stage from Latin and have no continuous line of descent; the labels 'popular' and 'learned' are due to the idea that the former are presumed always to have been present in popular speech whereas the latter have been introduced by the cultured strata of society as a result of 'learned' acquaintance with Latin and the classics. Popular and learned words may be expected to have broadly the following characteristics, therefore:

Popular
- have undergone all the sound changes expected
- are used in everyday speech
- denote basic, everyday notions

Learned
- are minimally adapted from Latin
- are more typical of written, educated language
- are more specialised in meaning and often introduce more subtle semantic discrimination

However, most words are not so easy to categorise in this way. It can also quickly be seen that many 'learned' words are very common in all registers of Spanish today (see 25.3.3), although it is probably the case that the incidence of such words increases with the formality of the register, and some seem to have passed very quickly into common usage (9.3.11, 11.3.12). And since the period of 'learned' borrowing probably antedates even the oldest 'Romance' texts, antiquity of attestation is no guarantee of the popular nature of a word (see 9.0).

A number of words which are otherwise 'popular' in nature exhibit irregularity in their phonetic development (see 7.1.2). The term 'semilearned' has sometimes been used to label such irregular changes, the hypothesis being that learned influence somehow retards or interferes with the normal processes of phonetic evolution. Indeed, in some cases, this is a very plausible explanation: the word *espíritu*, which, despite its 'regular' prothetic /e/ (see **Keypoint: consonant groups**), shows no other change that might be expected (the reduction of the proparoxytone, see **Keypoint: stress**, or the lowering of final /u/ to /o/); however, the association with Lat. SPĪRĬTU[S], familiar from the Latin formula for the Trinity (IN NŌMINĒ PĂTRĬS ET FĪLĬĪ ET SPĪRĬTU SANCTĪ 'in the name of the Father, and of the Son and of the Holy Spirit') must have been extremely strong, and many words associated with Christianity often show such abnormal developments. But the case is much more difficult to make in other instances. The term 'semilearned' is therefore used cautiously in this book.

Another, less problematic, complication that arises in distinguishing learned and popular words is that some words which appear to be 'learned' have undergone popular developments. Learned borrowings often included, even after basic accommodation to the sound pattern of Castilian, sequences which were atypical of the language and thus awkward to pronounce. Sometimes the adjusted pronunciation remained as the standard (e.g. *acento* < Lat. ACCENTU[S] < √CĀNO), and sometimes the learned spelling was restored (see 23.1.2); sometimes variant spellings and pronunciations of such words are visible today, such as *transformar~trasformar*, *examen* pronounced [eksamen] or [esamen]. A convenient, though not commonly used, term for learned words which display such phonetic adjustment is 'semipopular', which I have adopted in this book. Sometimes a doublet development has taken place, the semipopular word having one meaning and the 'restored' word another, as in *respetar* 'to respect' and *respectar* 'to concern'.

Further reading

Wright (1976); Badia (1973).

lenition

In the western Romance-speaking world, the intervocalic plosive consonants of Latin undergo a series of changes which can be characterised as involving articulatory weakening, a process which is often called lenition. These changes are:

- a geminate consonant becomes a single consonant
- a voiceless plosive becomes a voiced fricative
- a voiced plosive becomes either a voiced fricative or disappears altogether (this change appears to be irregular)

They may be conveniently tabulated as follows:

	Bilabial series	*Alveolar–dental series*	*Velar series*
Latin:	pp/p/b	tt/t/d	kk/k/g
Spanish:	p/β/β or ɸ	t/ð/ð or ɸ	k/ɣ/ɣ or ɸ

Examples:

CŬPPA > *copa*	GŬTTA > *gota*	SĬCCU[S] > *seco*
LŬPU[S] > *lobo*	LĀTU[S] > *lado*	MĪCA > *miga*
BĬBĔRE [BĬBO] > *beber*	NĪDU[S] > *nido*	PLĀGA > *llaga*
SA(M)BŪCU[S] > *saúco*	FRĪGĬDU[S] > *frío*	RĒGĀLE [RĒGĀLIS] > *real*

Although it is convenient to group these changes together, weakening of the same kind has affected other consonantal changes in the history of Spanish, and seems to be an ongoing process in the language.

- The Latin geminates were all simplified. An apparent exception, the trill /r/, though a 'long' consonant, is not a geminate in Spanish, since it falls within one syllable only (thus *carro* < Lat. CARRU[S] is syllabified *ca + rro*, not as *car + ro*); furthermore, it occurs obligatorily in initial position, which is an impossible position for a true geminate to occupy (e.g. /roxo/ *rojo*).
- Latin intervocalic /s/ underwent voicing to /z/, though subsequently the opposition between /s/ and /z/ present in the medieval language was neutralised as /s/ (see **Keypoint: the sibilants of Old Castilian**).
- Voicing also takes place within consonantal groups, e.g. the /k(k)/ of Lat. ECCLĒSĬA becomes /g/ in Sp. *iglesia* (3.1.5).
- The intervocalic fricatives of modern Spanish show a marked tendency to weaken, especially in some dialects and in certain contexts. The past participle [aðo] ending is now almost universally pronounced [ao] or even [aw], and in Andalusia and much of Latin America the total suppression of [ð] is common (see 27.1.3, 30.1.3, 32a.1.1). [ɣ], [β] and [ɾ] are also liable to weakening to the point of total disappearance.

mismo

MSp. *mismo* (also *mesmo* in Old Castilian and dialectally in Modern Spanish) is generally taken to derive from ?MET IPSĬ(SSĬ)MU[S], a pronominal construction based on the following elements: (a) the pronoun IPSE, which had the emphatic meaning of '-self' in Latin, (b) the superlative inflection -ĬSSĬMU[S], reduced to -IMU[S] (the form IPSĬSSĬMUS is widely attested in Latin), (c) the suffix -MET, which was attached to the personal pronouns in some of their cases for emphasis. Thus we may imagine that ?ĔGOMET IPSĬSSĬMUS would have been a very emphatic way of saying 'I myself' (perhaps in spoken register where such hyperbolic expression is frequent); we suppose that such an expression was then presumably reanalysed as ĒGO METIPSĬ(SSĬ)MU[S] to be the origin of Sp. *yo mismo*.

Mismo also expresses in Spanish (as does the cognate Fr. *même*) the notion of identity ('same'), which is rendered in Latin by another pronoun ĪDEM (formally a combination of the anaphoric pronoun ĬS and the suffix -DEM). These two notions are very close semantically. In Spanish they are distinguished in adjectival use to a certain extent by the position of the adjective (*el mismo hombre* 'the same man'/*el hombre mismo* 'the man himself'), and in pronominal use by stress (thus *el mismo* 'the same one', *él mismo* 'he himself').

monosyllabic verb forms

In Modern Spanish, there are four first person singular present tense verb forms which are stressed on the ending rather than the stem (because they are or originally were monosyllables), *soy* < SUM (7.2.5), *doy* < DO, *voy* < VĂDO (33.2.2) and *estoy* < STO. They also differ from other first person singulars in that in the modern language they end in -*oy* rather than -*o*. The third person form *ha* also develops to *hay* in its existential sense of 'there is/are' (11.2.1).

The origin of these endings in -*y* has aroused much controversy. One explanation is that the Old Castilian adverb *y* 'there' became cliticised to the verb and was reanalysed as part of the verb itself as *y* gave way to the fuller phonetic form *allí* which is the form used in Modern Spanish. This provides a very plausible explanation for *hay*, which is naturally associated with such a locative notion (cf. the continuing presence of the cognate Fr. *y* in Fr. *il y a*), though it is less clear how analogical extension could have taken place to the first person singulars, especially since the other monosyllabic third person singulars (*va* and *da*) and the inflection-stressed *está* have not followed suit. Another explanation is that in the four first-person forms, the context of a following tonic personal pronoun *yo* may have led to reanalysis, *so yo* being reconstrued as *so(y) yo*.

palatalisation

Latin had no consonants which were articulated in the palatal area of the mouth. In the Romance languages, this gap is filled: Old Castilian has the 'new' palatal consonantal phonemes /ʃ/, /ʒ/ and /tʃ/, together with the palatalised consonants /ʎ/ and /ɲ/, as well as /ts/ and /dz/, which had been produced by a process of palatalisation.

Palatalisation is in some instances an obviously assimilatory change in which certain consonants, when in proximity to a front vowel, themselves become palatal or palatalised. One particularly frequent context of such palatalisation is where a consonant is followed by an unstressed front vowel in hiatus, usually referred to as 'yod' by Romance linguists.

In other instances palatalisation takes place without there being any obvious front vowel or yod present. A number of both primary and secondary consonantal groups palatalise in this way (see **Keypoint: consonant groups**). Some commentators speak of a 'secondary yod' being created in such cases.

The following is a list, with examples, of the main palatalisations that took place in Castilian. It is organised in such a way that the sources of the 'new' palatal consonants of Castilian can be identified.

Latin	Castilian	Example
k^{e/i}-	ts > θ	CAELU[M] > *cielo*
-kj-	ts~dz > θ	BRĂCHIU[M] > *brazo* (spelling with ç in Old Castilian suggests /bratso/)
-tj-	ts~dz > θ	RATĬONE [RĂTĬO] > *razón* (spelling with z in Old Castilian suggests /radzon/); PLŬTĔU[M] ≥ *choza* (spelling with ç in Old Castilian suggests /tʃotsa/) (see also 9.3.9)
-k^{e/i}-	dz > θ	DĪCIT [DĪCO] > *dice* (OCast. *dize* /didze/)
-skj-	ts > θ	ASCĬŎLA (√ASCĬA) > *azuela*
pl-	ʎ	PLĒNU[S] > *lleno* (7.1.2)
kl-	ʎ	CLĀMO > *llamo*
fl-	ʎ	FLAMMA > *llama* (10.1.5)
-ll-	ʎ	CĂBALLU[S] > *caballo* (4.1.6, 7.1.6)
-lj-	ʎ > ʒ > x	ĂLIĒNU[S] > *ajeno* (4.1.6, 7.1.1, 9.1.4)
-t'l-	ʔʎ > ʒ > x	VĔTŬLU[S] > *viejo* (OCast. [βjeʒo] > MSp. [bjexo])
-k'l-	ʔʎ > ʒ > x	ŎCŬLU[S] > *ojo* (OCast. [oʒo] > MSp. [oxo]) (2.15, 5c.1.1)
j-	ʒ > x or ɸ	IŎCOR ≥ *juego*; IĂNŬĀRĬU[S] > *enero*
-ks-	ʃ > x	FLUXU[S] > *flojo* (8.1.3, 12.1.1, 20.1.1)
g^{e/i}-	j or ɸ	GĔLU[M] > *hielo* [jelo]; GERMĀNU[S] > *hermano* [ermano]
-g^{e/i}-	j	FŬGIT [FŬGĬO] > *huye*
-gj-	j or ɸ	CORRĬGĬA > *correa*
-dj-	j	ADIŬTO > *ayudo* (1.1.4, 2.15)
-j-	j	CŬIŬ[S] > *cuyo* (/j/ is sometimes lost: PĒIŌR(E) > *peor*)
-nj-	ɲ	SĔNĬORE [SĔNĬOR] > *señor* (4.1.6, 8.1.2)
-gn-	ɲ	COGNĀTU[S] > *cuñado* (4.1.6, 15.3.3)
-nn-	ɲ	ANNU[S] > *año* (8.1.2)
-mn-	ɲ	SŎMNU[S] > *sueño* (3.1.7, 7.1.4)
-kt-	tʃ	NOCTE [NOX] > *noche* (4.1.1, 14.1.1, 15.1.3)
-^ult-	tʃ	MULTU[S] > *mucho* (2.7)

Since these consonants were innovations in Romance and not paralleled in Latin, they posed difficulties for medieval scribes. Below is a table of the equivalences most widely found:

Phoneme	Spelling
/ts/	ç intervocalically, after a consonant and usually initially; z finally.
/dz/	z
/ʃ/	x
/ʒ/	j, i, g, gi
/tʃ/	ch
/ʎ/	ll (sometimes l, especially in earlier texts), li
/ɲ/	nn, ñ (an abbreviation of nn)

the passive

In Latin, the passive is a morphological category of the verb, clearly indicated by a set of very distinctive inflections, the perfect tenses of the passive being, unusually for Latin, formed periphrastically by the past participle plus a form of the verb SUM: the latter is the model which has survived into the Romance languages, though the periphrastic form has been reanalysed so that the time-reference of the verb SUM (|| Sp. *ser*) is the same as when it is used as a freestanding verb (thus Sp. *son amados* means 'they are (being) loved' rather than 'they have been loved', which was the meaning of Lat. ĂMĀTĪ SUNT).

The chief functions of the Latin passive were as follows:

- Passivisation is a convenient way of making the object of the corresponding active verb the topic of the sentence, since it becomes the syntactic subject of the passive verb.
- The passive is a device which is frequently used when it is desired to leave the agent unidentified, since expression of an agent is optional.
- Some intransitive verbs came to be used in the passive in Latin to express the notion of an indefinite subject, e.g. ĪTUR 'someone goes'.
- Sometimes the passive was a purely formal category in Latin. Deponent verbs, e.g. LŎQUOR 'to speak', were entirely passive in form though not passive in meaning in any of the above ways, and semi-deponent verbs, e.g. AUDĔŌ, AUSUS SUM 'to dare', were similarly passive in their perfective forms only.

In modern spoken Spanish the *ser* + past participle construction is relatively rarely used and is more typical of written registers of the language. The reflexive is a more versatile inheritor of the above passive functions; not only does it function as a passive, but it has also come to be used in Spanish to express an indefinite subject, with both transitive and intransitive verbs. It is also, like the Latin passive, sometimes nothing more than a formal verbal category, as in the obligatorily reflexive verb *arrepentirse* 'to repent' (see **Keypoint: the reflexive**). However, the reflexive is restricted as a passive in two important ways. First, it cannot freely take an agentive phrase (and some purist authorities today would say it never can do so) and it certainly cannot be used if the involvement of an agent, even if not explicitly present, is necessarily implied. Thus a sentence such as **América se descubrió (por Cristóbal Colón) en 1492* is unacceptable: the discovery of America necessarily implies a discoverer (but see 12.2.9, 16.2.1). Second, since the reflexive has a large number of different functions in Spanish, a meaning other than the 'passive' sometimes takes priority: thus *Juan se afeitó* means 'John shaved (himself)' rather than 'John was shaved'.

Moreover, *ser* is only one of the passive auxiliaries available in Spanish; other verbs available are *estar* (22.2.4), *andar*, *ir* (21.2.2) and *venir*. Each of these verbs has a different aspectual value, which is often difficult to render adequately in English translation.

Related keypoints: periphrastic verb-forms; reflexive; *ser* and *estar*.

the perfect

The paraphrase consisting of Lat. HĂBĔO + past participle formed an analytic perfect tense with transitive verbs in Romance. Its origin lies in the expression of literal possession by HABĔO, with the past participle acting as an adjective qualifying the direct object, so that Lat. °HĂBĔO LITTĔRĀS SCRIPTĀS would have meant 'I have the letters (here), written'. Implicit in this construction was the notion of completion of an activity (perfective aspect), i.e., 'I have got the letters written', and this is the basis for the Romance perfect verb form. With intransitive verbs a parallel construction involving the verb 'to be' (SUM + past participle) developed. Here the past participle, again originally adjectival, agreed with the subject of the verb, so °SYLVĬA INTRĀTA EST would have meant literally 'Sylvia is in a state of having entered', similarly expressing perfective aspect, i.e. 'Sylvia has entered'.

Modern Spanish has completely grammaticalised the *haber* + past participle construction. *Haber* is now used as the perfect auxiliary for all verbs, whether transitive or intransitive, so we have both *he escrito las cartas* and *Silvia ha entrado*. The past participle does not agree in either case, but is invariably masculine singular. The verb *haber* has ceased to have full lexical meaning as a verb of possession (having been replaced in this function by *tener* < Lat. [TĔNĔO]). In Old Castilian, however, remnants of the situation described above can be observed. Many intransitive verbs have *ser* as their perfect auxiliary (cf. 4.2.5) and their intransitive past participles usually agree with the subject; the transitive past participles of verbs conjugated with *haber* sometimes agree with the direct object (cf. 4.2.4, 6.2.4, 8.2.10); *haber* has full lexical meaning as a verb of possession.

Related keypoints: periphrastic verb forms; **the pluperfects of Old Castilian**.

periphrastic verb forms

Several universally used Romance verb-forms have developed from periphrastic constructions (see **Keypoints: future and conditional**; **the perfect**), but Spanish is particularly rich in other verbal paraphrases which have often quite subtle semantic nuances.

Haber de + infinitive was frequent in Old Castilian and in the Golden Age as a future-referring form (15.2.5), though it also retained deontic modal nuances of obligation or commitment (20.2.12, 22.2.8). The use of *haber* in this way recalls the Latin paraphrase that was the origin of the Romance inflected future. It survives strongly in both these functions in Latin America (Kany 1951: 152–5 and 28.2.6), where it can also express epistemic modality (*¿Ha de ser posible?* = Pen. *¿Será posible?* 'Can it be possible?'), and the inflected future is used correspondingly less than in the Peninsula. In Peninsular Spanish, *haber de* + infinitive is nowadays restricted to literary usage; deontic modality is expressed by *tener que* + infinitive (formerly *tener de*, see 13.2.5, 17.2.6; also 9.2.8) and epistemic modality by the inflected future; future reference is expressed periphrastically by *ir a* + infinitive (also available in Latin America), formerly without the preposition *a* (see 21.2.2, 33.2.1).

Among the other verbal paraphrases available in Modern Spanish are *estar para* + infinitive (future), *acabar de* + infinitive, *tener* and *llevar* + past participle (past), *estar*, *ir* and *llevar* + gerund (continuous: cf. 6.2.2), *soler* + infinitive (habitual: cf. also 18.2.6). See also **Keypoint: the passive**.

'personal' *a*

In Modern Spanish, some, but not all, direct objects are marked by the preposition *a*. The designation 'personal *a*' is due to the fact that in a large number of cases, *a* is used with direct objects which refer to persons or other nouns (pets, cities, abstract concepts) which can be viewed as person-like or 'personified' in some way. The use of the 'personal' *a* of modern Spanish is not reducible to such a straightforward semantic principle, however. It also serves to denote a particular individual as opposed to someone hitherto unidentified, so that there is a contrast between *Busco una secretaria* and *Busco a una secretaria*: when the personal *a* is used it indicates that I am looking for a particular secretary, a person whose identity I already know. The 'personal' *a* is also related to the 'strength' of the verb (this is what Kliffer 1984 calls 'kinesis'): there is a contrast between *Tengo un hermano*, which indicates nothing more than a relationship of possession, and *Tengo a mi hermano en casa*, in which *tener* has a clear effect on *mi hermano*: 'I'm keeping my brother at home' (cf. 7.3.8). At the same time, the 'personal' *a* seems to be used in a disambiguating function: the difference between *el alumno que vio el profesor* and *el alumno que vio al profesor* is precisely that *el profesor* is the subject of *vio* in the first phrase and its object in the second (cf. 7.2.11). It is particularly used with verbs which denote a relation of precedence or order between two like nouns, e.g. *jueves sigue a miércoles* (cf. 16.2.2).

The history of the 'personal' *a* has been approached from both a semantic and a syntactic point of view. In its earliest use, it seems to be primarily semantically motivated, and to be a marker of respect or deference (see Hatcher 1942; Ramsden 1961 and examples in 7.2.10). Its use in a disambiguating role has been related to the relatively 'free' word order of Spanish, since marking with *a* allows freedom of movement to the direct object of the sentence without compromising the signalling of object case-function.[4] Since the incidence of 'personal' *a* increases steadily from the times of the earliest Castilian texts onwards, careful textual study allows us to chart its use and to assess such explanations.

Further reading

Contreras (1978); Green (1977); Harris (1978:19–20); Hatcher (1942); Kliffer (1984); Ramsden (1961).

personal pronouns

Although elaborate rules have sometimes been given to account for the phonetic developments of Latin personal pronouns to the modern Romance forms, it is perhaps more appropriate to think of their development as the emergence of a limited number of phonetically distinctive forms which were based on the opposition between /o/, /a/ and /e/, and which formed a new kind of system in Romance. For example, although phonetically *me* can be derived from MĒ (accusative) and *mí* from MIHI (dative), *me* has both a direct or indirect object function (corresponding to both Latin accusative and dative), and the characteristic function of *mí* as a prepositional object form is not obviously associable with the Latin dative,

---

4 Harris (1978: 19–20), Green (1977: 26). A measure of the acceptance of this view is its uncritical adoption by Penny (1991: 102–3). In a later article, however, Green (1988: 114–5) suggests that the characteristic 'freedom' of Spanish word order is attributable to the possibility of moving the grammatical subject, VO order remaining relatively firmly fixed.

since the majority of prepositions in Latin took the ablative or the accusative. Spanish in fact offers interesting evidence of ongoing category-shifting, there being much variation today in the uses of *lo*, *la* and *le*. *Le* is often used as a direct object pronoun (*leísmo*, see 10.2.7, 12.2.1, 20.2.10, 24.2.2, 37.2.6); less widely, *la* is sometimes used as a feminine indirect object pronoun (*laísmo*, see 24.2.2).

Tonic and atonic pronouns

In Romance, a distinction emerged between tonic (stressed, disjunctive) and atonic (unstressed, clitic) forms of the personal pronouns. Thus *me*, *te*, *se*, *lo*, *la*, *le*, *los*, *las*, *les* and modern *nos* and *os* are atonic: they cannot receive contrastive stress, and they must always appear with a verb-form, occur in a particular place with respect to the verb, and stand in a particular order if there is more than one of them (see **Keypoint: clitic pronoun position**). *Yo*, *tú*, etc., and the prepositional forms *mí*, *ti*, etc., can receive contrastive stress, and can occur independently of a verb (–*¿Quién lo hizo?* –*Yo*. –*¿A quién se lo dio?* –*A mí*.), see 7.2.8.

Second person forms of address

Another development in Romance is the discrimination of formality within the second person. Two strategies are used to achieve this, both evidenced at different times in Castilian.

•   The use of plural for singular to indicate politeness (*vos* functions as a polite singular form as well as being a plural form in Old Castilian, see also 9.2.1, 12.2.5, 13.2.8, 14.2.3, 18.2.1).
•   The use of third person forms to refer politely to a second person. *Usted* in Spanish derives from the courtesy formula *vuestra merced*, which gained currency in the fifteenth and sixteenth centuries; its corresponding atonic forms are the third person pronouns, see 18.2.1, 20.1.3, 20.2.2, 22.2.1, 24.2.1).

First and second person plural

Distinctive tonic first and second person plural forms (*nosotros* and *vosotros*) developed in the fifteenth century and are now standard in Modern Peninsular Spanish, see 16.2.4, 17.2.1. *Nos* and *vos*, which were not distinguished in this way in Old Castilian, survive as atonic forms only, the latter with the loss of its initial /β/ (see 11.2.2, 29.1.3 and **Keypoint: the 'b/v' merger**).

Voseo

In Latin America, Old Castilian *vos* was completely lost as a second person plural form. In those areas of Latin America which exhibit *voseo*, *vos* survives as a second person singular form, though its corresponding atonic form is *te*; the corresponding verb form is in some areas a derivative of the Old Castilian *vos* form and in others the old *tú* form. Such developments produce a 'mixed' system of second person reference, therefore; see Chapter XII, introduction, 13.2.2, 13.2.8, 18.2.1, 30.2.1, 39.2.5. The second person familiar plural *vosotros* is nowhere used in Latin America and a distinctive second person plural verb form is correspondingly absent.

Further reading

Hodcroft (1994); Líbano Zumalacárregui (1991).

the pluperfects of Old Castilian

Old Castilian was rich in pluperfect tenses. There were two analytic pluperfects formed from the imperfect and preterite of *aver (ser)* + past participle: *avía fecho/era entrado, ovo fecho/fue entrado* (the latter is usually nowadays called the 'past anterior'). But Old Castilian also retained a synthetic pluperfect deriving from the pluperfect of Latin (Lat. FĒCERAT > OCast. *fiziera*), the form that was later to be reanalysed as an imperfect subjunctive (see **Keypoint: conditional sentences**, and 13.2.1, 14.2.5, 20.2.4, 23.2.2). The process of reanalysis is gradual, and it is often difficult to pigeon-hole this verb form into one functional category rather than another: to avoid difficulties of this kind, it is referred to as the '*-ra*' form.

How these three pluperfects were used can only be resolved by close textual study. It is likely that there was a dependency between the tense of the main clause verb and that of the subordinate clause verb, as follows:

Subordinate clause verb	*Main clause verb*
avía fecho	imperfect, conditional (see 6.2.4)
ovo fecho	preterite
fiziera	*-ra*

Further reading

Hermerén (1992); Lunn (1991); Wright (1929).

por and *para*

The modern distribution of *por* and *para* has systematised a semantic distinction in Spanish which was not made in Latin. *Por* appears to have functions of both Lat. PER (associated with movement through, cause, means or manner) and PRŌ (associated with substitution, favour, goal). The first Old Castilian form of modern *para* is *pora* (9.2.5, 10.2.13), which appears to derive from a Latin combination PRŌ AD or PER AD in which the dominant idea was directionality or purpose, although the phonetic detail of this adaptation is far from clear. Eventually *para* encroaches on the semantic area of *por* (see 11.2.6) until it has the domain we see today, a domain which is in fact quite well delimited as pertaining to purpose or destination: *por* continues to be associated with such meaning only in some set usages with verbal complements such as *luchar por* + infinitive, *esforzarse por* + infinitive.

Further reading

Riiho (1979).

possessives

Modern Spanish makes a number of distinctions between tonic (stressed) and atonic (unstressed) forms of the possessive, the latter (*mi(s)*, *tu(s)*, *su(s)*) always being used before a noun and the former (*mío/a(s)*, *tuyo/a(s)*, *suyo/a(s)*) being used after a noun, on their own, or with the definite article to form a prominal expression. Historically, *mi*, etc are phonetically reduced forms of *mío*, etc.

The modern system differs from that of Old Castilian, where we find the forms *mío/a(s)*, *to/a(s)*, and *so(s)* used both before and after the noun, although already the 'reduced' forms *mi*, *tu* and *su* were used exclusively before the noun (6.2.1). Up until the sixteenth century, the definite article was sometimes used with a possessive before the noun (e.g. *las sus fijas*, 7.2.1; see also 8.2.7, 11.2.13). Although it has been suggested (Cano Aguilar 1997: 142) that the use with the article was stylistically marked or emphatic, this is not always self-evident (cf. 8.2.7). The close study of texts may have further insights to yield, but provisionally it seems that usage is perhaps governed by considerations of metre or euphony, or is otherwise free, before the modern distribution becomes established.

The multiple meanings of *su(s)* in Modern Spanish ('his', 'her', 'their', 'your (sg. and pl.)') have probably led to the occasional use with *su(s)* of disambiguating phrases consisting of *de* + personal pronoun, e.g. *su libro de él* (cf. Kany 1951: 47–8 and see 30.2.7).

The tonic adjectival possessives have developed a number of functions in Modern Spanish: (a) in address, e.g. *Muy señor mío*, *amigo mío*, (b) with the indefinite article, to mean 'of mine, etc.', e.g. *un libro tuyo* 'a book of yours' (contrast the expression of this notion in Old Castilian, see 10.2.8), (c) increasingly in prepositional phrases, e.g. *detrás mío = detrás de mí* (this usage is particularly advanced in Latin America, see Kany 1951: 44–6), and (d) what is sometimes described as an 'affective' or 'emphatic' meaning which is difficult to render in English translation (see 28.2.3).

preterite stems

The preterite stem (e.g. *pus-* in *puse*, etc.) is the basis not only of the preterite tense in Spanish but also of the past subjunctive in *-se*, the *-ra* form and, in Old Castilian, of the future subjunctive (see **Keypoint: the future subjunctive**). Preterite stems generally have their origin in the perfect stems of Latin (thus, for the verb *decir*, *dij-* < DĪX-); but they are subject to a great deal of metaphony and analogical change.

- A number of otherwise regular preterites of the *-ir* verb type change /e/ and /o/ in their stem to /i/ and /u/ respectively in the third person singular and plural: *pedir: pidió, pidieron*; *morir: murió, murieron*. Many 'strong' preterite stems (i.e., preterites which are stressed on the stem in the first and third persons singular, e.g. *querer: quise, quiso*) also contain the vowels /i/ or /u/ throughout their preterite paradigm: *dije, hice, quise, satisfice, vine*; *anduve, cupe, estuve, hube, pude, puse, supe, tuve*, plus the *-uje* verbs such as *reduje*. Some of these can be derived by more or less regular sound changes from Latin origins: see 7.2.13, 8.2.1.

- The person/number inflections of many 'strong' preterites are the same, the first and third persons singular being distinct from the 'regular' inflection-stressed preterites (*-e, -o* as opposed to *-é/-i, -ó/-ió*).
- There is evidence that some 'strong' preterites considerably changed their form by analogy. The perfect of Lat. STŌ was STĔTĪ , and this (with metaphony) yields *estide* in some Old Castilian texts. The modern form *estuve*, however, has no identifiable historical origin and is probably formed by analogy with other strong preterites. The verb *andar*, whether deriving from Latin AMBŬLO or AMBĬTO (see 10.1.3, n.11), would have had a regular perfect in Latin, yet it shows the form *andide* in Old Castilian, which is analogical with *estide*, and in Modern Spanish is *anduve*, which is analogical with *estuve* and *tuve*.

the reflexive

In Latin, the reflexive had the following functions:

1   The pronoun, acting as either a direct or indirect object, refers literally to the subject of the verb, and the verb continues to have its usual literal meaning:

SĒ IPSUM AMAT
'He loves himself'

2   The reflexive construction can still be construed as in (1), but it appears to have a conventional, or specialised, meaning in which the verb often seems to be impressionistically weaker than in its other uses, e.g.

RĔCĬPE TĒ AD NŌS (Cicero)
lit: 'Draw yourself back to us', i.e., 'come back'.

3   A middle voice, indicating that something gets done (without envisaging the involvement of an agent), and which it is impossible to interpret literally as in (1) or (2):

MĀLA RŎTUNDA TŌTŌ ANNŌ SERVĀRE SĒ POSSUNT (Palladius)
'Round apples can be kept for the whole year' (it is impossible for apples *lit*. to 'keep themselves')

4   In late Latin, we also find instances of a dative or even an accusative pronoun being used with intransitive verbs; these constructions have no possible literal interpretation:

AMBŬLĀVIMUS NŌBĪS PER HEREMUM (Ant. Placent., Itin., 36)
'We went through the desert'

Spanish preserves all these functions and extends the use of the reflexive still further:

5 The middle voice function has extended to the point of making the reflexive nearly synonymous with the *ser* + past participle passive (see **Keypoint: the passive**). Although there is some puristic resistance to this in the modern language, examples from earlier texts confirm this impression (see, for example, 12.2.9, 16.2.1).

6 Perhaps as the result of a reanalysis of this passive function, the reflexive also comes to be used as an impersonal verb form indicating an indefinite or non-specific subject (19.2.4, 22.2.7).

7 The reflexive may simply add a nuance of meaning to the verb, and in this usage the verb can be either transitive or intransitive (4.2.7, 25.2.10). Historically, this is probably an extension of the dative function in (4) above.

Further reading

Pountain (2000a).

relatives

The Latin relative pronoun showed the same case-distinctions as other nouns and pronouns; Spanish has a number of relative elements (*que*, *quien(es)*, *el que*, etc., *el cual*, etc., plus the adjectival *cuyo*) the usage of which is complex and subject to considerable variation.

- A distinction between subject *qui* and object *que* can be observed in some early texts (see 3.2.2), but it is generally unknown in Castilian from the thirteenth century onwards, *que* being used for both. *Qui* is used with personal reference in some texts, but in Castilian is increasingly rivalled by *quien*, a derivative of the accusative form QUEM (6.2.7, 7.2.4, 8.2.2). By the sixteenth century an analogical plural *quienes* had developed (but see 24.2.6): *quien* and *quienes* were increasingly used for exclusively personal reference, especially as a prepositional case form. Thus a new kind of distinction arose in Spanish.
- The Lat. genitive CŪIŬS was the origin of Sp. *cuyo*, which was reanalysed as an adjective (see 23.2.5).
- The Latin interrogative/relative adjective QUĀLIS also came to function as a relative pronoun, originally with no article (see 2.14.2, 9.2.4). The addition of the article may have been motivated by the need to express gender and number reference in the relative pronoun, which facilitated the use of complex syntax in literary style; similarly, *que* also came to be used with the article (*el que*, *la que*, etc.).

However, in the spoken language *que* is by far the most frequent of the relatives, and is often used on its own where more careful written expression would demand one of the other forms, e.g. with a preposition: contrast spoken *es una mujer que no le gusta el café* with formal *es una mujer a la que/a quien no le gusta el café* (see 12.2.6, 20.2.5).

ser and *estar*

The forms of the Spanish verb *ser* derive variously from the Latin verbs SUM 'to be' and SĔDĔO 'to sit'. Spanish *estar* derives from Lat. STO 'to stand (of a person or thing)', also 'to stay, remain'. The general history of *ser* and *estar* in Spanish can be seen as the encroachment of *estar* on the referential area and functions of *ser*, and much of this process can be traced through examples of usage as recorded in texts.

The main stages of the development of *estar* that can be observed are:

* Associated with the position of animate subjects, with a locative adverb complement. In the modern language, *estar* is used in connection with all types of location, but *ser* persisted for some time in a locative function (4.2.8, 10.2.1), especially for inanimate subjects (12.2.10) and in the meaning of 'to get to a place'. See also 21.3.1.
* Associated with what may be called 'figurative' or 'metaphorical' position, such as states of mind, predicaments, etc. The complement may be a locative adverb or a past participle (12.2.10).
* With a past participle complement, associated with the notion of a state of affairs (but note the continuing use of *ser* in 20.2.5).
* With adjectival complements when the adjective denotes a state of affairs (but *ser* continues to be used with a number of such adjectives into the seventeenth century).
* With adjectival complements to indicate a non-inherent property of the subject.
* With adjectival complements to indicate an impression.

Ser with adjectival complements thus comes to be associated with an inherent property of the subject. Modern Spanish has contrasting examples such as *la pregunta es vacía* 'the question is an empty one = it's an empty sort of question' vs. *el cuarto está vacío* 'the room is empty' (emptiness is not an inherent property of rooms in general).

Further reading

Bouzet (1953); Pountain (2000b); Stengaard (1991b).

the sibilants of Old Castilian

The Old Castilian sibilant system was reduced very substantially in the course of the sixteenth and seventeenth centuries. The data are not straightforward, however: frequent variation in spelling in Old Castilian texts makes the assessment of textual data problematic and betokens some early trends towards merger (see 9.1.8, 12.1.1). The evidence of texts in non-Roman scripts (5b.1.2, 14.1.2) also offers problems of interpretation. Judeo-Spanish (33.1.1, 33.1.2, 34.1.1) is of considerable value and interest because it preserves more of the Old Castilian sibilant oppositions than does any mainstream variety of Modern Spanish, though there have been mergers in Judeo-Spanish too. None the less, it seems clear that

Old Castilian in principle distinguished seven sibilant phonemes, which subsequently underwent merger and change as shown below:

The medieval sibilants

OCast.	ts/dz	s/z	ʃ/ʒ	tʃ
MSp.	θ	s	x	tʃ
Examples:	*braço* /bratso/	*passo* /paso/	*dixo* /diʃo/	
	> *brazo*	> *paso*	> *dijo*	
	fizo /fidzo/	*rosa* /roza/	*muger* /muʒer/	
	> *hizo*	> *rosa*	> *mujer*	

The affricate /tʃ/ remained constant, but the three voiced/voiceless pairs have all developed into voiceless consonants in the modern language. The position of articulation of /ts/ and /dz/ has moved forward from the alveolar area to the dental /θ/ and that of /ʃ/ and /ʒ/ has moved back to the velar /x/. A good deal of controversy surrounds the reasons for this change; but we may conveniently envisage it as involving, on the one hand, the reduction of a phonemic system which was under-utilised (there were relatively few crucial minimal pairs based on the voiced/voiceless sibilant oppositions) and, on the other, the better discrimination of phonemes which were articulatorily very close (indeed, there are many examples of exchanges among these sibilants in the course of the history of the language (see 15.1.4)).

In Andalusia, the process of reduction went a step further with the neutralisation of the opposition between /ts/ and /s/, and between /dz/ and /z/: either as /s/ (*seseo*, see 27.1.1), generally articulated as a coronal [s], like the English [s], rather than the apico-alveolar [ş] of standard Castilian, or as /θ/ (*ceceo*). *Seseo* is also general in Latin America (Chapter XII, introduction, 28.1.1, 29.1.1).

Further reading

Alonso (1967); Lantolf (1979); Martinet (1951–2).

stress

In Latin, word-stress follows a highly predictable pattern in that it is regularly related to syllable structure and vowel length. Words of two syllables were always stressed paroxytonically, that is, with the stress on the penultimate syllable, e.g. MĬSĔR. Words of more than two syllables were stressed on the penultimate syllable if this syllable was 'long', and otherwise on the antepenultimate syllable. A 'long' syllable was one which ended in a long vowel, a diphthong (/aw/, /aj/ or /oj/), two consonants, or a single consonant in implosive position: thus the word DĬSCRĒTŬM consists of a sequence of 'long' + 'long' + 'short' syllables and CŌGĬTŌ of the sequence 'long' + 'short' + 'long'; these two words would be stressed respectively on the penultimate (DĬSCRĒTŬM) and antepenultimate (CŌGĬTŌ). No Latin words of two syllables or more were stressed oxytonically, i.e., on the final syllable.

Spanish differs in type from Latin in a number of ways. First of all, stress is not predictable on the basis of the phonological shape of the word: indeed, we can find the same phonological sequence stressed in a number of different ways to yield different meanings, e.g. *término* 'end (noun)', *termino* 'I finish', *terminó* 'he/she finished'. Second, a Spanish word of more than one syllable can potentially be stressed oxytonically (other examples are *papel, configurar, rubí, canté*), which was an impossible pattern in Latin.

A number of factors account for these changes.

- The loss of distinctive vowel length (see **Keypoint: vowels**) meant that the regular relation between vowel length, syllable length and stress was lost.
- Phonetic erosion, especially the loss of final *-e*, meant that the last syllable of a Latin paroxytone was sometimes lost, leaving an oxytonically stressed word. Thus Lat. MĀIŌRE [MĀIŌR] > Sp. *mayor*. (See **Keypoint: final** *-e*.)
- A large number of proparoxytones underwent syncope of the penultimate syllable, e.g. CŬBĬTU[M] >?/cobdo/ > *codo*. This must have reduced the number of proparoxytones in early Spanish very considerably, and if the process had been thoroughgoing, it might have resulted in a regular stress pattern for Spanish, with any word ending in a vowel being paroxytonically stressed and any word ending in a consonant being oxytonically stressed. However, enough proparoxytones probably survived to keep the pattern available, e.g. FĪCĂTU[M] > *hígado*, ?PARAMU[S][5] > *páramo* (other originally proparoxytonic survivals were such words as HŎSPITĒS [HŎSPES] > *huéspedes* (although erosion of the final *-e* in the singular eventually produced a paroxytone ending in a consonant: *huésped*). The stock of proparoxytonic words was subsequently built up through borrowings, chiefly from Arabic (e.g. Ar. *búnduqa* > Sp. *albóndiga*) and learnedly from Latin (e.g. EXERCĬTU[S] > *ejército*).
- Foreign words tended to be borrowed with their original stress pattern; there is evidence of this already happening in Latin (thus Gk εἴδωλον > Lat. ĪDŌLUM. Arabic once more provides many loanwords which are not stressed in accordance with the Latin stress rule: oxytones with a vocalic ending, such as *jabalí* 'wild boar' < Ar. *ŷabalī* 'mountain (boar)', and paroxytones with a consonantal ending, such as *alférez* 'standard bearer', 'ensign' < Ar. *f(aw)āris* 'horseman', 'rider'. Yet more paroxytones with consonantal endings have latterly been borrowed from English: *túnel, líder*, etc.

vocabulary – change in meaning

(This keypoint covers such a vast area of exemplification in this book that comprehensive reference would be cumbersome. Readers are therefore encouraged to follow up terms in ***bold italic*** in the index.)

This is a very complex area of language change, in which explanations are often highly speculative and unsystematic. Furthermore, in accounting for the history of a particular word or the expression of a particular concept, a number

---

5   This word is attested only in Latin from the north of the Iberian Peninsula and must be a borrowing into Latin from one of the pre-Roman languages of the region.

of factors acting in parallel can usually be identified, so that an individual example rarely relates exclusively to any one phenomenon. The following should be thought of as a guide to the major trends observable.

Vocabulary loss

- A change in the reference of a word may lead to loss if the word is not exploited for other purposes. A number of words pertaining to artefacts in the medieval world are obsolete for this reason in modern Spanish.
- A ***taboo*** concept (e.g. 31.3.1), such as bodily function, sex, death, birth, disability, association with superstition, misfortune, etc., may lead to avoidance of the word which refers to it and its replacement by a ***euphemism*** (e.g. 8.3.6).
- Some losses may be due to ***pruning of a semantic field*** which is, metaphorically speaking, overcharged, or particularly rich in near ***synonyms***. Latin makes a distinction between CRŬOR 'blood flowing from a wound' and SANGUIS 'blood (in general)', whereas in Spanish only *sangre* < SANGUĬNE [SANGUIS] has survived (see also 6.3.4).
- ***Phonetic weakness*** or erosion may lead to the replacement of a word. Very common in the history of Romance vocabulary are instances of words which were replaced by morphologically expanded forms: thus in Spanish Lat. ŎVIS 'sheep' was replaced by the originally diminutive ŎVĬCŬLA to give *oveja* (see also 6.3.9). A number of Spanish verbs derive from Latin verbs to which the ***inchoative suffix*** -ESCO has been added, probably for this reason (see, for example, 7.3.9).
- A much-discussed (and criticised) hypothesis concerning vocabulary loss (and gain) is that of the avoidance of homonymic clash. According to this hypothesis, if a pair of originally different words whose meanings it is important to distinguish would have developed the same form as a result of phonetic change, then one is replaced. The adoption of *cocinar* rather than *cocer* 'to cook', especially in Latin-American Spanish, can be seen as the result of homonymy of the latter with *coser* 'to sew' in *seseante* areas which pronounce both as [koseɾ].

Vocabulary gain

- The appearance of a new concept sometimes results in the appearance of a new word. This can occasion a gain in the number of distinctions made within a semantic field: when Ar. *nāʿūra* 'well with a wheel' is borrowed as Sp. *noria* to label this concept, it does not replace completely Lat. PŬTĔU[S] > Sp. *pozo*, which is the more general word for 'well', 'wellshaft' (cf. also 18.3.7).
- Foreign ***borrowing*** is a major source of lexical gain. The motivation for such borrowing is usually a notion particularly associated in some way with the foreign culture, though this is not always easy to establish: Sp. *blanco* is ultimately a borrowing from Germanic *blank*, which replaced the two Latin words for 'white', ALBUS 'white', 'bright' and CANDĬDUS '(shining) white' (see

5d.3.3). A special case of foreign borrowing is the extensive '***learned***' borrowing from Latin observable in Spanish (see especially 25.3.3). A less obvious form of foreign borrowing is the ***calque*** or use of a native element to model a word or expression taken from a foreign language. *Rascacielos* is a calque of Eng. *skyscraper* (see also 20.2.7). A semantic calque occurs when a native word changes or, more usually, adds to its meaning in parallel with a cognate foreign word; for example, Sp. *estrella* takes on the meaning of 'film star' in parallel with Eng. *star* (cf. 7.3.3).

• ***Morphological derivation*** is the source of much addition to Romance vocabulary. Suffixes are especially favoured (e.g. Sp. *tardanza* 'lateness' is a ***nominalisation*** formed by the addition of *-anza* < Lat. -ANTĬA to the adverb *tarde* < Lat. TARDĒ 'late'), but ***compounds*** (e.g. verb + noun combinations such as *abrelatas* 'tin-opener') are also fairly productive. ***Back-formation*** (e.g. 11.3.6) is the exploitation of a morphemic component not previously used in isolation. Such procedures tend towards greater ***transparency*** in the relation between morphological form and meaning.

• Phonetic motivation in neologism is also possible. ***Onomatopoeic*** creations are those in which the phonetic shape of the word corresponds (sometimes only conventionally) to the sound made by or associated with the activity or thing it denotes, e.g. *zumbar* 'to buzz'. Such sound-symbolism may be more indirect: see 7.3.4 and 10.1.5.

Change in meaning

Words may undergo ***widening of meaning*** without losing their original reference. Latin MŬLĬĔRE [MŬLĬĔR] has the meaning 'woman' while the notion of 'wife' is rendered by UXOR; Spanish *mujer* can denote both these notions (3.0). Conversely, words may be subject to ***restriction of meaning***, adopting a more specific meaning within the general area of their original reference (see, for example, 9.3.3). Change of meaning occurs when in either of these processes the original meaning is no longer perceptible: Sp. *anegar* 'to flood' derives from Lat. ĒNĔCO 'to kill (by torture, especially asphyxia)', which is in origin a reduction in its range of meaning; but it has now lost any association with torture, and does not necessarily imply any fatality.

• A number of changes of meaning seem to be caused by the pursuit of a more striking mode of expression:
  • ***Hyperbole***, or exaggeration (e.g. 6.3.5). As a result of hyperbolical use, some words undergo ***semantic weakening*** (or 'bleaching'), a process especially associated with a number of 'grammatical' words such as auxiliaries and copulas, which in the course of time have lost their full lexical meaning (see 6.3.6); though weakening can affect other words too (e.g. 18.3.10).
  • ***Self-deprecation***: Sp. *casa* 'house' derives from Lat. CĂSA 'hut', 'shack' (see 25.3.2). A consequence of this is sometimes the ***amelioration***, or ***promotion in register*** of a slang word to more generalised use (see 15.3.5).
  • ***Metaphor***: Sp. *esposas* 'handcuffs' was presumably in origin a metaphor for the indissoluble relation of matrimony between two people.

- It is generally considered that change of meaning only takes place when successive stages of the extension or restriction of meaning of a word are associated in some way. Such ***association*** is sometimes easily perceived, but if the word has been through a number of changes, the association can be opaque. Association may be of a number of types:
  - ***Metonymic***, or conceptual, ***association***: Sp. *boca* 'mouth' derives from Lat. BUCCA '(puffed out) cheek', 'mouthful', which partially overlaps referentially with the notion of 'mouth'. Sp. *bermejo* 'red' derives from Lat. VERMĬCŬLU[S] 'little worm', the word also used for the cochineal beetle which produced red dye. Sp. *boda* derives from Lat. VŌTA 'vows', the most significant part of a marriage ceremony (this kind of metonymic association, in which a part refers to the whole, is known as ***synecdoche***). Sometimes the association may be with a ***converse*** meaning (e.g. 20.3.7), a special case of which is ***change of valency*** in verbs (7.3.7).
  - ***Structural association***: An adjective regularly associated with a noun may come to have the meaning of the noun itself. Sp. *manzana* 'apple' is from Lat. (MALA) MATĬANA, a highly prized kind of apple (probably named after Gaius Matius, a well-known horticulturalist). A more complex example is Sp. *misa* 'Mass', which is part of the final dismissal formula of the Mass, ITE, MISSA EST *lit*. 'Go, it [the offering] has been sent.' These are examples of ellipsis, or the omission of part of the original phrase. For another example, see 8.3.8.
  - Change of meaning in verbs may involve a change in valency: *aburrir* 'to bore' is a weak causative counterpart of its Latin etymon [ĂBHORRĔO] 'to shrink back from'.
  - Some associations are ***pragmatic-***, ***social-*** or ***historical-based***. Sp. *estraperlo* 'black market', derives from *Straperlo*, a roulette machine named after its owners, Strauss and Perlo, who introduced it into Spain in the 1930s. The machine was stacked in favour of the banker, and the word widened in meaning to denote fraudulent practice in general.
  - ***Phonetic association*** has also been proposed as a plausible explanation of change (see 22.3.8).

Structural change

Although it is often convenient to think of each word as having its own idiosyncratic semantic history (an approach perpetuated by the usual alphabetical layout of etymological dictionaries), it is sometimes possible to see that movements in lexical meaning within a particular ***semantic field*** may be contingent on one another in much the same way as some phonetic or morphological changes. For particularly clear examples, see 5d.3.4 and 13.3.2.

Further reading

Ernout (1954); Ullmann (1963).

vowels

Classical Latin orthography distinguishes five vowels (A, E, I, O, U), but on the basis of evidence from Latin poetry, the observations of contemporary grammarians and the subsequent history of the vowels in the Romance languages, we know that each of these five vowels could be either long or short, and that these differences in length could have phonemic value: thus there is a contrast in Latin between ŌS 'mouth' and ŎS 'bone' and between DĒCĪDO 'I fall down' and DĒCĪDO 'I cut off'. In common with widespread modern practice, such reconstructed vowel length in Latin is generally shown in this book. In the Romance languages, the number of vowel contrasts was initially reduced as a series of mergers between vowels of similar quality, the net effect of which was to produce a vowel system that no longer relied on length contrasts. In Castilian, the Latin vowels underwent the following general pattern of change:

Latin	Castilian			
	Tonic vowels	Examples	Atonic vowels	Examples
Ī /ī/	/i/	FĪLĬU[S] > *hijo*	/i/	MĪRĀRĪ [MĪROR] ≥ *mirar*
Ĭ /ĭ/	/e/	VĬCE [VĬCIS] > *vez*	/e/	PLĬCĀRE [PLĬCO] > *llegar*
Ē /ē/		PLĒNU[S] > *lleno*		MĒNSŪRĀRE [MĒNSŬRO] > *mesurar*
OE /oj/ (already sometimes written as E in Latin and hence probably undergoing early monophthongisation to /ē/)		POENA > *pena*		FOETĒRE (already FĒTĒRE in Latin) [FĒTĒO] > *heder*
Ĕ /ĕ/ (probably articulated as /ɛ/)	/je/	CĔNTU[M] > *ciento*		FĔRĪRE [FĔRĬO] > *herir*
AE /aj/ (which seems to have monophthongised to /ɛ/)		CAELU[M] > *cielo*		PRAESTĀRE [PRAESTO] > *prestar*
Ă /ă/	/a/	MĂLU[S] > *malo*	/a/	FĂRĪNA > *harina*
Ā /ā/		MĀTRE [MĀTER] > *madre*		CLĀMĀRE [CLĀMO] > *llamar*
Ŏ /ŏ/ (probably articulated as /ɔ/)	/we/	DŎMĬNU[S] > *dueño*		CŎNSTĀRE [CŎNSTO] > *costar*
Ō /ō/	/o/	PLŌRO > *lloro*	/o/	NŌMĬNĀRE [NŌMĬNO] > *nombrar*
Ŭ /ŭ/		BŬCCA > *boca*		SŬPĔRĀRE [SŬPĔRO] > *sobrar*
AU /aw/		AURU[M] > *oro*		AURĬCŬLA [AURIS] > *oreja*
Ū /ū/	/u/	FŪMU[S] > *humo*	/u/	MŪTĀRE [MŪTO] > *mudar*

Castilian emerges from these changes with a five-term vowel system: /i/, /e/, /a/, /o/, /u/, since it is possible to see the diphthongs /je/ and /we/ which derive from Latin /ĕ/ and /ŏ/ respectively as combinations of the vowels /i/ + /e/ and /u/ + /e/. An interesting feature of the Castilian vowel system is that it has the same number of tonic as atonic vowels, although /i/ and /u/ are relatively restricted atonically and are practically absent in final position.

The above must be regarded as a somewhat idealised account, since a number of factors conditioned the development of vowels in Castilian, without, however, changing the structural situation. The most important of these are:

- Tonic vowels were raised (closed) and diphthongisation was blocked before a palatal consonant or consonant + /j/ (we may surmise that /ĕ/ and /ŏ/ were raised respectively to /e/ and /o/ rather than remaining as /ɛ/ and /ɔ/). Thus SPĔCŬLU[M], in which the consonant cluster /kl/ produced by the reduction of proparoxytones evolves to the new palatal consonant /ʒ/ in medieval Castilian, became /espeʒo/ with /e/ rather than /je/; LŬCTA, in which the consonant cluster /kt/ palatalised to /tʃ/, became *lucha* with /u/ rather than /o/.
- A number of contexts appear to cause the reduction of the diphthong /je/ to /i/, e.g.:

    a following implosive /s/ (e.g. VĔSPĔRA > *víspera*, cf. also 21.1.4)
    a following /ʎ/ (e.g. SĔLLA > *silla*)

Texts show much variation with regard to a number of these developments. Thus *cuende* (see 10.1.4) is attested in contrast with the modern *conde*, and variant spellings such as *miior* and *meior* (modern *mejor*) are quite frequent, even within the same document.

Glossary of linguistic terms

(Cross-references to other entries are shown in **bold**.)

ablative   See **Keypoint: the case-system of Latin** (p. 263).

absolute construction   As used in this book, a noun phrase involving a non-finite form of the verb (present or past participle) which carries the meaning of a full clause, e.g. *terminada la sesión = cuando se terminó la sesión*. In Latin, such constructions were marked by the use of the ablative case (see **Keypoint: the case-system of Latin**, p. 263).

accusative   See **Keypoint: the case-system of Latin** (p. 263).

adstrate   Pertaining to the language of a culture which is equivalent in status, e.g. Arabic vis-à-vis Spanish.

adversative   Expressing opposition or contrast.

affective   Expressing an attitude, such as affection or disparagement.

affix   A general term for a bound **morpheme**. An affix may be word-initial (**prefix**), eg. *desafortunado*, word-internal (**infix**), e.g. *cantaría*, or word-final (**suffix**), e.g. *fácilmente*.

affricate   A combination, or coarticulation, of a **plosive** and a **fricative**, e.g. [tʃ].

agent   The performer of a verbal action: in an active sentence, the agent is typically the **subject** of the sentence; in a **passive** sentence, the agent is usually introduced by *by* in English and by *por* in Spanish.

allative   A **case**-function expressing the notion of 'motion towards'.

allophone   A variant form of a **phoneme**. Allophones are in complementary distribution, i.e., they never form **oppositions** with one another.

alveolar   Pertaining to the alveolum, or ridge between the upper teeth and the **palate**.

amelioration   See **Keypoint: vocabulary – change in meaning** (p. 292).

analogy   Parallel development of a form. Analogy is particularly apparent when an irregular form regularises, i.e., develops in parallel with the regular (**productive**) forms of the language.

analytic   Use of periphrastic (see **paraphrase**) rather than inflected forms.

anaphoric   Reference back to an element in the preceding discourse.

antecedent   See **relative clause**.

antonym   An opposite.

apheresis   Removal, or fall (of a sound).

apical   Pertaining to the tip of the tongue. The [ş] of standard Spanish is an apico-alveolar sound.

apocope   The loss of a final sound.

apodosis   The part of a conditional sentence which expresses the consequence: *si tengo dinero <u>compraré el libro</u>*. See **Keypoint: conditional sentences** (p. 265).

apposition   The juxtaposition of two nouns or noun-phrases which have the same syntactic function, e.g. <u>*Valladolid, lugar de nacimiento de Felipe II*</u>.

aspect   Impressionistically, the way in which an action or state is viewed: continuous, repeated, within fixed limits, etc.

aspirate   A sound chiefly consisting of the exhalation of breath, e.g. [h].

assibilation   Articulated as a **sibilant**: /r/ is so articulated (approximating to [z]) in a number of Latin-American varieties of Spanish.

assimilation   Making similar: sounds in close proximity often assimilate features of one another, and this can be an important factor in sound change.

association   Relatedness of meaning, see **Keypoint: vocabulary – change in meaning** (p. 292).

assonance   A rhyme based on correspondence of vowels alone, and characteristic of Spanish poetry (thus *lado* and *llano* assonate, with the vowel pattern *a–o*).

atonic   Unstressed.

attenuation   A weakening (of meaning).

augmentative   A form which indicates largeness (e.g. the Spanish **suffix** *-ón*).

auxiliary   A verb used with another, non-finite, form of a verb to form a **periphrasis**.

back vowel   A vowel articulated by the raising of the tongue towards the **velum**.

back-formation   See **Keypoint: vocabulary – change in meaning** (p. 292).

bilabial   See **labial**.

caesura   A pause made in a line of verse.

calque   See **Keypoint: vocabulary – change in meaning** (p. 292).

case   Semantic definition (case-function): the kinds of relationship that nouns have with the verb (e.g. **subject**, **direct object**, **indirect object**, instrument, etc.) or, for the **genitive**, with other nouns. Morphological definition: the distinctive inflected forms of a noun which broadly correlate with such semantic functions. See **Keypoint: the case-system of Latin** (p. 263).

cataphoric   Referring forwards to an element in the following discourse.

causative   Expressing the notion of causation.

ceceo   **Neutralisation** of the **opposition** between /s/ and /θ/ and its realisation as /θ/.

circumlocution   An expression which uses more words than are strictly necessary to convey an idea.

cleft   A sentence in which a constituent (usally an object or adverbial phrase) is introduced by the verb *to be*/*ser* and the rest of the sentence is introduced by a relative element, e.g. *Conocí a Juan en Madrid* (simple), *Fue en Madrid donde conocí a Juan*/*Donde conocí a Juan fue en Madrid* (cleft).

clitic   See **Keypoint: personal pronouns** (p. 284).

clitic-climbing   See **Keypoint: clitic pronoun position** (p. 264).

close   Describes a vowel which has a relatively small aperture, such as [i] or [u]; also known as high, because the tongue is raised.

code-switching Moving between two languages within the same discourse (see Chapter XIII, introduction).

cognate A parallel form, e.g. French *hiver* is cognate with Spanish *invierno*; both are **derived** from Lat. HIBERNU[S].

complement Traditionally, the 'object' of a copular verb, eg *Juan es médico*. In modern linguistics, the term is also (and predominantly) used to denote a clause (or a clause-equivalent such as an infinitive or gerund) which functions as the **subject**, **object** or prepositional object of a verb. The grammatical element which introduces a complement is known as a complementiser.

concessive Expressing the granting or conceding of a point.

connotation Additional, suggested meaning as opposed to literal, direct meaning.

contraction The amalgamation of two or more words as a result of shortening.

contrastive stress Stress used to set an element in opposition to another.

converse The reversal of roles, especially of **subject** and **object**. *Buy* and *sell* are converse terms, since if A buys B from C, C sells B to A.

copula A connecting verb: *ser* and *estar* are the copulas, or copular verbs, of Spanish. Copular verbs have **complements** rather than **objects**.

coronal Pertaining to the blade of the tongue. English [s] and Latin American [s] are articulated coronally.

count A type of noun which denotes an individual entity and can be pluralised, as opposed to a mass noun, which denotes a quantity.

counterfactual A condition which has not been or cannot be fulfilled: see **Keypoint: conditional sentences** (p. 265).

dative See **Keypoint: the case-system of Latin** (p. 263).

dental Pertaining to the teeth. [θ] is a dental consonant.

deontic See **modality**.

deponent See **Keypoint: the passive** (p. 281).

derivation Used in two senses in this book (and generally): (a) the historical development of a form; (b) morphological derivation or the creation of a form on the basis of another.

devoicing The process which produces an **unvoiced allophone** of a **phoneme** which is normally **voiced**.

dialect Linguistically it is impossible to distinguish meaningfully between the notions of language and dialect. The notion 'dialect of' is perhaps useful in referring to a regional or social variety of what is perceived to be the 'same' language (e.g. working-class Sevillian speech is a 'dialect' of Spanish). The standard language usually evolves as a prestige dialect for essentially political reasons.

diminutive A form which indicates smallness.

diphthong A sequence of two vowels in the same syllable. Either the first or the second vowel will be treated as a **semivowel**. The combination of semivowel + vowel (e.g. [je]) is a rising diphthong; the combination of vowel + semivowel (e.g. [ej]) is a falling diphthong.

direct object See **object**.

dissimilation Making different. A sound occurring in close proximity to a similar sound may change to achieve better differentiation.

dorsal   Pertaining to the body of the tongue.

doublet   A pair: *cualidad* and *calidad* is a doublet development (see also under **Keypoint: learned and popular, semilearned and semipopular**, p. 277).

dynamic   See **stative**.

elative   A case-function expressing the notion of 'motion away from'.

elision   Omission or abbreviation: used particularly of the loss of sounds in fast speech or in historical development.

ellipsis   A construction in which words are left out or implied.

epenthesis   The introduction of an extra medial sound.

epistemic   See **modality**.

etymological   Pertaining to the historical **derivation** of a word. Used of spelling which reflects the historical origin, or **etymon** of a word.

euphemism   The expression of an unpleasant or embarrassing notion by a more inoffensive substitute.

existential   Pertaining to existence or being: the Spanish verb *haber* and English *there is, there are* are existential expressions.

filler   A word or phrase used to gain time in speech.

flap   The single rapid contact of two organs of speech, e.g. the movement of the tongue across the **alveolar** ridge in Spanish [ɾ].

folk-etymology   See **Keypoint: vocabulary – change in meaning** (p. 292).

frequentative   Denoting the (frequent) repetition of an action.

fricative   A class of continuant consonants produced by organs of speech coming into close proximity, so that there is an acoustic impression of friction produced in their articulation, e.g. [v], [ʃ], [x].

front vowel   A vowel articulated by the raising of the tongue towards the **alveolar** or **palatal** area.

geminate   Double: Lat. VACCA has a geminate /kk/.

genitive   See **Keypoint: the case-system of Latin** (p. 263).

grammaticalisation   The exploitation of a word to indicate a grammatical function, a process which typically involves the semantic weakening or 'bleaching' of the word. An example of grammaticalisation is when a **periphrastic** construction loses its literal meaning; the Spanish future tense is an example of a fully grammaticalised construction while the use of *ir* + past participle appears to be partially grammaticalised (see **Keypoint: periphrastic verbforms**, p. 283).

hiatus   Two vowels occurring sequentially but belonging to different syllables are said to be in hiatus, e.g. *be̱-a̱-ta*.

high   See **close**.

homonyms   Words that sound the same. Also known as **homophones**.

homorganic   Articulated with the same organs of speech.

hyperbaton   Transposition of the normal order of words.

hyperbole   Exaggeration.

hypercharacterisation of gender   See **Keypoint: gender** (p. 275). The morphological marking of gender by an inflection in a word which **etymologically** has no such inflection.

hypercorrection   Inappropriate use of a form which exhibits a feature recognised as being higher in prestige than the speaker's own usage.

implosive   Closing a syllable: the /n/ of *entrar* is implosive.

inchoative   Denoting the beginning of an action.

indirect object   See **object**.

infix   See **affix**.

interjection   A word or expression which has no grammatical function but typically expresses emotion.

intervocalic   Occurring between vowels.

intransitive   Traditionally, a verb which does not take a direct **object**.

isogloss   A line on a map which separates an area where a change has taken place from another where it has not.

labial   A sound which involves closure or constriction of the lips, e.g. [b], [β]. Such consonants are also termed **bilabial**.

labiodental   Articulated with the lower lip and upper teeth, e.g. [f].

laísmo   Use of *la* as an indirect **object** pronoun.

learned   See **Keypoint: learned and popular, semilearned and semipopular** (p. 277).

left-dislocation   Movement of an element to the front of its sentence.

leísmo   Use of *le* as an direct **object** pronoun.

lenition   See **Keypoint: lenition** (p. 278).

lexical diffusion   The process of the generalisation of a sound change through the lexicon. Incomplete lexical diffusion may result in some words not undergoing the change.

lexicalisation   To become a member of the lexicon, typically used to describe a change in which a word with a **suffix** comes to be thought of as a word in its own right.

liquid   A class of continuant consonants which are not **fricative** and impressionistically have a 'flowing' sound: [l] and [r] are the most obvious members.

locative   A **case**-function expressing the notion of 'place at which'.

logographic   The written representation of a word by a mnemonic sequence of letters which do not constitute a **phonemic** representation.

loísmo   Consistent use of *lo* as a direct **object** pronoun, whether for things or people.

low   See **open**.

mass   See **count**.

metaphony   A change to a vowel generally caused by proximity to another vowel, whose features it adopts.

metaphor   A figure of speech in which one thing is called another which it resembles in some significant way.

metathesis   Exchange of places by two sounds, e.g. Lat. PĂRĂBŎLA > Sp. *palabra*.

metonymy   Use of a word in a transferred sense. See **Keypoint: vocabulary – change in meaning** (p. 292).

middle   See **Keypoint: the reflexive** (p. 288).

modal   A morphological category loosely correlating with **modality**. Indicative, subjunctive and sometimes also imperative are moods which are traditionally distinguished for Spanish. However, many verb forms have a range of modal meanings.

modality   A category of meaning associated with the truth-value of a proposition, e.g. statement, possibility, command. Two fundamental categories of modality are deontic (expressing necessity or obligation) and epistemic (expressing supposition).

monophthong   A vowel which is not divisible into smaller vocalic constituents.

morpheme   'Grammatical' definition: the smallest contrastive unit of grammar. 'Semantic' definition: the smallest contrastive unit of meaning. Morphemes can be free, i.e., constituting words in their own right, or bound, i.e., obligatorily attached to another morpheme.

morphological   Pertaining to **morphemes**.

morphological derivation   See **derivation**.

nasal   Pertaining to the nose. Nasal sounds are those in which the air passes through the nasal cavity as well as through or into the oral cavity.

neologism   A recently created word or expression.

neutralisation   Loss of a contrast (**opposition**), either diachronically or synchronically.

nominalisation   The process of **morphological derivation** by which a noun is created.

nominative   See **Keypoint: the case-system of Latin** (p. 263).

object   In semantic terms, an element of a sentence that is affected by the verb. Traditionally, direct object and indirect object are distinguished: indirect objects appear with verbs like 'give' ('Mary gave Joe [indirect object] a book [direct object]'). Prepositions are also said to take objects.

onomatopoeia   The phenomenon of the sound-pattern of a word reflecting its meaning. See **Keypoint: vocabulary – change in meaning** (p. 292).

open   Describes a vowel which has a relatively large aperture, such as [a]; also known as low, because the tongue is lowered.

opposition   A contrast, e.g. the opposition between **voiced** and **voiceless** consonants.

optative   Expressing a desire or wish.

palatal   Pertaining to the hard palate. A sound in the course of whose articulation there is a movement towards the palatal area.

paraphrase or **periphrasis**   Use of more than one word to express a grammatical notion, e.g. the periphrastic future in Spanish (*ir a* + infinitive).

parataxis   Strictly, the use of clauses without conjunctions, though also used to indicate absence of subordinate clauses.

paroxytone   A word stressed on the next to the last syllable.

partitive   Expressing a **mass** concept.

passive   See **Keypoint: the passive** (p. 281).

patient   The recipient of the verbal action, often a function of the direct **object**.

pejorative   A form which has an unfavourable or disparaging meaning. Some of the **affective suffixes** of Spanish are pejorative.

perfective   An **aspectual** category which typically expresses the completion of an action.

phoneme   The smallest contrastive unit of sound in a language.

plosive   A non-continuant consonant whose articulation is characterised by a complete closure of the vocal tract.

popular   See **Keypoint: learned and popular, semilearned and semipopular** (p. 277).

prefix   See **affix**.

pro-drop   See 7.2.8.

productive   A form-class which is continuing to add to its membership through **analogy** or **neologism**: the -*ar* verb conjugation of Spanish may be described as productive because many new verbs (e.g. *formatear, privatizar*) are constantly being added to it. A form-class which has typically shown expansion at some point in the history of the language (e.g. the *u–e* '**strong**' preterites of Spanish) may be said to be **semiproductive**.

proparoxytone   A word stressed on the antepenultimate (next but one to the last) syllable.

protasis   The part of a conditional sentence which expresses the condition: *si tengo dinero compraré el libro*. See **Keypoint: conditional sentences** (p. 265).

prothetic   An extra initial sound, e.g. the /e/ in Sp. *escuela* < Lat. SCHŎLA.

reanalysis   The construing of a syntactic or morphological structure in a different way.

register   A variety of language used for a particular purpose, e.g. colloquial, legal, journalistic, etc.

rehilamiento   The articulation of Spanish [ʎ] with an element of frication, which in its most extreme form reaches the **voiced fricative** [ʒ].

relative clause   A dependent clause which refers to a noun in the main clause. The noun in the main clause is the antecedent of the relative clause.

right-dislocation   Movement of an element to the end of its sentence.

semantic field   See **Keypoint: vocabulary – change in meaning** (p. 292).

semi-deponent   See **Keypoint: the passive** (p. 281).

semilearned   See **Keypoint: learned and popular, semilearned and semi-popular** (p. 277).

semipopular   See **Keypoint: learned and popular, semilearned and semi-popular** (p. 277).

semiproductive   See **productive**.

semivowel   A vowel-like sound which has consonant-like properties. The two semivowels of Spanish are [j] and [w].

seseo   **Neutralisation** of the **opposition** between /s/ and /θ/ and its realisation as [s].

sibilant   A category of consonants which give the acoustic impression of hissing, such as [s], [z], etc.

sinalefa   The running together of two vowels which are separated by a word-boundary into one syllable, e.g. *me_ha-bló*.

sociolect   A socially defined variety of speech.

speech community   A group of people who speak what they recognise to be the same language or dialect.

stative   Denoting a state of affairs (as opposed to **dynamic**, denoting an action).

strong   Irregular.

subject   The noun or noun-phrase with which the verb agrees in person and number; it often has the **case**-function of **agent**.

substrate   Pertaining to the language of a culture which is inferior in status: Basque is said to be a substrate to Latin during the Romanisation of the Iberian Peninsula.

suffix   See **affix**.

supine   A verbal noun (a category of Latin grammar).

syncope   The loss of medial sounds.

synecdoche   A figure of speech in which the name of a part refers to the whole, e.g. *las faldas* referring to 'women'.

synonym   A word meaning the same as another. However, it is doubtful whether a pair of words are ever completely synonymous, and it is usually more accurate to speak of 'near synonyms'.

synthetic   The converse of **analytic**: use of a single **inflected** form to express a grammatical notion.

taboo   Superstitious or obscene connotations. Taboo words are prone to replacement by **euphemisms**.

temporal   Pertaining to time or tense.

tonic   Stressed.

topic   The element of an utterance which is the focus of the speaker's attention and about which something is said (the comment). The topic of a sentence is often information which is already known about (given information).

topicalisation   A syntactic or other device to bring an element in a sentence into prominence, particularly noticeable when that element is not the subject of the sentence.

transition relative   A relative pronoun used in a conjunction-like way (see 2.15 and 18.2.4).

transitive   Traditionally, a verb which takes a direct **object**.

transparency   Parallelism between form and meaning.

trill   A repeated **flap**.

unvoiced or **voiceless**   A sound in which the vocal cords do not vibrate.

valency   The capacity of a verb to take particular combinations of **case**-functions. **Transitive** and **intransitive** are different valencies.

velar   Pertaining to the velum or soft palate at the back of the mouth.

vocalisation   Becoming a vowel: certain consonants, e.g. **implosive** [l], are particularly prone to this process.

vocative   See **Keypoint: the case-system of Latin** (p. 263).

voiced   A sound in which the vocal cords vibrate.

voiceless   See **unvoiced**.

voseo   See **Keypoint: personal pronouns** (p. 284).

yeísmo   **Neutralisation** of the opposition between /j/ and /ʎ/ as /j/.

yod   See **Keypoint: palatalisation** (p. 280).

Bibliography

(* See Acknowledgements, p. xviii for explanation.)

Adams, J.N. (1994) 'Wackernagel's Law and the position of unstressed personal pronouns in Classical Latin', *Transactions of the Philological Society* 92: 103–78.

Agencia Efe, (1985) *Manual de español urgente*, Madrid: Cátedra.

Alarcos García, E. (1954) *Gonzalo Correas: Arte de la lengua española castellana*, Madrid: CSIC.

Alarcos Llorach, E. (1948) *Investigaciones sobre el Libro de Alexandre*, Madrid: CSIC.

Alarcos Llorach, E. (1953) Review of Stern 1953, *Archivum* 3: 242–50.

Alarcos Llorach, E. (1994) *Gramática de la lengua española*, Madrid: Real Academia Española/Espasa-Calpe.

Alcoba, S. (1987) *Léxico periodístico español*, Barcelona: Ariel.

Alemany Bolufer, J. (1915) *La antigua versión castellana del Calila y Dimna cotejada con el original árabe de la misma*, Madrid: Real Academia Española.

Allen, W. S. (1978²) *Vox Latina*, Cambridge: University Press.

*Alonso, A. (1949²) *Castellano, español, idioma nacional: historia espiritual de tres nombres*, Buenos Aires: Losada.

Alonso, A. (1951) 'Sobre métodos: construcciones con verbos de movimiento en español', in *Estudios lingüísticos: temas españoles*, 230–87, Madrid: Gredos.

Alonso, A. (1967²) *De la pronunciación medieval a la moderna en español*, Madrid: Gredos.

Alonso, D. (1962) 'B=V, en la Península Hispánica', in 'Fragmentación fonética peninsular', *ELH*, I, Suplemento, 135–209.

Alonso, M. (1986) *Diccionario medieval español desde las Glosas Emilianenses y Silenses (s.X) hasta el siglo XV*, 2 vols, Salamanca: Universidad Pontificia.

Alvar, M. (1953) *El dialecto aragonés*, Madrid: Gredos.

Alvar, M. (1955) 'Las hablas meridionales de España y su interés para la lingüística comparada', *Revista de Filología Española* 39: 284–313.

Alvar, M. (1976) *El dialecto riojano*, Madrid: Gredos.

Alvar, M., Llorente, A. and Salvador, G. (1961–73) *Atlas lingüístico-etnográfico de Andalucía*, 6 vols, Granada: Universidad de Granada.

Alvar, M. and Mariner, S. (1967) 'Latinismos', in *ELH*, II, 3–49.

*Alvar, M. and Pottier, B. (1983) *Morfología histórica del español*, Madrid: Gredos.

Amastae, J. and Elías-Olivares, L. (eds) (1982) *Spanish in the United States. Sociolinguistic aspects*, Cambridge: Cambridge University Press.

Arniches, C. (1915³)[1908] *Gazpacho andaluz*, Madrid: Velasco.

Note: Superscript numbers refer to edition.

Artigas, M. (1935) *Los libros de la Madre Teresa de Iesus: fundadora de los monasterios de monias y frayles Carmelitas descalços de la primera regla en Salamanca, 1558*, Edición facsímil, Madrid: Biblioteca Nueva.

Asín Palacios, M. (1943) *Glosario de voces romances registradas por un botánico anónimo hispano-musulmán, siglos XI-XII*, Madrid-Granada: CSIC.

Ayerbe-Chaux, R. (1977) 'Las memorias de doña Leonor López de Córdoba', *Journal of Hispanic Philology* 2: 11–33.

Badia Margarit, A.M. (1973) 'Por una revisión del concepto de «cultismo» en fonética histórica', in *Studia hispanica in honorem R. Lapesa*, Madrid: Gredos, 1: 137–52.

Bahner, W. (1966) [1956] *La lingüística española del siglo de oro*, Madrid: Ciencia Nueva.

Bakker, P. (1997) 'Notes on the genesis of "caló" and other Iberian para-Romani varieties', in Y. Matras, P. Bakker and H. Kyuchukov (eds) *The Typology and Dialectology of Romani*, Amsterdam: Benjamins, 125–50.

Barbolani de García, C. (1967) *Juan de Valdés, Diálogo de la lengua*, Messina-Florence: D'Anna.

Barbolani de García, C. (1982) *Juan de Valdés: Diálogo de la lengua*, Madrid: Cátedra.

Besses, L. (1906) *Diccionario de argot español, ó lenguaje jergal gitano, delincuente profesional y popular*, Barcelona: Sucesores de Manuel Soler.

Besso, H.V. (1964) 'Situación actual del judeo-español', in *Presente y futuro de la lengua española: Actas de la Asamblea de Filología del I Congreso de Instituciones hispánicas, Madrid, junio 1963*, Madrid: OFINES, 307–24.

Bickerton, D. (1981) *Roots of Language*, Ann Arbor: Karoma.

Bickerton, D. and Escalante, A. (1970) 'Palenquero: a Spanish-based creole of northern Colombia', *Lingua* 24: 254–67.

Blake, R.J. (1988) 'Ffaro, Faro or Haro?: F doubling as a source of linguistic information for the Early Middle Ages', *Romance Philology* 41: 267–89.

Blecua, J.M. (1969) *Don Juan Manuel: El Conde Lucanor*, Madrid: Castalia.

Borrow, G. (1843²) *The Zincali: or, An Account of the Gypsies of Spain. With an original collection of their songs and poetry, and a copious dictionary of their language*, London: John Murray.

Bouzet, J. (1953) 'Orígenes del empleo de "estar"', in *Estudios dedicados a Menéndez Pidal* 4: 37–58, Madrid: CSIC.

Boyd-Bowman, P. (1975) 'A sample of sixteenth-century "Caribbean" Spanish phonology', in W.G. Milan, J.J. Staczek and J.C. Zamora (eds) *1974 Colloquium on Spanish and Portuguese Linguistics*, Washington: Georgetown University Press, pp.1–11.

Brunet, M. (1962) *Montaña Adentro*, in *Obras completas*, Santiago de Chile: Zig-Zag.

Buñuel, L. (1980) *Los olvidados*, Mexico: Ediciones Era.

Cacho Blecua, J.M. and Lacarra, M.-J. (1987) *Calila e Dimna. Edición, introducción y notas*, Madrid: Castalia.

Canellada de Zamora, M.-J. and Zamora Vicente, A. (eds) (1970) *Antonio de Torquemada: manual de escribientes*, Madrid: Anejos del *Boletín de la Real Academia Española*, 21.

*Cano Aguilar, R. (1997³) *El español a través de los tiempos*, Madrid: Arco.

Cañas, J. (1988) *Libro de Alexandre. Edición*, Madrid: Cátedra.

Carrino, F.G., Carlos, A.J. and Mangouni, N. (1974) *The Gaucho Martín Fierro (1872) by José Hernandez. A Facsimile Reproduction of the First Edition with a New English Translation*, Delmar, New York: Scholars' Facsimiles and Reprints Inc.

Castiglione, B. (1942) [1534] *El Cortesano, Traducción de Juan Boscán, Estudio preliminar de M. Menéndez y Pelayo*, Madrid: CSIC.

Castiglione, B. (1972) [1528] *Il Libro del Cortegiano, a cura di Ettore Bonora, commento di Paolo Zoccola*, Milan: Mursia.

Chicharro, D. (1994¹⁰) *Santa Teresa de Jesús: Libro de la vida*, Madrid: Cátedra.

Company Company, C. (1985) 'Los futuros en el español medieval: sus orígenes y su evolución', *Nueva Revista de Filología Hispánica* 34: 48–107.

Company Company, C. (1994) *Documentos lingísticos de la Nueva España. Altiplano-central*, Mexico City: UNAM.

Contreras, H. (1978) *El orden de palabras en español*, Madrid: Cátedra.

Corfis, I.A. and O'Neill, J. (eds) (1997) *Early Celestina Electronic Texts and Concordances*, Madison: Hispanic Seminary of Medieval Studies.

*Cor. = Corominas, J. and Pascual, J.A. (1980–91) *Diccionario crítico etimológico castellano e hispánico*, 6 vols, Madrid: Gredos.

*Covarrubias Orozco, S. de, (1977) [1611] *Tesoro de la lengua castellana o española*, Madrid: Ediciones Turner.

Craddock, J. (1973) 'Spanish in North America', *Current Trends in Linguistics* 10: 305–39.

Crews, C.M. (1935) *Recherches sur le judéo-espagnol dans les pays balkaniques*, Paris: Droz.

Criado de Val, M. (1955) *Índice verbal de* La Celestina, *Anejo LXIV, Revista de Filología Española*.

Cuervo, R.J. (1893) 'Las segundas personas del plural en la conjugación castellana', *Romania* 22: 71–86.

Dutton, B. (1980) *Gonzalo de Berceo, obras completas. 2: los milagros de Nuestra Señora, estudio y edición crítica*, 2nd edn, revised, London: Tamesis.

Eberenz, R. (1991) 'Castellano antiguo y español moderno: reflexiones sobre la periodización en la historia de la lengua', *Revista de Filología Española* 71: 79–106.

ELH = M. Alvar, A. Badía, R. de Balbín and L.F. Lindley Cintra (eds) (1960–7) *Enciclopedia Lingüística Hispánica*, Madrid: CSIC.

Emiliano, A. (1993) 'Latín y romance y las glosas de San Millán y de Silos: apuntes para un planteamiento grafémico', in Ralph Penny (ed.) *Actas del Primer Congreso Anglo-Hispano, I, Lingüística*, Madrid: Castalia, 235–44.

Ernout, A. (1954) *Aspects du vocabulaire latin*, Paris: Klincksieck.

Esgueva, M. and Cantarero, M. (1981) *El habla de la ciudad de Madrid*, Madrid: CSIC.

Fernández-Ordóñez, I. (1994) 'Isoglosas internas del castellano. El sistema referencial del pronombre átono de tercera persona', *Revista de Filología Española* 74: 71–125.

Fontanella de Weinberg, M.B. (1992) *El español de América*, Madrid: Mapfre.

Fries, D. (1989) '*Limpia, fija y da esplendor*': la Real Academia Española ante el uso de la lengua', Madrid: SGEL.

Fuente, V. de la (ed.) (1873) *Vida de Santa Teresa de Jesús*, Madrid: Sociedad Foto-tipográfico-católica.

Galmés de Fuentes, A. (1955–56) 'Influencias sintácticas y estilísticas del árabe en la prosa medieval castellana', *Boletín de la Real Academia Española* 35: 213–75, 415–51; 36: 65–131, 255–307.

Galmés de Fuentes, A. (1983) *Dialectología mozárabe*, Madrid: Gredos.

Gamillscheg, E. (1932) 'Historia lingüística de los visigodos', *Revista de Filología Española* 19: 117–50 and 224–60.

García Gómez, E. (1952) 'Veinticuatro jarŷas romances en muwaššaḥas árabes', *Al-Andalus* 17: 57–127.

García Gómez, E. (1975²) *Las jarchas romances de la serie árabe en su marco*, Barcelona: Seix Barral.

Gerli, E.M. (1992) 'Poet and pilgrim: discourse, language, imagery, and audience in Berceo's "Milagros de Nuestra Señora" ', in E. M. Gerli and H.L. Sharrer (eds) *Hispanic Medieval Studies in Honor of Samuel G. Armistead*, Madison: Hispanic Seminary of Medieval Studies, 139–51.

Gilman, S. (1961) *Tiempo y formas temporales en el 'Poema del Cid'*, Madrid: Gredos.

Gómez-Moreno, M. (1954) 'Documentación goda en pizarra', *Boletín de la Real Academia Española* 34: 25–58.

González Muela, J. (1954) *El infinitivo en El Corbacho del Arcipreste de Talavera*, Granada: Universidad de Granada.

González Muela, J. (1970) *Alfonso Martínez de Toledo: Arcipreste de Talavera o Corbacho, edición*, Madrid: Castalia.

Granda, G. de (1978a) 'La desfonologización de /R/-/R-/ en el dominio lingüístico hispánico', in Granda 1978b, 69–79.

Granda, G. de (1978b) *Estudios lingüísticos hispánicos, afrohispánicos y criollos*, Madrid: Gredos.

Granda, G. de (1991) *El español en tres mundos. Retenciones y contactos lingüísticos en América y África*, Valladolid: Universidad de Valladolid.

Granda, G. de (1994) *Español de América, español de África y hablas criollas hispánicas: cambios, contactos y contextos*, Madrid: Gredos.

Green, J.N. (1977) 'How free is word order in Spanish?', in M. Harris (ed.) *Romance Syntax: Synchronic and Diachronic Perspectives*, Salford: Salford University, 7–32.

Green, J.N. (1988) 'Romance creoles' in M. Harris and N. Vincent (eds) *The Romance Languages*, London: Croom Helm.

Green, O.H. (1953) 'Celestina, Aucto I: "Minerva con el can"', *Nueva Revista de Filología Hispánica* 7: 470–4.

Green, O.H. (1956) 'Lo de tu abuela con el ximio (Celestina: Auto I)', *Hispanic Review* 24: 1–12.

Grimes, B.F. (ed.) (1999) *Ethnologue: Languages of the World*, Dallas: Summer Institute of Linguistics.

Gumperz, J.J. (1970) 'Verbal strategies in multilingual communication', in Monograph series on Language and Linguistics, 21st Annual Round Table: Washington: Georgetown University Press.

Hamilton, R. (1953) 'Juan de Valdés and some Renaissance theories of language', *Bulletin of Hispanic Studies* 30: 125–33.

*Harris, M. (1978) *The Evolution of French Syntax. A Comparative Approach*, London: Longman.

Harris, T.K. (1994) *Death of a Language: The History of Judeo-Spanish*, Newark: University of Delaware.

Hart-González, L. (1985) 'Pan-hispanism and subcommunity in Washington DC', in Elías-Olivares *et al.* (ed.) *Spanish Language Use and Public Life in the United States*, Berlin/New York: Mouton, 73–88.

Hatcher, A.G. (1942) 'The use of *a* as a designation of the personal accusative in Spanish', *Modern Language Notes* 57: 421–9.

Heger, K. (1960) *Die bisher veröffentlichten 'jaryas' und ihre Deutungen*, Tübingen: Niemeyer.

Hermenegildo, A. (ed.) (1985) *Lope de Rueda: Las cuatro comedias*, Madrid: Taurus.

Hermerén, I. (1992) *El uso de la forma en 'ra' con valor no-subjuntivo en el español moderno*, Lund: University Press.

Hernández Chávez, E., Cohen, A. and Beltramo, A. (1975) *El lenguaje de los chicanos*, Arlington: Center for Applied Linguistics.

Hernández, C., de Granda, G., Hoyos, C., Fernández, V., Dietrick, D. and Carballera Y. (eds) (1991) *El español de América. Actas del III Congreso Internacional de El Español de América, Valladolid, 3 a 9 de julio de 1989*, Valladolid: Junta de Castilla y León.

Hill, J.M. (ed.) (1945) *Poesías germanescas*, Bloomington, Indiana: Indiana University Publications.

Hitchcock, R. (1977) 'Sobre la "mama" en las jarchas', *Journal of Hispanic Philology* 2: 1–9.

Hodcroft, F.W. (1994) '¿A mí un "él"?: observations on "vos" and "él/ella" as forms of address in Peninsular Spanish', *Journal of Hispanic Research* 2: 1–16.

Holm, J. (1988–9) *Pidgins and Creoles*, 2 vols, Cambridge: Cambridge University Press.

Huerta Tejadas, F. (1954–6) 'Vocabulario de las obras de don Juan Manuel', *Boletín de la Real Academia Española* 34: 285–310 and 413–51; 35: 85–132, 277–94 and 453–5; 36: 133–50.

Jauralde Pou, P. (1990) *Francisco de Quevedo: 'El Buscón'*, Madrid: Castalia.

Jones, A. (1988) *Romance 'Kharjas' in Andalusian Arabic 'Muwaššaḥ' Poetry*, London: Ithaca Press.

Jungemann, F.H. (1955) *La teoría del sustrato y los dialectos hispano-romances y gascones*, Madrid: Gredos.

*Kany, C.E. (1951²). *American-Spanish Syntax*, Chicago: University Press.

Kany, C.E. (1960a) *American-Spanish Euphemisms*, Berkeley: University of California Press.

*Kany, C.E. (1960b) *American-Spanish Semantics*, Berkeley: University of California Press.

Kasten, L., J. Nitti and Jonxis-Henkemans, W. (1997) *The Electronic Texts and Concordances of the Prose Works of Alfonso X, El Sabio*, Madison: Hispanic Seminary of Medieval Studies.

*Keniston, H.M. (1937) *The Syntax of Castilian Prose*, Chicago: University Press.

Kliffer, M.D. (1984) 'Personal "a", kinesis and individuation', in P. Baldi (ed.) *Papers from the XIIth Linguistic Symposium on Romance Languages*, Amsterdam: Benjamins, 195–216.

Labov, W. (1994) *Principles of linguistic change*, Oxford: Blackwell.

Lantolf, J.P. (1979) 'Explaining linguistic change. The loss of voicing in the Old Spanish sibilants', *Orbis* 28: 290–315.

Lapesa, R. (1940) *Juan de Valdés: Diálogo de la lengua*, Zaragoza: Ebro.

Lapesa, R. (1951) 'La apócope de la vocal en castellano antiguo. Intento de explicación histórica', in *Estudios dedicados a R. Menéndez Pidal* 2: 195–226.

Lapesa, R. (1960). 'Sobre el texto y lenguaje de algunas jarchyas mozárabes', *Boletín de la Real Academia Española* 40: 53–65.

Lapesa, R. (1962) 'Sobre las construcciones "El diablo del toro", "El bueno de Minaya", "¡Ay de mí!", "¡Pobre de Juan!", "Por malos de pecados"', *Filología* 7: 169–84.

Lapesa, R. (1975) 'De nuevo sobre la apócope vocálica en castellano medieval', *Nueva Revista de Filología Hispánica*, 24: 13–23.

*Lapesa, R. (1981⁹). *Historia de la lengua española*, Madrid: Gredos.

Lapesa, R. (1985a) [1971] 'Sobre el origen de la palabra "español"', in *Estudios . . .*, 132–7.

Lapesa, R. (1985b) [1983] 'Mozárabe y catalán o gascón en el "Auto de los Reyes Magos"', in *Estudios . . .*, 138–56.

Lapesa, R. (1985c) 'Contienda de normas en el castellano alfonsí', in *Estudios . . .*, 209–25.

Lapesa, R. (1985d) *Estudios de historia lingüística española*, Madrid: Paraninfo.

Las glosas emilianenses (1977) Madrid: Servicio de Publicaciones del Ministro de Educación y Ciencia.

Lass, R. (1990) 'How to do things with junk: exaptation in language evolution', *Journal of Linguistics* 26: 79–102.

Lázaro Carreter, F. (1949) *Las ideas lingüísticas en España durante el siglo XVIII*, Madrid: CSIC.

Lázaro Carreter, F. (1980) *Francisco de Quevedo: 'La Vida del Buscón'*, 2nd edn, Salamanca: University Press.

Lenz, R. (1928) *El papiamentu: la lengua criolla de Curazao. La gramática más sencilla*, Santiago de Chile: Balcells.

Lenz, R. (1940) 'El español en Chile', *Biblioteca de Dialectología Hispanoamericana* 6: 79–208, Buenos Aires: Universidad de Buenos Aires.

Líbano Zumalacárregui, Á. (1991) 'Morfología diacrónica del español: las fórmulas de tratamiento', *Revista de Filología Española*, 71: 107–21.

Lida de Malkiel, M.R. (1950) *Juan de Mena, poeta del prerrenacimiento español*, Mexico City: Publicaciones de la Nueva Revista de Filología Hispánica.

Lipski, J.M. (1985) *The Spanish of Equatorial Guinea: The Dialect of Malabo and its Implications for Spanish Dialectology*, Tübingen: Niemeyer.

*Lipski, J.M. (1994) *Latin American Spanish*, London: Longman.

Lloyd, P.M. (1979) 'On the definition of Vulgar Latin', *Neuphilologische Mitteilungen* 80: 110–22.

*Lloyd, P.M. (1987) *From Latin to Spanish*, Philadelphia: American Philosophical Society.

Lope Blanch, J.M. (1969) *Juan de Valdés: Diálogo de la lengua*, Madrid: Castalia.

Lorenzo, E. (1971) *El español de hoy: lengua en ebullición*, Madrid: Gredos.

Lunn, P.V. and Cravens, T.D. (1991) 'A contextual reconsideration of the Spanish -ra "indicative" ', in S. Fleischman and L.R. Waugh (eds) *Discourse Pragmatics and the Verb: The Evidence from Romance*, London: Routledge 147–63.

Luria, M. (1930) 'A study of the Monastir dialect of Judeo-Spanish based on oral material collected in Monastir, Yugoslavia', *Revue Hispanique* 79: 325–583.

Macpherson, I.R. (1967) 'Past participle agreement in Old Spanish: transitive verbs', *Bulletin of Hispanic Studies* 44: 241–54.

Malkiel, Y. (1959) 'The Luso-Hispanic descendants of POTIŌ', in F. Pierce (ed.) *Hispanic Studies in Honour of Ignacio González-Llubera*, Oxford: Dolphin Book Co., 193–210.

Malkiel, Y. (1974) 'Distinctive traits of Romance linguistics', in D. Hymes (ed.), *Language in Culture and Society. A Reader in Linguistics and Anthropology*, New York: Harper & Row 671–88.

Malmberg, B. (1971) [1958] 'Le passage castillan *f > h* – perte d'un trait redondant?', in *Phonétique générale et romane*, The Hague / Paris: Mouton, 459–63.

Marciales, M. (ed.), Dutton, B. and Snow, J.T. (1985) *Celestina: Tragicomedia de Calisto y Melibea, Fernando de Rojas. Introducción y edición crítica*, Tomo I, *Introducción*, Urbana/Chicago: University of Illinois Press.

Marcos Marín, F. *et al.* (*c.*1993) ADMYTE (Archivo Digital de Manuscritos y Textos Españoles), vol.1, Madrid: Micronet SA.

Martinet, A. (1951–52) 'The devoicing of the Old Spanish sibilants', *Romance Philology* 5: 133–56 (also, in a French version, in Martinet 1955, 297–325).

Martinet, A. (1955) *Économie des changements phonétiques*, Berne: Francke.

Martínez Gil, F. (1998) 'On the spelling distinction "*b* vs. *u/v*" and the status of spirantisation in Old Spanish', in J. Lema and E. Treviño (eds) *Theoretical Analysis on Romance Languages: Selected Papers from the 28th Linguistic Symposium on Romance Languages (LSRL XXVI), Mexico City, 28–30 March 1996*, Amsterdam: Benjamins, 283–316.

Martínez Ruiz, J. (1974) 'Un nuevo texto aljamiado: el recetario de sahumerios en uno de los manuscritos árabes de Ocaña', *Revista de dialectología y tradiciones populares* 30: 3–17.

Mayáns y Siscar, G. (1737) *Orígenes de la lengua española*, Madrid: J. de Zúñiga.

Mazzocco, A. (1997) 'The Italian connection in Juan de Valdés's "Diálogo de la Lengua" (1536)', *Historiographia Linguistica* 24: 3, 267–83.

Méndez Plancarte, A. (ed.) (1952) *Obras completas de Sor Juana Inés de la Cruz II. Villancicos y letras sacras*, México-Buenos Aires: Fondo dc Cultura Económica.

Menéndez Pidal, R. 1908–11. *Cantar de Mio Cid. Texto, gramática y vocabulario*, 3 vols, Madrid: Bailly-Baillère.

Menéndez Pidal, R. (1942) 'El estilo de Santa Teresa', in *La lengua de Cristóbal Colón*, Madrid: Espasa-Calpe.

Menéndez Pidal, R. (ed.) (1955) *Primera Crónica General de España que mandó componer Alfonso el Sabio y se continuaba bajo Sancho IV en 1289*, Madrid: Gredos.

Menéndez Pidal, R. (1961) *Poema de Mio Cid. Facsímil de la edición paleográfica por Don R. Menéndez Pidal*, Madrid: Barbazan.

Menéndez Pidal R. (1962a) 'Sevilla frente a Madrid', in D. Catalán (ed.) *Miscelánea Homenaje a André Martinet. III Estructuralismo e historia*, Tenerife: Universidad de La Laguna, 99–165.

Menéndez Pidal, R. (1962[11]b). *Manual de gramática histórica española*, Madrid: Espasa-Calpe.

Menéndez Pidal R. (1971[2]) *Crestomatía del Español Medieval*, I, Madrid: Gredos.

*Menéndez Pidal, R. (1976[8]) *Orígenes del Español. Estado lingüístico de la Península Ibérica hasta el Siglo XI*, Madrid: Espasa-Calpe.

Menéndez Pelayo, M. (1894) 'De las influencias semíticas en la literatura española', in *Obras completas*, VI, 193–217.

Mesonero Romanos, R. de (1851) *Escenas matritenses*, Madrid: Imprenta y Litografía de Gaspar Roig.

Michael, I. (ed.) (1976) *Poema de Mio Cid*, Madrid: Castalia.

Milroy, J. (1992) *Linguistic Variation and Change. On the Historical Sociolinguistics of English*, Oxford: Blackwell.

Mondéjar, J. (1980) 'Lingüística e historia', *Revista Española de Lingüística* 10: 1–48.

Montero Cartelle, E. (1992) 'La trayectoria cronológica y modal de la expresión concesiva "maguer(a) (que)" ', in M. Ariza, R. Cano, J.-M. Mendoza and A. Narbona (eds) *Actas del II Congreso Internacional de Historia de la Lengua Española*, Madrid: Pabellón de España SA, I: 701–10.

Montero Cartelle, E. (1993) 'Las construcciones concesivas pleonásticas y el modo en el castellano medieval y clásico', in P. Carrasco *et al.* (eds.) *Antiqua et Nova Romania: Estudios lingüísticos y filológicos en honor de José Mondéjar en su sexagesimoquinto aniversario*, Granada: Universidad de Granada, I, 163–92.

Montesinos, J.F. (1928) *Juan de Valdés: Diálogo de la lengua*, Madrid: Espasa-Calpe.

Montgomery, T. (1991) 'Interaction of factors in tense choice in the "Poema del Cid" ', *Bulletin of Hispanic Studies* 68: 355–69.

Morel-Fatio, A., (1900) *Ambrosio de Salazar et l'étude de l'espagnol en France sous Louis XIII*, Paris: Picard/Toulouse: Privat.

Mozos Mocha, S. de los (1973) *El gerundio preposicional*, Salamanca: Universidad de Salamanca.

Naylor, E. (1983) *The Text and Concordances of the Escorial Manuscript H.III.10 of the Arcipreste de Talavera of Alfonso Martínez de Toledo*, Madison: Hispanic Seminary of Medieval Studies.

Niederehe, H.-J., (1987) *Alfonso X el Sabio y la lingüística de su tiempo*, Madrid: SGEL.

Ornstein-Galicia, J.L. (1981) 'Varieties of southwest Spanish: some neglected basic considerations', in R.P. Durán (ed.) *Latino Language and Communicative Behavior*, Norwood, NJ: Ablex Publishing Corporation 19–38.

Oroz, R. (1966) *La lengua castellana en Chile*, Santiago: Universidad de Chile.

Pastor, J.F. (1929) *Las apologías de la lengua castellana en el siglo de oro*, Madrid: Compañía Ibero-Americana de Publicaciones.

Pattison, D. (1967) 'The date of the CMC: a linguistic approach', *Modern Language Review* 62: 443–50.

Penfield, J. and Ornstein-Galicia, J.L. (1985) *Chicano English: an Ethnic Contact Dialect*, Amsterdam: Benjamins.

Penny, R.J. (1972) 'The re-emergence of /f/ as a phoneme of Castilian', *Zeitschrift für Romanische Philologie* 88: 463–92.

Penny, R.J. (1976) 'The convergence of B, V and -P- in the peninsula: a reappraisal', in A.D. Deyermond (ed.) *Medieval Hispanic Studies Presented to Rita Hamilton*, London: Támesis Books, 149–59.

Penny, R.J. (1990) 'Labiodental /f/, aspiration and /h/-dropping in Spanish: the evolving phonemic values of the graphs "f" and "h" ', in D. Hook and B. Taylor (eds) *Culture in Medieval Spain: Historical and Literary Essays Presented to L.P. Harvey*, London: King's College, 157–82.

*Penny, R.J. (1991) *A History of the Spanish Language*, Cambridge: Cambridge University Press.

Penny, R.J. (1996) 'Judeo-Spanish varieties before and after the expulsion', *Donaire* 6: 54–8.

Penny, R.J. (1997) 'The language of Gonzalo de Berceo, in the context of peninsular dialectal variation', in I. Macpherson and R. Penny (eds) *The Medieval Mind: Hispanic Studies in Honour of Alan Deyermond*, London: Támesis, 327–45.

Penny, R.J. (forthcoming) *Variation and Change in Spanish*, Cambridge: Cambridge University Press.

Pla Cárceles, J. (1923) 'La evolución del tratamiento "vuestra merced" ', *Revista de Filología Española* 10: 245–80.

Poitrey, J. (1983) *Vocabulario de Santa Teresa*, Madrid: Universidad Pontificia de Salamanca-Fundación Universitaria Española.

Pountain, C.J. (1983) *Structures and Transformations: The Romance Verb*, London: Croom Helm.

Pountain, C.J. (1985) 'Copulas, verbs of possession and auxiliaries in Old Spanish: the evidence for structurally interdependent changes', *Bulletin of Hispanic Studies* 52: 337–55.

Pountain, C.J. (1994) 'The Castilian reflexes of "abhorrere/abhorrescere": a case-study in valency', in C. Lupu and G. Price (eds) *Hommages offerts à Maria Manoliu-Manea*, Bucharest: Pluralia/Logos, 122–48.

Pountain, C.J. (1998a) 'Gramática mítica del gerundio castellano', in A.M. Ward (ed.), *Actas del XII Congreso de la Asociación Internacional de Hispanistas, Birmingham 1995. I. Medieval y Lingüística*, (Birmingham: University Press), 284–92.

Pountain, C.J. (1998b) 'Learnèd syntax and the Romance languages: the "accusative and infinitive" construction with declarative verbs in Castilian', *Transactions of the Philological Society* 96(2): 159–201.

Pountain, C.J. (2000a) 'Pragmatic factors in the evolution of the romance reflexive (with special reference to Spanish)', *Hispanic Research Journal* 1: 5–25.

Pountain, C.J. (2000b) 'Capitalization', in J.C. Smith and D. Bentley (eds) *Historical Linguistics 1995: Volume One, General Issues and Non-Germanic Languages. Selected Papers from the Twelfth International Conference on Historical Linguistics, Manchester, August 1995*, Benjamins: Amsterdam and Philadelphia, 295–309.

Pritchard, R.T. (1986) *Walter of Châtillon: the Alexandreis*, Toronto: Pontifical Institute of Mediaeval Studies.

Quilis, A. (1980) *Antonio de Nebrija. Gramática de la Lengua Castellana. Estudio y edición*, Madrid: Editora Nacional.

Ramsden, H. (1963) *Weak Pronoun Position in the Early Romance Languages*, Manchester: Manchester University Press.

Ramsden, H. (1961) 'The use of "a" + personal pronoun in Old Spanish', *Bulletin of Hispanic Studies* 38: 42–54.

*Real Academia Española (1963) *Diccionario de Autoridades*, Edición facsímil, 3 vols, Madrid: Gredos.

Rico, F. (1978) *Nebrija frente a los bárbaros*, Salamanca: University Press.

Riiho, T. (1979) *'Por' and 'para': estudio sobre los orígenes y la evolución de una oposición prepositiva iberorrománica*, Helsinki: Societas Scientarum Fennica.

Ríos de Torres, R.E. (1991) 'El habla negra en textos ibero-americanos y su prolongación lingüística sistematizada', in Hernández *et al.* (eds), pp.1321–33.

Rivarola, J.L. (1976) *Las conjunciones concesivas en español medieval y clásico. Contribución a la sintaxis histórica medieval*, Tübingen: Niemeyer.

Rohlfs, G. (1966) *Grammatica storica della lingua italiana e dei suoi dialetti: Fonetica*, Turin: Einaudi.

Romaine, S. (1982) *Socio-Historical Linguistics: Its Status and Methodology*, Cambridge: Cambridge University Press.

Rosenblat, A. (1977) *Los conquistadores y su lengua*, Caracas: Universidad Central.

Rubio Cremades, E. (1993) *Ramón de Mesonero Romanos: Escenas y tipos matritenses*, Madrid: Cátedra.

Russell, P.E. (1991) *Fernando de Rojas: La Celestina*, Madrid: Castalia.

Salvá, V. (1867⁹). *Gramática de la lengua castellana según ahora se habla*, Paris: Garnier.

Sánchez A.B. (1925) 'Las versiones en romance de las crónicas del Toledano', in *Homenaje ofrecido a Menéndez Pidal*, Madrid: Hernando, I, 341–54.

Sánchez, R. (1982) 'Our linguistic and social context', in Amastae and Elías-Olivares, 9–46.

Sarmiento, R. (ed.) (1984) *Gramática de la lengua castellana 1771, edición facsímil y apéndice documental*, Madrid: Editora Nacional.

Seco, M. (1970) *Arniches y el habla de Madrid*, Madrid: Alfaguara.

Seifert, E. (1930) ' "Haber" y "tener" como expresiones de la posesión en español', *Revista de Filología Española* 17: 233–76 and 345–89.

Sephiha, H.V. (1986) *Le judéo-espagnol*, Paris: Editions Entente.

Sinclair, A. (1977) *Valle-Inclán's 'Ruedo Ibérico'*, London: Tamesis.

Smith, C. (ed.) (1972) *Poema de mio Cid*, Oxford: Clarendon Press.

Sola-Solé, J.M. (1975) 'El "Auto de los Reyes Magos": ¿impacto gascón o mozárabe?', *Romance Philology* 29: 20–7.

Steel, B. (1976) *A Manual of Colloquial Spanish*, Madrid: SGEL.

Stengaard, B. (1991a) 'The combination of glosses in the "Códice Emilianense 60 (Glosas Emilianenses)" ', in R. Wright (ed.) *Late Latin and the Romance Languages in the Early Middle Ages*, London: Routledge, 177–89.

Stengaard, B. (1991b) *Vida y muerte de un campo semántico. Un estudio de la evolución semántica de los verbos latinos 'stare', 'sedere' e 'iacere' del latín al romance del S.XIII*, Tübingen: Niemeyer.

Stern, S.M. (1948) 'Les vers finaux en espagnol dans les muwaššaḥas hispano-hébraïques', *Al-Andalus* 13: 299–346.

Stern, S.M. (1953) *Les chansons mozarabes. Les vers finaux (kharjas) en espagnol dans les 'muwashshahs' arabes et hébreux*, Palermo: Manfredi.

Thompson, E. (1969) *The Goths in Spain*, Oxford: University Press.

Tiscornia, E.F. (1925–30) *Martín Fierro comentado y anotado*, Buenos Aires: Coni.

Ullmann, S. (1963) *The Principles of Semantics*, Oxford: Blackwell.

Valle, J. del (1996) *El trueque 's/x' en español antiguo. Aproximaciones teóricas*, Tübingen: Niemeyer.

Valle-Inclán, R. del (1971) [1928] *El ruedo ibérico. Viva mi dueño*, Madrid: Alianza.

Vigara Tauste, A.-M. (1992) *Morfosintaxis del español coloquial: esbozo estilístico*, Madrid: Gredos.

Whinnom, K. (1954) 'Spanish in the Philippines', *Journal of Oriental Studies*, 1, 129–94.

Whinnom, Keith, (1956) *Spanish Contact Vernaculars in the Philippine Islands*, London: Hong Kong University Press and Oxford University Press.

Whinnom, K. (1966) 'The relationship of the early editions of the "Celestina"', *Zeitschrift für romanische Philologie* 82: 22–40.

Willis, R.S., Jr. (1934) *El Libro de Alexandre. Texts of the Paris and Madrid Manuscripts Prepared with An Introduction*, Princeton: University Press/Paris: Presses Universitaires de France.

Wright, L.O. (1929) 'The indicative function of the -ra form', *Hispania* 12: 259–78.

Wright, R. (1976) 'Semicultismo', *Archivum Linguisticum* 7: 13–28.

Wright, R. (1982) *Late Latin and Early Romance in Spain and Carolingian France*, Liverpool: Francis Cairns.

Wright, R. (1986) 'La función de las glosas de San Millán y de Silos', in J.C. Bouvier (ed.) *Actes du XVIIe Congrès International de Linguistique et Philologie Romanes, IX*, Aix-en-Provence: Université de Provence, 209–19.

Wright R. (ed.) (1991) *Latin and the Romance Languages in the Early Middle Ages*, London: Routledge.

Zamora Munné, J.C. and J. Guitarte (1982) *Dialectología hispanoamericana*, Salamanca: Almar.

Zamora Vicente, A. (1967²) *Dialectología española*, Madrid: Gredos.

Index of topics (excluding keypoints)

Index of words

Tagalog

Turkish

Welsh